Oral and Literary Continuities in Modern Tibetan Literature

Studies in Modern Tibetan Culture

Series Editor: Gray Tuttle, Columbia University

Advisory Board

Lauran Hartley, Columbia University (literature)
Isabelle Henrion-Dourcy, Université Laval (anthropology)
Kurtis Schaeffer, University of Virginia (religion)
Emily Yeh, University of Colorado at Boulder (human geography)

The *Studies in Modern Tibetan Culture* series focuses on Tibetan culture and society from the early modern period of the seventeenth century to the present. The first series on modern Tibetan studies by a scholarly press, it explores how modernity manifests in a wide range of fields, not only religion, but also literature, history, economy, anthropology, media, and politics. It seeks to bring rarely heard and important Tibetan perspectives to a wider audience by publishing fresh analyses of yet unexplored source materials ranging from census and yearbook databases to auto/biographies and ethnographic fieldwork, as well as original translations of poetry, biography, and history.

Titles in Series

The Nine-Eyed Agate: Poems and Stories by Jangbu and translated by Heather Stoddard
Labrang Monastery: A Tibetan Buddhist Community on the Inner Asian Borderlands, 1709–1958 by Paul Kocot Nietupski
The Hidden Life of the Sixth Dalai Lama by Ngawang Lhundrup Dargyé and translated by Simon Wickham-Smith
The Disempowered Development of Tibet in China: A Study in the Economics of Marginalization by Andrew Martin Fischer
The Social Life of Tibetan Biography: Textuality, Community, and Authority in the Lineage of Tokden Shakya Shri by Amy Holmes-Tagchungdarpa
The Rise of Gönpo Namgyel in Kham: The Blind Warrior of Nyarong by Yudru Tsomu
Oral and Literary Continuities in Modern Tibetan Literature: The Inescapable Nation by Lama Jabb

Oral and Literary Continuities in Modern Tibetan Literature

The Inescapable Nation

Lama Jabb

LEXINGTON BOOKS
Lanham • Boulder • New York • London

Published by Lexington Books
An imprint of The Rowman & Littlefield Publishing Group, Inc.
4501 Forbes Boulevard, Suite 200, Lanham, Maryland 20706
www.rowman.com

6 Tinworth Street, London SE11 5AL

Studies of the Weatherhead East Asian Institute, Columbia University The Studies of the Weatherhead East Asian Institute of Columbia University were inaugurated in 1962 to bring to a wider public the results of significant new research on modern and contemporary East Asia. http://www.columbia.edu/cu/weai/weatherhead-studies.html

British Library Cataloguing in Publication Information Available

Library of Congress Cataloging-in-Publication Data

Jabb, Lama.
Oral and literary continuities in modern Tibetan literature : the inescapable nation / Lama Jabb.
     pages cm. — (Studies in modern Tibetan culture)
Includes bibliographical references and index.
ISBN 978-1-4985-0333-4 (cloth) — ISBN 978-1-4985-0335-8 (paperback)
     — ISBN 978-1-4985-0334-1 (electronic)
1. Tibetan literature—20th century—History and criticism. 2. Identity (Psychology) in literature. 3. Tibet Autonomous Region (China)—Civilization. I. Title.
PL3705.J33 2015
895'.409—dc23

2015009104

Portrait of Dhatsenpa Gonpo Tsering. Courtesy of Dhatsenpa Gonpo Tseing and Tamsin Leeper.

In memory of my beloved cousin and mentor, poet and essayist
Dhatsenpa Gonpo Tsering (1963–2013)

Contents

Acknowledgments

I could not have written this book without the kindness, generosity, assistance and insight of others. The names of those who have helped me are too numerous to list here, but to mention a few, first and foremost I would like to express my enormous debt to all the Tibetan scholars, writers, and poets I have referred to, cited, and reviewed here. Without their intellectual dynamism and the imaginative fecundity with which they have forged and tempered the vitality of the Tibetan language, this work would have never seen the light of day.

Since I work on the Tibetan language, but write in English, I have received invaluable assistance from both Tibetan- and English-speaking friends and colleagues. Along with my brothers Aga Norchung Tashi, Akhu Lhundrup, and Aga Tashi Rabten, I would like to thank Hungchen, Jangbu, Hortsang Jigme, Sangdhor, and Kyabchen Dedtrol for unstintingly sharing with me their vast knowledge of Tibetan religion, history, and literature. I owe an immense debt to my late cousin Dhatsenpa Gonpo Tsering and my Tibetan teacher Chapdak Lhamokyab who have remained a constant source of intellectual and emotional support ever since they risked life and limb to deliver me over the Himalayas as a young boy. Heartfelt thanks to Thupten Gyatso, and Kate and Tsedup Karko for their constancy in friendship and continued encouragement.

I would also like to extend my gratitude to my inspirational university teacher Kathryn Dean for familiarizing me with Western thought and modern political theory and giving me the confidence to go on and pursue a doctorate degree. Many thanks are also due to Ulrike Roesler, Heather Stoddard, Linda Flores, and Tsering Dhondup Gonkatsang for discerning comments and morale-boosting. Special thanks to George FitzHerbert and Jane Caple for proofreading many of the chapters and for their illuminating suggestions and encouragement. I also wish to acknowledge my indebtedness to recognized authorities on Tibetan literary studies in the West whose works I have engaged with here. To name but a few, I have found the writings of Pema Bhum, Lauran Hartley, Matthew Kapstein, Nancy Lin, Françoise Robin, and Tsering Shakya particularly stimulating.

This volume is a revised version of my DPhil thesis and I would like to express my gratitude to the University of Oxford and the Oriental Studies Faculty for providing a vibrant academic environment. In particular I am indebted to my supervisor Charles Ramble for his wise guidance, erudition, and persistent urging for the publication of this book. I am deeply grateful to Wolfson College for awarding me its first ever Junior Research Fellowship in Tibetan and Himalayan Studies, which has given me precious time for revision. My sincere thanks to the Dalai Lama Trust and the Ti se Foundation, whose generous financial support made the Fellowship possible in the first place.

Thank you to Gray Tuttle and the advisory board of the *Studies in Modern Tibetan Culture* for deeming my manuscript worthy of publication in this pioneering series, and to my editors at Lexington books, Brian Hill and Brighid Klick, for their patience, professionalism, and the speedy publication of this book.

I owe a huge debt of gratitude to my tribe, clan, and family back in Tibet for their abiding affection and belief in me. I am eternally grateful to my parents, Dolma Kyil and Kalsang Jinpa, for bringing up a family of fourteen through the darkest period of Tibetan history and still managing to nourish us with love and care. If this book bears even the faintest trace of their dignity, bravery, and wisdom I will be happy. Finally, from the depths of my heart and bones I would like to thank my sons, Mila and Samba, for their love, patience, and for keeping me sane during the seemingly endless hours of research and rewriting, and my wife, Jemima, for her unfailing support, many sacrifices, and deep love throughout and without whom my academic endeavors would never have borne fruit let alone the completion of this book.

As a Tibetan adage goes "consult others but decide yourself" [*gros gzhan la dris/ thag rang gis chod*], I have benefited tremendously from the insightful advice of many friends, colleagues, and teachers whose brains I have picked unashamedly over the years. What is useful in this book is largely due to the outcome of such consultation. However, I am entirely to blame for the inaccuracies, misinterpretations, and inconsistencies that might be found here although I have tried diligently to avoid them. Therefore, I would like to embrace the age-old Tibetan authorial convention of encouraging and eliciting from erudite minds, criticisms of the limitations of this work, and correction of its faults. Thank you.

Chapter 1

Introduction

The Persistence of the Past
in Modern Tibetan Literature

སྐྱབས་པ་ཐམས་ཅད་ཀུན་མ་ཡིན། །
ང་ནི་ཀུན་མའི་རྒྱལ་པོ་ཡིན།།

All scholars are thieves
I am the king of thieves
Gungthang Tenpai Dronme (1762–1822)[1]

Despite the traumatic sociopolitical experience of Tibetans in the twentieth century and the ongoing precarious state of their nation in the new millennium, Tibet remains a living culture. To paraphrase Shakespeare, Tibet continues to be a breathing part of this breathing world. As is the case in many contemporary societies with a long history, Tibet's past stretches far into unfamiliar and unexplored distance. In the current volume I will demonstrate that this past has a profound influence upon modern Tibetan language literature[2] and national identity in a variety of ways that warrant serious academic attention. Modern Tibetan literature provides a critical voice against Chinese colonial power, as well as against conservative elements within Tibetan society. Existing research takes the 1980s as the point of "birth" of modern Tibetan writing and presents this period as marking a "rupture" with traditional forms of literature. This introductory chapter outlines two key arguments of my book: that such an interpretation ignores the genres, themes and concepts derived from Tibet's rich and diverse oral traditions and the continuing influence of Indic literature and indigenous forms of narrative on new styles and literary devices within poetry and fictional writing. A survey of Western texts shows a neglect of the contribution made by Tibet's literary traditions and traditional modes of oral composition to its "new" literary practices. There are a few exceptions, but these are predominantly concerned with the legacy of classical Tibetan literature to the neglect of indigenous literary precedents and oral

1

art forms. Sketching an overview of my book this chapter will, therefore, outline the literary legacies of *mgur* (poem-songs), Indian-derived *kāvya* poetics and oral tradition.

Such an approach highlights the second principal theme of my book in that it reveals a reinforcement of Tibetan national identity that entails a multiplicity of narrative modes embracing contemporary and traditional literary texts, enduring oral art forms, audiovisual expressions, and a complex interplay of all these. Moreover, leading writers' frequent recourse to past artistic conventions and living oral traditions is itself a form of remembering and reinscribing the Tibetan nation. Tibetan national consciousness is reinforced not just through cherishing the memories and practices of the past in writing, but also through reusing or upholding older forms of narrative in innovative ways. It is important to note here that by Tibetan national identity I do not mean the product of a sovereignty-orientated "political nationalism." In my opinion it goes beyond this state-centric notion as it is a strong collective consciousness generated by a sense of nation embedded within a bewildering range of interconnected factors such as historical memories, cultural forces including literary production, territorial bonds, and the lived experience of the present.

BEYOND RUPTURE

The tendency to view the Chinese colonial takeover of Tibet[3] as the principal determinant of new Tibetan literature and the temporal location of this development in the early 1980s have a restrictive impact upon contemporary Tibetan literary studies. Many prominent scholars of Tibetan literary studies attribute the emergence of modern Tibetan literature to the relatively liberal policies adopted by the Third Plenum of the Eleventh Chinese Communist Party Congress in 1978, which relaxed the Party's restrictions on artistic production.[4] Dhondup Gyal, a Tibetan scholar and a prolific writer, who produced innovative literary works in the late 1970s and early 1980s, is seen as the founding father of modern Tibetan literature. While the immediate aftermath of the Third Plenum is undoubtedly a watershed moment in the development of modern Tibetan literature, an excessively narrow focus on this period has tended to obscure the influence of earlier literary works and figures. It limits the scope of research and overlooks the deep fertile ground within which new literary practices are rooted.

In his PhD thesis on new Tibetan literature, Tsering Shakya also embraces this general periodization and states: "In the 1960s, and more importantly in the 1980s, when a new literature emerged as a force, it did so as rupture rather than as an evolving process."[5] This rupture was caused by a point of crisis triggered by China's colonial rule of Tibet, which brought about a radical transformation in Tibet's cultural production. Chinese rule and the dramatic sociopolitical transformations it unleashed were pivotal in the development of modern Tibetan literature. Nevertheless, an overwhelming emphasis on external causal factors and a search for a fissure with the past leave little room for exploring the enduring legacy of traditional literary forms and oral modes of narrative. Such an argument although insightful only serves as a partial explanation. The drastic changes in Tibetan society and politics affected by the CCP do not necessarily imply a clean break with the past in terms of contemporary literary practices. The link between the past and present is rendered opaque by the sheer magnitude of the sociopolitical transformations. However, underneath the bewildering chaos of historical events, social reforms, and political campaigns in the latter half of the twentieth century lie hidden subtle, yet vital, cultural and literary continuities.

Dhondup Gyal, although credited with being the father of modern Tibetan literature, himself contends in his seminal work on the poetic form known as *mgur* that literary innovation entails tremendous collective labor on the part of generations of writers and artists, as well as a process of critical evaluation. In his view no individual author could achieve such a grand task alone no matter how distinguished he or she might be. He states:

> An innovative literary form cannot be established within a short period of time. Neither can it be formulated by a person of distinction. The birth and development of an innovative literary form requires sustained evaluation of all the experiences regarding literary practices and a reliance upon the laborious toil of numerous artists and writers. Furthermore, it is also conditioned by several factors, such as traditional literature and the artistic quality of a writer. The establishment of an innovative literary form is contingent upon the collective effort of a generation or many generations.[6]

This is not dissimilar to T. S. Eliot's idea of historical sense or "the consciousness of the past" which he sees as a *sine qua non* for the making of a great poet.[7] Alak Gungthang (Gung thang Bstan pa'i sgron me) underscores a similar point in his famous tongue-in-cheek comment that "All scholars are thieves / I am the king of thieves."[8] This suggests that the ability to borrow from great literary traditions and scholars for the creation of one's own work is the defining hallmark of erudition: to be an outstanding artist takes a certain degree of "depersonalization," entailing the appreciation of past literary luminaries.[9] Contemporary Tibetan literary innovation likewise draws heavily on a substantial cultural heritage, thus attenuating the view that new Tibetan literature represents an abrupt break with the old. It is not being asserted here that the present is at the mercy of the past: on the contrary, the two shape each other. Hence Eliot observes that the past is "altered by the present as much as the present is directed by the past."[10]

Tibetan intellectuals within Tibet were among the first of the few scholars to have taken note of the continuing influence of Tibetan literary traditions upon new literary practices. Sangye Kyab, a Tibetan editor, acknowledges this productive interplay in a preface written for a series of anthologies of modern Tibetan literature. After paying mandatory tribute to the Third Plenum, Sangye Kyab celebrates modern Tibetan literature for its aesthetic achievements and literary innovation and for drawing on Tibetan traditional literature, social conditions, and cultural history. He believes the innovative use of Tibetan spoken and written languages by modern Tibetan writers not only preserves Tibetan literature as a whole but acts as an inspiration for its further advancement.[11] Literary innovations are not seen as a radical break with the past. Rather they are thought to be an effective way of preserving Tibetan language, culture, and history in the aftermath of the Cultural Revolution. Viewed through this lens, contemporary Tibetan literature functions as a new social bond which reinforces Tibetan identity through literary acts of preservation and innovation.

Lauran Hartley is also aware of this persistent influence of past great literary figures and feels uneasy with the concept of a sharp historical rupture. In her doctoral thesis on contemporary Tibetan literary discourse she opines that "the unprecedented emergence of a discourse regarding Tibetan literature in the 1980s does not represent an absolute historical rupture."[12] Her perceptive observations of literary greats in the period preceding the Communist era and monastically trained traditional scholars who cooperated with the colonizing power confirms evident continuities between literary productions of the immediate past and the present.[13] Indeed, this belief reflects a consensus among the immediate post–Cultural Revolution Tibetan intellectuals who are heavily indebted to such great figures. The evolution of modern Tibetan literature is unimaginable without the contribution of these traditional scholars. However, the literary influence and inspiration of the past is not confined to these two groups of intellectuals. Factors influencing contemporary writers can be traced back to eras that long predate the Chinese takeover of Tibet. Matthew Kapstein and Nancy Lin also make refreshing observations of continuity with respect to Dhondup Gyal's work, but they focus on the classical Tibetan literary tradition and do not explore it in depth or with regard to other categories.[14] The creative and critical writings of modern literary practitioners bear witness to the influence of both classical Tibetan literature, and also of oral narratives and different traditions of *mgur*. Influence is a term fraught with ambiguities, but here I understand it as the connection between the artists and artistic creations of the past and those of the present. It entails an individual writer's active relationship with the literary and oral traditions.

POETIC REVERBERATIONS OF *MGUR*

Historical endurance, simplicity of style and language, colloquialism, metric flexibility, and a sense of spontaneity alongside accessibility and popular appeal establish *mgur* as a recognizable genre. Genre is a problematic term in literary studies in general, but here I employ it as an established and identifiable literary category marked by a set of features that distinguishes it from other kinds. However, this does not mean genres are mutually exclusive. The boundaries between such categories remain porous and undefined. As such, while classifying *mgur* some scholars differ in their emphasis with regard to specific features such as its secular or religious content. Others trace its origins to *dohā* and *Caryāgīti*, poetic spiritual songs of Indian siddhas, and note the influence of Indian *kāvya* conventions.[15] While acknowledging its association with other types of poetry in this book I understand *mgur* incorporating both the ancient songs of warrior kings (*btsan po'i mgur*, *gter mgur*) as well as spiritual experiential songs (*rnam mgur* or *nyams mgur*). This broad conception concurs with the interpretations of leading Tibetan scholars and poets such as Dhondup Gyal and Ju Kalsang, who stress *mgur*'s embrace of both secular and religious subject matter along with its ancient origins, flexible metrics, vernacular diction, spontaneous pithiness, and contemporary content.[16]

Modern Tibetan literature shares similar features with *mgur* in both its ancient form (*gna' mgur*) and as yogic experiential songs (*nyams mgur*). Modern Tibetan prose and poetry are not confined by the strict metrical styles and ornate idioms of Indic poetics. Similarly, the *mgur* genre, although predominantly metrical, is less rigid and is generally free of ornate diction and poetic ornamentation. As in modern Tibetan poetry, expression of subjective experience—be it sacred or profane—is a principal attribute of *mgur*. Before underlining the continuing legacy of Indic poetics it would be revealing to consider *mgur* as a literary precedent in its own right. Dhondup Gyal's scholarly attention to *mgur* is telling, and its impact on his innovative writing is more than evident in his insightful MA thesis on the history of *mgur* and its characteristics.[17] Throughout his thesis he shows genuine appreciation of *mgur* for its unique style, vernacularism, communicative efficacy, aesthetic beauty, and poetic potentiality for the future. His study demonstrates the enduring popularity of *mgur* throughout the ages among Tibetans from all walks of life. Warrior kings, ascetic yogis, scholar lamas, and ordinary people have employed it to express themselves and portray their respective socio-historical milieux. In contemporary Tibet, writers like Dhondup Gyal embrace *mgur* as a poetic mode of expression.

As already stated *mgur* is characterized by its simplicity of language and style. From existent traditional oral songs one can infer that in its ancient form *mgur* was a song composed entirely of ordinary speech.[18] Its affiliation with simple vernacular idioms has remained one of its defining features. We can thus find the *mgur* genre still flourishing throughout Tibet in the form of contemporary folk songs. An appreciation of *mgur* and other popular oral art forms makes it abundantly clear that they were influential in Dhondup Gyal's employment of simplicity of language and style in his own creative writings. He values *mgur* because it can be easily composed as well as understood by ordinary people, without having to conform to any abstruse literary theories and principles.[19] In contrast, while accepting the contribution of Indic poetics to the advancement of Tibetan poetry, he bemoans the total subservience to it that retarded literary progress and innovation. Dhondup Gyal contends that the failure to produce poetic innovations that were easily accessible to ordinary people lies with the elitist tendencies inherent within the restrictive conventions of the Indic *kāvya* tradition. He believes that *kāvyic* poetics of Tibetan literature served the literati with a refined taste but grew progressively estranged from the ordinary Tibetan people.[20] For Tibetan poets then, the attraction of *mgur* lies in its popular appeal as a simple yet beautiful idiom which overcomes some of the formal constraints of *kāvya* poetry.

Numerous examples can be cited to demonstrate the continuing influence of *mgur* on contemporary Tibetan writing. It is sufficient for the moment to draw attention to the following blog poem:

Machu Diary, Six Entries.
As the sand consumed the little yakhair tent
No chance to behold the dappled sunlight
Even holding my face against the sky
There is no way to tell the time[21]

To a hollow mountain
Making many an incense offering
I wished there was a way to wipe off
The frowns of the angry territorial deity

Yesterday we screamed out cries
Before the iron fortress, gateless
Today we pour out our hearts
Before the old lady, toothless

To the song sung on the mountain top
Response comes none
There is no point to go on
Feeding the fine grey steed

You are a poet
A broom moving in the street

I too am a poet
A windhorse stuck to the ice[22]

I'll not cross the bridge
For soldiers guard the bridge
I'll not greet the soldiers
For soldiers bear guns[23]

This is written by Kyabchen Dedrol, a distinguished young poet who was a leading member of the self-styled "Third Generation" (*mi rabs gsum pa*) literary movement, which will be explored in chapter 5. Unlike the majority of his poetry, which employs free verse form, it is composed in the style of the 6th Dalai Lama's *mgur* or traditional Lhasa love songs.[24] This genre predominantly features four-line stanzas with each line constituted of three trochaic feet. Here each stanza is a daily entry. The language is simple yet clear and fluid. The content is current and deals with the repressive situation in Tibet in the immediate aftermath of the protests that rippled across the Tibetan plateau in 2008. Infusion of a poetic form traditionally employed for romantic expression and witty banter with political content makes it evocative and furnishes it with a sense of immediacy. This poem is a poignant and potent expression of an author's subjective perspective on Tibetans' collective experience of colonial rule.

Recurrence of phrases and images might give it a deceptively unrefined appearance but one can sense a strong subversive element and a refusal to accept coercive authority that comes in the form of gun-toting "soldiers," "soldiers," and "soldiers." The use of epistrophe manages to convey the massive numbers of military personnel who flooded the Tibetan plateau in response to the 2008 protests, and who became a ubiquitous feature of Tibetan landscape.[25] This use of repetition is a salient feature of *mgur* poetry and it generates a sense of unity, familiarity, and intimacy within the poem and underscores the urgency of the message. Its function is captured by the Tibetan saying: "One must emphatically repeat what is urgent/And a hundred times recite the Holy Dharma."[26] This epigram also brings out another type of repetition taking place outside the poem itself—that has a sustaining and preserving use. It repeats the traditional poetic form of *mgur* and this act of repetition contributes to the survival of the latter. Through the employment of simple and memorable internal rhymes, alliterations, and a familiar rhythmic pattern it reuses and sustains an old poetic form.[27] It is therefore more than a poem that responds to an event caused by colonial repression. It is also an indication of the ongoing engagement of contemporary Tibetan poets with their literary tradition that I wish to highlight in this volume. Thus *mgur*'s inherent attachment to simple language and style makes it an effective mode of cultural transmission and political communication to this day. The presence of *mgur* in modern Tibetan writing in various aspects will feature in subsequent chapters.

Another salient feature of *mgur* that might have functioned as a literary precedent to modern Tibetan poetry is its more than occasional use of poetic stanzas characterized by lines of unequal length. Strict metrical composition governs the *kāvyic* poetry that dominated the Tibetan literary scene for centuries until the emergence of Tibetan free verse. *Kāvyic* metrics prescribes that stanzas be composed of symmetrical lines which have an equal number of syllables or feet while conforming to a variety of technical schemes and set imageries.[28] *Mgur* adheres to a freer mode of metrical arrangement which on many occasions permits lines of unequal length. Dhondup Gyal was observant of *mgur*'s more relaxed form of metrics and he introduced to Tibetan literature free verse, which jettisons the highly demanding and restrictive *kāvyic* metrics. He does not explicitly profess the influence of the recurrent asymmetrical metrics of *mgur* on his own innovative literary style. However, it is telling that he should acknowledge the poetic potential of *mgur*'s liberal metrics, which, he contends, can be employed to render contemporary Chinese poetry into Tibetan without undermining either the style or content of the original composition. This is because *mgur*'s flexible metrics is able to reflect the uneven lines and maintain the literary form of the original.[29] Although Dhondup Gyal encountered the genre of free verse through the Chinese language it is apparent that he drew on the poetic resources of *mgur* so as to innovate the Tibetan *vers libre*. Ju Kalsang, a distinguished Tibetan literary critic and poet, also acknowledges *mgur* as a literary precedent when he counters criticism leveled at modern Tibetan poetry. In a critical essay on Tibetan poems of antiquity found among the Dunhuang manuscripts, he argues that the asymmetrical metrical form of *mgur* represents an ancient Tibetan literary tradition and demonstrates that free verse is not a mere imitation of a foreign literary genre.[30]

In terms of style one can easily detect the similarity between *mgur*'s use of asymmetrical metrics and modern Tibetan free verse. Both ancient and modern forms contrast sharply with *kāvyic* poetry, as the following examples illustrate.

For the sire is beloved
Birds too big perish on spear tips
Hares too big adorn boot collars
Annihilation[31]
Royal entombment
No more obstacles, nor their traces
Dunhuang *mgur*[32]

In the crystal clear immaculate ocean
Leisurely glides the lady of the swans
Such a sight divests the journeying full-moon
Of its beauty in the clear, cloudless autumn sky
Gedun Choepel[33]

I've No Tears
Neither like snow, nor like rain
This morning from the skies of Tsongkha
Something unnameable is falling ever so softly
Is it the last tears you've left for this world?

Dissolved into space
Blended into clouds
The person who could frolic yesterday

The butterlamp extinguished
The scripture also closed up
Has the consciousness wrapped in white silk
Fallen like snow in the Pure Land?

I've no tears to shed
Not because I don't miss you
But when extremely sad
To shed tears is quite another matter
Khawa Lhamo (aka Metok Tso)[34]

The *mgur* in the first citation is from the Dunhuang manuscript known as *The Old Tibetan Chronicle*.[35] It is about the assassination of a mythic king—Drigum Tsenpo—and a celebration of the vengeful deeds of his descendants. Its archaic terminology cannot conceal an uncanny resemblance in form to the cited free verse dirge by Khawa Lhamo (Kha ba lha mo—Goddess of Snow), an up-and-coming Tibetan woman poet.[36] This abstract elegy laments a snuffed-out life with intense anguish. It mourns "something unnameable"—a coded allusion to the activism of fiery self-immolations spearheaded by the Tibetan clergy inside Tibet since 2009.[37] Thus the ancient *mgur* and Khawa Lhamo's free verse differ in the use of language, but they share the poetic feature of metrical flexibility and are equally contemporary in the choice of subject matter.

The stanza by Gedun Choepel (1903–1951) is equally distilled but the stylistic difference is immediately noticeable. A proper understanding of it requires familiarity with the Indian literary legacy. Observing technical and aesthetic principles of *kāvya* poetry, it is composed of four finely wrought lines of equal length. It uses a particular type of simile known as

"ornaments of parallelisms" (*sbyar ba'i rgyan*) which is part of a large stock
of decorative devices of poetic language called "ornaments" (*rgyan*). *Sbyar
ba'i rgyan* employs multivalent imagery to infuse a poem with a double sense
while also drawing parallels between two disparate things.[38] Gedun Choepel's
stanza can, therefore, be construed as either celebrating the beauty of a graceful swan, or more likely that of the Goddess of Melody, Sarasvati. According
to Indic mythology Sarasvati was born of the melodies emanating out of the
ocean thanks to the will of the divine creator, Brahmā, who is also known as
"the Swan Chariot" (*ngang pa'i shing rta*).[39]

The fact that modern Tibetan poetry draws on *mgur*'s simplicity of language and style does not mean, however, that it is free from *kāvyic* influence.
A cursory reading of the great yogic poems themselves reveals that even
the *mgur* tradition felt the impact of *kāvya* to a considerable degree. As the
following section will show, contrary to received scholarly opinion, modern
Tibetan literature has also not shaken off the *kāvyic* literary tradition.

ENDURANCE OF *KĀVYIC* POETICS

Indic literary influence on Tibetan intellectuals can be traced back to at
least as early as the time of the Tibetan empire and the early transmission of
Buddhism to Tibet in the eighth century.[40] Following the collapse of the
Tibetan empire, the Indic literary tradition flourished in Tibetan during the
thirteenth and fourteenth centuries, spearheaded by the intellectual endeavors
of the great adept, Sakya Paṇḍita (1182–1251) as exemplified by his book,
Entrance Door for the Learned.[41] His promotion of Indic classical learning with its particular emphasis upon *kāvyic* poetics was followed by many
literary creations remodeled on fundamental Indian literary works and their
translations, such as *Kāvyādarśa* (*Snyan ngag me long—Mirror of Poetics*),
Meghadūta (*Sprin kyi pho nya—The Cloud Messenger*), *The Tales of Rāmāṇa*
(*rA ma Na'i rtogs brjod*).[42] These works have in turn inspired numerous
Tibetan writers throughout Tibetan history with the exception of the artisti-
cally barren decade of the Cultural Revolution. Matthew Kapstein accurately
observes that "the Indian influence on Tibetan literature began more than
twelve centuries ago and has been felt ever since."[43]

The revival of classical Tibetan literature in the early 1980s inside Tibet,
triggered by the restoration of monastic education, publications of traditional
literary texts and high school and university courses in classical literature,
left a lasting legacy on modern Tibetan literature.[44] This is evident both in
the creative writings and analytical commentaries of leading writers. For
instance, many distinguished scholars including Dungkar Lobsang Trinley
and Ju Kalsang employ theoretical and technical categories expounded by

kāvyic poetics when interpreting and evaluating the *mgur* genre and other poetic expressions.[45] In a paper on *mgur* traditions Pema Bhum finds this trend irksome and takes issue with Tibetan intellectuals' failure to find alternative theoretical paradigms.[46] Dhondup Gyal also adopts *kāvyic* classifications of poetic figures of speech and aesthetic experience (*nyams 'gur*) as conceptual tools in his commentaries on the poetic properties of *mgur*.[47] Although he is credited for blazing a new path for Tibetan literature Dhondup Gyal's pedagogic as well as creative writings demonstrate a sustained interest in classical Tibetan literature and its biding influence. In a review of Dhondup Gyal's collected writings Kapstein, one of the first Western scholars to comment on the Tibetan pioneer's keen interest in classic Tibetan literature, notes that his creative writing shows that he "struggled to find a new voice not by rejecting Tibet's literary past, but by immersing himself within and revaluing it."[48]

Dhondup Gyal's commitment to the Tibetan literary tradition is apparent in the sustained attention he accords to classical poetical texts such as *The Tales of Rāmāṇa*,[49] and the 5th Dalai Lama's *kāvya*-influenced historical work, *The Tibetan Annals: Song of the Spring Queen* (*Bod kyi deb ther dpyid kyi rgyal mo'i glu dbyangs*).[50] His writings on classical Tibetan literature occupy a considerable part of his oeuvre, which includes retelling and translation of the Rāmāyaṇa tale, commentary notes on classical texts, and his own compositions influenced by the *kāvya* tradition. Nancy G. Lin sees his work on the Rāmāyaṇa as part of an ambitious project to revive as well as reform Tibetan literature in the aftermath of the Cultural Revolution. She observes that Dhondup Gyal regarded the Rāmāyaṇa as "a suitable narrative to affirm the legitimacy and continuity of the classical Tibetan literary tradition."[51] His selective approach (*blang dor*) shows his appreciation of this classical text while being audacious enough to jettison obscure Indic terminology and mythological references. His rewriting of the Rāmāyaṇa tales and interpretative commentaries on other classical Tibetan texts made them easily accessible to a new Tibetan generation who knew little about the Indic literary legacy. Most of all his immersion in Tibetan literary classics helps to dispel the notion that he rejected traditional authority to embrace a modern genre of literature. Although he is critical of classical Tibetan literature, he sees it as a vital ingredient for the reconstruction of Tibetan literary identity in a modern age. This represents an overall trend among Tibetan intellectuals who view classical Tibetan literature as both problematic and reinvigorating. Kapstein is aware of this proclivity and observes that an *Indianité* voice in Tibetan literature "has been at once reaffirmed and contested in contemporary Tibet."[52]

Even Dhondup Gyal's most pioneering poem, *Waterfall of Youth* (*Lang tsho'i rbab chu*), which introduced the genre of free verse as a defining feature of modern Tibetan poetry, displays the imprints of the *kāvya* tradition. In fact, it appears he only wrote five free verse poems. The majority of his poems are written in the classical style, be it at times informed by *mgur* genre and traditional oral literature. Even some of the images and phrases he uses to invoke the visual and aural sense of splendid beauty and the sweet melody of the *Waterfall* are Indic.

Behold!
Foamy waves white and pure
Ringlets of light, peacock feather tips
Parrot plumage
Patterned brocade
The bow of Indra

Hearken!
The sound of the flowing water, clear and sweet
The melody of youth, songs of the fragrance-eaters
Strains of Brahmā
Voice of Sarasvati
Chords of the cuckoo[53]

Compound expressions like peacock feather tips, parrot plumage, patterned brocade, and the bow of Indra (the rainbow) are employed to induce the visual beauty of the sparkling and spraying *Waterfall*. Songs of the fragrance-eaters (*dri za—gandhaarva*), strains of Brahmā, the voice of Sarasvati, and chords of the cuckoo invoke the melodious sound of the cascading *Waterfall*.

These are recurring motifs and kennings of classical Tibetan literature, employed to convey visual and aural beauty. Admittedly these images here refer to the beauty of a new and promising generation, but they nonetheless remain stereotypical representations. These are images only familiar to a literatus whose taste has been shaped by Indic literature. These features of Dhondup Gyal's most innovative poem have not been underlined to question his avant-garde credentials, but to underscore the continuity of the classical past. As noted by many, his *Waterfall* is undoubtedly an expression of "the burning desire for freedom, modernism and innovation"[54] as well as a resolve to face the challenges of a new age. It also conveys his ideal of change based on preserving and reinforcing the strengths of the past, while also embracing the opportunities of the present for a better Tibet. This approach—that synthesizes the past and the present—can be detected underneath the rhetoric of progress and relentless forward march of the poem. The poem lists the ten traditional Tibetan sciences (fields of knowledge), and asks what should be done to advance them. The *Waterfall*'s answer is to embrace modern scientific and technological progress and ideas of change. We should therefore not be surprised to hear more than a rumbling echo of classical Tibetan literature in the works of an author who sought to refine Tibetan literary production through preservation as well as reform.

As will be shown in the subsequent chapters the current of *kāvya* can be felt in a variety of forms and places. The *kāvya* tradition has not only had an impact on modern Tibetan free verse poetry, but also continues to be a prominent component of contemporary literary production. This is demonstrated by the proliferation of literary forums in the form of journals and websites that publish a considerable quantity of *kāvya* poetry. Another noteworthy development is the increasing use of the *kāvya* form to tackle current Tibetan affairs. This raises the question of whether poetry written in conformity with *kāvyic* theoretical and technical principles, but with topical content, should be classified as modern or traditional. The distinction between tradition and modernity is not as clear-cut a rupture as some seem to suggest. Contemporary *kāvyic* verses express present-day concerns through traditional forms. One example of the numerous verses that could illustrate this assertion is a four-line stanza printed on the inside cover of a 2009 music album. This verse also appears as the last statement of the moving visual images that accompany the songs in the album. The album is a music video (DVD) of Amdo *rdung len* (Tibetan guitar songs) entitled *Tears of the Great Land* (*Sa chen po'i mig chu*), which is a reference to the tragic aftermath of the 2008 protests in Tibet.[55] To avoid Chinese censorship the title of the album is deliberately mistranslated into Chinese as *dà měi gù xiāng, Great Beautiful Homeland,* a formulation employed to deflect Chinese gaze.

As great deeds radiate out of the holy footprints
Displaying images of unforgettable memories
Savage is the treachery that rots the heart of truth
But vain would it be to prevent the fruition of justice

By Jamphal

The translation fails to capture the technical brilliance of the stanza but it leaves no doubt in the reader's mind about whom the poem is addressed to. Its message is for both Tibetan people and the Chinese authorities, urging the former to believe in the eventual triumphant "fruition of justice" and warning the latter about the futility of the use of coercive force. Pop art sheds light upon the current situation in Tibet as it reveals Tibetans' experience of modernity through cultural consumption. The cited stanza, like countless other contemporary verses, echoes the style of Gedun Choepel. Gedun Choepel was one of the first modern Tibetan intellectuals to apply the traditional *kāvya* form to contemporary secular subject matter. A lasting literary legacy results from his innovative and lucid writing style, which fuses classical Tibetan literary conventions with vernacular speech, animated by his critical worldview and rebellious spirit.

GEDUN CHOEPEL: LITERARY LOCUS OF OLD AND NEW

Gedun Choepel is a giant of the Tibetan intellectual world standing on the cusp of the Tibetan modernity. His works display continuities of past literary traditions and innovative qualities that keep contributing to contemporary Tibetan literary arts. Even a cursory survey of contemporary Tibetan writing reveals the influence of his prose and verse styles as well as his critical outlook on life. While much has been written on Gedun Choepel, the literary legacy of his essays has been overlooked.[56] These articulate, novel and succinct pieces of writing remain scattered throughout his collected works.[57] In fact, along with Tharchin, Gedun Choepel should be recognized as a pioneer of Tibetan journalistic prose and essay form as demonstrated by their writings for one of the earliest Tibetan newspapers, *Tibet Mirror* (*Gsar 'gyur me long*).[58] Gedun Choepel embraced this modern literary form with alacrity.[59] The flexibility, open-endedness, and freedom associated with the essay both in terms of form and choice of subject matter along with the essay as "the critical form par excellence"[60] suited Gedun Choepel's propensity for criticism.

His short pieces of writing on subjects ranging from the snow lion and warrior kings to Tibetan language are informative, witty, fluid in diction and structure, personal in tone and unconventional in style. He enhances the essay with the perfection of a long-established Tibetan literary convention known as "verses of respite" (*ngal gso'i tshig*) by either framing them between finely crafted verses or scattering such captivating gems throughout the text. These interval verses not only give the reader respite from the complexity of a subject, but their poetic beauty, wit, occasional humor, and general profundity whet one's appetite for more. The communicative efficacy and artistic appeal of his essays lie in his ability to combine what William Hazlitt described as conversational and literary styles.[61] Donald Lopez briefly comments on this conversational tone in Gedun Choepel's unique prose style,[62] but remains silent regarding his role in the development of the Tibetan essay. To paraphrase Oscar Wilde, Gedun Choepel is an essayist who turns critical commentary into a creative, artistic performance.[63] He is a critic who is an artist in his own right. His short analytical essays noticeably depart from the conventional prose style, characterized by interminably ponderous passages formed of complex sentences and formal phraseology, not to mention uniformity and conformity of content.

Gedun Choepel's stylistic essays are mirrored by influential modern literary practitioners, including Dhondup Gyal, in both form and content.

Dhondup Gyal's essays on the Tibetan imperial period, complete with "verses of respite," bear witness to Gedun Choepel's direct influence.[64] His keen interest in Tibetan history, historical documents, and classical Tibetan litera- ture mimics Gedun Choepel's revision of Tibetan history. Gedun Choepel was a liminal figure on the cusp of the Tibetan modern age, who had recourse to Tibet's imperial past to reconstruct a sense of national identity. He was the first Tibetan scholar to revise Tibetan history through a critical apprecia- tion of the Dunhuang manuscripts—a revision that continues to reinforce the national consciousness of contemporary Tibetan intellectuals.[65] The stirring verses interspersed throughout his unfinished Tibetan history, *White Annals* (*Deb ther dkar po*) are to this day a source of intellectual inspiration and patriotism for Tibetans.[66] In some ways Dhondup Gyal continued this proj- ect, reinforcing his arguments by using a lucid prose style and pithy interval verses inherited from Gedun Choepel and, at times, directly quoting Gedun Choepel's verse as seen in his essay on the term *spur rgyal*.[67] Of course, he is not alone in imitating Gedun Choepel. Ju Kalsang, who openly confesses to Gedun Choepel's impact on his writing, interweaves his essays with verses and phrases that breathe out Gedun Choepel's literary influence. His essay on modern Tibetan poetry, one of the first critical commentaries of the kind, punctuated by and framed in distilled Gedun Choepel–esque stanzas, is a case in point.[68] The prose writing of Tsaba Danyuk, one of the finest contemporary Tibetan essayists, smacks of Gedun Choepel's style and spirit as he infuses it with quotations of Gedun Choepel and imitations of his verse.[69]

Gedun Choepel's literary and intellectual influence is also palpable in the writings of Sangdhor. He is one of the most iconoclastic and distinguished Tibetan writers to have emerged in Tibet in the new millennium. His status as a former recognized reincarnation (*sprul sku*; a status he has renounced) and ex-monk makes his temerity in attacking cherished beliefs and estab- lished social norms, including Buddhism, astounding. His professed athe- ism and relentless attacks on Buddhist philosophy and practices in his book *Audacity* (*Rtul phod*) have turned him into almost as controversial a figure as his hero, Gedun Choepel.[70] He calls the entire teachings of the Buddha "Eighty-Four Thousand Heaps of Lies" in a poem of the same title. This title caricatures and pillories Buddhist doctrines, famously known as the Eighty-Four Thousand Heaps of Dharmic Sermons (*chos kyi phung po brgyad khri bzhi stong*). The poem ridicules the conviction that these teach- ings are the genuine word of the Buddha when in fact it took centuries to commit them to writing. He contends that the fallibility of oral transmis- sion to record information and ideas verbatim, and the impulse of sectarian scholars to adulterate what had been handed down, undercut the authentic- ity of what is viewed as Buddha Dharma. The elaboration and fabrication of these assumed doctrines by subsequent followers through the written word in countless volumes further obscures them. The central thrust of the poem asserts that the Buddhist canon is a creation of collective imagination resulting from centuries of intellectual mendacity. This might be a worn-out argument within wider global narratives that criticize the validity of world religions, but its shock value in a religious society like Tibet should not be underestimated. The poem concludes by drawing a parallel between the Gesar epic and Buddha Dharma to suggest that a conviction in either of them is grounded in equally specious reasoning:

Just as the mythic Gesar epic was born
So-called Buddha Dharma came to be
If Joru's white willow cane is not real[71]
How real can Buddha's imprinted wheels be?[72]
Just as Joru is inferred as really being existed
So is Buddha inferred as really being existed
Just as in beholding the peg that tethers the horse of Joru
Why should one be amazed at beholding the Buddha's eating bowl?[73]

This verse mirrors the witty mocking style of Gedun Choepel's metric compositions and the line of reasoning found in his famous lecture on the Middle Way philosophy of the Indian Buddhist adept Nagarjuna, *Klu sgrub dgongs rgyan*.[74] Gedun Choepel's succinct, fluid style and skeptical attitude inform much of Sangdhor's prose and poetry. Sangdhor's frequent citations of and allusions to Gedun Choepel demonstrate that Gedun Choepel not only acts as an inspiration for his artistic creativity but also for his self-proclaimed humanistic outlook on life. In an essay on Gedun Choepel's aforementioned controversial lecture, Sangdhor interprets it as a non-Buddhist philosophical tract and admits that it informs his atheism and humanism.[75] Although Sangdhor frequently eulogizes Gedun Choepel and acknowledges Gedun Choepel's profound influence on him, his writing reflects contemporary Tibet and has a flavor of its own. As his poetry displays the continuity of past literary and oral traditions as well as an innovative style and vigorous criticism, it will be commented upon in the thematically arranged chapters to come.

There is no indication of Gedun Choepel's influence subsiding, as is evident in numerous literary pieces appearing in the latest forum for Tibetan literature—the proliferating Tibetan language websites and blogs.[76] A respondent to a short article on the history of Baltistan and its relation to Tibet that appeared on the Tibetan Khabdha website[77] posted the following comment in verse. It is clearly influenced by Gedun Choepel's lyrical style and his scholarly interest in the Tibetan empire. It stresses Baltistan's similarity to Tibet in terms of territory, people, and language and history before sounding a plaintive note in the last two lines:

Sabre peaks of snow rock mountains tower into the sky
Here and there the ebb and flow of green turquoise lakes
Through the deep ravined valleys rivers hasten along
It seems like an entrance into the highlands of Tibet
Sixty percent of the populace are Tibetan descent
Ancestry as well as language approximates Kham
Thus opines, scholar Jamphun Gyatso
Song and dance corresponding to Indic tradition
Religion and rituals practiced the Islamic way
Many a Middle-Eastern feature and complexion
The tattered skin of the dead white Snow-lion
Shredded into pieces remains everywhere strewn
Two-armed Gonpo[78]

Nostalgia for a lost Tibetan imperial age, which now resembles the tattered and scattered skins of the mighty and mythical national totem of Tibet, the snow lion, shapes collective memory. Impassioned, a fellow contributor expresses his admiration for this distilled verse in which he could hear the wandering melody of the wanderer Gedun Choepel's songs.[79] Thus classical Tibetan literary tradition steeped in *kāvya* poetics continues to exert its influence upon contemporary writers.

INFUSION OF ORALITY

Another neglected issue in the study of modern Tibetan literature is the complex interplay between the Tibetan oral tradition and literary creativity. Scholars researching the relation between orality and literacy note how great literary works are embedded in oral traditions and how the former cannot be studied without appreciating their indebtedness to the latter.[80] As in other cultures characterized by a coexistence of orality and literacy there is a high degree of "oral residue"[81] within the modern Tibetan literature. This important yet overlooked feature will be highlighted in my volume through various aspects. For now it is sufficient to point out that oral art forms function as a source of inspiration for literary innovation as well as an effective vehicle for social criticism. These two elements can be found in Kyabchen Dedrol's blog poem cited above. It is an attack on Chinese rule inside Tibet in the meter and melody of the traditional Lhasa love song. It not only employs a traditional lyrical form but also draws on conventional visual imagery to portray the contemporary Tibetan experience of fear and persecution. Kyabchen Dedrol's chosen image for the current situation inside Tibet is "the gateless iron fortress"—a popular Tibetan epithet for Hell.[82] Hell, which has always been an archetypal image in Tibetan arts, acquires a new archetypal usage in modern Tibetan poetry as it is repeatedly used to depict Tibet's current political experience.[83]

It must be pointed out that the appropriation of the oral tradition by modern writers is not a simple case of raiding the riches of the oral world for new usages. Neither is it a conscious restoration or revival of old oral art forms epitomized by the endeavors of Irish revivalists like W. B. Yeats who engaged in cultural nationalism by resuscitating Irish folk culture in art.[84] In the case of Tibet orality and literacy coexist and commingle. The presumed demarcation between them blurs beyond perception in genres like *mgur*, popular ritual texts, religious teachings, or the Gesar epic. For instance, the Tibetan epic narrative displays its presence in modern Tibetan literature in a multiplicity of ways while at the same time being narrated by living bards to a wide, mostly nonliterate audience. It is also published in print and multimedia formats and its protagonists, including King Gesar himself, are worshiped as deities.[85] It is, therefore, important to keep this living oral background in mind when we detect Gesar in the works of writers who would have themselves encountered the Tibetan epic through both the spoken and the written word. One such writer is Sangdhor, and most of his innovative poems are written in an eclectic style drawing on Tibet's oral and literary traditions, Buddhist texts, and contemporary writings. In a poem playfully entitled *It's a Story as Well as a Song* he borrows the meter, diction and mood of a self-vaunting Gesar song to wax lyrical about his own writing. The poem is composed of twelve four-line stanzas and the following excerpt should be sufficient to convey an overall feel of it:

I'm the fine halo of my own mind
And dark of night does not delight me
I'll leave fast and bid you "farewell"
I'll flee far and wish you "happiness."

What if I, whose every word is worth
A hundred sheep, were killed by a nark
Before being a pawn against the Red Party?
For this reason too Danma will retreat.

What if I, whose every syllable fetches
A hundred horses, were maimed in a trap
Before getting to fall for freedom?
For this reason too Danma will retreat.

What if I, whose every writing sells for
A hundred *dri*,[86] were finished off by a snare
Before getting to die for the truth?
For this reason too Danma will retreat.[87]

The poem is subtitled "When Avoiding a Drunkard." Sangdhor turns a real-life altercation with a belligerent inebriate into an occasion to sing the merits of his poetry.[88] He goes on to value his poetry over that of older, more established poets like Ju Kalsang. His refusal to be drawn into violent confrontation over trivial matters is inspired by Danma ('Dan ma), one of the principal heroes of the Gesar epic. Of all the fearsome warriors of King Gesar the Tibetan oral sources regard Danma as the consummate hero, celebrated for being endowed with all the necessary heroic qualities (*dpa' kun 'dzoms tsha zhang 'dan ma*) of bravery, strength, resourcefulness, and wisdom. Other warriors might be graced by some of these merits but not by all. For instance, Gyatsa (Rgya tsha), King Gesar's half-brother, is admired for his courage but derided for his impetuous stupidity. The poet takes on the very identity of Danma,[89] who, according to popular belief, only fights for the common good of a community (*spyi chos*) rather than for self-interest (*sger chos*). Hence embedded within the poem is the question of what cause is worth sacrificing one's life for like a "pawn." The poet prefers to be killed by "the Red Party" for "freedom" and "the truth"—that is, for both the cause of Tibet and intellectual enquiry. Thus ingrained ideals associated with a hero of Gesar epic in oral culture infuse a modern poem with national consciousness.

Alongside this ideology associated with Danma the meter and language of Sangdhor's poem are also informed by the Tibetan epic narrative. It is written in the popular eight-syllable metrical line of Gesar songs or *mgur* genre with a catalexis in the first foot and a dactyl for the fourth and last foot. Its language is given a pastoral feel with formulaic oral phrases like "a hundred *dri*" indicating priceless value and nomadic idioms like *sa mda'*, which loses its earthy sense when rendered into English as "trap."[90] The overall self-congratulatory tone of the poem seems to clash with its public-spirited ideal but it is a tone set by an age-old category of Tibetan self-vaunting songs and other oral utterances. This convention proves to be an effective vehicle for imparting Sangdhor's youthful conceit and playing down the literary merits of other poets:

Generally in Tibet, this land of melodious speech,
No person is incapable of singing mediocre songs.
Yet so far there isn't anyone like me who can spray
Mind essences out from the bathing pool of melody.[91]

Thus Tibet's oral tradition reveals itself in various manners in its contemporary poetry in which the Tibetan nation looms large. As will be shown in the following chapters oral art forms also permeate Tibetan fictional writing. For instance, Tsering Dhondup (Tshe ring don grub), who employs nomadic colloquialisms, bases a famous short story on a single episode of the Gesar epic. Chapter 3 will demonstrate that with poetic éclat he mimics its plot, language, and critical spirit in their entirety to censure both Chinese political authority and the corruption of Tibetan clergy.

CONCLUSION: CURRENTS OF THE PAST AND THE NATION

The currents of literary past and oral tradition detected in modern Tibetan writing through the endurance of *kāvya* and *mgur*, Tibetan literary greats and oral sources are also marked by frequent references to a Tibetan nation. Scholars and political authorities disagree over what exactly Tibet is.[92] While being aware of this contested notion of Tibet, following a prevailing Tibetan convention this book recognizes it as being constituted of *chol kha gsum*, three key provinces. This landmass roughly corresponds to the Tibetan plateau and is composed of Tibetan territories now incorporated into five different Chinese provinces. Such a concept of Tibet is based upon Tibetan subjective consciousness expressed through a variety of utterances, myths, rituals, historical narratives, beliefs, traditions, political expressions, and cultural and territorial bonds. This Tibet is also coterminous with the actual territory of the core part of the Tibetan empire. As the next chapter shows this is a Tibet that overlaps with the Tibetan identity evoked in modern poetry and fictional writing. Closely related to this is the term Tibetans, which is also contested. When I refer to and make assertions in the name of Tibetans in this work I mean most Tibetans or nearly all Tibetans from this Tibet formed of three integral regions.

One of the most distinguishing characteristics of modern Tibetan literature is an overwhelming concern with the history, language, and ongoing plight of this Tibet under Chinese rule. The following thematically arranged chapters will bring into focus this aspect along with the interplay between the old and new. All the chapters will delve into hitherto unexplored themes and issues and shed light upon Tibetan literary production. My exploration of topics ranging from popular music, Tibet's critical tradition, and cultural trauma to radical and erotic poetries reveals that in modern Tibetan literary creations, past and present mingle with artistic fecundity and social criticism along with an expression of national consciousness.

As Françoise Robin observes, modern Tibetan literature negotiates Tibetan cultural identity within and subtly against official Chinese discourse and cultural policies as well as among Tibetan intellectuals working under colonial conditions.[93] However, in doing so it appeals to Tibetan culture, history, and traditional forms of narrative as it seeks to create a modern voice or voices. Pervasive political control of literary production through surveillance, imposed self-censorship, well-publicized strict guidelines, and the overall repressive condition under which writers perform their task, mean we need to be acutely aware of double meaning, ambiguities, and coded language concealed within their writings. Writing under such trying circumstances entails strategic decision making and political calculations in the use of literary genres, forms, devices, language, and subject matter.

As such my research will endeavor to reveal some of these complexities by drawing upon insights afforded by a variety of Western theoretical sources. These range from political reflections on the nation and sociological investigations into cultural trauma to philosophical and literary contemplations of metaphor and theories of storytelling. This multi-perspectival approach, which especially benefits from the disciplines of political studies and literary theory and criticism, is supplemented by concepts enshrined in Tibetan works on literature, history, and religion and from the Tibetan oral tradition. Different genres of oral literature such as storytelling, folk songs, balladry, and proverbs are cited to illustrate their impact on modern literary production, and at the same time they are also employed as conceptual tools for providing fresh insights. For instance, proverbs that capture the Tibetan experience, worldview, and wisdom are used as pithy statements for offering a new perspective on literary practices. Traditional forms of oral narrative and poetry are accentuated also because they accord more opportunities for writers to question the colonial power with remarkable audacity. This is made abundantly clear by the creative interrelationship between contemporary poetry, folk tradition, and popular music that mixes the vernacular and the literary.

In the spirit of Gedun Choepel's "verses of respite" it is fitting to end this introductory chapter with a popular song from Tibet that confirms the currents of the past within the creativity of the present. It is a protest song that became an overnight sensation thanks to mobile phone technology. Following its release the singer was detained for a short while before being released, to public adulation. The song is a dirge mourning the death of protesters during the nationwide rebellion in 2008 and the subjugation of the Tibetan nation that began in the 1950s. However, at the same time it is an implicit celebration of Tibetan political agency and assertion of national identity through the very recent historical experience of Tibet. This song is composed of poetic lyrics drawing on folk songs, collective memory, and modern political vocabulary. It is delivered through the popular medium of the *rdung len* genre and disseminated through the modern multimedia technology of CDs, the Internet, and smartphones. This ultimately captures contemporary Tibetan cultural creativity where poetry, music, and national sentiments fuse. The song begins by narrating the persecution of the colonized natives and ends by mourning the deaths of global citizens. In common with many Tibetan oral and literary statements the following lyric associates the arrival of Chinese Communists and their subsequent rule in Tibet with violence, persecution, and bloodshed. Such a portrayal contrasts sharply against the repeated Chinese claim of "the Peaceful Liberation of Tibet."[94] Conscious of the norms of universal human rights, the Tibetan political identity expressed here is both local and global. Like many modern Tibetan lyrics, this song demonstrates the neglected interplay between older forms of narrative and the latest artistic expressions in Tibet, which will be explored further and more deeply in the next chapter:

The year Nineteen Fifty-Eight
The year when the bitter enemy arrived in Tibet
The year when venerable Lamas were imprisoned
We live in terror of that year

The year Nineteen Fifty-Eight
The year when the brave were bloodied
The year when the innocent were imprisoned
We live in terror of that year

The year Two Thousand and Eight
The year when innocent Tibetans were tortured
The year when the citizens of the earth were killed
We live in terror of that year
Tashi Dhondup (2008)[95]

NOTES

1. This famous phrase has acquired a proverbial status in Amdo. It is attributed to the great Lama scholar, Gungthang Tenpai Dronme, but doubts remain as to its origin. It is generally interpreted as a self-critical, derisive remark condemning scholarly compositions that make spurious claims to originality. All the translations of Tibetan texts in this book are by myself unless otherwise stated.

2. While mindful of the arguments about whether works written in non-Tibetan languages can be classified as Tibetan literature, for reasons of clarity and depth my book only treats literary creations written in Tibetan. It is informed by a conviction that one cannot speak of Tibetan literature without dealing with the Tibetan language. For Tibetan debates concerning what language is constitutive of Tibetan literature see Hartley 2003: 258–79. On Tibetan writers writing in Chinese see Lara Maconi 2008: 173–201 and Yangdon Dhondup 2008: 32–60.

3. In agreement with authors such as Tsering Shakya, Lauren Hartley and Françoise Robin, I believe that contemporary Tibetan literary arts are produced under colonial conditions, although they are not necessarily produced directly in response to those conditions. Communist China's control of Tibet bears many of the key features of colonialism. Territorial annexation of Tibet began with military aggression, followed by classic colonial policies of settlement, stranglehold of indigenous cultural

production, political repression, ideological indoctrination, and economic exploitation, which have marginalized Tibetans in their homeland. For one of the earliest documents describing the Chinese takeover of Tibet as a "colonization" manoeuvre see Radio Free Europe's report on Tibet: June 4, 1957. Even the Chinese leadership once employed such idioms of colonialism. In a rare public admission of the failure of Chinese policy on Tibet, in 1980 an exasperated Hu Yaobang, then the Party General Secretary, likened the situation in Tibet after three decades of Chinese rule to colonialism (Tsering Shakya 1999: 382). However, it must be noted that some commentators on modern Tibet such as Barry Sautman (2006: 243–65) disagree that Tibetan experience under Chinese rule amounts to colonialism. Yet other Tibet experts such as Carole McGranahan interpret Tibet's encounter with British, American and Chinese communist empires as "out-of-bounds" Tibetan imperial experiences that question the prevailing "analytics" of empire in the present (Stoler and McGranahan 2007: 18–19, 26–27; McGranahan 2007: 173–209, 2010: 37–52).

4. Tuttle 2007: 154. Pema Bhum 1999: 113, Tsering Shakya 2008: 64–67, and Robin 2007: 23.

5. Tsering Shakya 2004: 41.

6. Don grub rgyal [1985] 1997 Vol V: 519–20.

7. Eliot [1927] 1932: 17.

8. See note 1.

9. Eliot [1927] 1932: 17.

10. Ibid., 15.

11. Sangs rgyas skyabs 1991: 2–5.

12. Hartley 2003: 16.

13. Hartley 2008: 3–14, 2003: 104–52.

14. Kapstein 1999, Lin 2008.

15. Jackson 1996: 372–74; Sørensen 1990: 15–16 and Sujata 2005: 77–93.

16. 'Ju skal bzang 1990: 36–38; 'Ju skal bzang 1990: 36–38. For similar definitions of *mgur* see Rgya ye bkra bHo 2002 (ed.): 58–79; 'Ju skal bzang 1990: 67–98; Dge 'dun rab gsal 2001: 27 49.

17. Don grub rgyal [1985] 1997 Vol V: 316–601.

18. Rgya ye bkra bHo 2002 (ed.): 58–79; 'Ju skal bzang 1990: 67–98; Dge 'dun rab gsal 2001: 27–49.

19. Don grub rgyal 1997 [1985] Vol V: 345–46.

20. Ibid., 350–51. See Kapstein (2003: 792–793) for an English translation of this passage.

21. Traditionally Tibetan nomads measured time by tracing sunlight coming through the tent skylight: a Tibetan sundial where the time indicator is sunlight itself, rather than the shadow of a sunlit object as in the West.

22. Windhorses (*rlung rta*) are prayers and symbolic images printed on small slips of thin paper, which are thrown into the air during fumigation rituals (*bsang mchod*), or when passing through sacred or strategically important places. For the mythic and ritual significance of *rlung rta* for Tibetans see Samten Karmay 1998: 413–22.

23. Skyabs chen bde grol December 14, 2008.

24. K. Dhondup 1981; Sørensen 1990.

25. Smith 2010, ICT 2009 and TCHRD 2008.

26. *Gal bo che la nan bshad/ dam pa'i chos la brgya tshar. Brgya tshar* can literally be translated as "a hundred times," but it is also a plural word and could mean more than a hundred times.

27. For instance, *sgo med* (gateless) and *so med* (toothless) and *brgal* (cross) and *mjal* (greet/meet) in third and sixth stanzas are obvious internal rhymes. The use of alliteration is also noticeable in several places; that is, the letter *tha* in *nyi thig* (sunlight), *mthong rgyu* (to see/to behold) and *rtsi thabs* (way/method of calculation) in the first stanza; and the letter *gya* in *gyi ling gyo rgyal* (fine gray steed) in the fourth stanza.

28. Out of the many Tibetan commentaries on *kāvya* poetics the current book mostly consults Bod mkhas pa 2004, Bse tshang Blo bzang dpal ldan 1984, Dung dkar Blo bzang 'phrin las 2004 Ka, Tshe tan shabs drung [1981] 2005 and Bsam gtan rgya mtsho 2009. For English translations of *Kāvyādarśa* see Eppling 1989 and Dandin 1964.

29. Don grub rgyal 1997 [1985] Vol V: 512.

30. 'Ju skal bzang 1987.

31. *Bla brdungs* connotes annihilation of an enemy, entailing the pulverisation of both corporeal and spiritual existence. See Gyaye Tabo's commentary on the loaded meaning of this term (Rgya ye bkra bHo [2000] 2008: 908–11).

32. Cited in Don grub rgyal 1997 [1985] Vol V: 356–57.

33. Dge 'dun chos 'phel 1994: 406.

34. Kha ba lha mo 2012.

35. *Tun hong yig rnying shog dril* PT1287.

36. Although sometimes pennames are used for reasons of anonymity by contemporary Tibetan writers, in most cases the real identity behind them is already known and as such they function as important supplementary identity markers. As pseudonyms are deliberate poetic statements that utter nativistic proclivities, personal ideals, and ideological outlooks I have translated them into English where possible. For a short observation of the significance of Tibetan pennames see Pema Bhum 2008: 141–44.

37. On February 27, 2009, Tapey, a young monk from Kirti Monastery, self-immolated in protest against Chinese rule. On April 16, 2013, Chuktso, a young mother from Zamthang, set herself on fire for the same reason. Between these two dates, spanning just over four years there have been 115 similar acts inside Tibet of which 98 have resulted in death. For the latest information on self-immolation protests visit the website of the Tibetan Centre for Human Rights and Democracy (TCHRD) http://www.tchrd.org and also consult its *Annual Report 2012*. For a collection of articles on the issue see McGranahan and Litzinger (eds.) 2012 and Buffetrille and Robin (eds.) 2012.

38. See Bod mkhas pa (2004: 307–14) and Bse tshang Blo bzang dpal ldan (1996 [1984]: 593–631) for commentaries on *sbyar ba'i rgyan*.

39. Sarasvati is also associated with a swan mount. She is also known as *tshang pa'i sras mo*, the daughter of Brahmā (*The Great Tibetan-Chinese Dictionary* 1993). It is, therefore, highly probable that Gedun Choepel's phrase *ngang pa'i bu mo* carries a mythological allusion referring to Sarasvati.

40. Dung dkar Blo bzang 'phrin las 2004 Ka: 4–6; Kapstein 754–76; Dge 'dun rab gsal 2001: 50–83.

41. See Bo thar bkra shis chos 'phel dang Ngag dbang chos grags (1998) for this text with interpretative commentaries. Also, see David Jackson (1987) for a study of a section of this work.

42. For *Snyan ngag me long* see Dung dkar Blo bzang 'phrin las (2004 (1982), Bod mkhas pa (2004); Bse tshang Blo bzang dpal ldan (1996 [1984]) and (Szántó 2007: 209–55); for *Sprin kyi pho nya* and its commentaries see Dor zhi gdong drug snyems blo (1988), and for a translation of and commentaries on *The Tales of Rāmāṇa* see Don grub rgyal (1997: Volume I, IV, V, VI).

43. Kapstein 2003: 749.

44. Hartley 2003: 172–82; Stoddard 1994: 132–44; Upton 1999: 17–23. See Bse tshang blo bzang dpal ldan 1984, Dung dkar Blo bzang 'phrin las 2004 (Ka) and Tshe tan zhabs drung [1981] 2005 for some of the most influential books for the revival of classical Tibetan literature in the 1980s.

45. Dung dkar Blo bzang 'phrin las 2004 Ka: 4–12; 'Ju skal bzang 1987.

46. Pad ma 'bum 1994 Ka: 645.

47. Don grub rgyal [1985] 1997 Vol V: 522–82.

48. Kapstein 1999: 46.

49. Don grub rgyal 1997 Vols I, IV, V, VI.

50. Don grub rgyal 1997 Vols V, VI.

51. Lin 2008: 88.

52. Kapstein 2003: 751.

53. Don grub rgyal [1983] 1997 Vol I: 130–31.

54. Tsering Shakya 2004: 192.

55. Nam mkha' dang Dar mtsho 2009.

56. For an appreciation of Gedun Choepel's intellectual stature see Hor gtsang 'jigs med 1999, Lopez 2006, Rdo rje rgyal 1997, Stoddard 1985, Rak ra bkras mthong thub bstan chos dar 1980, Schaedler 2005, Me lce 2010, Huber 1997: 297–318 and Hartley 2003: 104–23; 2008: 4 10.

57. Dge 'dun chos 'phel 1994 Vols I and II.

58. Tharchin founded *Tibet Mirror* in 1925 and remained its editor till 1963 when it was closed down. 70 percent of this historic paper's full run is made available online by Columbia University Libraries. See Thar chen 1925–1963: http://www.columbia.edu/cu/lweb/digital/collections/cul/texts/ldpd_6981643_000/.

59. See Lopez (2006: 15–17) for an English translation of one of Gedun Choepel's essays penned for *Tibet Mirror*, "The World is Round or Spherical."

60. Adorno 1984: 166.

61. Hazlitt 1998: 192. On Hazlitt's conversational prose style fusing art and criticism see Paulin 1998: vii–xxiv.

62. Lopez 2006: 13.

63. Wilde 1961: 38–119. In his philosophical reflection upon the essay Lukács (1974: 1–18) also perpetuates this notion by defining essay as a critical art form.

64. Don grub rgyal 1997 Vol III: 3.

65. Dunhuang manuscripts are a large cache of ancient documents discovered at a cave complex in Dunhuang, the Chinese province of Gansu in the early twentieth

century. They are predominantly in Chinese and Tibetan and are a valuable source for studying early Tibetan history, religion, and society. The International Dunguang Project provides digital images and catalogues of these manuscripts on its website http://idp.bl.uk.

66. Dge 'dun chos 'phel 1994 Vol III: 205–300.

67. Don grub rgyal 1997 Vol III: 8.

68. 'Ju skal bzang 1991.

69. Tsha ba mda' smyug 2011.

70. Seng rdor 2008.

71. Gesar was known as Joru when he was a fatherless young boy. It is said he used "a white willow cane" as a horse because he and his mother were too poor to possess a real one.

72. It is believed that a Buddha bears Thirty-Two Sacred Signs or Features. These include marks of a wheel symbolizing Dharma impressed on the soles of the feet and palms.

73. Seng rdor 2008: 16.

74. Dge 'dun chos 'phel 1994 Vol II: 271–376. See Lopez (2006) for an English translation of and commentary on this controversial lecture on the Middle Way, *dbu ma*.

75. Seng rdor December 29, 2008.

76. The general dissemination and reception of modern Tibetan literature are enriched and made complex by the fast-developing Internet and telecommunications technology. Many of the works referenced in this book including this poem are made available through a variety of mediums ranging from conventional vehicles to the latest mode of Internet-enabled communication. In addition to already established forms of diffusion such as books, journals, newspapers, and school and university textbooks, modern Tibetan literature is being circulated via websites, blogs, Internet, and mobile technology of social media. Individual writers and readers share, exchange, discuss, and distribute literary works through online social networking services like Facebook, microblogging sites like Twitter and Weibo, and audiovisual and text messaging applications like WeChat. It is too early to ascertain, but these latest mediums will have a serious impact on the size and composition of the audience and reception of literary works. The extensive reach, immediacy, usability, multimedia functions, and user empowerment associated with such communicative modes make repercussions ineluctable. For instance, services like WeChat (used by a great number of Tibetans both inside and outside Tibet) utilize audio, visual, and text messaging, thereby making its literary content accessible to a wider public, including illiterate nomads and farmers. The audience is no longer formed of merely students, monks, and practicing writers and poets. My emphasis on the literary text does not permit me to investigate this issue in depth, but it deserves serious attention in future research on the reception and audience of modern Tibetan literature.

77. Dge 'dun rab gsal 2009.

78. Mda' tshan pa 2009. Two-armed Gonpo (Mgon po phyag gnyis pa) is another pen name of Dhatsenpa, aka, Dhatsenpa Gonpo Tsering, a respected exile-based Tibetan poet and essayist.

79. See comment number 20 posted by a certain Palma Yangsang (Pad ma yang sangs) at http://www.khabdha.org/?p=1913&cpage=1.

80. Ong 1982: 77, Lord 1991: 32.

81. A term coined by Ong (1982: 36) to denote the enduring features of orality in the literate world following the introduction of writing.

82. *Lcags mkhar sgo med.*

83. For Hell as a reoccurring image in modern Tibetan poetry see Lama Jabb 2012: 80–81.

84. For the concerted effort exerted by the newly established Irish state and intellectuals in the promotion and preservation of folk culture as part of modern Irish national identity formation see Giollain 2005: 225–44. For Yeats's contribution to Irish cultural nationalism characterized by an endeavor to revive pre-conquest Gaelic folk culture see Hutchinson and Aberbach 1999: 501–21, Aberbach 2007: 92–94.

85. For online literature and art on Gesar epic and ritual texts for propitiating King Gesar as a deity visit http://www.gesar8.com/. For the orality of the Gesar epic see FitzHerbert 2009: 171–96.

86. *Dri ('bri)* is the Tibetan word for a female yak.

87. Seng rdor August 13, 2010.

88. Private communication, October 30, 2012.

89. Ibid.: In this conversation Sangdhor conveyed to me: "One could say that in this poem the consciousness (*rnam shes*) of Danma has transmigrated into me, the poet."

90. *Sa mda'*, literally "earth arrow," is a booby trap containing concealed sharp weapons instead of explosives.

91. Ibid. This conceited tone is somewhat reminiscent of Thonmi Sambhota's self-congratulatory song (Ngag dbang rgya mtsho 1988: 21) and Sakya Paṇḍita's famous praise for his own intelligence and scholarly achievements (Kapstein 2003: 777).

92. Van Schaik 2011: xv–xxiii, McGranahan 2010: 48–52, Tsering Topgyal 2012: 35–36.

93. Robin 2008: 162–63.

94. The use of terms like "Chinese takeover," "colonial rule," and "repression" in my volume reflects this Tibetan perspective and my own perception of the mid-twentieth-century Sino-Tibetan encounter.

95. This and many of Tashi Dhondup's songs of dissent can be accessed at http://www.youtube.com/watch?v=kP5jT2K15Ms&feature=related. Tashi Dhondup received a fifteen-month prison sentence in 2009 for releasing a politically charged album entitled *Rmra kha med pa'i gcar rdung* (*Torture without Scars*).

Chapter 2

Singing the Nation

Modern Tibetan Music and National Identity

ངས་དེ་རིང་ཁྱེད་ཚོ་གླུ་ཞིག་ལེན།།
སྐད་ཡོད་གི་ཟེར་ནས་སྐྲངས་ནེ་མིན།།
ཁྱེད་དགའ་གི་ཟེར་ནས་སྐྲངས་ནེ་ཡིན།།

I'll sing you a song today
Not to flaunt my voice
But I'll sing to please you[1]

An unwelcome effect of the scholarly preoccupation and public fascination in the West with Tibetan Buddhism is that other salient aspects of contemporary Tibetan culture are often neglected. Modern Tibetan music is one such overlooked cultural phenomenon which offers many insights onto a people undergoing drastic transformations, while also illuminating the complex influence of Buddhism on the creative output of the contemporary Tibetan laity. In tandem with modern Tibetan literature, popular music indicates the tentative formation of an embryonic public space within which Tibetans are expressing their common concerns and collective identity under difficult political circumstances.[2] Popular songs provide a channel for voicing dissent, while also reinforcing Tibetan national identity by evoking images of a shared history, culture. and territory, bemoaning the current plight of Tibetans and expressing aspirations for a collective destiny. This is done through the public performance and dissemination of songs with musical accompaniment that mix poetic language and melodious voice. To use a concept of Karl Deutsch, popular music is an effective and wide-reaching "communicative facility" that stores, recalls, and transmits information and ideas in a predominantly oral society like Tibet. As with written poetry, its power lies in its inherent ability to effect delight in the audience. Tibetan popular music, like contemporary literature with which it is closely interlocked through lyric writing,

29

is one of the artistic means through which Tibetans imagine themselves as a nation. It is also a mode of subversive narrative that counters the master narrative of Chinese state power and its colonial conception of Tibetan history and society. This chapter provides a close reading of a sample of typical contemporary lyrics so as to give weight to such an assertion. It underscores the overall argument of this volume by demonstrating how a modern art form that combines musical melodies with a fusion of oral and literary languages is employed in the reconstruction of Tibetan national identity.

STRUMMING SONGS

Modern Tibetan music has a comparatively short history. Like all modern music, it is in a state of constant change and development. Although its roots can be found in traditional musical instruments, melodies, and folk songs, it largely departs from Tibetan folk music traditions and can safely be deemed a distinct genre. Having stated this, its relationship with the past is varied and much subtler. There is a harmonious, be it at times faint, echo which links it to traditional Tibetan music in terms of melodies, messages, lyric composition and specific performers. In its embryonic stage, modern Tibetan music was deployed to serve Chinese state propagandist purposes during the 1960s and 1970s. Tseten Dolma's (Tshe brtan sgrol ma) songs in praise of Chairman Mao and the Chinese Communist Revolution exemplify this early phase.[3] In the 1980s, Tibetan music, like modern Tibetan literature, found breathing space and tentatively freed itself from serving purely propagandist purposes. With an incremental assertiveness it began to express the collective concerns and identity of a people under colonial conditions. Palgon (Dpal mgon) from Amdo and Dadron (Zla sgron) from Lhasa were pioneering figures of the 1980s and 1990s who blazed a path for later Tibetan singers and musicians.[4]

Modern Tibetan music comes in a variety of forms. It ranges from songs sung in Tibetan and Chinese accompanied by Western musical instruments such as electronic synthesizers, and fusions of traditional Tibetan music with Indian or Western melodies, to subversive Tibetan rap. This chapter focuses on a type of popular Tibetan music called *Dranyen Dunglen* (*sgra snyan rdung len*) from the Amdo region of Tibet, which I would argue is one of the most potent artistic modes of communication in contemporary Tibet.[5] The name means "strumming and singing" (*rdung len*) and is performed with the musical accompaniment of a traditional Tibetan guitar (*sgra snyan*) or mandolin. The genre is commonly referred to simply as *dunglen*. Palgon, widely considered the father of this genre, started playing and mentoring some exceptional protégés like Dubay (Bdud bhe) and Doray (Rdo red) during the early 1980s.[6] *Dunglen*'s popularity spread far and wide through radio and cassette tapes in the 1980s and multimedia formats in the new millennium. Palgon's catchy melodies and nationally conscious lyrics have served as an inspiration to thousands of aspiring *dunglen* players across Eastern Tibet. The popularity of *Dunglen* music has spread beyond Amdo to Kham and Lhasa and even among the Tibetan diaspora.

While being mindful of the musical element of *Dunglen* songs this chapter specifically focuses on the lyric with its poetic qualities as a fundamental component of *Dunglen*. Here the lyric is understood in its original sense as a poem written to be sung. *Dunglen* lyrics are mostly written poetic statements carried far and wide by the singing voice, musical instruments, and modern communications technology. Although *Dunglen* songs are mostly heard rather than read they are widely available in their written form. Many of the lyrics are composed by literate individuals and appear in printed form on the inside of the album cover or if there is an accompanying music video they are vividly subtitled in large fonts. Like lyric poetry in general *Dunglen* lyrics are verses characterized by brevity, a first-person speaker, plain speech, poetic figures and the passionate expression of subjective thoughts and emotions. They are mostly short, simple, and expressive metrical compositions that employ a mix of vernacular and literary idioms. This poeticity combined with the musical element widens the reach of *Dunglen* as a vehicle of personal expression and as a locus of Tibetan national identity formation. These are my chief reasons for including a popular music genre in a study on modern Tibetan literature.

TIBET: AN AGGREGATE OF COMPONENTS

Before analyzing three *dunglen* songs, I will briefly clarify how national identity is understood in this chapter and throughout the volume. If we look at identity through the Buddhist concept of dependent origination (*rten 'brel*), it arises in dependence on a multiplicity of interacting causal factors and cannot exist on its own as an independent entity. Like all phenomena it is an aggregated entity (*'du byed kyi phung po*).[7] Similarly, a huge variety of interlinking factors shape the identity of a people. This identity is formed by distinguishing one collective entity from another or others through contrasting features as well as by observing their shared values and characteristics that establish links between different peoples. The identity of a people therefore needs to be defined both in its dynamic relation to other culturally distinct collectivities and in its perceived unique historical and cultural attributes and lived experience. I believe that national identity is formed through historical, cultural, and political encounters with the other as well as through shared culture, common historical experience and memories and long-established myths, rituals, beliefs and symbols that foster collective self-awareness. Unlike modernists

I do not understand it and nationalism (the ideology and political movement closely associated with it) as mere inventions of the modern age. Political aspirations—not necessarily preoccupied with the state—play a vital role in the formation and perpetuation of national identity. However, this political dimension is only a single (be it a key) aspect of national identity which—as Anthony D. Smith has observed—is also "a collective cultural phenomenon."[8] Therefore, among the multiple factors that shape the Tibetan national identity it is necessary to look to Tibet's interaction with other nations as well as its past and recent histories and cultural elements that generate an enduring sense of community and solidarity.

In its project to identify and fix ethnic groups as minority nationalities (Ch. *shǎoshù mínzú*) within the modern Chinese state, the Chinese Communist Party (CCP) drew on what Joseph Stalin called "four commons" when he defined a nation as "a historically constituted, stable community of people, formed on the basis of a common language, territory, economic life, and psychological make-up manifested in a common culture."[9] On top of these essential characteristics, the CCP added "customs and historical traditions" as shown by the following statement, which still informs its concept of nation: "The distinctive attributes of a nation as represented by modern scientific research are commonalty of language, culture, customs and historical tradition, a certain stage of socio-economic development, and a certain pattern of territorial distribution."[10] Cultural forces are crucial even in this highly politicized official perspective. In his definition of nation Smith also stresses similar features when he categorizes it as "a named human community residing in a perceived homeland, and having common myths and a shared history, a distinct public culture and common laws and customs for all members."[11] Tibetan possession of these national attributes is evident but understanding Tibetan national identity requires looking beyond these to collective memory and public will.

Formation of a nation entails more than a few essential features. In his celebrated essay, "What is a Nation?" Ernest Renan did not accord much importance to such common features and instead defined nation as "a soul or spiritual principle" that is constituted by collective memories of the past and the collective will in the present to live as a community "to perpetuate the value of the heritage that one has received in an undivided form."[12] Victories, defeats, happiness and suffering of a people form what he refers to as "a rich legacy of memories." Stressing that common suffering is more cohesive than joy, Renan states: "Where national memories are concerned, griefs are of more value than triumphs, for they impose duties, and require a common effort."[13] Indeed, the songs reviewed here make it apparent that remembrances of past victories and tragedies and an aspiration for a shared future play a crucial role in the formation of contemporary Tibetan identity.

This aspiration often takes the form of a political community, but such a community does not always mean the creation of a state. Max Weber, while stressing the vital role of common memories in the formation of national identity, notes that a collective will to live together entails an ambition for a political community, which for him means a state. Acknowledging the ambiguity of the term nation, Weber defines it as "a community of sentiment which would adequately manifest itself in a state of its own; hence, a nation is a community which normally tends to produce a state of its own."[14] In a similar vein, Ernest Gellner sees the realization of a political community in the form of the centralized modern state as inextricably linked to nation formation. Nationalism, he states, is "primarily a principle which holds that the political and national unit should be congruent."[15] As will be shown in my analysis of *dunglen* songs, Tibetans' longing for a shared future plays a crucial part in the formation of their national identity. Nevertheless, the political manifestation of this aspiration is not as straightforward as Gellner and Weber's state-centric approaches suggest. In terms of political institutions, this aspiration is manifested either through a desire for a sovereign state (*rang btsan*), or a devolutionary demand for a "meaningful autonomy" (*don dang ldan pa'i rang skyong ljongs*) that guarantees a high degree of self-rule for Tibetans in a community of their own within the constitutional framework of the People's Republic of China.

I am not claiming that the concept of the state is irrelevant to the Tibetan case, but am noting that the collective aspirations of people do not inevitably or always entail the creation of a sovereign political community. National movements engage and negotiate with the state but do not always seek to realize what Gellner describes as a "marriage of the state and culture" so as to ensure that the former protects and diffuses the latter.[16] Political communication and cultural socialization can of course be undertaken by agencies other than a Weberian state laying claim to the monopoly of legitimate violence within a specific territory. Karl Deutsch agrees that a people with shared values and aspirations do pursue political power, but he gives greater prominence to the fact that their community is made possible by effective "communicative facilities" such as beliefs, customs, and language subsumed under a socially standardized system of symbols.[17] These are cultural elements that provide a given people with cohesion and continuance. Modern Tibetan music is one such facility that stores, recalls, interprets, reapplies, and transmits information and ideas about a particular community that does not possess a centralized political authority of its own.

To recapitulate, national identity is constituted of a common sense of history, culture, territory, collective memories, and a will to live in a community of shared values, beliefs, myths and symbols. Modern Tibetan music as a "communicative facility" encapsulates all these constitutive elements and thus reinforces Tibetan national consciousness. Tibetans, through their shared historical and cultural experiences, are the principal agents in the construction of a pan-Tibetan identity. Contemporary Tibetan music, by glorifying, mythologizing, and celebrating historical achievements, evoking past and present sufferings and the real or perceived uniqueness of a Tibetan plateau culture steeped in Buddhism, is an important medium or vehicle in this reassertion of Tibetan collective identity. This will be demonstrated in the following section through an analysis of extracts from three *dunglen* music videos.

SAVORING SONGS

Although Tibet has boasted a literate "high culture" over some twelve centuries, it remains a predominantly oral society in which the sung word has a wider scope and more profound impact than the printed word. Few ordinary rural Tibetans, who make up the large majority of Tibetan population and are the target audience of *dunglen* music, are capable of understanding the complex symbolism or coded intellectual idiom used by literary poets. However, the popularity of contemporary music with its novelty and catchy melodies helps to spread the message of even highly literary lyrics far and wide. This is enhanced by the use of colloquial language, clear enunciation of sentences against the backing of a single, simple yet rhythmic instrument like *dranyen*, the Tibetan guitar or mandolin.

The first *dunglen* extract examined here is a song entitled *An Ingrained Dream* (2005) performed by one of the most influential and politically conscious of *dunglen* singers.[18] This song is far more complex than it first appears. The folksy, slow-paced melody of the song, combined with an optimistically prophetic voice tinged with sadness, evokes intense emotions. However, as with other songs in the *dunglen* genre, it is the lyrics that ultimately determine a song's popularity. Audiences pay particular attention to the expressiveness, poetic quality, and currency of *dunglen* lyrics and, increasingly, their patriotic elements or public-spiritedness. In Tibetan popular parlance this much-loved type of *dunglen* has come to be known as "guitar songs of the national pride" (*la rgya'i rdung len*). In the following extract, the lyric is a *mélange* of literary topoi and vernacular speech.

An Ingrained Dream
Last night in my first dream I dreamt
At the peak of the Machen snow mountain in the east
Two turquoise-maned snow lion cubs at play
With a Golden Wheel in their grasp

Last night in my second dream I dreamt
On the Golden Throne of the Sacred Fortress

A Lama imbued with compassion
Gave me a Dharmic sermon

Last night in my third dream I dreamt
In this snowy land of Tibet
I sang a little song of celebration
Upon the reunion of Tibetans

Last night in my fourth dream I dreamt
To this region of snowy Tibet
Returned the Lord of the Realm
Emerging from the sublime Potala Palace

Like most songs of the patriotically informed *dunglen* genre, this song is rich in symbolism of political and historical import. The singer is very well known and was detained by the Chinese authorities several times for singing politically suggestive songs. Employing symbols that reinforce Tibetan national identity, he begins by evoking the image of the banned Tibetan national flag, itself a rich system of symbols (Figure 2.1).[19] The Tibetan national flag is popularly known as the Snow Lion Flag (*gangs seng dar cha*) because it displays a snowcapped mountain and two snow lions as its centerpiece. *Machen*, aka, Amnye Machen, is regarded as one of the most sacred mountains of Tibet.[20]

Reference to it in the song under review is an obvious allusion to the snow mountain on the Tibetan flag. In Amdo, where Amnye Machen is situated, many people refer to it as "the soul mountain of snowy Tibet" (*bod gangs can*

Figure 2.1   The Tibetan National Flag, also known as the Snow Lion Flag. Flag of Tibet, public domain from Wikimedia Commons.

gyi bla ri). As a historic and popular pilgrim site, it is a sacred hub attract-
ing Tibetans from afar and functions as a nationally cohesive force. Amnye
Machen, also known as, Magyal Pomra, *Rmra rgyal sbom ra*, the ancient
mountain deity and mythical ancestral figure who is believed to reside there, is
worshiped daily across Tibet.[21] It must be noted that the name of the mountain
and that of the deity are interchangeable. The Tibetan Bon religion regards
him as one of the Nine Primordial Tibetan Deities in charge of guarding Tibet
(*bod srid pa chags pa'i lha dgu*). Amnye Machen is also regarded as the soul
mountain (*bla ri*) of the legendary Gesar, the supernatural hero of the Tibetan
epic narrative, which is itself another Tibetan national "marrow." When the
Dalai Lama was awarded the U.S. Congressional Gold Medal in 2007, many
Tibetans celebrated the occasion by flocking to this holy mountain.

The two young lions with "a Golden Wheel in their grasp" evoke the image
of the pair of snow lions on the Tibetan national flag, the mythical national
totems of Tibet. On the Tibetan flag the snow lions are depicted hoisting up a
blazing tricolored jewel with one pair of arms, while holding a swirling jewel of
wish-fulfilment at ground level with the other pair. The former denotes Tibetan
reverence for Buddhism and the latter signifies adherence to the divine and
secular ethical codes grounded in Buddhism. In the song, the "Golden Wheel"
grasped by the snow lions as they play has a similar significance in that it is
a well-known motif for the teachings of the historical Buddha.[22] The Dharmic
wheel and youthful energy of the lions are suggestive of an emergence of a
new generation of Tibetans conscious of their cultural and historical heritage.

Similar allusions are made to the Tibetan flag in other forms of popular art
as demonstrated by a typical poster displayed in many family homes in Amdo
(Figure 2.2).[23] The collage of a snow mountain, snow lions, and the Dharmic
wheel echoes the images visualized at the outset of the song. The poster also
features superimposed pictures of the Dalai Lama and the disappeared 11th
Panchen Lama (the public display of such images is banned in Tibet),[24] who
flank the snow-clad peak under the arch of a magnificent rainbow, which
signifies the fulfilment of wishes.

The rainbow as a Buddhist symbol denotes spiritual liberation (that is,
"the attainment of the rainbow body," *'ja' lus thob pa*), but here it implies an
earthly political liberation. This rainbow corresponds to the leitmotif of the
song, which entertains the realization of a "dream" for Tibetans. It is a very
similar "dream" that the poster and its caption refer to:

In the sacred realm encircled by snow mountains
May the strung jewels of infinite wonder and profundity,
The twinned Dalai and Panchen Lamas
Assume the religious and secular powers of Tibet,
And may all sentient beings be graced with peace.

Figure 2.2 A popular poster from Amdo, 2007. Author's own.

The significance of the song's dream motif becomes more apparent in the second, third and fourth stanzas, which allude to the Dalai Lama and his return to the Potala Palace, the seat of political and religious power in Tibet. The Dalai Lama returns home to resume the "combined political and spiritual authority" (*chos srid zung 'brel kyi bdag dbang*). He gives a "Dharmic sermon" and returns to the Potala Palace as the rightful "Lord of the Realm," that is Tibet. With his return the Tibetan longing for the reunion of Tibetans separated since the Tibetan uprisings in the 1950s is also achieved. As already noted, the song is entitled *An Ingrained Dream* and dream is the recurring motif of the lyric. This motif emphasizes a deeply embedded aspiration to regain a homeland, or what Renan and Weber refer to as the strong will of a people to live in a collectively cherished community of their own. It also entails a desire to give political expression to a cultural identity.

Tibet's past, present, and future converge in this "dream." The songwriter's evocation of Amnye Machen, and by extension its mythic deity, is not simply a retrieval of ancient myth for public-spirited artistic use, which the Irish folklorist Standish O'Grady sees as a form of restoring myth to the people.[25] Amnye Machen has a mythic origin but, as already mentioned, is still worshiped daily and remains a unifying part of a living culture. Juxtaposition of powerful and prevalent Tibetan symbols both in the lyric and the visual images that accompany the song on the music video (that is, soaring snow mountains, sweeping grasslands, blue skies, the Potala Palace, massive religious gatherings, and devout *khatak*-offering[26] pilgrims) link this living present to an immemorial past and fuses both with a vision of a better future Tibet. Even Benedict Anderson, who embraces a modernist concept of nationalism, acknowledges that "[I]f nation-states are widely conceded to be 'new' and 'historical,' the nations to which they give political expression always loom out of an immemorial past, and still more important, glide into a limitless future."[27] This song expresses a political aspiration for the stateless nation of Tibet, firstly by invoking the Tibetan national flag and an ancient and living Tibetan national deity. This is immediately followed by a spiritual and political longing for its highest incarnate lama, in whom once again Tibet's past, present, and future come together.

Such an observation makes one take notice of the ambivalent role of Buddhism with regard to the formation of Tibetan national consciousness. Buddhism remains a defining attribute of Tibetanness and is one of the central forces that inform popular *dunglen* songs. This is despite the fact that the central tenets of Buddhism contradict the concept of an exclusive identity, national or otherwise. Concepts such as emptiness, dependent origination (interdependence), and universal compassion negate the existence of the unique self upon which the modern notions of individual and national sovereignty are premised. *Rang med*, or nonexistence of self, can hardly be reconciled to the modern political concept of *rang btsan*, or supremacy of self, which is the Tibetan term for national sovereignty.[28] The Buddhist cosmological concepts of karmic justice and interdependence inform Tibetan understandings of the world.

Nevertheless, despite this propagation of Buddhist universalism, Tibetans retain a strong sense of communitarian distinctiveness and a passion to form a community of their own, if not necessarily national sovereignty.[29] Association of Buddhism with Tibetans' shared sense of consciousness is not a modern phenomenon. It can be traced back to the distant past. The idea of Tibet as the divine dominion of Avalokiteśvara (*Spyan ras gzigs kyi gdul zhing*) has its genesis in the Dharma kings of the Tibetan empire.[30] In the contemporary age the relationship between Tibetan identity and Buddhism remains undiminished if not redoubled, as evidenced by the nationally unifying leadership of the Dalai Lama, the series of protests across the Tibetan plateau in 2008 initiated by Buddhist clergy, and the bewildering spread of self-immolations since 2009.[31] One finds the creation of an exclusive identity, which many modern Tibetan songs celebrate, thanks partly to a religion with a cosmic worldview of intricate interdependence.

The second song extract demonstrates how *dunglen* can act as an effective vehicle for conveying the current sociopolitical issues of Tibet. It is called

Tibetan Finery (2007) and sung by a prolific young singer noted for his expressive lyrics and distinctive voice. This song is again slow-paced and sung in a deliberately quiet melodious voice. It carries a deferential tone with an assertive undercurrent. The lyrics are written in a vernacular idiom and willfully reiterative to hammer home its central message.

Tibetan Finery

I'm a singer who loves Tibet
I sing pure Tibetan songs
Not that I can't sing in a foreign tongue
But within my heart resides Tibetan pride

I'm a singer born in Tibet
I wear rosaries around my neck
Not out of a lack of gold, turquoise or coral
But within my heart lies the behest of the Lama

I'm a singer in the Land of Tibet
What I wear is woven of cotton and wool
Not that I don't possess the skins of leopards and otters
But because our Venerable Lama advised us so

Once again the song demonstrates and encourages Tibetan attachment to a nation or common cultural territory called "Tibet," as the primary refrain of the song. The singer reminds the audience that he was born in Tibet, lives in Tibet, speaks Tibetan, loves Tibet, and sings in Tibetan. Every single line of the first stanza features the term *bod*, Tibet or Tibetan. Thanks to the use of repetition— a unifying and emphatic device in both oral and written poetry—the very being of the singer and, by extension, that of Tibetan listeners, becomes infused by Tibet. This subjective consciousness of being Tibetan through language, territory, and "love" for a cultural entity is instrumental in forming national sentiments. The song also contrasts "pure Tibetan songs" against those sung in "a foreign tongue" thus expressing attachment to the Tibetan language as well as mocking those Tibetans who sing in foreign languages, especially Chinese. This contrast reinforces an ideal of pureness or authenticity, appealing to deeply embedded emotions, wherein lies its strength. It also shows Tibetan resistance against the assimilationist policies of the Chinese state, which exercises a hitherto unknown foreign stranglehold on Tibetan cultural production. The gentle pace of the song and silver-toned voice belie the assertiveness and resolution of the lyrics. As there is a strong perceived threat to the survival of the Tibetan language under the Chinese rule this particular singer is widely admired for deliberately choosing not to sing in Chinese.

The central symbol of the song, expressed in its second refrain, is the word lama. It is a clear reference to the Dalai Lama. This explains the overall deferential tone of the singing voice, which a Tibetan would usually reserve for paying homage to a senior Buddhist lama. This song is a celebration of a wide-scale political and environmental movement on the Tibetan plateau, which started in February 2006, prefiguring the Tibetan uprising in spring 2008 and acts of self-immolation initiated in 2009 in all their intensity, geographical scale, and composition of participants. In January 2006, at a public teaching in India, the Dalai Lama denounced the Tibetan tradition of adorning *chubas* (*phyu pa*)[32] with endangered animal fur and urged all Tibetans to cease the practice. He dramatically declared to a gathering of over ten thousand devotees: "I am ashamed and don't feel like living when I see all those pictures of people decorating themselves with skins and furs."[33] One should not underestimate the gravity of this message to Tibetan devotees, who could not bring themselves to even contemplate the natural demise of their exiled leader let alone to be a cause of it. Although the Dalai Lama's teachings are banned in China, there were many pilgrims from Tibet among the worshipers who would carry the news back. The Tibetan response to the message of their exiled leader was immediate.

As a show of obedience, public burnings of endangered animal furs started the following month in Amdo Rebgong, in today's Qinghai province. This sparked off an intense Tibet-wide campaign and put an end to an age-old tradition in a matter of a few months. As this campaign combined environmental activism with Tibetan political dissent it was widely reported in the international media.[34] Renunciation of a traditional chic fashion was correctly interpreted as an expression of unfailing allegiance to the Dalai Lama. Conscious of this fact and perceiving it as a threat to its territorial sovereignty, the Chinese state resorted to coercing Tibetans to wear fur in an effort to counter the Dalai Lama's influence.[35] The lyrics of this *dunglen* song are a reiteration of this allegiance and a pledge to carry on the anti-fur campaign. Unlike the Tibetan *dunglen* artists who, prior to the public burning of animal furs, used to dress lavishly, the music video that accompanies the song features the singer in simple modern attire without excessive jewelry. The projection of this unpretentious self-image underscores the immediate impact of the Dalai Lama's words in the very person of the singer, not to mention his fellow countrymen. As the lyrics demonstrate, the song also advocates that Tibetan identity can be kept alive by dressing humbly in traditional clothes "woven of cotton and wool" and wearing a rosary, without the need to fall back upon the traditional fur-trimmed costumes and jewelry, which had become frivolously extravagant.

This dress code of humility is also observed by our next *dunglen* singer, who sings a beseeching song, *Lady* (2007) addressed to Tibetan women in general. It is written by a certain Migdra (Rmig sgra), Hoof-beats. Although the singer is a newcomer to the *dunglen* scene his song is worth examining for it typifies many of the politically charged songs inside Tibet. It has simple yet memorable lyrics and an upbeat melody. The music, voice, and words fuse into a rhythmic collage reminiscent of the hoof-beats of mounted horses breaking into a canter. It is tempting for a Tibetan listener to imagine that the riders are none other than the legendary Tibetan armies the song evokes.

Lady[36]
Lady, Lady
Lady of Utsang!
Please don't go, please don't go,
Listen to me! Listen to your big brother!
For it's time to safeguard the political sovereignty
Of Ganden Phodrang, the "Blissful Palace."
Please Lady don't go,
And stay with me.
Please stay with me.

Lady, Lady
Lady of Kham!
Please don't go, please don't go,
Listen to me! Listen to your big brother!
For it's time to command the armies of the Chushi Gangdrug,
The "Four Rivers and Six Ranges."
Please Lady don't go,
And stay with me.
Please stay with me.

Lady, Lady
Lady of Amdo!
Please don't go, please don't go,
Listen to me! Listen to your big brother!
It's time to behold the blessed face of the Wish-fulfilling Gem.
Please Lady don't go,
And stay with me.
Please stay with me.

This song evokes the prevalent and unifying notion of Tibet as an integrated territory, constituted of three *Cholkas*, or provinces, *bod chol kha gsum* (Figure 2.3). The geographical division of Tibet into three principal components has its origins in the distant past. According to written records, the term *Cholka-sum* appears to have been used at the latest by the mid-thirteenth century during the height of the Sakya rule. It is quite apparent that this term is modeled on even earlier sources. When the *Kachem Kakholma* (*Bka' chems ka khol ma*), one of the oldest and most cited Tibetan history books, identifies Tibet as the divine dominion of Avalokiteśvara it describes

Tibet as composed of three regions rich in biodiversity. This book, which is believed to have been written no later than 1049,[37] conjures up a vision of Tibet that precedes human civilization: the upper region is a terrain of snow and rock mountains with roaming carnivores and herbivores; the middle part is a zone of rocky meadows and woods teeming with primates and bears; and the lower area is an expanse of lakes, forests, and grasslands abounding in species of birds and quadrupeds including elephants and semi-aquatic mammals.[38] Many Tibetan historical texts echo this earlier description of Tibet when they refer to the upper part of Tibet as the Three Rings of Ngari, the middle part as Four Horns of U-Tsang, and the lower section as the Six Ranges of Dokham or Three Zones of Dokham, denoting the regions of Kham and Amdo. Metaphorically, Ngari is said to resemble a reservoir lake, U-Tsang channels, and Dokham fields. This symbolic irrigation system fuses *Cholka-sum* into Tibet giving it a territorial integrity as life-giving waters flow from Ngari through U-Tsang to the fertile fields of Kham and Amdo.[39]

As the song shows, the idea of a territorially integrated Tibet is an enduring one. It was this Tibet that in 1253 Kublai Khan, the first emperor of the Yüan Dynasty, offered to Sakya Pakpa Lodro Gyaltsen as the latter's dominion after receiving a tantric initiation from the Tibetan Lama for the

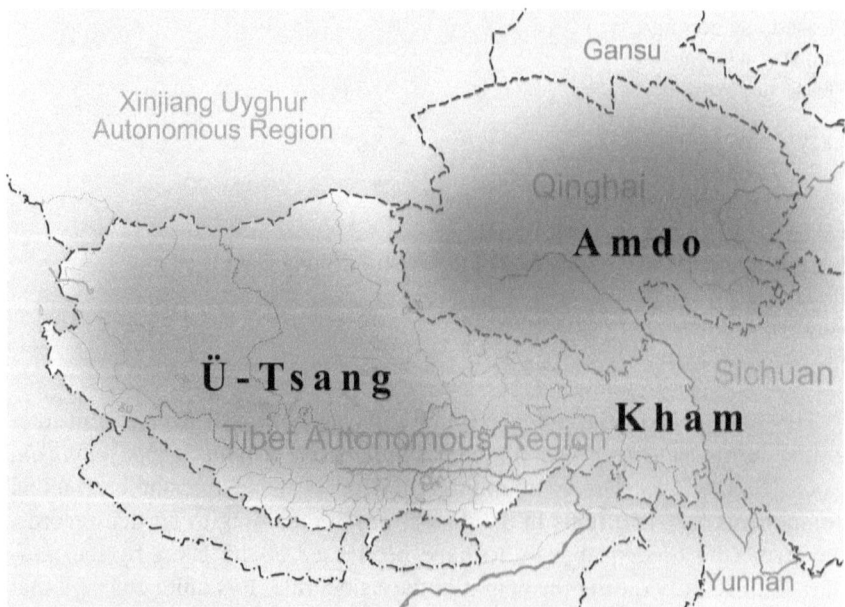

Figure 2.3   Map showing the "Three Provinces" of Tibet. Modified by Kmusser from two maps originally created by Keithonearth and Gruschke. Available under Creative Commons on Wikimedia Commons.

second time.[40] It was this Tibet that the Great Fifth and Thirteenth Dalai Lamas aspired to restore and rule, following in the footsteps of the Tibetan imperial kings. As will be shown in the following section, there is absolutely no doubt that Tibet, constituted of *Cholka-sum*, was etched into the Tibetan imagination and part of common parlance well before the establishment of Communist Chinese rule. This Tibet roughly corresponds to the Tibetan plateau and is what Tibetans mean by *bod* even today. The *dunglen* song, *Lady*, utilizes such a perception of Tibet to remind Tibetans of a glorious past and to call for a concerted effort for its emulation. A unique feature of each Tibetan province is evoked in order to make this appeal.

At the very outset the song jogs the collective historical memory of Tibetans by recalling the Great Fifth Dalai Lama's Ganden Phodrang government (*dga' ldan pho brang*, the Blissful Palace), which was situated in Lhasa, U-Tsang Province. The Fifth Dalai Lama is a nationally unifying figure. He is renowned for his distinguished service to Tibet including its reunification in the mid-seventeenth century.[41] By evoking the image of this celebrated Tibetan political institution, which was established in 1642 and persisted until 1959, the song not only remembers a specific political community of the past, it also entertains an idea of its restoration in the future. Although the jurisdiction of Ganden Phodrang was roughly confined to central Tibet, this wished-for restoration envisions an extension of it to cover the entire Tibet. This is what many theorists of nation recognize as the will to live in a political community of shared values. In fact, the song refuses to acknowledge the current political reality that Ganden Phodrang has been exiled and its power sapped. The lyrics imply that it is still in charge of Tibet although its sovereignty or sovereign jurisdiction, *srid mtha'*, is in dire need of protection.

The second stanza recalls a very recent event in Tibetan history—the military campaigns of the Chushi Gangdrug (*Chu bzhi sgang drug*) against the advancing Chinese Communist forces in the 1950s and 1960s. The lyricist selects this historic movement for its evocative power as well as its association with the second Tibetan province of *Kham*. The name Chushi Gangdrug translates as Four Rivers and Six Ranges,[42] indicating that its members were predominantly from Kham, where most of these famous Tibetan landmarks can be located. This organisation is also known as *Tensung Danglang Magar* (*Bstan srung dang blangs dmag sgar*), the Voluntary Force for the Defense of Dharma. This guerrilla movement was initiated as a reaction against the bloody crackdown on Tibetan resistance to CCP reforms in Kham and Amdo in the mid-1950s. It was formed in 1956 and its military campaigns finally came to an end in 1974. It was partly financed by the CIA from 1957 until 1968.[43] The military operations carried out by the agents of Four Rivers and Six Ranges, former Tibetan nomads, farmers and traders, have acquired a mythic status and continue to fire the imagination of young Tibetans.

Although the soldiers of the Chushi Gangdrug laid down their arms long ago, this song imagines commanding its armies once more, yet again expressing an aspiration to recapture an imagined sovereign nation, through violent means if necessary.

The song concludes by invoking the name of the exiled 14th Dalai Lama, who was born in the third Tibetan province, Amdo. As in the previous songs, the Dalai Lama is not mentioned by name to avoid Chinese censorship and political trouble for the singer, but as the "Wish-fulfilling Gem" (*yid bzhin nor bu*).[44] Although this is an epithet usually associated with the Dalai Lama, it is sufficiently ambiguous to allow for an argument that it refers to another senior lama in case of political interrogation over the lyrics. The music video of the song synchronizes an image of the late 10th Panchen Lama with the utterance of this honorific title as another deflection. He is paying homage to Jowo Shakyamuni, the most venerated statue of Buddha in Tibet, which is also known as the "Wish-fulfilling Gem" (*jo bo yid bzhin nor bu*). Despite these deflections, the identity of the holy person is clear for a devout Tibetan listener in tune with the political message of this song. That the producers go to such great length to conceal the identity of their exiled leader when the song openly calls for the resurgence of "the armies of the Chushi Gangdrug" may seem perplexing but it reflects the hidden nature of Tibetan subversion within contemporary China. Like James Scott's "hidden transcripts," assertive messages are conveyed, but only to their targeted audience "behind the back of the dominant."[45] They do not seek open confrontation but build tacit community solidarity. The central message of the song is a call to Tibetans to regain a Tibet constituted of three *Cholkas* by restoring Ganden Phodrang, enthroning the Dalai Lama and safeguarding it by military means, Chushi Gangdrug.

THAT SWEET HOME OF SNOW

The conceptualization of Tibet as a vast snowy land constituted of three zones has been embedded in the Tibetan psyche for a long time. This homeland long lodged in the Tibetan imagination, written word, and common parlance demonstrates that it is not an invention of the modern age. Nor is it a product of the Chinese occupation of Tibet. There is a common intellectual consensus that the concept of native territory or homeland plays a pivotal role in the formation of national consciousness. Distinguishing nation from a state or an ethnic community, Anthony D. Smith places emphasis on its territorial dimension when he writes that a nation "must reside in a perceived homeland of its own, at least for a long period of time, in order to constitute itself as a nation" with a shared culture and an aspiration for nationhood.[46] It is also this attachment to a perceived sacred, ancient, and uniquely sublime land, which is a recurring theme in many of today's *dunglen* songs. The Tibetan concept of homeland transcends immediate tribal and regional boundaries as well as the administrative demarcations established by the contemporary Chinese state. This "delocalization in the imagination"[47] of Tibetans can be traced as far back as the Tibetan empire and has also been reinforced by the current collective experience of Chinese rule.

The idea of Tibet as a "land of snow" or a "land encircled by snowcapped mountains" permeates historical and religious texts, classical and contemporary Tibetan literature, and traditional oral narratives and ordinary speech. For example, a passage from *The Old Tibetan Chronicle*, which describes the descent of the first Tibetan mythic king, Nyatri Tsenpo, displays a self-centric spatial representation of Tibet, characteristic of pre-Buddhist Tibetan thinking, when it celebrates Tibet as:

Center of the sky
Middle of the earth
Core of the continent
Ring of snow mountains
Source of all rivers
High peaks, pure earth[48]
A great land where
Men are born wise, brave
And devout
Where flourish horses ever so swift[49]

The *Kachem Kakholma*, another early Tibetan historical source, intersperses its text with the phrase "Tibet—the Land of Snow" so frequently that it resonates in the ear long after reading. For instance, the chapter on the origin of the Tibetan race uses the phrase no less than sixteen times with slight variations.[50] Another frequently cited prophetic verse from the famous *Kadam Scriptures* (*Bka' gdams glegs bam*) gives what is typical in Tibetan histories: a depiction of the Snow Land of Tibet as divinely chosen—the dominion of Avalokiteśvara, indicating the arrival of Buddhism in Tibet:

To the north of Eastern Bodhgaya
Lies the *Purgyal*[51] land of Tibet
High mountains like celestial pillars
Low lakes like turquoise *maṇḍala*
Snow mountains like crystal *stūpa*
Golden mountains of amber meadows
Sweet fragrance of medicinal incense
In autumn bloom, flowers golden
In summer bloom, flowers turquoise

Oh! Avalokiteśvara!
The Lord of snow mountains
Your dominion lies in that land
In that dominion live your converts-to-be![52]

This is an excerpt from a prophetic song of *ḍākinīs* which goes on to give a list of sacred landmarks inside Tibet. The historicity of such prophesies can be questioned but that is beside the point. Alongside their legitimizing power they have a unifying quality on a national scale. For instance, the above quotation is cited in many religious and historical texts not only to invoke Tibet as a chosen land but also to weld different parts of Tibet into a sacred territorial integrity.[53] While underlining the "chosenness" of Tibet, different Tibetan religious figures interpret aspects of this prophesy to legitimize their respective denomination and their own native holy sites. Thus it functions as a grand narrative in which Tibet is the hub that holds all the spokes of different narrative strands together and intact. Each spoke is a flexible symbol that can be identified with almost any holy locality inside Tibet.

The great monk-scholar and poet Shangton Tenpa Gyatso (Zhang ston bstan pa rgya mtsho, 1824–1897) continues this line of thinking in an instruction text on "*Kadam* Heart-Essence" (*Bka' gdams snying gi thig le'i man ngag*). He recognizes the great Labrang Monastery (his own seat of learning) as one of the sites alluded to in the aforementioned prophesy.[54] The notion of "chosenness" is also demonstrated by the intertextuality of Shangton's manual, which is interwoven with the very verse cited above. Its beginning typifies many Tibetan religious texts that bury Tibet deep within them:

Dominion of the Lotus-Holder, the Land of Snow,
Loved and possessed by the Compassion Treasures:
The Father and the Son—Atisha and Dromton.
Homage to you, may your compassion hook me![55]

As already noted the idea of Tibet as a land of snow is not confined to historical or religious texts. It is also pervasive in oral expressions, the impact and reach of which, given that Tibet is still a primarily oral society, far transcends that of textual sources. A stereotypical Amdo wedding recital (*gnyen bshad*) gives prominence to the snowy features of Tibet, reiterating metaphorical idioms found in the above verses:

Yes! Let me praise the lie of the solid land, the flow of the pristine rivers and the formation of the high snow mountains of Tibet—this Land of Snows. In its upper region, the Three Rings of Ngari resemble a crystal *stupa*-like snow mountain; in its middle region, the Four Horns of U-Tsang[56] are like a snow lion flaunting the turquoise mane around its neck; in its lower region, the Six

Ranges of Dokham blaze like a tigress and her cub. The majestic Machen snow mountain is like a crystal pillar soaring into the azure sky. The Snow Mountain of Ultimate Victories[57] is like a silver banner fluttering in the wind. The runaway expanse of the Blue Lake[58] is like the azure sky fallen upon the solid earth.[59]

Within these grandiose and recurring images are allusions to Tibet's snow-peaked sacred landscape and past military prowess. U-Tsang, known for its association with the four great divisions of the Tibetan imperial army and Dokham, where many imperial battles were fought, garrisons stationed and later settled, are likened to the physical beauty and ferocity of feline beasts. Ngari, the home of holy Mt. Kailash, represents Tibet's snow-enshrined sacredness. This sacredness is emphasized further as the nuptial recital continues to list one great snow mountain of Tibet after another before launching into the main section. Many Tibetan ballads contain similar passages. One of the most famous bandit ballads begins as follows:

Beneath the celestial stars, moon and sun
Lies Tibet where high mountains compete.
Looking up, beholding that mountain
There in that misty mountain,
Reside I, the Long-necked Yidak,[60]
Whose tale is endless to tell,
Whose deeds are never done.[61]

A traditional oral ode to the tribal land of Mayshul (*dme shul*) in the Upper Rebgong region of Amdo once again demonstrates the centrality of the Tibet image in its narrative. Before praising the beauty, natural resources, and the bravery of its people, first and foremost it locates their land:

Beneath the tent of the azure sky
Atop the fine mat of the solid earth
Inside Tibet, the Land of snow mountains[62]

These citations could be expanded upon endlessly and form an inexhaustible repertoire of enduring historical concepts and symbols which call into question the fashionable notion that the idea of a common nationality is an invention of the moderns.[63] Versed in the discourse that views nation and nationalism as products of modern invention, Gellner states: "The cultural shreds and patches used by nationalism are often arbitrary historical inventions. Any old shreds and patches would have served as well."[64] There are, of course, many cases of deliberate "inventions of tradition" involving reappropriations of long lost symbols and rituals for nationalistic ends as demonstrated by Eric Hobsbawm and others.[65] However, as shown by the concept of Tibet found in the above examples and the cited *dunglen* lyrics, this is not always the case. The continuity with the past cannot be dismissed as mere use of ancient material for novel nationalistic purposes. Whether or not such an idealized, mythologized Tibet conforms to historical facts is a moot point. Besides, as demonstrated by ethno-symbolists such mythical and symbolic cultural elements are as vital for the formation and persistence of nations as any material or organizational factors.[66] Time-honored affection for an ancestral homeland provokes emotive political loyalty and generates a deep sense of national solidarity. It is this and similarly overlooked fluid continuities from the past that partially explain Tibet's enduring cohesive dynamism in the absence of a state of its own that might, in Gellner's idiom, provide a "political roof" for preserving its national culture.[67]

Closely associated with this concept of Tibet is the political reality and idea of exile, which entails if not total loss then at least partial loss of that idealized home. An exile's predicament, sense of alienation, and acute homesickness are commonly recognized features of a forced life in a foreign land. What is little acknowledged is the other side of the exile coin, at least in the case of Tibetans: the sense of loss, anguish, and predicament experienced by those who are left behind in a troubled homeland. This experience of exile by those who are *not* in exile is characterized by pain of separation, the current plight, and a longing for a banished leader and reunion with exiled compatriots. Exile thus plays an influential role in the formation of modern Tibetan national consciousness, as is evident from its impact upon contemporary Tibetan artistic output such as songs, poetry, and fictive narratives. These artistic productions make it plain that exile is a powerful transnational force in the reconstruction of Tibetan national identity inside contemporary Tibet. Homeland, exile, and loss of identity are inextricably intermeshed as shown by the following prose poem by Jangbu, one of the most acclaimed modern Tibetan poets.[68]

Homeland

Our homeland is the liberating property of a term in the dictionary of the future that may only reach us from a remote place after many years. Inside that term the river is forever ebbing away while the fish, seizing the opportunity presented by the distant flow of the river, are pursuing ready formed particularities in the distance. After many years, when they meet in a foreign land they will nurture a new home by an old philosophy[69] and will have forgotten the past intimidations, massacres and betrayals, and may speak to their children of a distant river of ancient times and a distant borrowed home of the future. Upon pondering this, those who lost their homeland may only then pay attention to their homeland.

In essence, homeland is our own body and the fragmentary explanation upon which the body itself relies.[70]

Following the advice of Cleanth Brooks, I will not maul and distort the meanings this poem communicates with clumsy paraphrases.[71] Allowing the poem to speak for itself, it is sufficient to say that loss of political power at home results in an experience of exile akin to that felt by Tibetan refugees in foreign lands, even if one corporeally exists in Tibet. The acclaimed Tibetan writer Woeser speaks of a similar national psychology when she opines that regardless of their place of residence all Tibetans are exiles "in body and spirit." The exile of the Dalai Lama is a constant reminder of that assault on the Tibetan body in the 1950s and Woeser underscores this when she writes: "Every time His Holiness the Dalai Lama speaks to Tibetans in India or in other countries he frequently repeats the words *tsenjol* (exile) and *tsenjolpa* (an exile), and the deep impression left by these two words has become a significant identifier of the Tibetan people post-1959."[72] The Dalai Lama, the Tibetan community, and government in exile indeed occupy a special place in the imagination of Tibetans still inside Tibet, who make up 97 percent of the Tibetan population. Many follow the incessant global travels of His Holiness and his every deed unflaggingly. The naming of Dharamsala as "Little Lhasa" is not a mere cliché. With the flight of Tibetan refugees to India, the center of Tibetan political identity shifted beyond the Himalayas. Although Dharamsala possesses no economic and military hard power, it does enjoy soft power. In the eyes of many Tibetans, political legitimacy to rule Tibet resides there.

Charles Ramble has traced the shifting centers of Tibetan identity throughout the ages and noted the pivotal role India still plays.[73] Influenced by Bon cosmology, pre-Buddhist Tibetans saw Tibet occupying the center of the world, as evident in the extract from *The Old Tibetan Chronicle* cited above. The advent of Buddhism turned Tibet into a self-styled region of barbarians (*mtha' 'khob kyi yul*) in dire need of a Buddhist liberation. Tibet's spiritual center shifted to India, the Land of Spiritually Exalted Beings (*rgya gar 'phags pa'i yul*).[74] I would argue that the flight of the Dalai Lama and the *Ganden Phodrang* government has reinforced this spiritual locus by also shifting the center of political legitimacy. India captured and still captures the imagination of Tibetan Buddhist devotees, but it now also fuels the political imagination of Tibetan artists and activists. Under colonial conditions the narration of exile in Tibetan imaginative writing, including songs and poetry, becomes a form of remembrance, resistance, and living. "The struggle of man against power," writes Milan Kundera "is the struggle of memory against forgetting."[75] *Dunglen* songs are part of this struggle. They counter the Chinese colonial narrative of Tibetan history and society by remembering the silenced tragedies of a very recent past and a living present. Singers and songwriters remember through a creative fusion of music and oral and literary arts, with far-reaching consequences.

FUSING LITERARY AND ORDINARY SPEECH

Dunglen songs have a popular reach even though many of the impassioned lyrics are at times conspicuously literary. This popular reception is achieved through a fusion of literary and ordinary speech in lyric writing, and in performance through enunciation of the words in the most prevalent accent accompanied by explanatory visual images. The contrived style of some *dunglen* lyrics seems to exemplify the Formalist definition of literature as an "organized violence committed on ordinary speech."[76] Through the use of literary devices and deliberate crafting, ordinary language is transformed, intensified, condensed, inverted, and made unfamiliar to a plain speaker. For instance, the lyrics of *An Ingrained Dream* are versified using a combination of formal phraseology and spoken language, with greater emphasis on the latter. However, even this song employs the complex classical synonym "Harbor Palace of the Pure Realm" (*zhing dag pa gru 'dzin pho brang*) as a substitute for the Potala Palace. This is the classical Tibetan translation of the Sanskrit term *Potala,* but it is only in circulation among literate Tibetans. According to Buddhist mythology, Mount Potala is the abode of Avalokiteśvara situated on an island south of Sri Lanka.[77] The Potala Palace in Lhasa was named after it. This mythological allusion would fail to signify the Potala Palace to non-literate Tibetans if it were not accompanied by the term *phodrang* for palace and the music video featuring the signified. Although an excessive reliance on formal phraseology and classical Tibetan poetics would no doubt undermine the popular reach of *dunglen,*[78] moderate use of highly literary terms is valuable in articulating politically sensitive issues and ideas.

A synthesis of literary and ordinary speech enables *dunglen* songs to function as a communication link between Tibetan intellectuals and the ordinary people, thereby bringing them into a cohesive discourse. Something like Gramscian "democratic centralism" is at work here, with an "organic unity" between the intellectuals and ordinary people ensured through constant communication and interaction.[79] The intellectual keeps abreast of the concrete realities and basic necessities on the ground through "active participation in practical life, as constructor, organizer," and as "permanent persuader."[80] Through a combination of formal phraseology and ordinary speech many *dunglen* songs express deep emotions, anxieties, and grievances that concern ordinary Tibetan people. It is this ability to organize and coherently articulate many unexpressed feelings, ideas, and issues of the ordinary people that makes *dunglen* an effective mode of communication in contemporary Tibet. The intellectual lyricists are highly sensitive to the current situation in Tibet and conscious of Tibetan historical experience and cultural heritage.[81] As a result, their songs not only express a variety of emotions but also convey political ideas and ideals, such as national pride and national liberation, back to the listening masses.

As already pointed out, the message of the sung word transcends the confines of the written word in Tibet, where oral transmission is still the dominant mode of communication. Radio, CDs, television, mobile phones, and various multimedia formats deployed for the diffusion of *dunglen* music have ushered in what Walter J. Ong calls an epoch of "secondary orality." The "secondary orality" is rightly perceived as more extensive and the communal sense it fosters is much larger because it embraces electronic modes of communication and incorporates existent technologies of writing and printing.[82] Its reach is even further extended, deepened, and made more complex by a constantly changing plethora of smart communications technology such as mobile phones and computers with twenty-four-hour Internet connection. Such a phenomenon is a constitutive component of a nascent public sphere where Tibetans engage in discussions, critique established sociopolitical authorities, and negotiate their identity through a diversity of artistic means including modern Tibetan music. As we have seen, visual images of historical landmarks, unifying public figures, and familiar daily activities supplement the melody and message of the songs as well as augmenting their entertainment value. We should not be fooled by the unpolished and unprofessional appearances of these music videos into thinking that they have little effect upon the audience. It is true that at times they appear to be a jumble of randomly selected images. The moving image is sometimes completely out of synchronicity with the music, the singing voice, and the subtitled lyrics in the video. There is no use of color coordination and saturation to make the video slicker and more streamlined. There are also many technical problems with the audio quality. Despite the lack of these postproduction touches, which are hallmarks of Western pop videos, images are chosen and assembled with conscious deliberation. Snow mountains, lakes, historical monuments, religious festivals, grasslands and horse races, and so forth are archetypical images that inform the perceived singularity of Tibetans.

In this clinging to symbols of Tibetan identity one can sense a Tibetan denial of the Chinese presence. The majority of modern Tibetan music videos and album covers, unless they are for Chinese state propaganda, have few visual images that indicate Chinese authority or presence. Some Chinese artists' portrayal of Tibet also denies the political presence of the Chinese. For example, this can be clearly seen in Dadawa's controversial album, *Sister Drum* (Ch. *Ā jie gŭ*).[83] Targeting mainland Chinese consumers, the producers use the spiritual and mystic image of Tibet as the artistic springboard for the female vocal. The slick, high-quality visual images devoid of any Chinese presence project a vision of Tibet as an exotic fantasyland, but they may also be seen as an inadvertent acknowledgment of a past Tibet independent of Chinese influences. Ironically in this case, the imagination of some Chinese and Tibetan artists concur but for different reasons. For the former it might be an attempt to escape from a spiritually vacuous and materially avaricious society, or part of Chinese identity construction vis-à-vis the "other." For the latter it is an aspiration to regain a homeland where there is no role for any foreign power.

CONCLUSION: SONGS OF JOY AND WOE

The *dunglen* genre has been flourishing since the early 1980s. Although this chapter emphasizes the politically suggestive songs, these constitute only a part of the *dunglen* genre and the variety of subject matter it tackles. Yet, for nearly three decades there has been a proliferation of nationally expressive songs; even a cursory overview of some of the lyrics produced since the birth of the *dunglen* reveals that its patriotic content grows as the years pass. In the songs of the early 1980s, one finds many archetypal images and topoi referring to Tibet and Tibetans as a collective identity, but less frequently and less explicitly than is the case today. Songs have progressively become more audacious and expressive over the decades in spite of the fact that singers and lyricists responsible for such songs face serious political reprisals. The coded language and ambiguity of earlier songs have given way to more explicit expressions of nostalgia for past glories and aspirations for their emulation. These songs are informed by complex systems of beliefs and values deeply embedded in Tibetan society alongside textual knowledge and traditional oral narratives. They in turn inform the Tibetan audience and have become a vital mode of cultural communication and production, serving a patriotic socialization of contemporary Tibetans. The expressiveness of modern Tibetan music and its preoccupation with common concerns turn it into what Durkheim, following Albert Schaeffle, refers to as social "tissues" or "social bonds" that facilitate national solidarity.[84]

Modern Tibetan music, which fuses the vernacular and literary language, is one of the many communicative modes currently deployed to narrate the Tibetan nation from the margins of the contemporary Chinese state. This process of narration entails a reconstruction of Tibetan national consciousness that draws on Tibet's past, present, and future. This is characterized by a critical attitude toward the Chinese authorities. As will be shown in the next chapter, antiauthoritarianism inherent in modern Tibetan artistic creations also attacks the established Tibetan norms and practices, but not without embracing Tibet's critical tradition. While appreciating the significance of these qualities we should also not forget that the communicative efficacy of *dunglen* resides in its ability to delight and console its audience through its mix of melodious voice, poetic words, and musical accompaniment. It consoles a people experiencing the political loss of their nation. Ultimately it adheres to the old Tibetan adage:

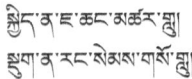

When happy sing songs of tea, wine, and mirth
When sad sing songs of self-consolation

NOTES

1. From a traditional Tibetan song.

2. The public space or public sphere is a contested political notion, but here it is understood as a discursive space where private individuals come together to discuss matters of public concern. It is a space that is relatively autonomous from the state and is critical of it. For a classical discussion of it see Habermas 1992.

3. Yangdon Dhondup 2008: 287–89.

4. For an informative article on contemporary female Tibetan singers including Dadron see Henrion-Dourcy 2005: 195–258.

5. See Yangdon Dhondup (2008: 285–304) and Stirr (2008: 305–31) for discussions of other types of popular Tibetan music. On the production and consumption of modern Tibetan music, including examinations of Tibetan cultural identity and nationalism see Morcom 2008: 259–85, 2010: 385–418.

6. A collection of Palgon's songs along with music charts can be found in Dpal mgon 2010. This volume also features an informative introduction in which Palgon stresses the importance of the traditional Tibetan guitar, originating from Ngari (western Tibet) and the vital role of Gungthang Rinpoche in the birth of *Dranyen dunglen*.

7. Charles Ramble (1990: 196–97) uses a similar analogy in his anthropological account of the social tradition in Buddhist societies.

8. Smith 1991: vii.

9. Cited in Dawa Norbu 1988: 338; and also see Gladney 2004: 9–10.

10. Norbu 1988: 338. For the influence and endurance of this definition see a Chinese state document entitled *Speeches on Nationality Policies* (rgyal khab mi rigs las don u yon lhan khang gi srid jus zhib 'jug khang 1979) and 'Ba' ba phun tshogs dbang rgyal 2009.

11. Smith 2010: 13.

12. Renan [1882] 1990: 19.

13. Ibid., 19.

14. Weber 1994: 25.

15. Gellner [1983] 2006: 1.

16. Gellner 1998: 50–58.

17. Deutsch 1994: 26–29.

18. The songs explored here are well circulated and remain publicly accessible. However, due to their subversive nature and the potential reprisal it might incur the identity of this and other singers are kept confidential.

19. For an explanation of the symbolism of the Tibetan national flag visit: http://tibet.net/about-tibet/the-tibetan-national-flag/ For an informative piece on the provenance of the Tibetan national flag, see Jamyang Norbu December 27, 2007.

20. Some of the sacred and ritual texts on Amnye Machen can be found in A bu dkar lo et al.: 2008. For the significance of Amnye Machen as a pilgrimage site see Buffetrille 1997 and 2003.

21. In Denkhok area of Kham (in today's Dege, Sichuan province) every year a sacred dance, *'cham*, is performed featuring Magyal Pomra surrounded by lesser local deities on Tibetan New Year's Eve. He is regarded as the principal regional deity and as such Amnye Machen mountain remains an object of daily worship and occasional pilgrimage for the local Khampas. I am grateful to Jamji, a Tibetan artist from Denkhok, for this information.

22. For instance, sermons of the historical Buddha are popularly known as *chos 'khor* (dharmic wheels). As wheels can also symbolize *chos srid zung 'brel* (combined political and spiritual authority) here the "Golden Wheel" might, in addition, bear a political significance.

23. I am indebted to Emilia Sulek for drawing my attention to this poster.

24. This is the child (Gedun Choekyi Nyima) recognized by the Dalai Lama as the reincarnation of the 10th Panchen Lama on May 14, 1995. The Chinese authorities rejected this recognition and immediately seized the boy and his parents, whose whereabouts are still unknown. Through an elaborately staged ceremony the CCP recognized another boy, Gyaltsen Norbu, as the reincarnation of the 10th Panchen Lama on November 12, 1995. For issues and events surrounding the Panchen Lama dispute see TIN and HRW/Asia (1996: 52–66) and an illuminating paper by Robert Barnett (2008: 353–421) on the complex selection procedure and the use of new technologies of cultural communication and production by both parties for legitimating authority.

25. Eagleton 1999: 33–34.

26. *Khatak* (*kha btags*) a scarf, usually white in color, offered in greeting people or in religious and secular ceremonies. It symbolizes sincerity, respect, reverence, loyalty, and trust.

27. Anderson [1983] 1991: 11–12.

28. In his reflection on the significance of mountain worship on the formation of Tibetan national identity, Karmay Samten also notes this incompatibility of Buddhism with political nationalism: "Nationalism requires will, self-assertion, self-identification, and self-determination, and these notions have no place and receive no respect in Buddhist education as we know it" (1998: 424).

29. For analytical literature on the role of Buddhism in the formation of Tibetan national identity and Tibetan political struggle, and Chinese reaction against it see: Schwartz 1994, Dreyfus 2003: 492–522, 2002: 37–56, TCHRD 2008, Sperling 1994: 267–84, Germano 1998: 53–94, Kapstein 1998: 95–119 and TIN & HRW/Asia 1996.

30. For early Buddhist mythological accounts of Avalokiteśvara's spiritual conquest of Tibet see Dpa' bo gtsug lag phreng ba 1986: 105–46; Smon lam rgya mtsho (ed.) 1989: 1–57, and Davidson 2004: 64–83. Also see Dreyfus 2003: 492–522 for the importance of treasure texts and Buddhist deities such as Avalokiteśvara in the formation of an early Tibetan collective identity.

31. For information on Tibetan self-immolations see chapter 1, footnote 37.

32. Traditional Tibetan overgarment.

33. Quoted in Ridder & Collins 2006.

34. Many international news media outlets saw this anti-fur movement in terms of Tibetan discontent with the Chinese rule in Tibet and their show of loyalty to the Dalai Lama: Hilton 2006, Spencer 2006, Phayul 2006, and Wildlifeextra.com 2009.

35. Ridder and Collins 2006, McCartney 2007 and Yeh 2012: 408–18.

36. The spelling mistakes in the music video have been corrected in this chapter.

37. *Bka' chems ka khol ma, Royal Testament of the Pillar,* is believed to be a treasure text which contains the testament of the Tibetan emperor, Songtsen Gampo. It is said to have been concealed in one of the pillars inside the Lhasa Jokhang Temple and later discovered by Atisha in 1049. See editor Smon lam rgya mtsho's preface 1989: 1–3 and Dung dkar Blo bzang 'phrin las 2002; 1–2 for a brief description and dating of the text. In his analysis of Tibetan kingly cosmogonic narrative Ronald M. Davidson (2004: 67, 78–80) dates it to the twelfth century.

38. Smon lam rgya mtsho (ed.) 1989: 47.

39. For an explanation of *Cholka-sum* and the internal territorial divisions of respective provinces see Dung dkar Blo bzang 'phrin las 2002: 1430–31; Brag dgon pa Dkon mchog bstan pa rab rgyas: 1982: 1–2 and Zhwa sgab pa Dbang phyug bde ldan 1976: 26–7. Although tripartite division of Tibet has been in vogue for a long time the boundaries between different regions were and are never clear-cut. They are porous and blur into each other. For an analysis of the term *Cholka-sum* and the age-old tendency to divide Tibet into three different realms in Tibetan historical narratives see Hor gtsang 'jig med 2009: Vol 1: 195–240.

40. Zhwa sgab pa dbang phyug bde ldan 1976: 281–83 and Shing bza' skal bzang chos kyi rgyal mtshan 1992: 653.

41. The legacy of the Great Fifth Dalai Lama is acknowledged by many scholars but to name a few: Samten G. Karmay 1998: 504–22, Dawa Norbu 2001: 65–85, Zhwa sgab pa dbang phyug bde ldan 1976: 397–463, Dung dkar blo bzang 'phrin las 2002: 677–78, and Laird 2006: 152–84. For accounts provided by the Great Fifth himself see Samten G. Karmay's [2014] translation of his autobiography *The Illusive Play.*

42. For a breakdown of this list of names see Dung dkar blo bzang 'phrin las 2002: 824.

43. Aspects of this violent Tibetan resistance are still shrouded in mystery but recent accounts can be found in Andrugtsang Gompo Tashi 1973, Sarin and Tenzing Sonam 1998, Knaus 1999, Dunham 2004, Tsong kha lha mo tshe ring 1992–2008, and McGranahan 2010.

44. *Yid bzhin nor bu* is an honorific term signifying reverence to a sacred entity.

45. Scott 1990: xii.

46. Smith 2010: 13.

47. Bulag 1998: 173–79.

48. This is a borrowing of Hugh Richardson's translation of the Tibetan phrase *rI mtho sa gtsang.*

49. This extract is from PT1286. A Tibetan transcription of PT1286 can be found at http://otdo.aa.tufs.ac.jp/archives.cgi?p=Pt_1286. For a translation of a longer

passage from PT1286 including this extract see Snellgrove & Richardson (1995: 24). For similar quotations expressing Tibetan geo-spiritual self-representations see Zhwa sgab pa dbang phyug bde ldan (1976: 17–18) and Macdonald (1971: 190–391).

50. Smon lam rgya mtsho (ed.) 1989: 45–57.

51. Purgyal, *pur rgyal*, is an old epithet for Tibet. Tibetan scholars disagree over the etymology of the term but for an analysis of it see Don grub rgyal 1997, vol 3: 1–13.

52. Cited in A ti sha 2006: 239–40.

53. For instance, adhering to a historical tradition Zhwa sgab pa dbang phyug bde ldan (1976: 17) cites it in his highly influential political history of Tibet.

54. Zhang ston bstan pa rgya mtsho 2004: 47–48. Shangton might be echoing the 2nd Jamyang Shepa (1728–1791) who sees Labrang Monastery and its surrounding landscape in the famous prophetic verse from *Kadam Scriptures*. See the latter's biography of the 1st Jamyang Shepa (1648–1722) for identification of specific sites (Kun mkhen 'jigs med dbang po 1987: 155–63).

55. Ibid., 40.

56. *Dbus gtsang ru bzhi* can alternatively be rendered into English as Four Divisions of U-Tsang reflecting its initial military connotation.

57. This is the name of a mountain in Northeastern Tibet (*gangs dkar phyogs las rnam rgyal*). It appears to be an outlier of Kunlun Mountains (*khu nu la'i ri rgyud*) and can be located in today's Themchen county, Qinghai. Some argue that it is called *gangs dkar phyogs las rnam brgyad*, the Eight-peaked Snow-mountain. For a discussion of this mountain initiated by Mda' tshan pa (2010) visit: www.khabdha.org/?p=7601. I am grateful to all the contributors.

58. *Mtsho sngon khri shor rgyal mo* is another Tibetan term for *mtsho sngon po*, the Blue Lake (Kokonor). A more literal translation would be "The Blue Lake that Caused Ten Thousand Losses" or "The Blue Lake that Flooded the Land of Ten Thousand Families." Legend has it that when its primordial waters first gushed out of the earth to form a lake it burst forth to deluge a massive expanse of land inhabited by ten thousand nomadic families.

59. A written version of this nuptial recital can be found in Karma mkha' 'bum dang Bkra shis rgyal mtshan (eds.) 1995ka: 65.

60. The real name of this particular bandit was Bsam grub rgya mtsho, but he was and is better known by the nickname Yi dwags ske la, meaning the long-necked or scrawny-necked hungry ghost.

61. For a written version of this ballad see Karma mkha' 'bum dang Bkra shis rgyal mtshan (eds.) 1995kha: 47. For an account of this bandit and his sociopolitical milieu see Lama Jabb 2009.

62. Karma mkha' 'bum dang Bkra shis rgyal mtshan (eds) 1995kha: 87.

63. See Dreyfus 2003: 492–522 for an account of Tibetan collective sense of identity predating the modern age that critiques this extreme modernist conception of national identity.

64. Gellner [1983] 2006: 55. I concur with Smith [1998: 45] when he counters this argument by stressing the complexity of the cultural heritage of a given ethnic community. He notes that the binding, collective quality of preexistent cultures cannot be reduced to "traits" or "shreds and patches."

65. Hobsbawm and Ranger (eds) 1983.

66. Leoussi and Grosby (eds) 2007.

67. Gellner 1998: 53.

68. Heather Stoddard has translated a substantial number of Jangbu's poems and short stories (see Jangbu 2010).

69. *Byed thabs snying ba zhig* can be more literally translated as "an old method." Here philosophy in its connotation as a theory or attitude that guides one's behavior is preferred.

70. Ljang bu 2001: 23.

71. Brooks 1959: 256.

72. Woeser 2009: 10.

73. Charles Ramble; *"From 'Centre of this Earth' to 'Barbarous Borderlands' and back again: spatial self-representation in Tibetan politico-religious discourse,"* Friday 13, November 2009, Wolfson College, University of Oxford.

74. Tibet as the chosen dominion of Avalokiteśvara found in the mythology of ancient texts like *Kachem Kakholma* gives it a special status, but it does not wrest away the spiritual authority from India.

75. Kundera 1982: 3.

76. Quoted in Eagleton [1983] 1996: 2.

77. Dung dkar blo bzang 'phrin las 2002: 562.

78. For instance, most Tibetan listeners would not be capable of appreciating the literary merits of Palgon's *Dunglen* rendition of Shelkar Lingpa's (1876–1913) famous poem, *Lha sa dran glu*, "A Song of Longing for Lhasa" (Shel dkar gling pa 2010: 195–990). It is a highly contrived classical composition adorned with phonetic figures (*sgra rgyan*) and formal phraseology.

79. Gramsci 1971: 188–90.

80. Ibid., 10.

81. In terms of lyric writing Tibetan intellectuals have been prolific ever since the birth of *dunglen*. *Dunglen* lyrics either originate from folk songs or are composed by poets and writers. To cite just two examples, many of Palgon's songs are written by monastic scholars, lay writers, and poets (Dpal mgon 2010). These include Gunthang Rinpoche, Manla Kyab, Sman bla skyabs (comedian, poet and prolific lyricist), Doray (teacher and *Dunglen* singer) and Ma O, Rma 'od (poet and senior government official). A similar picture emerges when it comes to a much younger generation of *Dunglen* singers such as Namkha. Some of the finest lyrics in Namkha's popular album *Kha ba can gyi glu ba, Singer of the Land of Snows* (Nam mkha' 2005) are penned by the likes of Ba Gocha, 'Ba' go cha (monk lyricist), Ringon Lamathar, Ri sgon bla ma thar (medical doctor and poet), Krilungtok, Khri lung rtogs (lyricist), and Wongtak Rilu, Wong stag ri lu (journalist and poet).

82. Ong 1982: 136–38.

83. Dadawa 1996. For an interview with the singer covering this album's controversial reception visit CNN at http://edition.cnn.com/2011/WORLD/asiapcf/01/19/talk.asia.dadawa/

84. Cited in Thom 1990: 37.

Chapter 3

The Tibetan Tradition of Social Criticism and Modern Tibetan Literature

བླ་མའི་མཆོག་ནི་མཚང་ལ་རྐོལ་བ་ཡིན།།
གདམས་ངག་གི་མཆོག་ནི་མཚང་ཐོག་ཏུ་འབེབས་པ་ཡིན།

The finest Lama attacks faults
The finest advice finds faults[1]

Speaking of Shakespeare, Ralph Waldo Emerson says: "The greatest genius is the most indebted man."[2] He is asserting the impossibility of artistic and intellectual innovation without the vital aid of tradition. An Eliotian "consciousness of the past" is an imperative for the forging of distinguished artists. Great modern Tibetan writers are also equally indebted to Tibet's artistic and intellectual past and living oral traditions. In their writing, one can say with William Faulkner "the past is never dead, it is not even past."[3] This is evident in the neglected impact of different forms of Tibetan oral narrative and traditional literature on Tibet's modern creative writing. This impact manifests itself in both innovative literary forms and injections of critical content in the form of social criticism. The overlooked Tibetan tradition of social criticism helps to repel the scholarly assumption that the Tibetan critical attitude is a product of the modern age.

This chapter will first briefly acknowledge the critical legacy of traditional Tibetan literary figures, *mgur*, and proverbs. Then it will proceed to focuses on the critical input from the Tibetan Gesar epic and romantic balladry. These predominantly oral genres are selected here because of their particularly enduring elements of social criticism and their artistic influence evident in contemporary writers. In both of these genres we see criticisms leveled at the perceived social and religious wrongs of Tibetan culture, but it must also be noted at the outset that these are by no means "revolutionary" genres: they do not seek a systemic overhaul of Tibetan society, unlike Chinese Communist

59

ideology and policies. An analysis of these materials illuminates the interplay between the orality of Tibetan culture and modern literary creativity. It also helps to question the prevailing idea that modern Tibetan literature marks a total rupture with the past while problematizing theoretical dichotomies such as the traditional and the modern.

TIBET'S CRITICAL TRADITION

There is a common tendency in academic literature to attribute critical commentary on sociopolitical practices found in modern Tibetan literature to Tibet's colonial experience since the 1950s.[4] This overlooks the critical tradition inherent in classical Tibetan literature as well as in different forms of oral narrative that predate the arrival of the Chinese Communists in Tibet. In a perceptive paper on the representation of religion in contemporary Tibetan fiction, Robin finds that Tibetan writers' portrayal of religion and religious figures underwent a transformation following the 1980s.[5] The earliest short story writers, such as Tsering Dhondup, were radically critical of the Buddhist clergy, partly due to the fact that they were writing in the aftermath of the Cultural Revolution. Over time, attitudes toward religion shift from what Robin classifies as radical anti-clericalism, to a selective rationalist approach that critiques overtly superstitious practices, rather than religious culture in its entirety. From the mid-1990s, a more positive reappraisal of Tibetan Buddhism starts to inform Tibetan fictive narrative. Robin ascribes such critical attitudes to the shifting cultural policies of the colonizing power and makes no mention of indigenous and traditional sources of critical thinking.

It is informative to look beyond colonial policy, education, and political control in general to find other antecedents to modern Tibetan writers' criticisms of superstition and unequal social relations. Many great Tibetan Lamas, yogis, and scholar monks have advised against superstitious practices throughout history and endeavored to distance Buddhism from the worshiping of worldly gods and spirits.[6] They have preached against the corrupting propensities of the Buddhist clergy in spiritual and material pursuits, as evident in such popular idiomatic expressions found scattered in their works: "It is not the pure Dharma that flourishes but worship of materialism."[7] A sharp, critical spirit has often been encouraged and celebrated in Lamas. For instance, an often quoted maxim attributed to Atisha singles out the ability to censure as the hallmark of a great Lama: "The finest Lama attacks faults/ The finest advice finds faults."[8] To name the works of just a few great itinerant Tibetan yogis, the songs and life stories of Milarepa (1052–1135), Drukpa Kunleg (1455–1529), Shar Kalden Gyatso (1607–1677), Shabkarpa (1781–1851), and Za Paltrul (1808–1887) are replete with similar critical content. The 6th Dalai Lama's self-criticism of halfhearted religious devotion or semi-monkhood in the following stanza is a pithy representative of this critical tradition, which is upheld by many Buddhist thinkers and practitioners to this day. Through self-criticism, a general phenomenon in Tibetan society is targeted:

Dark clouds with golden lining
Are harbingers of frost and hail
Monks neither lay nor religious
Are enemies of Buddha Dharma[9]

Another exceptional monk-scholar and poet, Shangton Tenpa Gyatso (1824–1897), continues this tradition in the carping epilogue to his famous tract of elegant sayings, which is a sublime paraphrase of Dromton's ('Brom ston, 1004–1064) already fine verses of advice.[10] These precepts are well-loved for their practical observations of life and their poetic beauty. Their popularity is attested by the fact that they have been republished several times. For instance, this text can be found in at least three anthologies of Tibetan literature which are widely circulated among monks, high school and university students, and the general public alike.[11] A couple of these influential anthologies were first published in the 1980s when new Tibetan literature, *gsar rtsom*, started to flourish. Thus it has been part of the literary diet of new writers over three decades. Some parts of this text have also been incorporated into a Tibetan language textbook for junior middle school pupils in Chinese state-run schools.[12] Therefore, one can presume that the following critical message has had a big audience:

The Lama known for his greatness and fame
Is never present when beseeched by the pillowed dying
The vulture that soars high in the blue sky
Circles over the corpse with its wings—flap, flap

The ritualist who forages for food offerings
Never ceases to move his mouth and hands
Pikas and mice on the ground and amidst the crags
Never cease to move their muzzle—nibble, nibble

The great yogi who roams through wild mountains
Wanders at villagers' doors collecting fistfuls of barley
The hungry wolf that roams the empty valleys by day
By night prowls the encampment's edge—sneak, sneak

Powerful men who crave after fame and status
Never tire though hardships accumulate on the way

The stag that wanders through high rock mountains
Never for a moment stays still—stumble, stumble[13]

The communicative efficacy of fine poetry is apparent in this extract which is composed in a distinctive *mgur* meter. This is one of the best-loved meters of Tibetan *mgur* poets. It is written in four-line stanzas. Each line consists of four feet: three trochees with catalexis in the first foot, and the fourth foot a dactyl. It goes: 1/10/10/100 in which 1 = stressed and 0 = unstressed. In the above verse the last line of each stanza is embellished with a Tibetan poetic device that is visually, aurally, and rhythmically descriptive in an untranslateable way—"*kho lhab be lhab be ro la 'khor*"—(*It*) *circles the corpse with its wings—flap, flap.* It is quite impossible to render the rhythm and expressiveness of these phrases into English. This rhetorical device is used in both oral and written composition and is at least, as ancient as the recorded Tibetan language itself. In its written form, it can be found, for example, in the archaic songs of Dunghuang manuscripts.

Commenting on these poem-songs Roger Jackson calls such traits "reduplicated or trebled onomatopoetic phrases."[14] In his analysis of a subversive recitation by the Bhutanese wandering bards Michael Aris calls these figures "that well-known poetic device of reduplicated syllables having no lexical value, employed to describe specific appearance or situations."[15] However, they are not just for conveying rhythmic sound or producing alliterative, syllabic meters. They are lexically rooted and are a nuanced imagistic representation of both abstract and concrete entities being described. On top of the onomatopoeic quality they add visual images of the action, scene, and object being described. This includes sensitive descriptions of specific motions or movements associated with the entities in question. Within them one finds the heightened sensibility of the poet and the vivid imagination of the reader. In the above verses, Shangton Tenpa Gyatso flaunts his technical brilliance and mastery of this expressive device as he takes issue with the hypocrisy, irresponsibility, avarice, and untrustworthiness of high Lamas, monk ritualists, ascetic yogis, and powerful men, who are likened to restless, hunger-driven vultures, rodents, wolves, and stags. Criticism is leveled against charlatans familiar in any time—a message as pertinent today as it was during the nineteenth century when the poem was composed.

Prompted by Alak Dorshi's (Dor zhi gdong drug snyems blo) contextualisation of Dhondup Gyal's censorious attitude to religion within this critical tradition,[16] Matthew Kapstein—in his reflections on Dhondup Gyal's short story, *Sprul sku*—acknowledges voices skeptical of Buddhist practices in pre-modern Tibet, but concludes that these were merely "the prerogative of the religious elite."[17] What is implied is that this critical scrutiny neither influenced the thinking of the traditional laity nor bequeathed anything to

Dhondup Gyal's skeptical outlook, which is thought to have been the product of a modern age. This suggestion reflects the assumption of a hermetically sealed dichotomy between the religious and the secular, and between the traditional and the modern. This, I would argue, is a difficult position to maintain when one considers the socio-artistic legacy of roaming, maverick yogis singing and preaching in a vernacular idiom in traditional Tibet,[18] and Dhondup Gyal's own immersion in this traditional legacy of critical verse. Michael Aris is acutely aware of this porous boundary between the sacred and the profane in traditional Tibet and discerns mutual borrowings between the tantric yogin and the peasant that make the line even less distinct. The spiritual songs of the tantric yogin, writes Aris, "often proclaimed the highest mystical insights in the meter of humble folk-songs, drawing their imagery from the world of the village and the tent. Peasants for their part introduced all kinds of Buddhist allusions and gestures into their songs and dances. In countless ways besides this we can observe how a sphere that was conventionally regarded as 'sacred' came to be penetrated by or absorbed into a sphere usually looked on as 'secular,' and vice versa." Dhondup Gyal inherited such a cultural world, albeit one seriously disrupted by the advent of the Chinese Communists in the 1950s and the chaos of the Cultural Revolution.

Besides, oral and vernacular transmission of *mgur* and Dharmic teachings alongside their written form further blurs the sharp boundary that is presumed to lie between a literate religious elite and their fellow illiterate devotees. Dhondup Gyal was brought up within a lay tantric community in Amdo where singing and reciting of *mgur* were part of its cultural legacy. He also made a seminal study of the *mgur* genre across history, for which he examined thirty hagiographical works and ten *mgur* collections by past scholars, which spanned several centuries.[19] Rumor has it that even his penname Rangdrol[20] ("self-liberation") reflects his cultural roots. It is said that although Dhondup Gyal refused his recognition as a reincarnate Lama (*bla sprul*) by some tantric practitioners from his village, he later adopted the term Rangdrol as pseudonym, which was his intended reincarnate Lama name.[21] Whether this account is apocryphal or not, it underscores Dhondup Gyal's links to a tantric community that had produced several influential masters and poets in the past.[22] Given these factors and the revelation that he was cared for in his minority, by his monk uncle, who helped him master literary skills including liturgical prayers and chants (*'don chog*),[23] it would be hard to imagine that his artistic creations were not influenced by Tibet's critical tradition and its literary heritage.

The expression of a critical attitude in traditional culture was not confined to the pronouncements of religious figures. It was, and is, prevalent in the ordinary speech of the laity, as can be seen in the following sharp Tibetan proverbs.

ལྷ་པ་མོ་པ་རྩིས་པ་གསུམ།།
འཇིག་རྟེན་ཁམས་ཀྱི་གཡོབ་རྒྱལ་གསུམ།།

Medium, diviner and astrologer
Are the three great liars of the world

ལྷ་བླ་མས་མི་གསུང་དགུ་གསུང་རེད།།
གསུང་ཕྱག་མོ་མི་འབབ་དགུ་འབབ་རེད།།

The diviner and the Lama say all sorts of things
Their prophesies and divinations foretell all sorts of things

ཤ་མ་ཟ་ཟེར་ནོ་བླ་མ་རེད།།
ཤ་གང་ཚོ་ཟ་ནོ་བླ་མ་རེད།།

It's the Lama who advises not to eat meat
Yet, the fattiest meat[24] is eaten by the Lama

བླ་མའི་ཨ་མ་དམྱལ་བར་སྐྱེ་ཡ།།
སྨན་པའི་ཨ་མ་སངས་རྒྱས་ཡ།།

The Lama's mother will be reborn in Hell
The Doctor's will attain enlightenment

རྐུན་པོ་གཡག་ལ་དགའ།།
བླ་མ་རོ་ལ་དགའ།།

The thief loves a yak
The Lama loves a corpse

གྲ་པས་དཀོར་འཇུ།།
རྨ་བྱས་དུག་འཇུ།།

The monk digests material offerings
The peacock digests poison[25]

A proverb, says Walter Benjamin, "is a ruin which stands on the site of an old story and in which a moral twines about a happening like ivy around a wall."[26] These and similar proverbs are born out of individual and collective experience of life, and they provide pieces of advice for specific situations. Furthermore, these pithy statements contain a critique of the conditions which gave them birth, conditions which in many cases still prevail in Tibetan society. The first and second of the cited proverbs are cynical about divinatory customs that have been, and continue to be, a prominent feature of Tibetan communities to this day. They highlight the hit-and-miss nature of these practices and mock the professed visionary powers of the practitioners. The third and fourth are directed at the hypocrisy and charlatanism of Lamas who abuse their power and status for personal gain at the expense of the faithful. The fourth proverb also derides a Lama's family and entourage symbolized by the mother. They are thought to be preoccupied with anticipating the riches their Lama might accrue when attending his duties rather than with the contributions he might make to the welfare of his flock. On the other hand a doctor's mother is thought to be more concerned with the efficacy of her son's medical care and the health of his patient. The fifth and sixth ridicule some Lamas' and monks' acquisitiveness by alluding to the wealth they amass from carrying out prayers and rituals for the dead. In short, these proverbs give counsel through criticism, by advocating the eschewal or removal of certain social practices. The stories from which such proverbs grew were indeed old ones, but they are certainly not yet dead. The walls around which their morals twine are still very much intact: hence the continued resonance of such messages in contemporary Tibetan society.

The critical voices encapsulated and dispersed far and wide by the Tibetan proverb are also present in the epic narrative of Gesar. Through its sheer popularity and vernacular accessibility the Tibetan epic deepens the impact and widens the reach of Tibet's critical tradition. The entire Gesar epic draws heavily on a multiplicity of proverbs, set phrases, and verbal and imagistic formulaic expressions. Gesar narrative not only makes use of proverbs but the poetic, distilled, and expressive utterances within it acquire proverbial status. In fact, it is often hard to ascertain what is or is not a proverb within this epic story. In it the listener and the reader encounter numerous adages, statements, and songs cynical about the Tibetan religious elite. These are couched in proverbial phraseology that is accessible to a wider audience. To cite but one example, in one of the most popular Gesar episodes, *The Battle of Hor and Ling* (*Hor gling g.yul 'gyed*), the great Hor warrior Shanpa—the Butcher—sings an acerbic song attacking pseudo-Lamas. It is a long song but the following excerpt is adequate to capture its critical content:

Now to turn to the story of the Lowly Lama:
His residence lies at the center of the village,
Provisions are offered by nieces and nephews.
For intimate company he keeps young girls,
As his inner circle whirl his wife and children,
And sons and daughters act as patrons and sponsors
He sows discord amongst married neighbors.
By day his eyes focus on the tip of his nose,[27]
By night he sneaks up to the patron lady,
And becomes the wrecker of his patrons' families.
He rolls the whites and blacks of his eyes around the sky,[28]
While inside he is anticipating his patron's gifts.
At the sight of his Master Lama he is jealous,

At the sight of food and wealth his mouth waters,
At the sight of misfortune and illness he is joyous,
At the sight of beautiful women he is lustful.
By the day he delivers corrupt teachings before his patrons,
By night he sneaks like a dog around girls' pillows.
Next day, by the pillowed head of the dead one,
He and his disciples ring bells and clash cymbals.
He is embarrassed in the presence of other Lamas,
Uneasy in the presence of fellow monks and friends,
And depressed in the presence of the dead.
Such is the story of the Lowly Lama.
The blessing of a materialistic Lama is like an arrow shot,
The consciousness of the dead is like a stone flung into darkness.
I have no need of such Lamas,
So if you happen to be such a Lama,
I, Shanpa, will definitely not receive the empowerment.[29]

Shanpa sings this song to Gesar, who—unbeknown to the fearsome Hor warrior and his fellow tribesmen—has miraculously turned himself into a Lama with a golden headdress surrounded by an impressive retinue. Gesar, disguised as this Lama, gives a fake empowerment (*dbang*) to the Hor tribe in order to hoodwink them with a ceremony of *dmu gab*, the spell of oblivion. Once a *dmu gab* is cast it causes a state of confusion in everyone and no one is capable of recollection or intelligent thinking. Shanpa doubts the true identity of the Lama and sings this barbed song attacking the charlatanism and avarice of "the Lowly Lama" in general. Within the cited episode Shanpa fails to undermine Gesar's scheme and ends up being overwhelmed by his irresistible magical and spiritual powers.[30] Nevertheless, the critical message of his song has not been cast into oblivion like the victims of *dmu gab*. The negative qualities listed in the song are antitheses of altruism, compassion, and wisdom prized in fine Buddhist masters. Nepotism, lechery, sexual deviancy, deception, cupidity, perfunctory performance of rituals, and feigned meditative mastery accompanied by actual spiritual diffidence that endow many so-called Lamas are identified as legitimate targets of attack.[31]

The Gesar epic mainly targets the deviancy and corruption of Lamas. However, the prose writings of some scholar Lamas feature social criticisms that go beyond this and even attack the system of reincarnation (*yang sprul*) itself. In his *Revealing the Truth about Reincarnations* Gungthang Tenpai Dronme ingeniously retells a story from the *Ro sgrung* genre, *Tales of the Corpse*, to launch a scathing attack on the *yang sprul* system which is depicted as "a lie that deceives self and other."[32] The story centers on a carpenter and an artisan who are antagonistic toward each other. They live in the dominion of a certain King Kunkyong (Kun skyong) whose late father now resides in heaven. The artisan plots to murder the carpenter by presenting King Kunkyong with a fraudulent letter purporting to be from his departed father, requesting that he be sent a carpenter to construct a temple in heaven. The artisan suggests burning the carpenter on a pyre so that the smoke will carry him to the intended destination. Upon hearing about this from the king, the carpenter realizes it is a ploy devised by the artisan, but nevertheless consents to the arrangements. However, on the appointed day the carpenter makes his escape through a tunnel dug beneath the pyre. After a month in hiding, protecting himself from the elements and bathing "in warm water and milk," he turns up before the king in a white silken garment, and with a very fair complexion. He then presents another letter to the king, also purporting to be from his late father, asking him to honor the carpenter for the excellent services rendered, and requesting that an artisan to be sent to heaven in exactly the same manner for finishing the temple paintwork. The king is overjoyed, and showers the carpenter with rewards including gold, silver, and different kinds of animals. He then summons the artisan and informs him about the new arrangements. The appearance of the carpenter makes the artisan think there is indeed a way of traveling to heaven, and his own avarice is whetted by the carpenter's newly gained wealth, so he eagerly complies with king's request. Unlike the carpenter, however, he does not escape the incinerating pyre.[33]

Gungthang employs the art of storytelling as a critical tool to shed light upon aspects of life that would otherwise remain obscure and unchallenged. Through the cited story he critiques a long-established Tibetan Buddhist institution of recognized reincarnation and encourages in the reader a skeptical perception of it. He makes it clear right from the outset, and in the following passage that this story is retold in order to expose a mechanism of self-deception that underpins this tradition:

> What does this analogy relate to? It is an analogy for those purported Lamas and holy persons of today who totally lack (spiritual) confidence yet amass wealth through providing rituals for the dead and the living and wish to be reborn to indulge that wealth.
>
> How is it analogous? The workings of one's mind are not obscured from oneself. Yet, the artisan Kunga deceives himself, whilst knowing full well that he could not fly a single handspan[34] into the sky, even as he lives an untroubled present life, let alone being able to travel to the heavens whilst being incinerated by fire on all sides. Likewise one's own experience concretely confirms that we neither have the freedom nor the ability to choose the span of our lives nor our departure for the next. This is the case even though, in the here and now, we possess human form and are blessed with favourable external and internal conditions and are fully endowed with intellectual faculties and ingenuity. Therefore, our own experience confirms that we do not have the freedom to choose the form of our next lives as we please, especially when we are swept away by karmic winds like a windblown feather and distracted by *Bardo* hallucinations.[35]

Gungthang goes on to stress at length that the wish to determine rebirth on the part of purported Lamas is driven by the same acquisitiveness that causes an agonizing death for artisan Kunga. Their professed ability to be reborn is a fabrication for the deception of the unthinking faithful. It is greed, delusion, and lunacy which make one invest so much energy, wealth, and effort in a child who has no connection with one whatsoever. This perverted form of altruism, says Gungthang, is ruinous for both the self and the other. Buddhist principles of karmic justice and pure altruism inform Gungthang's criticism but there is no doubt that he uses an engaging and powerful story to ridicule and attack blind belief in the easily corrupted tradition of so-called recognized reincarnation.

In a similar vein, in his autobiography, the Great Fifth Dalai Lama condemns the institution of succession by reincarnation as an instrument for amassing wealth and gaining social and political status. In characteristically sharp and forthright terms, he states that coteries of a deceased Lama are more concerned with finding the replacement than with his immediate demise. This is because the demise brings to an end the stream of dubiously obtained material offerings (*dkor nag*) that have been flowing uninterruptedly into the Lama's coffers. As a result, asserts the Great Fifth, in their mad rush to install the next incarnation, coteries fall prey to the concocted tales of ambitious parents.[36] The Great Fifth is also acutely aware of the political manipulation of the reincarnation system and as such, he caustically alludes to the sons of Mongol leaders being recognized as reincarnate Lamas in his own day.[37] The Great Fifth does not spare himself from this criticism either. In fact the above acerbic words begin with a self-critical comment expressing his inadequacy for the role of Dalai Lama. He views himself as an impostor occupying "the seat of his predecessors like a donkey in a leopard's skin."[38] As Samten Karmay has already observed, the Great Fifth frankly admits his failure to recognize any of the belongings of the previous Dalai Lama presented to him when he was subjected to traditional "tests" for authenticating his identity.[39]

It must be acknowledged that neither the Great Fifth's nor Gungthang's criticism had any impact on the persistence of their own reincarnation lines, let alone undermining the prevalence of the institution of reincarnation in Tibet as a whole. In fact, the Fifth Dalai Lama was himself responsible for actually creating new reincarnation lineages such as that of the Panchen Lamas.[40] The critical attitudes of these influential religious personalities might not have had immediate tangible outcomes, but radical ideas, which disturb established certainties, are sown. These are acts that have the potential to ripen into more nuanced consequences as time progresses. They can also be seen as precedents for the critical content of contemporary Tibetan fictional and factual writings. Even the Chinese Communist Party (CCP) has been seen to appropriate such critical voices to instil its antireligious attitude in young Tibetan minds. This is apparent in the selection of the Gungthang's piece just cited, in the Tibetan-language curriculum for junior secondary schools.[41] A brief introductory passage that prefaces the text is telling:

> We, Tibetan people, are a religious people. We are a people who have an established tradition of searching for *sprul sku* (incarnate Lamas). The history of searching for *sprul sku* spans several centuries, and during this time there have arisen many issues which have remained totally unknown to the faithful masses. In this lesson, the author not only exposes the secrecy surrounding *sprul sku* searches but also censures and ridicules conduct that deceives both self and other. Reading of this lesson must be followed by a comprehension of the author's viewpoint as well as studying his stylistic features and his line of reasoning that draws on examples.[42]

To presume, therefore, that the radical and rationalist attacks on traditional practices in modern Tibetan literature are merely the product of Chinese Communist ideology, state education, and antireligious policies, is in effect to deny critical agency to Tibetans themselves. The suggestion implies that Tibetans are incapable of self-reflection and critical thinking without colonial tutelage, or a forced encounter with something called modernity, which is clearly not the case. This is not to deny that modern sociopolitical conditions have played a pivotal role in bringing critical thought and practices to the fore in Tibetan literary culture. Radical shifts in social structure and power relations over the past decades have given unprecedented prominence and leeway to forces that critique old customs, ideas, and practices. Nevertheless, it would be a mistake to believe that such critical attitudes toward established beliefs and customs are the monopoly of the colonial power. This would imply that no form of social criticism existed in the pre-Communist world of Tibet, which is simply untrue. Tibet's critical tradition is evident in many art forms, ranging from classical and religious literatures to diverse oral creations such as the Tibetan epic that predate as well as coexist with, and continue to inform, modern Tibetan literature.

FLOW OF THE GESAR EPIC

Tibetan epic literature and balladry are genres which clearly demonstrate this point. Although this chapter focuses particularly on the critical element inherent in these popular genres, it should be noted that their influence on modern Tibetan literature is felt in a variety of ways. The Gesar epic (*ge sar sgrung*) and Tibetan balladry (*bstod sgra, rogs 'then*), like any other traditional oral compositions, cannot be fully appreciated without an understanding of their broader cultural dimensions. An appreciation of what John Foley calls "traditional referentiality"[43] and what David Buchan terms "received traditional diction"[44] is crucial for an in-depth insight. The figurative language, set themes and structural formulas, and stories of these oral art forms are set within a very broad cultural reference. This reveals shared culture as a system of customs, beliefs, and values that ultimately infuses meaning, and enables a rapturous union of storyteller/singer and audience. The complex cultural setting of oral compositions endows them with a collective cohesive quality. In his reflection on epic, Hegel emphasizes that a specific social world with shared moral values and worldviews presupposes its creation. As its prerequuisite, he states that "[t]he relations of ethical life, the bond of the family, as well as the bond of the people—as an entire nation—in war and peace—must all have been discovered, framed, and developed" so as to give birth to "the primitive epic."[45] Common cultural features provide social cohesion and give life to Tibetan oral narratives like the Gesar epic. These art forms in turn become a source of sustenance for modern literary creations.

The long, rich, episodic, and lyrical tradition of the Gesar epic is a great repository for modern Tibetan writers. Tsering Dhondup, a talented novelist and short story writer, wrote a famous story called *A Show to Delight the Masses,* which was based on Gesar's journey to Hell to deliver his notorious concubine, Atak Lhamo.[46] This particular episode is a typical example of the anti-clerical spirit of the Tibetan epic narrative mentioned above. In which some members of Tibetan clergy are subjected to the torments of Hell for their corrupt, decadent, and fraudulent conduct on earth.[47] However, the person in need of deliverance in Tsering Dhondup's satirical short story is a corrupt Communist county chief who dies suddenly in his office and ends up in court before the Lord of Death. There, he finds his earthly powers ineffectual for his defense. Due to his numerous misdeeds on earth, the threat of damnation looms. Upon receiving the news of his sudden death, a seedy local Lama travels to the twilight zone of the Lord of Death and rescues the Communist chief. The Lama undertakes the rescue mission so that the county chief can give official sanction to the recognition of the cleric's own nephew as another local Lama. After his deliverance the county chief returns to his nefarious dealings with a vengeance, only to be thrown into Hell once more at the end.

The satire critiques the corruption of colonial public offices as well as the traditional institution of reincarnation by highlighting their corruptibility. The story also implicitly satirizes the religious policy of the CCP—an atheist institution—that nevertheless claims legitimacy in its exercise of power over the selection of influential religious figures through the system of reincarnation, a concept based in Buddhist religious belief. Some might argue that such an attack on the reincarnation system is unprecedented in Tibetan literary history and might attribute it to the aiding and abetting of the Chinese Communist policies. Be that as it may, we should spare a thought for the fact that the institution of reincarnation was already the target of censorious comments in pre-Communist Tibet, as has already been pointed out. Like Gungthang, this modern Tibetan writer also uses storytelling as a critical vehicle. He utilizes the literary form of the short story modeled on the fantastical plot and poetic language of a Gesar episode to deliver a message similar to Gungthang's, and every bit as scathing.

The magical qualities and lyricism of Gesar are also more than apparent in the imaginative writings of Dhondup Gyal. His first short story, *Epic Bard, (Sgrung pa)*, which appeared in *The Qinghai Tibetan News* in 1979, revolves around an esteemed Gesar bard, *A khu sgrung pa*, whose life was tragically cut short during the Cultural Revolution.[48] The narrator of this very short story is a great admirer of the bard, who in turn is affectionate to him. However, the story begins ominously as the narrator approaches the bard who is standing beneath a wilting and discolored cedar tree with cawing crows, which was once the magnificent hub of their village. The bard is uncharacteristically reticent and distraught about something. It transpires that the cause of his anxiety is the sudden shift of the CCP's policy to outlaw religious worship as well as traditional singing in general and the telling of the Gesar epic: the onset of the Cultural Revolution. The bard refuses to surrender to such an unheard-of policy and goes on narrating the epic tales. After a lapse of three long, dark years the narrator then returns to a much bleaker village, with neglected fields full of weeds. He learns that in the violent campaign to sweep away "Gods, Ghosts, Demons and Obstructive Spirits," (*lha 'dre gdon bgegs*—the target of campaigns against conservative elements during the Cultural Revolution), the bard was labeled as "a counter-revolutionary through the telling of the epic narrative" and subjected to struggle sessions.[49] He died in agony as a result of relentless torture and forced deprivation. However, the story ends happily with the arrival of spring and the reemergence of the Gesar epic, signaling Tibetan cultural revival during the Reform Period. This short story seems to be the first fictional work in Tibetan to censure the destructive policies of that tumultuous decade. The audacious criticism of the Cultural Revolution is softened by toeing the Party line in laying the blame squarely on the "Gang of Four."

By frequently heaping praise on the Gesar epic, Dhondup Gyal makes it clear that he sees it as a life-giving force in terms of Tibetan national revival. At one point the eloquent narrator says that by the effective means of the Gesar epic, the bard had given courage and purpose to Tibetan youth throughout his life, revitalized the elder generations, and given people happiness and hope during times of despondency.[50] As the story comes to an end, the narrator mourns the bard in the following words of aspiration: "Ah, Bard! The 'Gang of Four' have tortured you and made your precious human body perish, yet the vitality of your Gesar epic blooms like spring flowers in the hearts of the Tibetan people."[51] The art of storytelling here comes to symbolize the Tibetan spirit and their struggle for cultural survival. Through the tale of a traditional oral storyteller, a Gesar bard, a modern storyteller not only summons the Tibetan epic narrative to the mind of the reader, but also captures the experience and trauma of a distraught Tibetan generation. As Walter Benjamin noted, the art of storytelling is "the ability to exchange experience."[52] The experience is both individual and collective because a storyteller constantly integrates others' experience. In *Epic Bard*, Dhondup Gyal narrates the tragic tale of an individual to encapsulate a traumatic collective experience during one of the darkest times in Tibetan history.[53] The short story remembers the cultural trauma by remembering a traditional mode of narrative, and this remembrance serves as a political criticism as well as a reinforcement of Tibetan collective consciousness.

The influence of the Tibetan epic and other traditional modes of narrative, is also pronounced in an unfinished story by Dhondup Gyal entitled *A Tale of Journeying through the Royal Tombs of the Warrior Kings (Btsan po'i bang so myul ba'i gtam rgyud)* which so far has not attracted scholarly attention.[54] This beautifully written fictional narrative borrows heavily from Gesar epic, *mgur* tradition, hagiographical genre, classical Tibetan poetry, Indic mythology, religious literature, Tibetan folklore and folk songs, and colloquial speech interspersed with proverbs. Traditional literary conventions and elements of oral narrative shape the overall form and structure of the story and heighten the magical elements of the content, where the narrator gets transported to phantasmagorical realms as he searches for the mythic celestial tombs of the Warrior Kings of the Tibetan Imperial Period. The narrator is a university student with a keen interest in old Tibetan history books, not very dissimilar to the author himself, who read Tibetan history at the Central University for Nationalities.[55] He lauds the historical and literary merits of *Bka' thang sde lnga*[56] in an effort to counter his roommate Tashi's skepticism of such discovered "treasure texts" (*gter ma*). Tashi is unconvinced, and refuses to listen when the narrator offers to read a passage concerning the burial of precious treasures for future Tibetan rulers during the Tibetan imperial age.[57] Dismissing this and other textual evidence, he ridicules the belief in such buried treasures, much to the narrator's chagrin. However, half in jest Tashi immediately assuages the narrator's indignation by singing a Gesar-style song complete with its unique melody:

When tranquil you're like White Tsangpa[58]
When enraged you're like Red Tamdrin[59]
Before the Great Lion King of Ling
I, the Butcher,[60] surrender my head and body

The small, black crow and I are alike
There is no good in killing a crow
Neither its feathers nor skin has any use
Please I beseech you to spare my life[61]

This is one of the many stylistic and thematic allusions to Gesar that can be found throughout the text. A year after the above altercation, the two interlocutors remain friendly roommates, but still disagree over the value of *Bka' thang sde lnga*, which inspires an adventurous tale as they take a Sunday siesta.

When the narrator falls asleep he encounters his roommate Tashi in a misty dream realm. Tashi urges the narrator to find the hidden treasures and tells him that the Emperor Songtsen Gampo is waiting to receive him. A sudden fall into a pitch-black pit leads to a gigantic subterranean world of magical incidents. He is rescued by a goddess with irresistible charm and metamorphic abilities. They part, love-stricken, after surfacing from the caves. She gives him a bracelet with magical powers as a souvenir. After a string of magical events and travels through fantastical landscapes, the bracelet changes into a fabulous horse charged with delivering him to heaven with the aid of a shape-shifting fawn and a great ascetic. At the gates of heaven he is seized by fearsome guards and taken to the court of heaven. He wishes he had possessed the resourcefulness, bravery, power, wisdom, splendor, cunning, and beauty of the heroes and heroines of the Gesar epic to get him out of this tight spot.

Unfortunately, both for the narrator and us, the author's untimely death left this fascinating tale incomplete. Dhondup Gyal might have intended to weave the lives of Tibetan warrior kings into the narrative as the tale unfolds in both heaven and on earth. The story reflects his endeavor to find novel literary techniques to gain truer representations of the Tibetan condition. In fact, Dhondup Gyal stressed the need to find a unique, coded technique for circumventing state censorship while being able to convey what is truly pressing on one's mind. He told Pema Bhum that he had not discovered such a technique yet, but had started writing a story about an encounter with Songtsen Gampo, who would admonish and counsel Tibetan youth.[62] Although, at the time, Pema Bhum did not know it, this was a reference to the story just summarized. Once again, we see that Dhondup Gyal was looking to the past for artistic inspiration.[63] In its language, style, and plot, in its allusions, and in the frequent use of magic, this unfinished story shows that the narration of the Tibetan imperial past entails if not restoration then at least serious recourse to Tibet's traditional and oral modes of narrative. Once again this specific way of storytelling engenders a communal sense of belonging as it simultaneously remembers collective history and revives older modes of narrative in the written word for a critical representation of the present Tibetan condition.

Following Franz Xaver Erhard's study of Jangbu's short story *Conscious-ness Born of the Shoulder Blade* (*Sog rus las mched pa'i rnam shes*) there might be a temptation to view this type of narrative as a Tibetan form of magical realism.[64] Magical realism, rooted as it is within living traditions of mythic beliefs and magical elements, is a useful literary technique for authors wanting to give expression to the sociopolitical realities in Tibet and to contest the narrative of Chinese colonialism. However, it is unwise to pigeonhole specific contemporary Tibetan fiction as magical realism without giving careful thought to classical Tibetan literature and the traditional forms of narrative which constitute the literary context of such work. Neither Erhard nor Schiaffini-Vedani, who speaks of a Tibetan import of magical realism, gives the matter such consideration.[65] The Tibetan genre of hagiography is replete with fantastical descriptions of flying Lamas with magical powers and miraculous abilities to defy the laws of nature while being immersed in Buddhist transcendental wisdom. Popular Tibetan folktales, such as *Tales of the Corpse*,[66] teem with a diversity of spirits and humans with transmogrify-ing abilities. They display an imaginative power that remains bound to the concrete realities of life on the ground, but can also break out into breath-taking magical realms. The epic literature of Gesar abounds in descriptions of the extraordinary deeds of supernatural heroes who act out their lives in constant engagement and frequent struggle with a great range of worldly and unworldly spirits. Although such magical or supra-mundane elements abound in the epic, the narrative remains ultimately rooted in the customs, beliefs, and social practices of the Tibetan people. Well before the CCP's assumption of control over Tibet and the influence of magical realism, this epic literature described a culturally diverse Tibet, steeped in a Buddhist worldview, Bon beliefs, and traditional folk religious practices. Magical realism as a foreign literary genre might have exerted influence on Tibetan writers, but Tibetan magical narratives and still surviving cultural norms and beliefs have consti-tuted an even stronger influence. To put it another way, if certain aspects of modern Tibetan literature are to be characterized as magical realist, it should be acknowledged that that peculiar blend—of magic and realism—is also one bequeathed by the Tibetan literary heritage.

The literary influence of the Gesar epic on modern Tibetan literature is not confined to contemporary fiction writing. A poem by exile-based Dhatsenpa posted on the Tibetan *Khabdha* website, loaded with political messages con-cerning the very survival of Tibet as a nation, displays more than echoes of the Tibetan epic. It uses the Gesar genre overtly as its vehicle.[67] It is written in the style of a typical Gesar song, complete with proverbs, metaphors, and imagery found in the epic tradition. It could be sung as well as recited with equal rhythmic and melodious effect. The song is entitled *Let's Have a Round Drum-like Discussion*. This might sound peculiar in English translation, but the image evokes a thorough discussion as perfect as a smooth and finely crafted drum. The singer ponders whether Tibetans should adopt advocacy of independence or of genuine autonomy as the means to overcome their current predicament. For the singer both cases are justifiable and frustrating in equal measure. The question is then left open-ended, with an urgent call for critical discussion informed by independent thinking. The song is thoroughly Gesar in style, imagery, and diction, but the subject matter is the most serious political question Tibetans are facing today. Modern Internet technology, as the medium of communication through which the song flows, also impinges on the style and audience of the song. Unlike a typical Gesar song in which the singer reveals his or her identity here, the singer exercises the right of anonymity that emboldens contributors to participate in chat rooms worldwide. The song is sung to friends of the Web, *dra grogs*, fellow users of the Tibetan chat website, *Khabdha*. This and other forms of contemporary creative writing in Tibetan demonstrate that the Tibetan epic is not only a living oral tradition but continues to contribute to cultural production in rich, diverse, and literary ways.

ROMANTIC BALLADRY: MINIATURE LYRICAL TRAGEDIES

To imply that the critical attitude of Tibetan writers was engendered by colonial rule or an assimilation of the colonial narrative of Tibetan history is itself an internalization of a colonial discourse that assumes that the colonizing power introduced enlightened and critical thinking to the colonized. In his study of Dhondup Gyal's work, Tsering Shakya contends that Dhondup Gyal's attack on traditional customs such as arranged marriage—an issue tackled in many of his short stories—reveals an assimilation of the colonizer's ideas regarding tradition, modernity, and Tibetan society. Reflecting on the critiques of traditional nuptial customs so often found in modern Tibetan fiction, Tsering Shakya states: "The new discursive formation surrounding marriage, family and patriarchal authority is a consequence of colonial rule, since freedom of choice in marriage was viewed as an emancipatory benefit of the new colonial authority."[68] This statement requires nuance. While it is one thing to argue that Chinese colonial rule helped to undermine traditional authority by officially sanctioning writers to attack old customs and beliefs, it is quite another to suggest that such critical voices owe their existence to the colonial condition. In fact, traditional social practices, especially those concerning marriage, were the targets of criticism in various forms of indigenous narrative well before the CCP asserted control over Tibet.

Indeed it is very likely that the theme of arranged marriage in Dhondup Gyal's writing was at least partly inspired by Tibetan romantic ballads, since such balladry, *rogs 'then*, is particularly strong among communities such as his own. For instance, the plot of *Ganji Karma* (*Rgan gya'i skar ma*), one of the most famous Amdo ballads, takes place not very far from his birthplace. Given that he was a fan and a keen performer of Amdo love songs (*la gzhas*) and his enthusiasm for other oral art forms,[69] it is hard to imagine that Tibetan balladry would have bypassed him. Many of these popular ballads narrate the tragic stories of star-crossed lovers who are prevented from realizing their matrimonial wishes due to parental power, tribal conflict, and unequal social relations.[70] These ballads function as a damning attack on patriarchal authority, tribal warfare, and corrupting tendencies of wealth and social status. Indeed the subject matter, critical qualities, and lyrical style of such ballads are reflected in some of Dhondup Gyal's most famous short stories, such as *The Frost-bitten Flower* (*Sad kyis bcom pa'i me tog*), *The Wild Yak and Tiger Plains* (*'Brong stag thang*) and *Chronic Disease of the Heart* (*Sems gcong*). In this Dhondup Gyal is not alone. Many of his contemporaries also demonstrate the stylistic, romantic, and critical influence of such traditional balladry. For instance, an exceptionally fine short story by Lhundrup (Lhun 'grub) entitled *Gait of the Black Hobbled Horse* (*Rta nag sgrog 'gros*) reads like a ballad in prose.[71] It narrates the misfortune that has befallen a poor family, whose son is driven to kill the son of a wealthy family who covets his beautiful wife and subjects him to public humiliation and intimidation. As in traditional ballads, the portrayal of the downtrodden and the wronged is used in fictional narrative as a way of attacking exploitative social relations.

Dhondup Gyal's short story *The Frostbitten Flower* criticizes similar conservative attitudes and social practices in Tibet in its attack upon the custom of arranged marriage.[72] The institution of the family, and the theme of frustrated love, are employed to reveal exploitative relations within a patriarchal system. Phuntsok, father of the heroine Lhakyi, is bent on honoring a pledge he had made as a young man to his blood brother, Akhu Nyima, who had saved him from certain death during a bandit attack. As a show of gratitude, Phuntsok promises that if his unborn child is a girl that she will be betrothed to Akhu Nyima's son, Rigyak. Rigyak happens to be the elder brother of our heroine's lover, Tsering. This dramatizes and complicates the story by creating misunderstandings, suspense, and tension. Upon discovering Lhakyi's love for his younger brother, Rigyak tries to make amends by dissuading his father, Akhu Nyima, but to no avail. Phuntsok's resolution to keep his word, and both fathers' stubborn adherence to the customary practice of demanding the eternal deference of children to parental authority, frustrate the two lovers, who then become estranged. For the female protagonist, the estrangement leads to the tragic events of her attempted suicide, sexual abuse, vagrancy, and finally her attempt to embrace the life of a nun. In romantic ballads dispirited lovers also frequently resort to suicide or renunciation of worldly life. However, unlike the majority of ballads with an unhappy ending, and in common with Dhondup Gyal's *Epic Bard*, this short story ends on a happy note, with the arrival of a cuckoo, the harbinger of spring. In spite of this happy denouement it shares the similar targets of social criticism with the Tibetan lyrical balladry.

In one archetypical romantic ballad, *Sertso and Lodroe Dawa* (*Gser mtsho dang blo gros zla ba*) two lovers rebel against parental authority because the female protagonist, Sertso, is married off to a wealthy stranger against her will. The combined force of human avarice and nuptial customs has an asphyxiating effect in terms of individual freedom. The Tibetan saying, "it is up to oneself either to bend oneself into a bow or straighten into an arrow,"[73] which celebrates free choice, rings hollow in this romantic ballad. Parental authority rules supreme. Sertso is treated as a lucrative asset for the augmentation of family wealth and social status. Her family is paid in gold, silver, and cattle for her reluctant hand. Gold and silver are delicately weighed in scales over patterned swathes of rare woollen and silken cloths. A flock of three hundred sheep is given to please the father, two hundred milch *dris* (female yaks) in their prime to please the mother, and thirty riding horses to satisfy the brother. Parental love and sibling affection evaporate in the presence of such opulence. The emphasis in the narrative on the offering of these assets for her procurement in the form of traditional wedding gifts underlines the fact that wealth is exchanged for human life. It shows how the use of euphemism in the language of these exchanges, for example reference to these assets as "compensations for maternal milk and paternal care (*ma'i nu rin, pha'i bskyang rin*)," helps to conceal their actual function—payments for the female body—and make such nuptial bartering appear more palatable.

Sertso excoriates parental disregard for the intimate feelings of an individual, she rails against emotional blackmail in the name of familial duty, and the tradition of exchanging one's daughter for property. The only option left for the lovers is to run away from their community. Tragically, their flight to Lhasa is abruptly cut short when their pursuers overtake them. The sudden arrival of the pursuit party catches the conversing and caressing lovers off-guard in their hideout amid the rocky canyons of the Machu River (Yellow River). The male protagonist, Lodroe Dawa, picks up his gun and prepares for a confrontation, but there is no time to act. All of a sudden a bullet fatally pierces his chest. Instead of returning home, Sertso faces death with a yearning wish to join her lover in the afterlife. She climbs up a steep rock face and plunges into the gorges where "the Machu River hurries to the Eastern sea / With its blue rapids spraying high into the sky."[74] Her last comments are a damning critique of her acquisitive family in particular, and the tradition of arranged marriage in general. She tells her dying lover that she does not wish to live in this world which denies her the freedom to love and live with him.

She pledges to join him in the afterlife, where they might enjoy such freedom. She sends the following bitter message to her parents and brother before taking her own life:

You pursuers, callous, heartless butchers
Cease your bloodthirstiness and hearken to me
Tell my loving father to ensure
He tends to his precious white sheep,
While I tend to the golden eyed-fish.
Tell my loving mother to ensure
She drinks the milk of young *dris*,
While I drink the waters of the blue Machu.
Tell my horse-loving brother to ensure
His mounts are fine steeds,
While mine will be the pristine river
If there is a compassionate deity
Providence will surely grace us lovers[75]

In *The Wild Yak and Tiger Plains* Dhondup Gyal once again deploys these stereotypical themes of Tibetan balladry to attack traditionalism and advocate social change.[76] This short story centers on romantic love, arranged marriage, and tribal feuding. In total disregard for long-running communal hostilities, a girl named Lhamo Tsering and a boy named Kalsang Gyal, from the feuding tribes of *'Brong* and *Stag*, fall in love. Tending their different flocks of sheep by day they sustain their tryst in the flowery meadows around the river that demarcates their tribes' respective territories. Lhamo Tsering's father has already betrothed her to Chagjam, a man from her own tribe, although she has pledged to marry her lover. The arranged marriage and the long history of blood feud, animosity, and mistrust between the two pastoral communities mean that the young lovers are at the mercy of traditional forces. Chagjam, himself reluctantly betrothed, is unwilling to force Lhamo Tsering into marriage. However, by evoking notions of shame and tribal honor, his father and kinsmen incite him to act when, one day, the lovers' secret rendezvous is discovered. The male protagonist is ambushed and beaten senseless. The ensuing situation threatens to escalate into a full-scale tribal confrontation. Bloodshed is only narrowly avoided thanks to the tireless work of one character, the newly appointed Communist Party secretary, who is a local Tibetan. However, he cannot resolve the conflict without the assistance of a local *geshe* (learned monk), who is respected by both the Party and the local people.

In this short story, echoes of the famous ballad *Ganji Karma* abound (as apparent in the summary below). What is novel is the character of a caring Tibetan Party secretary who has recently replaced the former Chinese incumbent. His endeavors and enlightened frame of mind, which overcomes old attitudes and antagonisms, combine to secure eventual conflict resolution. As a result, Tsering Shakya concludes that this figure represents colonial authority.[77] What is more, it is clear that the tribal conflict could not be resolved peacefully without the assistance of the old *geshe*. This *geshe* negotiates between the past and present, and between colonial authority and the colonized. The *geshe* is portrayed as someone who propagates the party's message to the people, while also catering to their social and (implicitly) their spiritual needs. He is versed in the five major traditional Tibetan sciences (fields of knowledge), and specializes in traditional medicines, which he dispenses to the rural populace. At the same time, he is a member of the annual regional congress, the resolutions of which he relays with great enthusiasm.[78] So both the *geshe* and the Tibetan party secretary dwell in what Homi Bhabha has called an "interstitial space" as they negotiate between, and engage with, disparate collective entities in both diachronic and synchronic fashion.[79] Within these in-between spaces they straddle the past and the present, and enable interaction between native and colonial power in the here and now. These liminal spaces thus connect seemingly polarized identities by facilitating engagement, negotiation, and contestation between them. Although Dhondup Gyal pays lip service to progressive party policy, which is a customary practice of writers during the 1980s, a more nuanced reading of the text shows that Tibetans remain the locus of agency in this fictional narrative. It also demonstrates that his portrayal of religious figures is not as negative as is generally thought. In contrast to the tragic narrative of ballads, this particular story has a happy ending. In the denouement the conflict is averted and the lovers reunited. Dhondup Gyal's notions of reform and progress are substituted for the device of catastrophe typically found in traditional love ballads as the ultimate criticism of detested old customs. Mirroring the coerced optimism of CCP ideology the message appears to be that social and intellectual progress averts the need to use the symbolism of death and suicide as social criticism.

Forbidden love, tyranny of patriarchal authority, and arranged marriage are also the driving themes of *Ganji Karma*.[80] As already noted, parallels can be drawn between this specific ballad and *The Wild Yak and Tiger Plains*. Tribal territorial disputes that plague Tibetan nomadic communities also loom large in this oral narrative. Two frequently encountered obstacles for the consummation of romantic love in Tibet are long-running communal animosity and deeply embedded paternal authority. As in *Romeo and Juliet,* two lovers from feuding tribes—Tsekyi, a girl from Rebgong, and Karma, a boy from Ganja— maintain their amorous trysts while grazing animals in idyllic mountain pastures.[81] In the sacred caverns at the White Rock of Ganja, a famous site for pilgrims and yogis, the lovers take a solemn oath before the great tutelary deity, Demchog (Bde mchog), to spend the rest of their lives together.[82] When the female protagonist, Tsekyi, informs her father of her intentions, he fumes with anger. He upbraids her, saying she should be ashamed of her conduct, and goes on to inform her that she has already been given away to a family within their own tribe. Meanwhile the simmering hostility between the two communities erupts into a tribal war. On the battlefield, the male protagonist, Karma, loses his life. The news of his death overwhelms Tsekyi with grief and an intense sense of despair as can be seen in the following extract:

My sweetheart is like the sun in the sky,
Grim Death has eclipsed him.
The sun in the sky will rise again,
Never again will I see my sweetheart.
My sweetheart is like the conch-white moon,
A demonic eclipse has claimed him.
The conch white moon will rise again,
Never again will I see my sweetheart.
Looking up, empty blue sky,
Looking down, empty solid earth.
In this earthly world beneath the sky,
All I had was my childhood sweetheart
My sweetheart was all I pined for.

She wants to be by her lover and care for him in the hostile realms of *Bardo*, but knows it will be impossible to encounter him in this liminal stage between death and rebirth. Instead, she decides that the best way to assist her dead lover would be to become a nun. Renouncing worldly cares, she pledges to undertake meritorious actions and recite Mani mantras for the rest of her life so as to ensure that the Three Jewels protect her lover:

Impermanent is the living world,
Insubstantial, the Samsaric home.
From this day forth, no attachment
Have I for this wretched world.
The great sacred White Rock of Ganja
Is the abode of one thousand *ḍākinīs*.
The infallible refuge of Ḍākinī Gungru,[83]
My sanctuary in this life and the next,
I will receive her as my root guru,
And take monastic vows to attain nirvana.

She cuts off her cascading tresses of hair and scatters them into the wind after her departed lover, who was the first and the last "keeper of her hair" (*skra bdag*) and becomes a nun.[84] Some might detect a note of escapism here, but at the heart of this lyrical ballad of love, death, and renunciation lies an attack on oppressive parental authority and communal violence. In a way, these ballads are an illustration of a damning Tibetan song (in the form of narrative poetry) that condemns patriarchal authority as follow: "Young maiden put all her trust in her father/ But she never knew he dealt in human beings!"[85] The potency of poetic lyricism, the extensive reach due to the oral nature of the narrative, and the currency of its subject matter makes balladry a powerful mode of social criticism.

Suicide and death are reoccurring themes in these popular ballads. On the surface, suicide might appear to indicate despair and surrender to old customs. Scratch beneath, and one finds this common pattern of recourse to suicide as an ultimate indictment of, and resistance to, established authority that tramples individual free choice. These ballads are miniature lyrical tragedies that both depict and critique prevailing conditions of life. They are tragic in the Aristotelian sense. They are an imitation of lives beset by misfortune and catastrophe, and this serves some cathartic purpose for the singers, audience and readers of the ballads alike.[86] The Tibetan adage: "To express is medicine and to repress is poison" conveys a similar sentiment.[87] However, they are not merely concerned with the discharge of pent-up emotions, or an attempt to find respite from tension and anxiety in life. Most of all, these ballads are tragic in a Romantic sense, in that they portray an individual's refusal to conform to stifling established norms. Friedrich Schiller, who epitomizes the Romantic perspective on tragedy, views individual freedom or free will and an antiauthoritarian attitude as principal features of tragedy. In *The Roots of Romanticism*, Isaiah Berlin observes that for Schiller, tragedy is not about inevitable suffering, but about resisting conformity. For him, Berlin states, "the only thing which can be regarded as properly tragic is resistance, resistance on the part of a man to whatever it is that oppresses him."[88] It is the exercise of individual freedom celebrated by the already cited Tibetan saying, which allows us either to bend ourselves into a bow or straighten into an arrow as we wish. As we have seen, similar concerns with subjective experience and individual freedom found in Tibetan balladry, reinforce its currency in modern Tibetan literary creations.

Ian Watt regards individual experience, which is always unique and new, as the hallmark of the modern Western novel.[89] The expression of personal emotions and thoughts is regarded as a defining feature of modern poetry since at least the age of Romanticism. Pema Bhum stresses the subjectivity of modern Tibetan poets as a distinctive attribute of their poetry.[90] Subjective consciousness might be a very modern theme or an attribute of modern literature, but it also features noticeably in traditional forms of narrative as has been shown. Admittedly unlike the modern novel, individual emotions and thoughts expressed in Tibetan balladry are not minutely particularistic.

In contrast to Watt's modern novel, balladry does not reject traditional plots, or general human types in its characterizations or set idioms, yet it still portrays individual human predicaments. Like the novel, it furnishes the narrative with psychological insight, but obviously without the same level of detail. It is condensed and distilled. The orientation of the Tibetan ballad toward the individual is seen in its very structure, which is composed of interrelated segments giving respective voice to at least two protagonists or more. The first-person mode of personal expression is not engulfed by a single all-encompassing narrative mode or by an omniscient third-person narrator. The similarity between the structure of *Ganji Karma* and Dhondup Gyal's *The Frost-bitten Flower* is apparent in that both tales allow each main character to speak for him- or herself. Tsering Shakya is attentive to this perspectivist structure of Dhondup Gyal's story, but draws comparison with Akira Kurosawa's film *Rashomon*, rather than looking to the literary precedents deeply embedded within Tibetan oral culture itself.[91] This attention to the individual is most prominent in the Tibetan epic narrative of Gesar where each character vocalizes through his or her own songs. In fact, many of the heroes not only sing individual songs but also have their own characteristic melodies.

These brief examinations of the Gesar epic and Tibetan balladry have helped to reveal the contribution that oral art forms have made to contemporary Tibetan literary production with regards to subject matter and their inclusion of critical commentary on social issues. The influence of oral narrative is, of course, not confined to these realms. It also makes an impact with regard to style, structure, plot, theme, and language. For instance, the lucid and lyrical style of Dhondup Gyal's prose echoes the poetic beauty and fluidity of oral creations such as balladry, love songs, and the Tibetan epic narrative. Tsering Dhondup also draws heavily from different modes of oral narrative in his fictional prose. This furnishes his writing with a natural fluidity and effective realism when portraying nomadic life, normally reserved for the spoken language.[92] In his already-cited short satire, *A Show to Delight the Masses*, not only does he extract the plot, structure, and prosimetric form (*bcad lhug spel ma*) from an entire episode of the Gesar epic, but also closely mimics its proverbial, rhythmic, and playful narrative style with finesse. As already mentioned, a parallel can be drawn between the perspectivist structure of *The Frost-bitten Flower* and that of many Tibetan ballads which give distinct voices to respective protagonists. The structure of Dhondup Gyal's *The Wild Yak and Tiger Plains* also bears signs of Tibetan oral poetic devices as its plot is framed between a love song and an auspicious concluding song, known as Tashi (*bkra shis*).[93] It is customary in Tibet to conclude a merrymaking occasion by singing such an auspicious song. Dhondup Gyal resorts to this very traditional formulaic structure to celebrate the successful conflict resolution within his narrative and to bring it to an optimistic end.[94]

Both Dhondup Gyal and Tsering Dhondup infuse their fictional prose narratives with proverbs, idioms, and set expressions to heighten the stories' expressive content and enrich them aesthetically. As an example, a randomly selected short story like *The Wild Yak and Tiger Plains* contains no less than fifty-two proverbs and set expressions of various lengths. Such expressions are integral to the linguistic warp and woof of the entire narrative. The use of these linguistic resources is naturalistic, and not contrived as in some less-accomplished writers. Most of all, these adages and formulaic expressions reflect the dialogue of rural characters, which the authors attempt to recreate. "Among the Ibo," writes Chinua Achebe in *Things Fall Apart*, "the art of conversation is regarded very highly, and proverbs are palm-oil with which words are eaten."[95] Substitute Ibo with rural Tibetans and palm-oil with *dri* butter, and we have an accurate picture of the ordinary language spoken by the "Tsampa-eaters." Many modern Tibetan writers employ everyday speech (characterized by simplicity and set expression) as a literary device to effect an impression of realism as well as to refine their style. The aforementioned authors are singled out to underscore the point in this paper but it is also a phenomenon prevalent among other writers.

It is clear that the use of simple, ordinary speech is a defining characteristic of modern Tibetan literature. This is not to claim that this attribute is unique to modern composition. On the contrary, it is a feature shared by both secular and religious *mgur*, the genre of elegant sayings, some hagiographies, and ritual texts. However, ordinary spoken language has never been so widely employed in written prose and poetry as in recent times. Wordsworth's adoption of "the real language of man in a state of vivid sensation" in his poetic compositions revolutionized English poetry.[96] It undermined the artificial and contrived conventions of poetic diction that prevailed in the pre-Romantic age, and succeeded in bringing the deeds and words of ordinary people to new prominence. With regard to Tibetan literary history it would be premature to declare that the vernacularizing tendencies in contemporary Tibetan literature might have artistic repercussions of Wordsworthian magnitude. However, it would not be far-fetched to claim that the everyday speech found in the different forms of oral narrative and among the ordinary people have had and will have a considerable literary impact. It remains a treasure trove for new literary productions and highlights the inextricable interplay that has always existed between orality and the written literature of Tibet.

CONCLUSION: A FERTILE *BARDO*

There has always been a complex, little explored, and mutually influential relationship between the spoken and the written word in Tibet throughout its literary history. Modern Tibetan literature compounds this complexity and makes it clear that it cannot be fully understood without an appreciation of its oral and textual roots in the past and its continuing dynamic interplay with living traditions of oral narrative. Emphasis upon the artistic and critical contributions of the past in this chapter is not a denial of the burdensome qualities of that past. Karl Marx's epigram, that "the tradition of all the dead generations weighs like a nightmare on the brain of the living" in his study of Louis Bonaparte's political ascendancy, and Harold Bloom's "anxiety of influence" underline the oppressive hold of the past.[97] Modern Tibetan literature is no different in facing such challenging powers and suffers accordingly. However, as Arendt's reading of Kafka's parable *"He"* illuminates, the past is not necessarily a force that pushes us back. Rather, it can be seen as a force thrusting forward against the future, while with human beings inserted in between.[98] By creating two antagonistic forces, the insertion of man breaks up the traditional notion of unidirectional temporal movement and results in a third "diagonal force," or a "non-time-space in the very heart of time." Such a space holds for humans the possibility of umpiring the fight between past and future while being rooted in the present.[99] Writers and readers of modern Tibetan literature alike occupy such a *Bardo*-like space between Tibet's past and its future. It is not that dissimilar from the liminal space inhabited by the *geshe* of Dhondup Gyal's *The Wild Yak and Tiger Plains*, who fruitfully negotiates between two opposing forces. This fertile realm is also borne out by the artistic articulation of Tibetan cultural traumas in the present, to which we will turn our attention next.

My brief reflections upon Tibet's critical tradition and some modes of traditional oral narratives reveal this "in-betweenness" and show that the Tibetan literary creations of the present cannot be known without recognizing the artistic legacies of the past. As so often, the point is enshrined in a Tibetan proverb:

གནའ་གཏམ་མ་བཤད་ན།།
ད་གཏམ་མི་ཤེས་གི།

Without talking about the past
The present cannot be known

NOTES

1. This is a popular maxim usually attributed to Atisha. It is frequently quoted in many Tibetan religious works but can be mostly found in the teachings and life stories of great *Kadampa* masters.
2. Emerson [1850] 1986: 458.

3. Cited in Arendt [1961] 1993a: 10.

4. Tsering Shakya 2004; 2008; Pema Bhum 1999; Erhard 2007; and Hor gtsang 'jigs med 2000.

5. Robin 2008: 148–70. See Dullha Gyal's PhD dissertation for an extensive discussion on "new Tibetan fiction" including the critical portrayal of religion (Bdud lha rgyal 2009).

6. There is also a rich tradition of critical folk and street songs in Himalayas. For a treatment of this subject see Aris 1987: 131–64 and Goldstein 1982: 56–66.

7. *Chos gsha' ma mi brin zang zing brin.*

8. In this statement the word "Lama," *bla ma*, carries its primary meaning as an accomplished spiritual master. However, depending on the context it also connotes the reincarnation of a holy person. As a result, sometimes it is interchangeable with the word *sprul sku* as in reincarnate Lama.

9. For a Tibetan interpretation of this and other songs by the 6th Dalai Lama see Dor zhi gdong drug snyems blo 2004: 47–70. For English translations and commentaries see K. Dhondup 1981 and Sørensen 1990.

10. Zhang ston bstan pa rgya mtsho 2004 Vol. 4: 279–87. This work is modeled on 'Brom ston rgyal ba'i 'byung gnas' secular aphorisms, *Mi chos gnad kyi phreng ba* [1988–1989] 2008; 2010: 77–81.

11. Kan lho bod rigs rang skyong khul rtsom sgyur khang 1984: 93–101; Blo bzang chos grags dang Bsod nams rtse mo (eds.) [1988–1989] 2008: 2010: 360–68 (This particular anthology remains part of the core reading for Tibetan graduate students in Chinese state-run Tibetan universities since its first publication. The fact that it has been printed four times is an indication of its popularity and influence.); and Karma 'phrin las (ed.) 2005: 35–43.

12. Ljongs zhing lnga'i skad yig rtsom sgrig Au yon lhan khang (ed.) [2005] 2008: 173–81.

13. Zhang ston bstan pa rgya mtsho 2004 Vol. 4: 286–87.

14 Jackson 1996: 371.

15. Aris 1987: 150.

16. Dor zhi gdong drug snyems blo [1987] 1997: 4–7.

17. Kapstein 2002:110.

18. Aris 1987: 138. Aris goes on to show that how these two realms converge on other levels of experience such as Tibetan Buddhist philosophy, religious practice and the political theory of the "Two Systems," *lugs gnyis*, which combines the spiritual and the political (1987: 138–34).

19. Don grub rgyal 1997 Vol. 3: 316–17; 316–601.

20. Rangdrol (Rang grol) is a typical epithet that features in the names of great tantric masters like Shabkar Tsogdruk Rangdrol (aka, Shabkarpa) and Gurung Natsok Rangdrol (1822–1874). The latter is a famous tantric master who shares his birthplace with Dhondup Gyal.

21. According to another hearsay account, Gyurmey ('Gyur med), the founder and first editor of the literary journal *Sbrang char, Light Rain,* gave Dhondup Gyal the penname (Pad ma 'bum 1994 Kha: 18–19).

22. Chos skyong 2005: 110.

23. Pad ma 'bum 1994 Kha: 9–10. Chos skyong 2005: 111, 113–14.

24. *Sha gang tsho* can be translated as "the choicest meat" but here this more literal rendering is adopted to reflect the overall negative connotation of this proverb.

25. *Dkor* denotes material offerings made to individual Lamas and monks or to their institutions. It usually carries a negative connotation because such wealth has been offered on the behalf of the dead. With regards to the diet of the peacock in Tibet as in India it is believed that peacocks can digest poisonous plants, which they transform into the iridescent colors of their feathers.

26. Benjamin [1970] 1999: 107.

27. An aspect of meditation pose.

28. A common posture for intense devotion and contemplation.

29. *Hor gling g.yul 'gyed* Vol. 2. 1980: 213–14.

30. A fascinating account of Gesar's transformation into a great Lama ensconced in a magnificent camp in order to put a *dmu gab* spell on the people of Hor can be found in *Hor gling g.yul 'gyed* Vol. 2. 1980: 184–229. *Dmu gab* is intended to cause forgetfulness, confusion, torpidity, ignorance, and other undesirable mental and physical effects, culminating in the total destruction of Hor.

31. The Tibetan epic is peppered with such critical statements. Just to cite a few Gesar episodes for similar damning attacks on corrupt Tibetan religious figures see *Byang bdud klu btsan* 2002: 23, *'Khrungs gling me tog ra ba* (1999: 36) and *Dmyal gling mun pa rang gsal* 1983: 60–65, 68–70, and 74–75.

32. Gung thang bstan pa'i sgron me 1984: 84–92, 2005: 2–9. There are many versions of *Ro sgrung* and uncertainty about the authorship of the corpus still prevails, although it is sometimes attributed to Arya Nagarjuna. For printed Tibetan versions see Dpal mgon 'phags pa klu sgrub 2006 and *Mi ro rtse sgrung* 1980. Different English renditions of some of these stories are offered by Benson 2007 and Yeshi Dhondup 2009. For an acclaimed French translation see Françoise Robin [2006] 2011. The origins of these stories are traced to the non-Buddhist Indian sources in the Vetala tales called *Vetālapañcaviṃśatikā*, which features twenty-five stories. A survey of these Sanskrit tales can be found in Sternbach (1976 vol. III: 2ff) and Warder (1992 vol. VI: Chapter XLVL).

33. This specific tale is known as *The Carpenter Kunga* (*Shing bzo kun dga'*), and a printed version of it can be found in *Mi ro rtse sgrung* 1880: 25–30. Gunthang's retelling slightly varies from this printed rendition and it might indicate that he consulted yet another version of *Ro sgrung*. An English translation of this story is provided in Benson 2007: 23–28.

34. Here "handspan" translates the Tibetan *mtho gang*. This is a common unit of measurement in Tibet. It is the linear distance between the tips of the thumb and of the middle finger on one's outstretched hand. This measurement is only about a millimeter shy of a Western "handspan," which is the distance between the tip of the thumb and the tip of the little finger of an outstretched hand.

35. Gung thang bstan pa'i sgron me 2007: 5. According to Buddhist belief *Bardo* (*bar do*) is the intermediate state between death and rebirth. This liminal stage plays a formative role in shaping one's future form of life and spiritual progress.

36. Ngag dbang rgya mtsho 1984: 248.

37. See Samten Karmay (1998: 507–08) for an English translation of this passage.

38. Ngag dbang rgya mtsho 1984: 248.

39. See Samten Karmay (1998: 508) for an English translation of this passage.

40. I am grateful to Samten Karmay for this information and for drawing my attention to critically pertinent passages in the Great Fifth's autobiography.

41. Ljongs lnga'i skad yig rtsom sgrig u yon lhan khang (ed.) 2005: 2–10.

42. Ibid., 2.

43. On the concept of "traditional referentiality" see Foley 1999.

44. Cited in Toelken 1986: 134.

45. Hegel 1975: 1052–53.

46. Tshe ring don grub 1996: 171–201. For an English translation of this short story and a brief introduction to the author see Hartley and Pema Bhum (2001: 58–77). There are different versions of the episode on Gesar's journey to Hell but Tsering Dhondup models his fictional narrative on *Dmyal gling mun pa rang gsal* 1983. I am grateful to the author's generosity for giving me his own copy.

47. Accounts of bloodcurdling punishments meted out to flawed Tibetan religious figures in the Gesar epic can be found in *Dmyal gling mun pa rang gsal* 1983: 60–65, 68–70, and 74–75.

48. Don grub rgyal 1997 Vol. 2: 318–28.

49. *Lha 'dre gdon bgegs*, (Gods, Ghosts, Demons and Obstructive Spirits) is the Tibetan rendition of Chinese slogan *niúguǐ shéshén* (Monsters and Demons), employed to attack anyone who was accused of holding on to old values and traditions during the Cultural Revolution. Struggle sessions (Tibetan—*'thab 'dzing*, Chinese—*pīdòu dàhuì*) are a political method of persecution and terrorization adopted by the CCP especially during the Cultural Revolution. During these sessions accused were subjected to public criticisms and brutal and humiliating treatments so as to break their spirit or sometimes even to execute them.

50. Don grub rgyal 1997 Vol. 2: 324–25.

51. Ibid., 327.

52. Benjamin [1970] 1999: 83.

53. For Tibetan experiences of the Cultural Revolution see Dawa Norbu 1997: 261–76; Tsering Shakya 1999: 314–47; Pad ma 'bum 2001, 2006 and Craig 1999: 166–95 and Arjia Rinpoche 2010: 74–106.

54. Don grub rgyal 1997 Vol. 2: 352–97.

55. Pad ma 'bum 1994: 17.

56. Gu ru U rgyan gling pa: [1986] 1997. *Bka' thang sde lnga* is considered an invaluable treasure text revealed in 1285 by Orgyan Lingpa, which consists of five books or sections dealing with Kings, Queens, Ministers, Translators and Paṇḍitas, and Gods and Ghosts respectively. A very brief introduction of it by Chab brag lha mo skyabs can be found on his blog: http://www.chapdaklhamokyab.fr/ཆབ་བྲག་ལྷ་མ/ བཀའ་ཐང་ས་ལ/, January 1, 2011. For an appreciation of its literary values see Rgya ye bkra bho 2002: 372–400. Parts of the books dealing with Kings and Ministers were translated into English by Frederick W. Thomas 1935: 264–88. For a list of other Western-language sources on *Bka' thang sde lnga* see Martin 1997: 53.

57. A fascinating account of the buried treasures can be found in the chapter 18 of the book concerning Kings in *Bka' thang sde lnga* (Gu ru U rgyan gling pa: 1986: 153–208). This chapter is entitled *On the Burying of Heritage Wealth for Future Royal*

Lineage (*Ma 'ongs rgyal brgyud nor skal ji ltar sbas tshul*). The location of these riches and the manner of their burying are described with minute and vivid detail. It makes sumptuous reading. No wonder Dhondup Gyal was struck by it. The sheer quantity and variety of the precious wealth is simply breathtaking.

58. Sanskrit: Brahmā.

59. Sanskrit: Hayagrīva

60. Bshan pa is an allusion to Sdig gcod shan pa rme ru (Meru, the Murderous Butcher), who is one of the most feared heroes of the Gesar epic. He is the self-same hero who sings the cited critical song about "the Lowly Lama."

61. Don grub rgyal 1997 Vol. 2: 356.

62. Pad ma 'bum: 1994: 21.

63. For arguments of Dhondup Gyal as a transitional figure see Lama Jabb 2011: 91–93 and Lin 2008: 86–111.

64. Erhard 2007: 133–46. Heather Stoddard translates this story as *Soul Born of A Scapula*. See Jangbu (2010: 124–29) for her English translations of this story and other writings by Jangbu.

65. Erhard 2007: 133–46; Schiaffini-Vedani 2008: 202–04.

66. Like many Tibetans as a young boy I was introduced to these fantastical tales through oral transmission. There were some of my favorite bedtime stories narrated by Aga Nori, one of my older nomad brothers. See footnote 32 above for bibliographical details for some printed versions of *Ro sgrung*.

67. Mda' tshan pa 2008.

68. Tsering Shakya 2004: 204.

69. Pad ma 'bum (1994: 22) witnessed Dhondup Gyal's liking for folk songs one night when the latter, after performing a few songs himself, challenged the assembled crowd to a witty, humorous singing contest. To his disappointment, no one took it up. At a literary workshop (*Literary Genres in Tibet*) in Paris organised by INALCO and TINEMO January 27, 2011 where I presented a section of this chapter, Jangbu, who knew Dhondup Gyal personally, also confirmed the latter's fondness for and familiarity with all types of oral performance. Dhondup Gyal had a huge repertoire of general folk songs, love songs, and proverbs, which he frequently used at social gatherings and in informal conversations.

70. See Bkra shis rgyal mtshan (ed.) 1997 for a collection of some romantic ballads in printed form.

71. Lhun 'grub [1982] 1991: 219–38. The title of the story alludes to a famous ballad about a black horse which was stolen and taken away to a faraway place. It finds its way home after an arduous trek through hostile territories even though it had three legs hobbled together. This also has a special musical melody in which arrangements of notes resemble the irregular gait of such a hobbled horse. As a child I often heard this captivatingly plaintive tune performed on a flute in Tibet.

72. Don grub rgyal 1997 Vol. 2: 218–88. *The Frostbitten Flower* was first published in 1982. For an English translation of it see Virtanen 2000: 31–74. Six years after the publication of this acclaimed short story Yangtso Kyi presented an equally powerful portrayal of paternal tyranny and forced marriage in her proverb-packed short story *Diary of the Grassland* (G.yang 'tsho skyid [1988] 2011: 69–81). An English translation of this by Lauran Hartley can be found in Yangtso Kyi 2000: 19–26.

73. *Rang lus 'dom pa gang po/ bkug nas gzhu gi gtong na/ drang mo mda' gi gtong na/ rang lag red.* A more literal English rendition would be: It's up to one to bend the single-fathom body of oneself into a bow or straighten it into an arrow.

74. *Chu rma chu dgu rung zhabs red/ rlabs sngon mo mkha' la 'phyo bzhin/ shar rgya mtsho'i phyogs la rgyug gi.*

75. For a printed version of this ballad visit http://www.sangdhor.com/list_c. asp?id=114, October 26, 2009.

76. Ibid., 193–217.

77. Tsering Shakya 2004: 204.

78. Ibid., 210–11, 215.

79. Bhabha 1994: 4–5.

80. A printed version of this ballad can be found in Bkra shis rgyal mtshan (ed.) 1997: 237–58. For a video production of it see Nub mtsho mi rigs sgra brnyan par skrun khang: 2003. This video can be viewed online at http://www.tbyouth.com/article/photo/20100808772.html, May 5, 2009. There are slight discrepancies between the printed version and audio and visual recordings.

81. Ganja, Rgan gya, is located in a lush grassland area north of Labrang monastery in Amdo.

82. *Bde mchog* is the name of a popular wrathful deity, known as Cakrasaṃvara in Sanskrit. For an explanation of the sacred significance of the White Rock of Ganja (Rgan gya'i brag dkar) see Zhang ston bstan pa rgya mtsho 2004 Vol.1: 458–77.

83. Ḍākinī Gungru (Gung ru mkha' 'gro) is a famous female incarnated Lama and she is the head of Dragkar (The White Rock) Monastery in Ganja. She is also regarded as the chief *ḍākinī* in charge of the sacred White Rock of Ganja. A brief account of her six successive incarnations can be found in Hor gtsang 'jigs med 2009 Vol. 3: 181–87; and Zhang ston bstan pa rgya mtsho (2004 Vol.1: 181–20) wrote a fascinating short biography of the 4th Ḍākinī Gungru, Dkon mchog rig 'dzin dpal mo.

84. *Skra bdag*, keeper of (her) hair is a frequently used Tibetan phrase in oral sources denoting the rightful husband of a lady or the love of her life.

85. *Sman bu mos blo rtse phu lu gtad/ pha mi btsong yin no ma shes zig.*

86. Aristotle 2001: 95; Nightingale 2006: 44–46.

87. *Kha nas phud na sman/ khog la bzung na dug.*

88. Berlin 2000: 79.

89. Watt 1957: 13.

90. Pad ma 'bum 1999.

91. Tsering Shakya 2004: 207.

92. Tshe ring don grub 1996; 1997; 2001; 2002 and 2006.

93. *Bkra shis 'jog* means to sing an auspicious song at the end of a festivity.

94. Don grub rgyal 1997 Vol. 2: 196–98; 214–17.

95. Achebe [1958] 1986: 5.

96. Wordsworth [1802] 2001: 648.

97. Marx 1978: 595; Bloom [1973] 1997: xi–xlvii; 5–16.

98. Arendt 1993a: 10.

99. Ibid., 11–13.

Chapter 4

Narration of Cultural Traumas in Modern Tibetan Poetry and Fiction

རྒྱུ་ནག་པོ་ཡར་ལོག།
རླུང་བསེར་བུ་ཐུར་ལོག།

Bitter enemies came up
Fierce winds blew down[1]

The plight of Tibet and the weight of its recent history are felt in contemporary Tibetan writing. The violent takeover of Tibet in the 1950s and subsequent Communist Chinese rule have been traumatic experiences that have left indelible marks on the Tibetan psyche. The Chinese state continues to control and shape the narrative of modern Tibetan experience, but in recent times Tibetan writers have been breaking (at great personal cost) a long-held silence through poetry, prose, and visual arts. Many of these writers received a hybrid education. They received modern education and statist indoctrination in formal Communist schools, but at the same time grew up listening to stories of the harrowing experiences of their parents or elders of their tribes and villages. Thanks to the unique experience of these writers, narratives that were confined to the private, oral sphere of the family hearth are now being transferred into the public space through the printed page and popular electronic multimedia. This chapter will explore some of their audacious writings, ranging from poetry and fiction to nonfiction prose, with special focus on Tsering Dhondup's novel *The Red Wind Scream* (*Rlung dmar 'ur 'ur*). These works demonstrate how the cultural traumas of the 1950s and the Cultural Revolution, which threatened the very survival of Tibetan culture, are now being remembered to reinforce Tibetans' collective identity. It should be acknowledged from the outset that as the concerned authors are from the Amdo region of Tibet they mainly depict the tragic events of their immediate communities. Such events were not necessarily repeated throughout Tibet in an identical way. Nevertheless, specific collective traumatic experiences are rearticulated synecdochically as the story of Tibet's encounter with Communist China.

Cultural trauma entails an originating event as well as subsequent interpretations and representations undertaken by those who directly experienced it, and by their descendants. Artistic remembrances of cultural traumas as shared sufferings reinforce a common Tibetan consciousness while they also question Chinese narratives of modern Tibetan experience. As the vitality of these public expressions originates in oral sources, I will also give a summary of my mother's account, in her own words, of our tribe's encounter with the Chinese People's Liberation Army in 1958. Her voice is only one of the many that breaks the forced silence of Tibetan history and listening to it serves to contextualize contemporary artistic utterances within the personal experiences that have become enmeshed with the fate of Tibet as a nation.

COHESIVE ENDURANCE OF CULTURAL TRAUMA

A traumatic cultural event engenders collective suffering, which in turn reinforces the national identity of a people. Renan was acutely aware of the cohesive force of shared experiences such as suffering, joy, and hope that constitute what he called a "rich legacy of memories" vital for nation formation. In his influential lecture *What is a Nation?* Renan emphasized that "suffering in common unifies more than joy does." He immediately added: "Where national memories are concerned, griefs are of more value than triumphs, for they impose duties, and require a common effort."[2] I concur with Renan and theorists of cultural trauma who stress the lasting impact of a horrifying occurrence on the memory of a people and their collective consciousness. The process of social mediation plays an important role in the remembrance of cultural trauma, but I believe cultural trauma is ultimately rooted in a concrete originating event. It cannot be presented as a mere social construction.

"Cultural trauma," posits Jeffrey C. Alexander, "occurs when members of a collectivity feel they have been subjected to a horrendous event that leaves indelible marks upon their group consciousness, marking their memories forever and changing their future identity in fundamental and irrevocable ways."[3] Alexander and others take a constructivist approach to cultural trauma which views it as something socially constructed rather than an unmediated spontaneous reaction to a sudden occurrence.[4] They emphasize the complex processes of mediation and representation to which an event is subjected before it comes to be perceived as traumatic by a collectivity.

Another central aspect of this constructivist approach is that an event is conceived as culturally traumatic when the process of social mediation presents it as a threat to collective identity. According to this belief, "real or imagined phenomena" are seen as traumatic because they are believed to have harmfully affected collective identity by abruptly disturbing a group's culturally patterned meanings.[5] Cultural trauma is thus viewed as the outcome of conscious representation of social pain as a fundamental threat to a group's sense of itself. Neil J. Smelser regards this perceived threat as a central attribute of cultural trauma and shows how the language of negative affect underlines this. He maintains that cultural trauma is experienced as a threat to a culture and that this engenders negative emotions in the personal identities of individuals who identify with that culture.[6]

The Tibetan encounter with Communist China in the 1950s, and the subsequent experience of Chinese rule in the form of the Great Leap Forward and the Cultural Revolution, can be understood as culturally traumatic within this theoretical framework. Tibetan representations of these sudden, radical, indelible, fundamental, and psychologically shocking changes are expressed in diverse interpretative modes ranging from private conversations to public discourses such as literature. However, awareness of the role of processes of representation and interpretation should not be exaggerated to the point at which the originating historical events in the genesis of cultural trauma are neglected.

Piotr Sztompka seems to advance a more nuanced constructivist conception of trauma when he acknowledges the role of a concrete originating event. "Trauma," says Sztompka, "like many other social conditions, is at the same time *objective* and *subjective*: it is usually based in actual occurrences or phenomena, but it does not exist as long as those do not become visible and defined in a particular way."[7] He goes on to emphasize the latter half of this statement by claiming that traumas are defined, framed, and interpreted within a framework of pre-existing meanings and cultural templates, yet the pivotal role of an actual event is undeniable. Ron Eyerman also underscores the centrality of mediation and interpretation but accepts that cultural trauma is "rooted in an event or series of events."[8] This acknowledgment is a crucial corrective to extreme constructivist tendencies, which tend to construe cultural traumas as mere cultural constructions while marginalizing the relevance of overwhelming historical occurrences. Although this chapter considers artistic reconstructions of Tibetan cultural trauma, I strongly believe that these reconstructions derive from concrete, historical occurrences rather than from some purely imagined events.

When Chinese Communist personnel and the People's Liberation Army (PLA) marched into Eastern Tibet (Amdo and Kham) in the early 1950s, they were confronted by an alien world with a distinct socioeconomic system, shared historical memories and cultural values and ties. Only a few years after their arrival, the Chinese Communists imposed socioeconomic changes in these Tibetan regions through what they called "democratic reforms" (*dmangs gtso bcos bsgyur*).[9] In the name of the socialist transformation of Tibet these measures were implemented to revolutionize the traditional Tibetan social system. They entailed confiscation of land and other forms of private property, suppression of the traditional Tibetan elite, collectivization programs alongside the establishment of class division, and the launching of class struggles (*gral rim 'thab rtsod*). Creation of cooperatives—later communes (*mnyam las can, thun mong can*)—affected all levels of Tibetan communities. Often violent "struggle sessions" (*'tham 'dzing*) against "class enemies" (*gral rim dgra bo*) targeted traditional Tibetan monastic and tribal leadership. "Struggle sessions" were a technique of persecution and denunciation which had been adopted by the CCP as early as the 1930s. The practice was refined through subsequent trials, into a highly efficient system of cruelty in "breaking" opponents and terrorizing the people. During these sessions, the accused were subjected to public criticisms and brutal, dehumanizing treatments entailing breaking their spirit and sometimes even execution.[10] As the entire Tibetan way of life came under attack, forced communist reforms were met with fierce resistance from 1956 onward. In the late 1950s, the unrest in Amdo and Kham escalated and spilt over into Central Tibet and became a catalyst for the famous Lhasa uprising in March 1959.[11] While the Chinese Communists carried out an indiscriminate crackdown against Tibetan farming and nomadic communities, Tibetan rebels put up pockets of resistance in their own tribal or regional territories throughout the eastern Tibetan plateau.

Although in some Tibetan places the rebellion continued until early 1960s, in Amdo it reached a crescendo in 1958. A secret Chinese military document records that there were 996 skirmishes between the Chinese army and Tibetans for the duration of just eight months in 1958 in the territories of Jonei, Thewo, Labrang, Machu, Watse, and Luchu alone. These are six counties in today's Gannan (Tib. kan lho) Tibetan Autonomous Prefecture, Gansu Province. According to this confidential document: "Because of incessant battles waged through night and day for eight months between mid-March and mid-September a complete victory was won with regards to quelling the revolt in Khanlo. Attached forces under our Command Headquarters fought 996 times. During which 21,141 rebels were eradicated, and 8,355 guns of various types, 11,579 knives and spears, and 2,755 horses were seized."[12] Although these statistics concern only a single Tibetan area, they indicate the intensity of military activity and the scale of resistance in eastern Tibet which has been little reported.

However, this widespread rebellion failed to block communist reforms let alone to drive out the Chinese. Chinese suppression of it, coinciding as it did with the Great Leap Forward, led to unprecedented Tibetan suffering—massacres, mass imprisonments, mass suicides, the destruction of monasteries, starvation, and radical sociopolitical restructuring along Marxist collectivist lines.[13] As a result, 1958 was a year of bewildering changes which radically and fundamentally transformed Tibetan communities in Amdo and became etched indelibly on the minds of local people. In Amdo parlance, it came to be simply known as *nga brgyad lo*, the Year of '58. This term not only denotes a perceived historical rupture, but also carries with it connotations of fear, disorientation, and unspeakableness. To many Tibetans, the mere mention of this year evokes memories of traumatic individual and collective experience. Inside Tibet these disturbing memories are mostly preserved and transmitted through private oral communications. The reproduction of such oral accounts in contemporary Tibetan literature brings them into a public space. As private narratives take on a public dimension, they become seamlessly interwoven into the collective narrative of the Tibetan nation.

DEMISE OF *DRONG*, THE WILD YAK

A careful reading of modern Tibetan literary works originating from Amdo reveals that the events of the 1950s are a recurring, central theme. Because of its sensitivity the presence of this theme is not always obvious. In many instances, it is dealt with implicitly, or encoded with great subtlety. In such cases it requires at least a certain degree of cultural sensibility and Tibetan historical consciousness to decipher their hidden messages. However, recently there have been more and more explicit references to the 1950s, especially 1958, as a traumatic historical juncture.[14] As a result, 1958, a tragic and momentous year in local Amdo history, functions as a common thematic thread that runs through particular works of contemporary Tibetan writers, giving these literary creations a sense of unity as it has done to the oral discourses over the decades. In the process of remembering, the 1950s and the year 1958 in particular have become literary identity markers of the Tibetan people as well as points of reference. For the Amdo people it was 1958 when the aggression of the PLA wreaked havoc throughout the region. Subsequently, this date has taken on a national significance as it is identified as "the year when the bitter enemy arrived in Tibet."[15] This is the case although in other parts of Tibet it is regarded as just another year of a tumultuous decade.[16]

Ju Kalsang makes an implicit allusion to the 1950s in his poem on Gedun Choepel. In this poem, Gedun Choepel is rediscovered only after the bloody rule of Mao. It addresses Gedun Choepel as follows:

When gradually the dark, poisoned smoke that belched
Out of the barrel of that murderous gun faded,
Your tomb
Was found at a bend in history.[17]

"The poisoned smoke" that concealed Gedun Choepel's grave came "from the barrel of the gun" that secured Chinese power in Tibet through "murderous" acts. Gedun Choepel passed away in October 1951 just a month after the PLA soldiers marched into Lhasa for the first time.[18] Ju Kalsang's poem intimates that the resultant violence and chaos left Gedun Choepel buried at that specific juncture in Tibetan history. Following the crackdown on the 2008 protests across Tibet, Ombar (oM 'bar)—"Burning Om"—a young Tibetan intellectual, is more forthright in his reference to this tumultuous period of Tibetan history. In a banned 2008 issue of *Eastern Snowmountain*, a Tibetan journal of social and literary commentary, he writes bluntly: "Many years ago an army of wolves bearing five stars on their foreheads arrived on this plateau." Through deceptive persuasions and sugared words, he continues, they duped the Tibetan clergy and power elites, and through aggressive military force armed with guns, cannons, and bombs they made bloody sacrificial offerings.[19]

Many Tibetan poets and writers of fiction are less forthright than Ombar when making reference to the 1950s. They employ metaphorical figures of speech to allude to this period with great efficacy and potency. The frequent use of metaphor has both practical and literary purposes. The ambiguity and multivalence of a metaphor are useful in evading censorship and the evocative power of the device is ideal for engendering heightened sensibilities. One of the favorite metaphorical images used in contemporary Tibetan poetry is *drong* (*'brong*) wild yak. The *drong* is celebrated for its untamed and untamable spirit, its bravery, stamina, perseverance, independence, and ability to survive in the unforgiving Tibetan wilderness. Because of these qualities and its perceived status as the most esteemed wild animal of Tibet the *drong* is used as an image to signify pre-1950s Tibetans and Tibet. In many modern Tibetan poems, the fall of Tibet and deaths of Tibetans are equated to the "defeat" or disappearance of wild yaks.[20] One can detect this in the following allusive poem by Mogru Sherab Dorje (Rmog ru shes rab rdo rje). The silenced history of modern Tibet whispers through the "grass" and "the wind and breeze" within this poem.

History Talk
As that herd of wild yaks were defeated like that
This mountain valley was emptied like this

On either side of that process
The heavy anguish of mountains and rocks was sown into the sky
The wandering dirges of rain and rivers roamed in every direction
But even when darkness rained upon the earth,
Deep within the lone black yakhair tent, countless
prayers and butterlamps were offered.

Children who lost their mothers
Were like tongues of flame in the wind
Like prayer flags on the mountain pass

As that herd of wild yaks were defeated like that
This mountain valley was emptied like this

On the night of a waning moon
I heard talk
That talk was amidst the grass and plants
That talk was on the wind and breeze
"That footloose lot are still hunters
The hunters are still in the mountains as before"

As that herd of wild yaks were defeated like that
This mountain valley was emptied like this[21]

To use a Tibetan phrase, like the rest of the world Tibet is constituted of an external container (*phyi'i snod*) and internal contents (*nang gi bcud*).[22] The physical environment—the container—treasures the living beings within it—the contents—and the two make an integral whole, fusing into a single living vitality. What Mogru's poem metaphorically suggests is that, deprived of wild yaks, Tibet has been emptied of its living contents. It becomes a place characterized by extinction. The Tibetan verb *stongs* in its past tense has two connotations here. It either means the "mountain valley" has emptied out or all its living beings have become extinct. Tibet's bloody "defeat" at the hands of Communist China in the 1950s is seen as a traumatic, earth-shattering event that signaled the fall of Tibet. This was an overwhelming historical occurrence that generated "heavy anguish," "wandering dirges," and orphaned children. The "history talk" that can be heard in the wild-yakless wilderness of Tibet reminds Tibetans of those free-ranging "hunters" that killed their immediate forefathers, and warns them that "the hunters" are still at large in the mountains—Tibet.

A similar urge to "talk history" can be detected in a long poem by Guru Dhondup entitled *Death*, which is a reflection upon the decline and imminent death of Tibet. Once again the image of the wild yak stands for the Tibetans who fell during the 1950s, as can be seen in the following extract:

Once upon a time
A tiger-like forefather of mine jumped off a great mountaintop
A leopard-like forefather of mine plunged suicidally into the depths of a great river
Many yak and wild yak-like forefathers also gradually seeped
Into the platter of this weapon blade-like great land

Since they entrusted their mournful melodies to the tongues of grass
The inner depths of this supreme mountain
Have become a tattered plastic bag for collecting tears[23]

Like "the wandering dirge" in Mogru's poem, Guru Dhondup's "mournful melodies" owe their genesis to the numerous violent deaths suffered by Tibetans. In common with other Tibetan poets Guru Dhondup refers to this historical occurrence as "the wound of history" (*lo rgyus kyi rma kha*). In the same way as Mogru's "history talk" is borne on the wind and grass, these plaintive melodies are sung by blades of grass. These predominantly rustic images emphasize the rural and oral sources of the stories and memories embedded within such poems. What Tibetans melancholically call "the sighing song of the long grass" (*'jag ma'i shugs glu*) disperses the tragic tales of the 1950s that have no voice within the official Chinese narrative of Tibet's absorption into Communist China. A favorite mantra of the Chinese Communist Party is that it has delivered Tibet from a dark, feudal past to a brightly lit present. For instance, one of the latest Chinese "white papers" on Tibet considers "the peaceful liberation of Tibet" over sixty years ago as "a milestone marking the commencement of Tibet's progress from a dark and backward society to a bright and advanced future."[24] Another official publication states: "The Society of old Tibet under feudal serfdom was even more dark and backward than in Europe in the Middle Ages."[25] The Chinese state has propagated its own conception of Tibetan history while endeavoring to stifle Tibetan counternarratives through its coercive apparatuses and its control over means of representation such as the mass media and the education system.

Reflecting on the inefficacy of attempts to repress the collective memories of traumatic events, Smelser acutely observes: "It is difficult to imagine anything like the complete success of an organized political effort to ban a major historical event or situation from memory, largely because it is impossible to control, even with extreme efforts, private oral intercommunication among citizens, between parents and children, and so on."[26] In spite of massive efforts, China has failed to silence the alternative Tibetan voice found within interpersonal oral communications, which provides narrative material and artistic inspiration to contemporary Tibetan writers as evident in the cited poems. The stories sung by the grass in the Tibetan countryside are now being consciously related through contemporary Tibetan poetry. As Guru Dhondup's poem on death progresses, we find its narrator terrified not of death itself, but of the silence it leaves behind—his horror at a mute posterity:

Even though in truth death is a blissful liberation
Today I don't want to die, dumb like this
After my silent death

My children and grandchildren would be orphaned
They would be dumb—incapable of speech, and lame—unable to walk

Like Mogru's poem, Guru Dhondup's *Death* also deliberately remembers the same haunting historical happening through the symbolism of the slaughtering of wild yaks. For such poets, poetry is an effective means of representing an alternative voice silenced within Chinese state-controlled media. In this way, Tibetan poets are what theorists of cultural trauma call "cultural carriers" who represent, articulate, and mediate a traumatic event.[27] The 1950s are represented poetically as the period of the demise of wild yaks. Poetic recollections of it as a cause of collective suffering serve to reinforce modern Tibetan national consciousness.

Before looking at other equally potent metaphorical expressions for the 1950s, another poem that revolves around the symbolism of wild yak is worth mentioning. Nyan's (Gnyan, Argali or Fearsome Spirit) now-famous poem *Notes on Remembering the Wild Yak* is a eulogy and a dirge rolled into one. Its laudatory tone extols an unyielding rebellious nature. Its elegiac undertone mourns the demise of a glorious past generation and notes the void left behind. In its entirety the poem remembers a past generation who have stood up against advancing Chinese forces in the 1950s. It is a long poem formed of ten parts. The following excerpts of five parts should be adequate to reveal its central themes and its overall assertive feel.

ONE
Before the blowing of the red wind, wild yaks stampeded across yonder pass.
Today my grandfather is staring at the pass, remembering
a wild beast called the wild yak.
Those slate rocks and wild pastures, once trampled under the hooves of wild yaks,
Who could have leveled them into uniformity and snuffed out their lives today?
Does that wild beast called the wild yak, over so many, many years gone by,
Today remain silent beneath this land under your feet?

Before the blowing of the red wind, wild yaks stampeded across yonder pass
Today my grandfather is staring at the pass, remembering
a wild beast called the wild yak.
What can be seen at the pass today are only a highway and concrete pylons.
The herds of wild yaks that held the sun and moon
between their horns, today are gone from sight.

TWO
No one has tamed the wild yak
No one could turn the wild yak into a slave-like domestic animal
As the wild yak is not broken it has no slave mentality.

The wild yak has an extremely stubborn character
The wild yak hates oppression and invasion
The wild yak dances upon the body of a murderer
The wild yak will lick the murderer to death[28]

The wild yak does not carry out sly attacks
The wild yak charges straight at the pointed gun of the hunter
The wild yak is ever ready to sacrifice its life leaping
over a cliff so as to defend its character
The wild yak has never experienced a lingering death
like the fate of a domestic animal with
A tightening noose round its neck

Because the wild yak enjoys strong internal solidarity
The wild yak seeks vengeance if a sibling is wounded
The wild yak bewails the bleeding wound of its sibling
The wild yak is an independent wild beast wherever it roams and resides

THREE
For the wild yak apart from naked self
The wild yak has no one to say "yes" to
The wild yak has no owner
The wild yak has no class

The wild yak has an unshakeable belief in itself
For the wild yak considers itself as the pride and youth of this land
It has never bowed down before anyone
The wild yak has no habit of bowing down

For the wild yak apart from naked self
The wild yak has no Protector
The wild yak has no Constitution
The wild yak has no herder wielding sling and club

FOUR
For dear life, for livelihood,
For freedom, for siblings, the wild yak is ever ready to rise up
Thus the wild yak has an absolute resolve to rise up against you
The wild yak turns a deaf ear to your violent guns

Invasion and oppression
Intimidation and enslavement
The wild yak resists all these before the human race
The wild yak is never among those who surrender to you
And the wild yak has a hard backbone that has never been saddled

. . .

TEN

Before the blowing of the red wind wild yaks stampeded across yonder pass
Today my grandfather is staring at the pass with a sorrowful heart and mind
Yet, following the wild yaks, the flow of conversations
From my grandfather and his generation is coming to an end

Grandfather is mourning the wild yaks instead of the human race
Is grandfather the only person who commemorates the wild yak?
Is the naked armed grandfather the only one?

In this harsh, derelict land, now there is not even a faint scent of the wild yak
No one raises the flag of the wild yak
Silent chests have distanced themselves from someone
And have completely forgotten yesterday's darkness and bloodshed[29]

This poem celebrates wild yaks' mobility and independence, its aggressive and protective spirit, its obstinacy and untamable nature. These are the perceived qualities of the old Tibetan generation. Almost every line of the poem features the term "wild yak": it is used sixty-six times and its reiteration becomes an integral part of the overall rhythm of the poem and seems to acquire the concentrated force of a Tibetan mantra. The common poetic device of repetition is employed here for generating emphasis and a sense of unity, intimacy, and imagistic concentration. However, the self-vaunting and defiant tone of the poem is moderated by the sobriety of two lines that recur several times: "Before the blowing of the red wind wild yaks stampeded across yonder pass / Today my grandfather is staring at the pass, remembering a wild beast called wild yak." Once again the vanishing of the wild yak and the stirring of "red wind" point to the 1950s as an abrupt historical juncture. The fall of Tibet and deaths of Tibetans are directly linked to the arrival of the "Red Chinese" (*rgya dmar*)—Chinese Communists. This encounter not only entailed loss of human lives but also devastating environmental degradation as the wild habitat of wild yaks now remains "leveled" and lifeless. As Guru Thondup observes in his poem, due to this encounter Tibet has "become a tattered plastic bag for collecting tears." Nyan's poem strikes a despondent note too as the poet wonders if his grandfather is alone in commemorating the wild yak. He moans that the wild yak spirit has deserted today's Tibetans who "have completely forgotten yesterday's darkness and bloodshed." However, like the other cited poems, Nyan's poem is an act of remembrance in itself. In fact, it not only publicly remembers a transformative historical event, but by doing so uses it to inspire fellow Tibetans as well as to establish it as an important aspect of modern Tibetan consciousness.

FACING THE MURDERER

As already apparent in the cited poems, contemporary Tibetan literature is characterized by an audacity to speak out, albeit often in a metaphorical idiom. The temerity of many contemporary Tibetan writers to present an alternative articulation of this most sensitive subject—Tibet's traumatic encounter with Communist China—separates them from their immediate precursors. Tibetan writers from the early communist rule till the early 1980s had to swallow their pain and pride and write eulogies to the conquering Chinese Communist Party (CCP). Although there were a few exceptions, most of the political poems of praise during these decades would have been the product of CCP compulsion.[30] The Tibetan critic Pema Bhum underscores this fact when he speaks of the common suffering caused by Chinese occupation, especially in the psyche of the Tibetans remaining inside Tibet. He writes: "All Tibetans, both inside and outside Tibet, share a common sorrow—their homeland is occupied by another. In addition to this, Tibetans inside Tibet bear the sorrow that comes from being forced to hide the anger they feel towards the plunderers of their homeland and the murderers of their fathers; they can never show their real face and must bow respectfully to those in power. There is also a special suffering for writers and poets. Suppressing the fire of hatred in their hearts and pretending to smile, they must use their pen, which is like their soul, to sing songs of praise to the bloody hand that murdered their fathers."[31]

However, as time progressed, contemporary Tibetan writers and poets now refuse to be silenced by this unprecedented suffering borne by Tibetan intellectuals. Now they dare to identify "the bloody hand that murdered their fathers" and question the legitimacy of this hand, the CCP, to continue its rule in Tibet. In an accusatory poem pregnant with historical and political implications, Guru Dhondup equates the communist power in Tibet with a self-imposed, tyrannical stepfather. This blog poem, suggestively entitled *Please Stepfather, Do Not Deceive Me*, traces the cold-blooded murder of his father to what Ju Kalsang calls in his poem on Gedun Choepel "a bend in history"—the 1950s.

Over fifty years ago
You killed my dear father
Killed with cunning, killed with cruelty
Although I was extremely young at the time I knew his face well
It is still terrifying and enraging to think of it now.

As you are actually so devious
Each sweet from your bag allured my childish mind.
Because you held me by my heart and lungs with just feigned smiles and flatteries,
I had to leave all the time and youth of my childhood in your lap nonchalantly

From then on
We became father and son without any blood ties
Whether I've loyalty or not, whether you've any affection or not
Initially I accepted you as a father out of fear

Finally, whether you cared for me or not, whether I trusted you or not
Because you're the first person who taught me how to walk
Gradually I accepted you as a father from the depths of flesh and bones
In my heart, only then did I believe that you were the sole person who cared for me

However, these days you've changed
If I told how, no one would believe it.
Dear stepfather, you're always pointing a steel barrel at me
And yelling that you're going to kill me if I don't remain silent
And asking me if I've forgotten your kindness for caring for me till now
And telling me that nothing good will come if I follow others and rebel
against the father
And telling me that if it hadn't been your care I would be an animal now

Dear stepfather, words do not have blades yet they cut human hearts asunder
Really, all I am talking about is my own welfare.

Dear stepfather, now I've realized everything clearly
In this environment, where deception and treachery devour one another
I've realized clearly that there is no one but myself to care for me.
Yet, either through karma or coercion, we've become father and son.
Please, as a father do not deceive me.
I can endure any deceptions
But for the deception of a father who pretends to care.
Dear stepfather, at least do not deceive me[32]

Although enshrouded in metaphorical language, this poem contains a concise account of modern Tibetan experience under the Chinese communist rule beginning from the early 1950s. For the narrator of the poem, it is an experience of murder, deception, coercion, intimidation, and yet more deception. He is forced into a father-son relationship with a stepfather who kills his real father and lures him with "feigned smiles and flatteries." At first "out of fear" and later out of a semblance of gratitude, the traumatized and deluded narrator accepts the stepfather as his father. It is hard not to detect the echoes of Chinese colonial tutelage in the figure of stepfather. As his acceptance is based on the shaky foundations of violence and fear, it has to be upheld through the constant use of coercive control. Once again, just as in Ju Kalsang's poem, power is exercised through the "steel barrel" of the gun as propagated by Mao. The poem seems to suggest that the CCP, or the Chinese state, symbolized by the stepfather, cannot gain legitimacy for its rule in Tibet. As such it resorts to its usual modus operandi—brute force and emotional blackmail—the same strategies that established its power on the Tibetan plateau in the first place. The poem is bold in its frank questioning of Chinese legitimacy, and contains overtly rebellious strains. However, it is more nuanced than it first appears. In its concluding part, it resignedly propagates a peaceful coexistence based on mutual understanding. This might also be an implicit acknowledgment of the Dalai Lama's "Middle Way Approach" (*dbu ma'i lam*), which advocates Tibet's peaceful coexistence with China under a single nation-state.[33] The poem appears to suggest that the tragic story that began in the 1950s can only be resolved by a fostering of sincerity and mutual acceptance. This distinctively compromising tone at the end of the poem tempers its otherwise embittered metaphorical expressiveness.

The dominant use of paternal figures within the poem to convey the theme of an alien usurpation of power might be construed as a gendered use of figurative language typical of a patriarchal society like Tibet. Although such an interpretation might be partly valid, here paternal images are employed not just to portray a violent power shift but also to allude to the bloody suppression of the Tibetan revolts during the 1950s in which it was the Tibetan male population which suffered most with regard to number of casualties. To put it bluntly, more fathers lost their lives than mothers during the rebellion. In some Tibetan areas, almost the entire adult male population was wiped out. Alak Tsayi, a respected Lama from Amdo, touches on this when he tells us that adult males became a rare sight in the areas surrounding his own birthplace Tsayi (*Tsa yus*) after 1958, and remained so throughout the 1960s. As a result, agricultural tasks usually reserved for men were undertaken by women and children.[34] Many Tibetans, including the men of my own tribe, refer to this phenomenon as "the time when all the males were exterminated leaving only the female folk behind" (*pho shul bcad nas mo shul la gtugs dus*). In popular vernacular parlance this period is identified as "the time when the Chinese raid (invasion) took place" (*rgya rgyugs dus*). In the already-cited essay, Ombar draws on similar set phrases when he describes the 1950s as being characterized by "deaths of men and horses; destruction of families; the fall of yak-hair tents; the extermination of males leaving only females behind; and a great tumult of violence and intimidation."[35] In Guru Dhondup's poem, the father image is used not to privilege male deaths, but to represent a specific aspect of the actual losses suffered by the Tibetan people. On the contrary, in both oral and written sources, some of the most powerful images evoked record deaths of women and children. For instance, when bearing witness to the destruction of entire communities, many accounts single out the heart-rending image of dead mothers still clutching their dead infants and still suckling them on their breasts.[36] In Mogru's *History Talk* the helpless children at the mercy of forces beyond their powers are in such a pathetic situation because they "lost their mothers."

METAPHORS OF THE UNSPEAKABLE

As evident in these examples, contemporary Tibetan writers employ meta-phorical and figurative language not only for its literary merits, but also for practical, political purposes. More often than not, these two functions—the poetic and the concealing or encoding—are inextricably intermeshed. Figura-tive language is endowed with polysemy, emotional charge, and evocative-ness alongside cognitive and aesthetic qualities. As a result, metaphor proves to be indispensable for an effective way to articulate sensitive issues in a heavily censored society that is under the constant surveillance of an ever-watchful state. While commenting on a specific form of classical Tibetan metaphor known as "exaggerated ornament" (*rab rtog gi rgyan*) Dhatsenpa emphasizes the ability of metaphor to give voice to the ineffable.[37] In her philosophical reflections on metaphor Hannah Arendt also singles out its capacity to carry over the ineffable. She brings into focus the vital role of metaphorical language in making manifest invisible thinking or speculative reasoning. It is believed that metaphor bridges the gulf between nonsensory matters and sense experience. Metaphor is thus crucial for the very process of thinking as well as for conveying this "image-less" mental activity.[38] Similarly Dhatsenpa finds in "exaggerated poetic ornament" that an inex-pressible profound state of mind, or a complex human emotion, is expressed through the attribution of animate qualities to inanimate, natural objects. This metaphor is somewhat akin to what is known as pathetic fallacy. In addition to an anthropomorphic treatment of nature and natural objects, the Tibetan "exaggerated poetic ornament" entails the ascription of human and nonhuman sentient characteristics to inanimate things or attribution of conscious human qualities to animal or inanimate objects. It is an exaggerated or distorted depiction of real entities and situations in high-flown metaphorical expres-sions. Artistic imagination produces an overblown description of a thing but this description is still rooted within reality.[39] Although its affected language at times overstretches one's imagination, as Dhatsenpa has noted, one of its chief purposes is to transmit what ordinary speech fails to convey.

In contemporary Tibetan writing, this poetic device is abundantly deployed to express the politically unspeakable and to articulate the indescribable shock and dismay experienced by Tibetans during the 1950s. In Mogru's poem, wind and grass talk about the silenced history of Tibet, rain and riv-ers sing "wandering dirges" and mountains bear "heavy anguishes." Within Nyan's poem lurks one of the most taboo subjects in contemporary China: the notion of Tibetan independence. It disregards the contested issue of a past Tibetan sovereignty by ascribing qualities of fierce independence, protective instinct, territoriality, vengefulness, and overall a unique collective identity to the vanished wild yak that is the fallen Tibet. All these ultrasensitive mes-sages are not necessarily comprehensible to an outsider. The functioning of metaphors within specific cultural templates or communal settings gives them an inaccessible quality. Ted Cohen maintains that a proper appreciation of a metaphor requires as prerequisites the formation of a community (irrespective of size) and the cultivation of cultural intimacy. A figurative use of language, he says, "can be inaccessible to all but those who share information about one another's knowledge, beliefs, intentions, and attitudes."[40] This aspect of metaphor enables what communist-era Polish writers called "Aesopian language"—the presentation of political discussion as imaginative works.[41]

The exclusive quality of metaphor makes it a useful device for circumventing censorship,[42] yet this instrumental dimension does not make it any less informative or less emotionally charged to an insider. Hayden White describes the historical narrative as "an extended metaphor" in that it is not an exact reproduction of the events it reports but, as in a metaphor, it points toward a set of culturally embedded images associated with the events. By doing so, just like a metaphor, it "charges our thought about the events with different emotional valences."[43] By "extended metaphors" White is talking about the representation of historical events in the fictional modes of Western literary culture such as tragic, comic, romantic, or ironic. However, as can be seen in the poems cited above, even ordinary metaphors conceal within them historical narratives charged with emotion. For instance, Nyan's poem is a story about wild yaks that ceased to stampede across a pass due to the stirring of a "red wind." The Tibetan word *zhogs*, stampede, alone evokes a multiplicity of images and emotions. The sheer multitude of wild yaks, their vitality and power. Their awesome presence resonates through their thundering hooves before they vanish into silence. This narrative value of metaphor, its power to bring to mind several images associated with an entity or an event, "charge of affect"[44] and its persuasive force are some of the principal reasons for its prominence in contemporary Tibetan poetry and fiction.

By far the most frequently used metaphor is red wind (*rlung dmar*) or a variant of it such as cold wind (*grang rlung*) or violent wind (*drag rlung*) or just wind (*rlung*). Often the term red wind or wind is followed by verbs such as *lding*, *g.yug* or *'tshub* denoting the stirring, blowing, and gusting of wind. As in Nyan's poem, in many works of contemporary Tibetan poetry and fiction, red wind signifies an abrupt historical juncture. Its color, signifying agitation and unpredictable abruptness, evokes the sudden and forceful entry of Chinese Communists into Tibetan areas in the 1950s. In some cases the image of wind or red wind is so recurrent throughout a literary work that it functions as its central unifying image. So through metaphor, the arrival of the "Red Chinese"—a shared traumatic experience—functions as a kind of unifying thread running through particular works of Tibetan creative writing. The use of wind as a literary image echoes the Tibetan saying that has come to encapsulate the arrival of the Chinese Communists on the Tibetan plateau and the resultant social chaos: "Bitter enemies came up/ Fierce winds blew down."[45] Though Tibetans were not and are still not permitted to talk openly and publicly about the traumatic events of the 1950s and the subsequent Communist rule, subtle literary representations of these events demonstrate the existence of a conscious recollection of this decade. This artistic remembrance is an active part of modern Tibetan collective memory and identity formation. It constitutes an important counternarrative that rejects the Chinese Communists' rose-tinted portrayal of modern Tibetan experience by remembering local Amdo tragedies and weaving them into Tibet's national history. The presence of red wind can be felt in both contemporary Tibetan poetry and fiction, but here a short story and a novel have been selected to underscore the stated points.

DYING IN THE WIND

In a short story entitled *Entrusting to the Wind* by Lhajam Gyal (Lha byams rgyal 2010) "a wild gust that blew over fifty years ago" blows throughout the entire narrative.[46] It almost scatters the main protagonist, a tantric practitioner, into oblivion were it not for the persistent memory of an elderly monk and the storytelling flair of his great-nephew, the narrator. This short story relates the death and funeral of an esteemed religious figure known as the Great Tantric Practitioner of Zurtsa. He is the late paternal great-uncle of the young narrator who bases his story on oral accounts given by an old monk called Lobsang. We learn that in 1958 the tantric master is deported to a prison in Tshadam (Tsha 'dam) and is incarcerated there for a decade.[47] After ten years of deprivation, hunger, thirst, and incessant hard labor, he is let out, stricken with a chronic stomach disease. His release coincides with the initial phase of the Cultural Revolution. Consequently, he is labeled as a "class enemy" and subjected to a series of intense "struggle sessions" entailing torture. During this time of "terrifying, howling red wind" the tantric master passes away while absorbed in deep meditation (*thugs dam la bzhugs nas*). Because no form of worship or religious practice was tolerated during this period, his horrified relatives try their best to undo his meditative pose so as not to arouse others' deadly suspicion. Their attempt to unlock his limbs proves futile and eventually they "entrust his corpse to the wind" as requested by the deceased. The dead body is exposed to the elements and "given to the birds" (*bya gtor*).[48] However, no vulture descends upon it and it remains like "a great yogin" in the cemetery. After seven days Lobsang pleads with the corpse that unless a sign is shown it will be buried instead. As soon as those words are uttered the meditation posture comes apart and the corpse "collapses like a pile of stones." Vultures come flocking, darkening the sky. According to Lobsang and local elderly people, this is not the end of the tantric master. They believe he has absolute control over the mobility of his consciousness (*rnam shes*) and has come back as his own great nephew. The narrator himself turns out to be the reincarnation of the great tantric practitioner.

The story does not make any explicit mention of the arrival of Chinese communists and their subsequent rule in Tibet. However, the use of metaphorical terms such as "wind" and "red wind" is very clear, referencing the arrival of an alien, disorientating force that is responsible for the premature death of the tantrist. The narrator's description of wind reveals his thoughts about an obliterating political force that he dares not name outright. The narrator muses:

I can't help thinking of the wind. Sitting silently before the old monk Lobsang I once again think of that wind, empty of form; the wind-like campaigns and the wind-like times. Now those gusts of wind (*rlung sha*) have blown and vanished in every direction of this land. What trouble has the wind brought? By all means, the wind has carried off my forefather to a certain dimension of time and he can no longer be seen.[49]

This is no ordinary wind but a wind that signifies a perceived historical rupture. Tracing the genesis of this wind to "over fifty years ago" and identifying 1958 as a crucial reference point make it unnecessary to name names of principal agencies. Throughout the story the narrator ponders repeatedly "what has the wind carried off?" and "what has the time carried off?" These rhetorical questions insinuate the loss of an entire Tibetan generation and the memory of their way of life, to wind-like, traumatic historical events.

Scratch beneath the surface of this fictional text and the overall tone of loss and despondency reveals a hidden spirit of defiance, survival, and remembering. This short story shows how the memory of a lost generation is kept alive through the art of storytelling. As storytelling acts as a form of remembrance, the narrator's "forefather" might have disappeared but his story is not forgotten. Although this is a fictional narrative it remains bound to real-life experience. When reflecting upon women and fiction Virginia Woolf stresses the close relationship between imaginative work and life. Unlike science, which is "dropped like a pebble upon the ground" says Virginia Woolf, "fiction is like a spider's web, attached ever so lightly perhaps, but still attached to life at all four corners."[50] The attachment of Lhajam Gyal's story to Tibetan life is nothing tenuous as shown by its evocation of historical situations and events. It records the traumatic death of a respected Tibetan religious figure (by extension the demise of a generation) and the bewildering experience of a community assaulted by a mighty impersonal force (the CCP or Chinese state) that unleashes "wind-like campaigns." In short, the story chronicles in writing what Tibetans underwent during the early Communist era. Although it is sketchy with regards to historical information due to the political sensitivity of the subject matter, its written form and electronic publication broaden the reach of content that is mostly preserved only in oral format.[51]

Lhajam Gyal's fictional text utilizes the modern literary form of short story but it relies heavily on information gleaned from oral sources. It is an oral narrative wrapped in written form. The author acknowledges his debt to oral narratives by giving a salient voice to an oral storyteller. A substantial proportion of the story is the reiteration of a tale repeatedly told by the old monk Lobsang, who himself directly experiences "the wind-like times." In almost every Tibetan family and community there is at least one oral storyteller like Lobsang, who uses story as a memory capsule to impart knowledge, experience, and testimonies of a traumatized generation. Leaving aside his audacity in tackling such hypersensitive subjects, the strength of *Entrusting to the Wind* lies in its embrace of this storyteller. "Experience which is passed on from mouth to mouth is the source from which all storytellers have drawn," observes Walter Benjamin. "And among those who have written down the tales, it is the great ones whose written version differs least from the speech of the many nameless storytellers."[52] By drawing on the experience of an oral storyteller Lhajam Gyal's story is also a tale about survival. In the short story the memory of the tantric practitioner survives within the oral narrative of Lobsang. Lobsang's tale is in turn preserved by the narrator. As the narrator is the great nephew of the tantric practitioner, he perpetuates the latter's bloodline. This survival narrative is given additional prominence by the concept of reincarnation. Not only does the lineage of the narrator's "forefather" find continuity through the body of the narrator, but his very consciousness survives in the person of the narrator. The notion of reincarnation, like the memory of a lost generation, survives "the terrifying, howling red wind" and continues to function as a vehicle of preservation, continuation and stability.

HOWLING RED WIND

The blowing of a "terrifying, howling red wind" also functions as the unifying image of the extraordinary Tibetan language novel *The Red Wind Scream*.[53] This is an audacious piece of work since it is the first serious Tibetan novel from Tibet to tackle the controversial historical events of Communist Chinese arrival in the 1950s and the Cultural Revolution. The novel came out in book form in 2006, but long excerpts from it were published as early as 2002. After publishing this book without official permission, its author, the famous fiction writer Tsering Dondup, was demoted from his post as head of the local county archives. Although parts of the book had already been printed in officially approved publications, the author's efforts to obtain an ISBN (compulsory for publication in contemporary China) for its release in book form were fruitless.[54] The official explanation for his demotion was his failure to follow legitimate publication procedures. He was warned not to get the novel published again and two boxes containing copies of it in his possession were confiscated along with his passport.[55] Although no further explanation has been given, the reasons for the author's punishment are clear: the novel questions the official Chinese narrative of modern Tibetan history and gives an unflattering portrayal of the CCP. *The Red Wind Scream* is the authorized English translation of the Tibetan title *Rlung dmar 'ur 'ur* but it might be better translated as *The Howling Red Wind* or *The Roaring Red Wind*. The title suggests a mighty, incessantly blowing, merciless red wind, representing the CCP or the Chinese state. It also indicates what Piotr Sztompka would categorize as a "traumatogenic change," a social change that is sudden in its speed, wide and comprehensive in its scope, radical, deep and fundamental in its impact upon social life and shocking to the mind.[56]

Any paraphrasing would not do justice to this rich, densely packed, and finely crafted novel. Nevertheless, a brief summary of it is necessary to appreciate the traumatic events that form its historical background. It also helps to reveal how these transformative events are represented and remembered as fundamental aspects of modern Tibetan experience which inform Tibetan collective consciousness. The novel has two parts and two principal settings, a nomadic community and a prison labor camp. The main protagonist of the first section is the local head Lama of Tseshung (Rtse gzhung) called Alak Drong (A lags 'brong), Wild-yak Lama. The narrative begins with a sarcastic and humorous description of Alak Drong as a vain and decadent Lama in the present. This is immediately followed by an account of his enthronement day when he was a young boy many years ago. A gust of red wind starts blowing on this day, signaling the imminent entry of "the Red Chinese." A work team of "the Red Chinese" arrives in Tseshung for the first time and camps outside the local monastery. Alak Drong, as the absolute leader of his nomadic community, meets the newly arrived head of the Chinese Communist work team, Aiguo Wang. The latter is the new representative of incomprehensible entities called *gung khran tang* (Ch. *Gòng chǎn dǎng*), the "Chinese Communist Party," and *krung go* (Ch. *Zhōng guó*) "Chinese State." These are Tibetan transliterations of Chinese terms that make no sense in Tibetan. Such alien concepts confound the Lama and he refuses to yield to this new authority when requested to do so. He believes his nomadic community is bigger than *krung go*. However, after being taken on an "outside" tour[57] the Lama nominally gives in to CCP authority and acquires an equally incomprehensible position called "Preparatory Committee Vice-Chairman" (*kru rin u yon gzhon pa*).[58] Everyone, including the learned and esteemed Dranak Geshe (Sbra nag dge bshes), finds this term unintelligible.

These humorously narrated initial bafflements pale into insignificance as the seemingly innocuous arrival of the "Red Chinese" then starts to send shock waves through the nomadic community, causing unprecedented bloodshed and turning society upside down. When gravely wronged local nomads revolt against the PLA, the latter crush them with disdainful ease and ruthless force in a single day. Along the banks of the Machu River, nomads suffer heavy losses. These poorly armed tribesmen are mowed down by automatic machine guns as the "red wind" rages. Men and monks who survive the assault are then herded up and arrested on the same day. It is simply referred to as "the Harrowing Day." The Lama is stripped of his traditional authorities and his newly acquired post. He is arrested and subjected to humiliating struggle sessions before being taken on a grueling, demeaning, disorientating journey to a distant concentration camp with many nomad men from his tribe. Monasteries are destroyed or desecrated, and religious scriptures are fed to the flames or turned into the soles of shoes. Prison life turns out to be horrifying, as prisoners are exploited and brutalized systematically with cruel and calculated efficiency. The systematically organized labor camp and its dehumanizing conditions are described vividly and with gruesome details, leaving little to the imagination. After a long torturous journey, Alak Drong and his fellow nomads arrive in a forested valley with a sprawling new prison camp housing inmates in their tens of thousands. The prison population is made up of different ethnic groups including Tibetans, Hui, Mongols, and what Tibetans call "White Chinese" (Chinese Guomindang members or sympathizers). The prisoners undergo a rigorous and bewildering regime of hard labor, psychological indoctrination ("political study classes") and physical and mental torture, as their bodies atrophy day by day under rapidly deteriorating prison conditions.

Afflicted by this turn of events and these appalling circumstances, the prisoners' sense of morality disintegrates and inmates resort to mutual distrust and betrayal, which the prison authorities exploit to the full. Eager to get his sentence reduced, Alak Drong double-crosses his loyal devotee Tsetra (Tshe bkra) who in turn informs on the Lama with a vengeance. Alak Drong even betrays his own beloved teacher Dranak Geshe, whose stoicism, probity, and belief in the Lama remain unshakeable. The great *geshe* dies in prison and departs "this hell on earth" with his knowledge and faith intact. As a formerly idyllic environment rich in diverse wild animals and plants is laid to waste in search of foodstuffs and raw materials, undernourished and maltreated prisoners begin to die in their thousands, and corpses litter the prison surroundings. In sum, prison life is characterized by punitive labor, thought control, total exhaustion, starvation, lingering death, and pervasive suicide. Environmental destruction and the aggravation of prison conditions are related in a particularly harrowing passage on the slaughtering of defenseless white geese and cranes on a desolate spring day. As the red wind blows fiercely, prison guards, also hit by the food shortages, encircle the unsuspecting birds and machine-gun them down. In an instant their "happy home is turned into a woeful graveyard." "At this time there is a sudden increase in the strength of the wind," continues the passage. "As the red storm raged birds wailed in the sky and people cheered on the earth. Bloodstains left by the weeping wounds of every white goose and crane formed a vivid sight, like the red flags on the snowplain. A fleeting glimpse of them caught by the surviving siblings will never fade away."[59]

Just when there seems to be a slight improvement in the prison situation, the Cultural Revolution arrives, unleashing more chaotic scenes. This political movement is said to be second only to "the Harrowing Day" in terms of mass deaths, imprisonments, suicides, and dehumanization. Alak Drong survives another ten years of harsh prison life amid Cultural Revolutionary fervor, struggle sessions, slogans, propaganda, and feigned love for Mao. He is finally released along with other surviving "historical prisoners" (political prisoners) with two bricks of tea as compensation for serving over twenty years of a prison sentence. As he crosses the bridge—over the once crystal-clear river now turned blood-red—he shouts: "Prison staff and common criminals, go on eating human flesh and drinking human blood!"[60] Thus Alak Drong's ordeal comes to an end, and the first section of *The Red Wind Scream* draws to a close. Throughout the first (and indeed the second) section the only constant is the merciless and unceasing red wind. One evocative passage describes the red wind as a violent, all-pervasive force formed of powerful gusts that lash out earth, sand, and rocks. The most frightening and dispiriting aspect of all is its roaring sound, which resembles "the simultaneous howling of thousands of hunger-stricken wolves in silent and expansive grasslands" and "the simultaneous screaming of slogans by tens of thousands of Red Guards in Tiananmen Square."[61]

While the first half of *The Red Wind Scream* recounts the arrest and the prison experience of Alak Drong, the second half concerns the fate of his nomadic community, which fares no better. It spans the period from "the Harrowing Day" in 1958, through the Great Leap Forward and the Cultural Revolution, to the beginning of Tibetan cultural revival in the early 1980s. The narrative relates the communized status of Tseshung and the overwhelming impact of launching one radical political campaign after another on its nomadic populace and newly arrived Chinese "Youths."[62] The "Youths" are sent from mainland China to carry out farming work in Tseshung. Initially they plow grasslands and plant many crops with great enthusiasm, and report fraudulently high yields. However, crop failure, harsh conditions, and starvation soon follow and cause many deaths, compelling them to flee in all directions and scavenge for scraps of food from sympathetic yet poverty-stricken nomads.

Communization of the traditional nomadic community entails collectivization of the means of production and the restructuring of its social organization. Different subtribes of Tseshung are classified as "people's communes,"
and clans within each subtribe are designated as "production brigades."[63] At
the lowest organizational level are "production teams" known as farming or
pastoralist teams. Forced "tented settlements with streets" also prove to be a
disastrous failure, leading to unprecedented hardship and food scarcity, and
a widespread famine. An already dire situation is further compounded by
incessant political study classes, harsh interrogations, struggle sessions, and
incomprehensible and ludicrous meetings. This tale of a traditional pastoralist
world being turned upside down by alien political ideas and modes of social
organization is mostly narrated through the interlinked life stories of Lobsang
Gyatso and Tashi Lhamo and their archenemy Lobsang Tsultrim.

Lobsang Gyatso and Lobsang Tsultrim were monk disciples of Dranak
Geshe. Lobsang Tsultrim bears an undying grudge against Lobsang Gyatso
because of the latter's superior intelligence and diligence when studying
religious scriptures during their childhood. Although both of them have
been forced to return to lay life, Lobsang Gyatso, who lost his father on "the
Harrowing Day," secretly keeps his celibacy. He is labeled as a *zhwa gon*,
"the Hatted One," because of his father's role in the revolt, his own former
monkhood and because he was the disciple and nephew of Dranak Geshe.[64]
Lobsang Tsultrim's life takes him on a different path as he is appointed as
the head of "Forward Brigade" which replaces his former clan. To everyone's horror he turns into a zealous revolutionary and a ruthless enforcer of
party instructions. Tashi Lhamo, who lost her brother and parents on "the
Harrowing Day," is an attractive and popular woman of strong character and
unshakeable loyalty. She rejects Lobsang Tsultrim's repeated advances and
has a fake marriage with Lobsang Gyatso so as to give him the appearance
of a layman while ensuring that his monastic celibacy is kept secret. With a
redoubled sense of jealousy, Lobsang Tsultrim gets Tashi Lhamo labeled as
a "reactionary" and subjects the couple to violent struggle sessions. He even
exposes Lobsang Gyatso to the dreaded mindlessness and confused fury of
schoolchildren who have been instilled with revolutionary fervor and violence. Although they are always the first target of every fresh campaign, their
mutual affection, integrity, and human dignity enable them to survive. Their
platonic relationship grows from strength to strength and starts exhibiting
faint signs of romance.

As a "hatted" couple they are not allowed to read books, but under the
pretext of studying Mao's works Lobsang Gyatso teaches Tashi Lhamo
how to read and then immerses her in Buddhist teaching and generates a
strong spiritual awakening in her. Even during the Cultural Revolution he
goes on giving her lessons on Buddhist ethics and philosophy—with grave

consequences. One day when yet another struggle session is carried out against them for trying to waterproof their ragged tent by covering it with an older tent, their tormentors discover a copy of *Lam rim*, *Stages of The Path*, a didactic Buddhist classic of the fourteenth century, which they had retrieved from a cave. This discovery triggers a wide-scale search through the entire nomadic community, and exposes more prohibited religious objects. Severe public beatings follow, causing more fear, injuries, and suicides. Meanwhile Aiguo Wang, who has been presiding over these chaotic scenes in Tseshung, loses power at the outset of Cultural Revolution, and dies in the labor camp where he had sent Alak Drong and others many years ago.

The presence of Mao comes to penetrate almost every aspect of the pastoralist community. Even when shopping for the New Year (*lo gsar*), nomads must set aside some funds out of what little they have, to buy "portraits and various souvenirs of Mao Zedong that have been growing year by year and now cover the surface of the earth." Revolutionary songs featuring Mao are sung during the pathetic Losar festivities. Mao's portrait must be displayed at workplaces where every morning and evening herders and milkmaids must "report" to it. Selected quotations from his works must be memorized and failure to do so results in criticism and damages one's livelihood. Tibetan women who used to voluntarily and effortlessly recite *Tara Praises* (*Sgrol bstod*)[65] from memory, now find it extremely difficult to learn these quotations by heart no matter how hard they try. This creates great mental anguish, which seems to them far worse than their heavy burden of physical labor. As a result, Mao's death comes as a great relief and signals the end of a tumultuous era.

The demise of Mao is mourned with great displays of public grief. However, the mourning is soon curtailed by the joyous celebration of the overthrow of the Gang of Four led by Jiang Qing who are accused of attempting to usurp power. These events lead to the fall of Lobsang Tsultrim and the rehabilitation of Lobsang Gyatso and Tashi Lhamo. Lobsang Tsultrim becomes a despised and alienated figure but he presently resurfaces as Alak Drong's trusted monk assistant. He is greatly involved in the rebuilding of the monastery and restoration of its religious practices. Even a decade after Alak Drong's release only a few monastic structures have been rebuilt and "the ruins of every monk's living quarters still face the sky as if asking someone for the repayment of debts." This sight and the surprised glances cast by people are unsettling for Lobsang Tsultrim, who has undergone a total ideological transformation. His servile and cunning traits remain undiminished as he ingratiates himself with his Lama's lavishly dressed and bejeweled consort, who shows an unhealthy interest in the financial affairs of the monastery.

Concurrently Tashi Lhamo persuades a hesitant Lobsang Gyatso to visit Alak Drong and get himself ordained again on the latter's re-enthronement day. Although Lobsang Gyatso has been eagerly waiting for such an opportunity for thirty years a sense of disillusionment besets him. He is not sure who would be a bona fide religious practitioner: a robed monk or a layperson with an impeccable sense of karmic justice. The sight of Lobsang Tsultrim in monastic robes and other former revolutionaries turned devout Buddhists disgusts him. Lobsang Gyatso's disillusionment is compounded by a strong sense of love and longing for Tashi Lhamo, who has made great sacrifices for him and with whom he has managed to weather those difficult decades. The loneliness and yearning induced by a single day spent away from her make him realize that it would be impossible to part company with her. Although Tashi Lhamo vehemently protested against it before he left for the monastery Lobsang Gyatso decides to return to lead a lay life with her. But upon his return he finds that Tashi Lhamo has renounced a lay existence to become a nun in the caverns of Kalden Hermitage. Lobsang Gyatso declares to her his intentions to lead a married life with her, but her determination to pursue a spiritual path is unshakable. When his pleas fail to sway her mind, he leaves her in the cave and "staggers out like a drunkard into the most aggravating and interminable, violent red wind." This wind that resembles "the violent shrieking of demons and ghosts" drowns the anguished wailing of Tashi Lhamo as Tsering Dhondup's novel comes to an end. The fictional narrative concludes, yet one cannot help but sense that the relentless red wind that howls throughout the novel goes on screaming beyond it.

DISJOINTED NARRATIVE

It must be pointed out that the narrative of *The Red Wind Scream* is nowhere near as temporally sequential or linear as in the above summary. Tsering Dhondup's novel is remarkable for its bold subject matter, seamless fusion of literary and vernacular language, verisimilitude, dark humor, and meticulous research based on oral and written material. It also stands out among Tibetan novels because of its experimental mode of narrative which is deliberately disjointed, fragmentary, and confusing. In the first half of the novel the narrative starts with a cynical description of Alak Drong in the present but immediately flashes back to his childhood. It does not linger in one place for long as it leaps forward to his prison journey and then hurries back to the encounter with "the Red Chinese." The Lama's carefree, unruly, and over-indulgent childhood is narrated with recollections of the arduous journey to prison followed by his actual prison experience. The description of prison life is in turn replete with flashbacks and foreflashes (flashforwards) that take us back and forth numerous times. The flashbacks transport us to "the Harrowing Day" or good old times well preceding that bloody encounter. Foreflashes bring us back to the seemingly interminable and soul-destroying conditions of the labor camp.

Similarly, the second part of the novel starts in the present with the revival of Tibetan Buddhism symbolized by the re-enthronement of Alak Drong. The narrative then promptly leaps back to the events immediately following "the Harrowing Day" and then creeps forward, narrating the interlinked fates of its three main protagonists against a chaotic sociopolitical background, often depicted nonchronologically. The narrative is frequently interrupted by both analeptic and proleptic accounts of events and characters. For instance typical proleptic phrases hint at the marriage of Lobsang Gyatso and Tashi Lhamo right at the beginning of the second part of the novel.[66] This anticipates the significance and the implications for the protagonists of something that is only revealed at a later stage in the narrative.[67] Analeptic statements in the form of flashbacks provide us with background information about characters already introduced, or earlier events. Lobsang Gyatso's reminiscences on his teacher and uncle, Dranak Geshe, transport the reader back to a time prior to the advent of "the Red Chinese." It paints a man of compassion, learning, stoicism, and humility produced by the traditional Tibetan monastic system, and also traces the genesis of Lobsang Tsultrim's bitter jealousy of Lobsang Gyatso to this period.[68]

Accounts of past events are thus interspersed and at times intermixed throughout the novel but not in their chronological order. They are interwoven within the overall fictional narrative but the order of telling does not reflect the order of occurrence. This mode of narrative is at times confusing but it does not affect the general fluidity and coherence of the novel. After reflecting upon various rearrangements in the telling of a story, Nelson Goodman observes: "Actually, although every narrative will survive some reordering, and some narrative will survive any reordering, not every narrative will survive every reordering."[69] The narrative of *The Red Wind Scream* not only survives many reorderings but its dislocated mode of telling also helps to mimic the oral accounts it is based on. As Alessandro Portelli points out, unlike a systematically relayed oral history, oral narratives are characterized by the narrating of events or experiences in fragments, episodes, and repetitions.[70] Its mode of telling is disjointed, unsystematic, jolting, and sketchy rather than highly ordered and sequential as in historical narrative. Tsering Dhondup seems to employ these features of oral narrative to depict sensitive historical events such as what he refers to as "the Harrowing Day" (*skyi g.ya' ba'i nyin mo*). This is a highly significant date both within the fictional novel and for the actual people of Sokpo, the nomadic community upon which some of the key elements of the narrative are loosely based. Although this is the key day which sets in motion the series of outrageous events that make up the entire narrative of the book, the day itself is only related in fragments scattered throughout the work.[71] This mode of narrative reflects the difficulty people have in speaking about traumatic experiences in a coherent and unbroken way over a long period of time. Telling the narrative in fragments also reflects the prohibited nature of the story, and the unspeakable horrors associated with it.

Besides featuring in oral traditions, nonlinear narrative is a favorite literary technique employed by modernist novelists such as Virginia Woolf, whose work (in Chinese translation) Tsering Dhondup read avidly. In a conversation with me Tsering Dhondup expressed his admiration for Woolf but went on to say that he did not undertake any conscious imitation of her disjointed narrative technique in *The Red Wind Scream*. He was quick to add that although no deliberate mimicry was attempted she might have influenced his novel without himself knowing it.[72] Indeed one does find parallels between Woolf's and Tsering Dhondup's depictions of temporality. While commenting on Woolf's disrupted portrayal of temporal experience in *Mrs. Dalloway* Paul Ricoeur observes that her "art here lies in interweaving the present, with its stretches of the imminent future and the recent past, and a recollected past, and so making time progress by slowing it down."[73] This statement applies equally to *The Red Wind Scream*, which is also constituted of different times woven into an integral whole that is fragmentary yet fluid. However, one should not be hasty in deducing from this similarity the assimilation of a modernist narrative device by Tsering Dhondup. In fact, when asked about the narrative style of *The Red Wind Scream* Tsering Dhondup told me that there was no conscious design or pre-planning. Rather, he said, it evolved out of the process of writing itself, which drew on the nonlinear and unpredictable features of oral storytelling.[74] Therefore, although one cannot rule out modernist literary influence entirely, it is what Michael Levenson calls "the will of the narrating mind at the instant of narration"[75] which has shaped Tsering Dhondup's mode of narration that disregards chronology. The very process of narration upsets sequential, linear narrative as the narrating mind jumps backward and forward in time and flits from one event to another in an infinitely random manner.

ROOTED IN ORALITY

The indebtedness of *The Red Wind Scream* to oral narratives is not confined to its disjointed and fragmentary mode of storytelling. The entire novel is steeped in orality. It draws heavily on oral sources for its historical material and in its use of mostly vernacular dialogue. Immersion in the Tibetan oral world also functions as a literary device to simulate the spontaneity of orality in the fictional narrative. It is also this reliance upon the experience and speech of what Water Benjamin calls "many nameless storytellers" that gives

Tsering Dhondup's novel its depth and critical edge as a counternarrative of modern Tibetan experience, Tibet at odds with the official narrative of the Chinese state. To an adult Amdo reader it is obvious that many of the anecdotes, episodes, and shocking descriptions of events and experiences related in the novel derive from actual oral accounts of Tibetans' first encounter with Chinese Communists in the 1950s and the subsequent developments. Indeed in a private communication the author informed me in categorical terms that most of the incidents in the novel were based on actual occurrences that had been preserved in oral narratives. "There are no lies in it," said Tsering Dhondup speaking of the controversy surrounding the publication of *The Red Wind Screams*. "And I was prepared to tell them (Chinese authorities) that if they questioned the historical veracity of my novel."[76]

Similar oral tales are recorded in rare nonfictional books published inside Tibet such as *The Joys and Woes of the Naktsang Boy* and *My Homeland and Peaceful Liberation*.[77] The former is a poignant memoir that recounts the sudden fall of a well-to-do nomadic family and the harrowing experience of two orphaned boys after their father died fighting the PLA while attempting to flee to Lhasa in 1958. The latter is composed of interview-based narratives that relate many tragedies that befell individuals and tribes as they came face-to-face with the might of the CCP. It was compiled and introduced by Rinzang (Rin bzang), whose efforts to tackle the silenced history of Tibet ended up in the personal tragedy of being physically silenced. Due to severe maltreatment in prison he lost the power of speech and can no longer lead an ordinary existence without permanent care. The prison experience left him with incapacitating physical and psychological damages.[78] Both of these courageous publications make horrifying yet informative reading as they chronicle indiscriminate crackdowns, massacres, destructions, mass imprisonments, torture, famine, and deadly political campaigns unleashed during the Great Leap Forward.

The Red Wind Scream differs from these books because of its obvious fictional elements in the drawing of characters, plots, and dialogues, and the deliberate fusion of literary and vernacular idiom. Stripped of these literary devices it reveals a narrative skeleton based on oral testimonies. To borrow Virginia Woolf's analogy once more, the spiderweb of this fiction is spun from real life experience that has been handed down orally from generation to generation. The examples are too numerous to be listed. From the depiction of the first encounter between Alak Drong and the "Red Chinese" and the rendering of horrendous prison conditions to the descriptions of the plight of the "Youths," struggle sessions, deprived living conditions, and the portrayal of reaction to Mao's death, all bear the imprints of oral transmission. Here it will suffice to cite the following example as an illustration of the rootedness of *The Red Wind Scream* in orality in its attempts to offer a realistic depiction of a traumatized community. As already mentioned, like most of his other fictional works, Tsering Dhondup loosely bases this novel on the Sokpo nomadic community in which he grew up. However, although Sokpo features prominently in the background, the novel is not specifically set among the Sokpo. Instead, the fictionalized narrative is national in its scale, and the plight of nomadic communities like the Sokpo is used to capture and represent a common Tibetan historical experience under the Chinese Communist rule. The Sokpo are a Tibetanized Mongol tribe in Amdo and the founding patron-tribe of Labrang monastery. The Sokpo lands correspond to today's Henan Mongol Autonomous County in the Chinese province of Qinghai.

The novel makes several references, mostly in snippets, to what it calls "the Harrowing Day." These fragments build up to paint a day of unprecedented horror, when the entire nomadic tribe revolted against the "Red Chinese" and fought a desperate one-sided battle with the PLA. The nomads' intention was to escape to the other side of the Machu River to undertake guerrilla warfare against the intruders, but the plan backfires terribly. Instead the day ends in carnage, widespread persecution, and mass arrests, marking in the collective memory of the community the tragic advent of a tumultuous era. The recurrent allusions to this day in the novel turn it into a historical reference point which exactly mirrors the significance of a similar day in Sokpo history. *The Red Wind Scream* records in written words what Sokpo people have retained in oral stories.

I too am from Sokpo and was brought up listening to such tales, so what follows is a brief account of "the Harrowing Day" given by my mother. My mother's description of this eventful day has been cross-checked against another testimony provided by a notable tribal elder, Kapthe. Kapthe is famously known as the Armless One because he lost his left arm fighting with the Chinese on that day. As a result, nowadays he claims, half in jest, that he sacrificed his arm on that day "for the sake of the Buddha Dharma and the welfare of a great number of people."[79] Although his fascinating tale has not been summarized here it provides supplementary information. Many Tibetans of my own and younger generations from Amdo, including the writers studied here, would have been exposed to similar stories. My mother's account of this day demonstrates the degree to which Tsering Dhondup's novel is orally embedded and, by extension, how Tibetan artistic representations of traumatic events are informed by those who directly experienced them. While Tsering Dhondup gives a general overview of "the Harrowing Day," my mother's recollections offer a particular firsthand description of that day. The version of her account provided here omits repetitions, digressions, interruptions, and minute details but remains faithful to the tone and speech of my mother as an oral storyteller.

It was the fourteenth day of the fourth month in the spring of 1958, a day before Buddha's birth, death, and enlightenment day according to the Tibetan lunar calendar. The entire Sokpo population, including its thirteen subtribes, were assembled in one place with all their possessions and livestock. Tibetan tribes from Golok and other places swelled their ranks. The plan was to cross the Machu River and form a military alliance with other Tibetan tribes against the PLA. Different subtribes were encamped in clusters on a plain near the riverbank. While women and children remained inside the camps men kept guard on surrounding mountaintops. They organized into military units according to existing subtribal divisions and took up strategic positions. The PLA carried out a surprise attack in a pincer movement just before dawn when it was still quite dark. They deployed overwhelming military force armed with cannons and machine guns.[80] An abridged version of my mother's account of this attack follows:[81]

> Just before dawn there were two gunshots from the opposite side of the camp and two things like red stars travelled across the sky. Apparently these were signals for each other to see if they were ready for the attack. Then there was a commotion of gunfire. It was like roasting barley. All types of guns, big and small, were going off. It was absolutely terrifying. Just the sound of it was enough. Our soldiers were called Divine Army of the Protector and Chinese soldiers were called Army from the Outside.[82] Most of our soldiers were surrounded from all sides and ambushed in the night. Most of them were either killed or wounded. Some of them still fought against the PLA soldiers on the mountain slopes or on the plain but they were totally outnumbered. The Chinese soldiers moved or halted in unison and they were carpeting the whole area. Some of our soldiers fought their way towards the riverbank but they were either killed or wounded in or around the banks of the Machu River. Very few of them made it across the river alive.

> Women and children took shelter in a forested place but we were under nonstop firing. People and horses were shot down all around us and we changed our hiding places from one tree to another. There was constant gunfire, bullets stripped off pieces of earth next to me, and leaves rained down as I cowered beneath trees. The fight went on all day. We tried to avoid capture but the Chinese came flooding upon us. We were later rounded up and driven back to the camp. On our march back we encountered the dead and wounded everywhere along the banks of the Machu River. They were scattered all over the place. It was a heart-rending and horrific sight. There were both familiar faces and strangers among the killed. The Dakmar tribe arrived at the campsite that morning as the Chinese raid took place so they did not have time to put up their tents. There were entire families wiped out in a single spot with freshly finished hearths. The injured were writhing and groaning in agony. Yaks were wandering about still fully loaded. One woman was killed in her headdress and with her baby still nursing at her breast. We were cornered right against the edge of the river. We could see Chinese soldiers shooting at people who were crossing over to the other side of the river. They laughed aloud every time they hit someone either in

midstream or on the other bank. They also opened fire on the nomad settlement on the other side of the river. Many people were shot down in the river or got carried off by its currents.

When we got back, the entire place was absolutely teeming with Chinese soldiers and chomping horses. They seized the abandoned family tents and were milling about. My mother, aunt, and I were together without grandmother. We had two small puppies at the time and they were still guarding our tent. When they saw us return they barked excitedly and came running to greet us. Their foreheads were bayoneted so they were gappy with tufts of hair missing. Some PLA soldiers were inside the tent and boiling something in our old cauldron covered with the lid of the milk barrel. There were also wounded soldiers with bandages and in tattered clothes amongst them. One would think they would have been ferried away somewhere but anyhow they were there. We pitied them too, as they had been brought here and made to fight by force. That night we slept cowering outside the tent as they cooked something over the stove.

The next morning everyone was rounded up in a large group near our encampment. Some people had already been rounded up the night before and grandmother was among them. While they were detained like that, two women gave birth among the crowd in the night. There were many wounded people with injuries to their heads or limbs and were bleeding profusely. The Chinese soldiers surrounded us with machine guns bristling with things. We thought they were going to shoot into the crowd but they were just posturing.

All the men were singled out of the assembled group and taken away to the county headquarters. From there they were taken further away to *laogai* (labor camps) in low-lying places. Most of them died there. Then we were ordered to move back to where we had come from. We did not go back for about two days because everyone was looking for the corpses of their loved ones. There were bodies strewn everywhere and everyone was helping each other in their search for the dead. Thanks to other people's help we found my cousin who was wounded in the head on the riverbank. As there were no men, women relatives looked after him and took care of his body when he died. It really was terrifying. Not just our tribesmen but everyone else was in the same situation. Women were just happy to find their dead sons or husbands and be able to expose their corpses to the elements (*ro shun phud*).[83] Those who got carried off by the river were never found. Such a terrifying thing happened to us that time.

On the banks of the Machu River they killed anyone they could kill and arrested anyone they could arrest. Some made it to the other side like my uncle but he was wounded and then shot himself. My father took to the hills. He carried out surprise attacks against the Chinese soldiers with his friends. After a while some of his friends were killed and he was wounded in the leg and captured with a friend. He faced struggle sessions with a wounded friend and the corpse of another fighter. Later my father died in detention without receiving any medical treatment. It was a terrifying time.

Locals refer to this event as "the massive massacre on the banks of the Machu River" (*rma kha nas kha btags dus*) or "the Chinese raid on the banks of the Machu River" (*rma kha nas rgya rgyugs dus*). This event took place near a landmark hill in today's Kizin Township, which is situated in Henan Mongol Autonomous County of Qinghai. Reflecting this location Alak Tsayi gives the event a toponym: the "Great Massacre at the Round Hill of Kizin."[84] In his meticulously researched volume on the Great Leap Forward, Frank Dikotter alludes to this event when he mentions open rebellion against the Chinese throughout eastern Tibet in 1958 that seriously strained PLA military resources in the region.[85] Almost every Tibetan nomadic tribe and farming communities have a "Harrowing day" or a similar date seared into their collective memory.[86] Oral narratives and rare historical texts and life stories such as Alak Tsayi's *The Tragedy of My Homeland* perpetuate this remembrance.[87] In so doing they generate a Foucauldian "countermemory" that challenges and contests hegemonic Chinese renderings of modern Tibetan history.[88] It is in these pervasive oral narratives, these carriers of "countermemory," that Tsering Dhondup embeds his novel. Like the alternative voices buried within them, *The Red Wind Scream* narrates a powerful, tragic human story while displaying a critical edge. It overcomes a state-enforced historical amnesia by capturing real lives through a creative fusion of the literary and the oral.

LOADED WITH CRITICISM

In a historicist reflection on the inextricable link between history and the novel, Irving Howe notes that the latter not only represents historical realities but undertakes a criticism of established values irrespective of authorial intention. The novel, with its mimetic depiction of the real, entails a subversive element. Howe writes: "What gets 'swept' into the novel are not just depictions of how we live now; it also draws upon the line of critical thought, the fund of literary allusions, the play of street sentiment, and sometimes the ideology of revolt." He goes on to say: "There is also a subterranean critical ferment, sometimes beyond the writer's intention. Once past the sorts of novels written for amusement or shock, a representation of life can rarely be separated from a criticism of values."[89] Likewise *The Red Wind Scream* represents lives of people under specific historical circumstances and criticizes the prevailing beliefs and values. As can be seen in the preceding paragraphs, it subverts the idiom of the CCP by appropriating for itself the discourse of popular dissent and revolt. In its narrative of "the Harrowing Day" we find the "play of street sentiment" and "the ideology of revolt." Whereas Rinzang's *My Homeland and Peaceful Liberation* chronicles the violent and traumatizing absorption of Tibetans into the PRC through the presentation of eyewitness testimonies,

Tsering Dhondup portrays this process through fictional representation. Both are equally expressive and retentive of shared traumatic memories and both are critical of the agencies considered responsible for them.

Although the CCP and its "helmsman" Mao are not named outright for explicit criticism in *The Red Wind Scream*, they are portrayed in a way which exposes their faults and turns them into objects of ridicule. Distinctively unflattering depictions present them as tyrannical, manipulative and ruthless powers responsible for untold suffering inflicted upon Tibetans. They are painted as being capable of psychologically transforming people beyond recognition or disciplining them into total, unquestioning submission. The case of Namgyal, an escapee prisoner, illustrates this point. Namgyal is arrested for no apparent crime and gets deported to the labor camp with Alak Drong and others from his tribe. He escapes midway by feigning death and makes it home on foot. He hides in the mountains by day and spends time with his newlywed wife and family at night. This coincides with the Great Leap Forward, and the situation back at home is "unspeakable" as the trauma of communization begins. The traditional community is upended by poverty, forced labor, and a flurry of political activities which encourage mutual informing, distrust, and betrayal, turning everyone against their neighbors. Even family members inform on and denounce each other. Thanks to "mutual love and affection" and a strong sense of solidarity shown by his family Namgyal survives with his freedom intact until his loyal wife is swayed by the prevailing ideological fervor of the Party. This surprising turn is revealed in the following excerpt:

> Unfortunately the power of indoctrination and campaigns cannot only annihilate the power of love and affection but it can also turn sensible people into madmen, the wise into fools, the brave into cowards, and human compassion into malevolence. So one day his wife suggested to him that he hand himself in and go back to prison.
>
> "What!" cries Namgyal in shock. "Are you possessed by the devil?"
>
> "No matter how many years it takes I'll definitely wait for you," replies his wife holding onto Namgyal's hand and shedding tears. "I have just requested to join the Communist Youth League. If my harboring of a criminal is discovered, then I might get labelled as a Hatted One let alone being able to join the Communist Youth League."
>
> "Harboring of a criminal? You tell me, what crime have I committed?"
>
> "If the Party says you've committed a crime then you've surely committed a crime."
>
> "What is this so-called Communist Youth League?"
>
> "It's a glorious organization. It's the supporter and the successor of the Party."[90]

Namgyal's wife tries to convince him that his voluntary surrender would be met with leniency. Namgyal is scared and shocked by her reasoning and refuses to comply. To his consternation, his wife then betrays him in the name of the Party, and Namgyal ends up in prison after being subjected to routine struggle sessions.[91] In this way, the author shows how, beginning with the Great Leap Forward, the Chinese state, hardly distinguishable from the CCP, penetrated the very heart of private space, the family. This was only made possible by the commune system. Jack Gray has observed that the commune "became a means to thrust the power of the State directly into the village for the first time in Chinese history."[92] This assertion is equally applicable to the Tibetan society. Although in theory the Great Leap Forward was launched to counter state bureaucracy and encourage locally initiated economic empowerment, in practice it only helped deepen state penetration—with crippling effect. Most of all, as seen in the above excerpt, it furnished the Party with totalitarian powers to obliterate the private sphere of the family and the individual. Unfortunately Tsering Dhondup's novel does not provide us with adequate psychological depth and details regarding the reduction of the individual into an unthinking political tool that spouts party slogans. CCP's devastating use of terror and indoctrination is underlined as capable of shaping human conduct, but no attempts are made to explore the psychological impact of these techniques in its minute details.

The Party is thus portrayed as absolute, God-like chairman Mao at its helm. Once again *The Red Wind Scream* does not directly criticize Mao in unambiguous terminology, but instead one finds sardonic depictions of the cult of his personality and his dictatorial powers. In the following memorable passage which describes the bizarre daily ritual of reporting aloud to a portrait of Mao, he is revealed as an object of worship which verges on religious zeal. The passage is worth quoting in its entirety as it is descriptive of the harsh conditions during the Cultural Revolution. By then nomadic communities had already been systematically organized into ever smaller units under the organizational level of commune.

Each production brigade is divided into either five or six teams in accordance with the size of its population and livestock. Every four or five women form a unit of milkmaids. Each unit also has a male yak-herder. In winter each nomadic settlement has a square yak pen made with walls of rammed earth or layered turf. In one of the corners of each yak pen there is something resembling a casket. It is made of fresh, later frozen, yak dung measuring about a square meter and inside each is pasted a portrait of Mao. Every morning and evening each person from each team has to stand before it raising their arms in salute and solemnly carry out "morning request for instructions and evening report":

"Dear Great Teacher and Great Chairman, Great General, Great Helmsman Mao Zedong, Today we shall keep your correct instructions firmly in our mind and shall attentively study your works, and we shall diligently carry out more milking and shall tend the cattle well, and thus we shall definitely make contributions to the country and the collective!" Each syllable is thus enunciated either by the team leader or a progressive. Everyone else repeats after them like first graders being taught language by a primary school teacher. In the evening it goes: "Dear Great Teacher and Great Chairman, Great General, Great Helmsman Mao Zedong, Today we have kept your correct instructions firmly in our mind and have attentively studied your works, and we have milked seventeen litres of milk (or seven or eight, or twenty or thirty). We have also made sure no cattle were lost to either wolves or class enemies, and we have thus made contributions to the country and the collective." During the three seasons of spring, summer and autumn the team leader's family brings out their framed portrait of Mao Zedong and hangs it from the guy rope and then (everyone) must perform as above. One time the team leader's family forgot to take the frame inside after carrying out "the evening report." The family head who was given to cracking jokes, next morning said with a slight laugh: "Oh no, Chairman was left outside. Hope he wasn't frightened by the many gods and ghosts that were all around last night!" Someone heard his joke and reported it (to the authorities). As a result, he was labelled as a Hatted One and subjected to struggle sessions that made sure he would never laugh again. His wife was also dismissed as the head of the milkmaid unit. She cried for several days and whinged and blamed her husband for several years, so that eventually they had to divorce.[93]

Such worship of Mao was taking place throughout Tibet and China and it reached a fever pitch during the Cultural Revolution. The absurdity and pervasiveness of this phenomenon is recorded in firsthand Tibetan accounts such as Arjia Rinpoche's autobiography *Surviving the Dragon* (which contains revealing chapters on the impact of the Great Leap Forward and the Cultural Revolution on the daily existence of Tibetans), and Rinzang's *My Homeland and Peaceful Liberation.*[94] Blind obedience to Mao was effected through countless meetings, struggle sessions, political study classes, propaganda, and the compulsory observation of daily rituals like above. Like the rest of contemporary China, Tibet was flooded with Mao's pictures, books,[95] and memorabilia and Tibetans had to immerse themselves in "Mao Zedong thought." As Arjia Rinpoche notes, Mao's statue was "the only statue that people could worship."[96] Although state and party apparatuses helped to create Mao's cult of personality he himself was the genesis of it. In a speech in March 1958, responding to Nikita Khrushchev's attack on Stalin, Mao demanded total allegiance by stating that the "correct cult of personality" should be rightly revered. Mao declared: "What is wrong with worship? The truth is in our hands, why should we not worship it? . . . Each group must worship its leader, it cannot but worship its leader."[97] Dikotter finds that Mao secured backing for the launch of the Great Leap Forward through consecrating his own cult of personality which made senior leaders grovel to Mao through humiliating self-criticisms and public display of reverence to his leadership.[98] In the above passage Tsering Dhondup is merely recording this widespread worship of Mao in the written word. He does so with sarcasm and jocularity as can be seen in its emphasis on the string of grandiose epithets and the family head, who forever loses his sense of humor.

Although *The Red Wind Scream* is replete with harrowing descriptions of the human condition, the pervasive presence of Tsering Dhondup's trademark humor makes it a surprisingly enjoyable read. His deft mix of humor and tragedy stands out along with his technical competence and flair for threading together a good story. As evident in the above excerpt, humor is not used to trivialize a serious subject matter but to expose and censure certain manmade circumstances. It is a lighthearted yet profound and critical way of presenting traumatic experiences. To cite one example, through the description of a struggle session, Tsering Dhondup contrasts the old world against the new. He injects humor into a tragic situation to narrate the confusion caused by the overthrow of the traditional tribal system by the Chinese state. It takes Tashi Lhamo and Lobsang Gyatso four frugal years to amass enough sheepskins to make a decent *chuba* for the latter. Not long after donning his new sheepskin *chuba* for the first time, Lobsang Gyatso is taken to another nomadic settlement for a vicious struggle session. He returns with his new Tibetan robe shredded and in pieces. In his tattered clothes he resembles a "youth" mauled by a pack of wolves and the pathetic sight reduces fellow nomads to tears.[99] Even Lobsang Tsultrim—who usually does not think twice about subjecting Lobsang Gyatso to countless, inhuman struggle sessions, is incensed and moved by a hitherto unseen sense of tribal loyalty. "It's alright to subject a person to a struggle session, but why shred his clothes?" fumes Lobsang Tsultrim. "Those dog-shit eaters are taking revenge on our settlement because of a feud from the old society. This is bullying. I'm going right now to get the *chuba* compensated for. Unbelievable . . ."[100] However, a low-ranking PLA officer is the head of the work team at the other nomadic settlement. When he retorts to Lobsang Tsultrim that his request was equivalent to providing protection for a "class enemy," the latter has no option but return empty-handed. Although he could not avenge the shredded *chuba*, Lobsang Tsultrim is sure that this incident has nothing to do with "class hatred." In his opinion its genesis lies in the blood feud between the two tribes that was left unresolved because of "Liberation." Incidentally many years later this dispute is settled by Alak Drong and the two feuding tribes are reconciled. However, no mention is made of the shredded *chuba* incident that took place during the Cultural Revolution.[101]

To me it appears that beneath this tragicomic depiction lies the clash of two different worlds, the tribal system of traditional Amdo society and the political modernism of Communist China. Traditional knowledge, concepts and modes of social organization could no longer make sense of what was taking place on the ground, thus marking the sudden emergence of a new modern world. Here modernity is marked by the failure of the old to explain and cope with the new.[102] The "shock of the new" wreaks havoc on traditional modes of social organization and disrupts established categories of perceiving the world. As in the case of many colonized nations for Tibetans the modern is also associated with "'foreignness,' domination, and violence."[103] The traditional tribal organization was no match for the highly centralized and complex political community. Institutionally and practically, the tribal system was not equipped to deal with the bureaucratic modern state. The idea and practice of blood feud persists but it is seen as ineffectual against an impersonal, all-powerful state. Hence what transpired during the Great Leap Forward and the Cultural Revolution is conveniently forgotten like the shredded *chuba* incident. By tracing the origins of traumatic historical events to this encounter between two different worlds, *The Red Wind Scream* not only remembers forgotten incidents but also recaptures the sociopolitical circumstances that enabled them. By bringing to the fore, right at the outset of the novel, the baffling initial encounter between Alak Drong and Wang Aiguo, the representative of unheard-of agencies called *Zhungguo* and the Chinese Communist Party, it captures a historical situation. Milan Kundera maintains that a great novel imparts invaluable experiential knowledge by grasping the "human content" of a historical situation.[104] It may not be an exaggeration to contend that Tsering Dhondup's novel boasts such a "human content" with its rich, diverse and perceptive representation of Tibetan life under traumatic historical conditions. It records the experiences of Tibetan people as well as environmental degradation. In short it narrates the destruction of Tibet's container (*snod*) and traumatization of its contents (*bcud*) triggered by the arrival of Chinese Communists in the 1950s.

CONCLUSION: BONES THAT REMEMBER

The frequent use of metaphors such as "red wind" and "wild yak" and their status as unifying imageries demonstrate how cultural trauma serves as a rallying point for the Tibetan people. By alluding to collective sufferings and maintaining and sustaining collective memories of them, these figurative expressions reinforce Tibetan solidarity. Poetic and fictional representations of cultural trauma derive from originating historical events. These artistic rearticulations are heavily dependent upon the oral stories passed down from those who directly experienced a traumatic situation. In the written word contemporary Tibetan writers continue a long-running act of remembrance that starts in orality. The indelibility of cultural trauma is generated by the radical, fundamental, and shocking impacts of sudden social change; however, it is also constituted by deliberate recollections of them through private oral communication and through the public medium of creative writing. In the memorable passage of *The Red Wind Scream* when hungry prison guards mow down unwary white geese and cranes on a bleak spring day, their snow-swept habitat is splattered with blood. The vivid blood marks resemble the "red flags" dotted across the snowplain. Referring to these scarlet spots Tsering Dhondup writes: "A fleeting glimpse of them caught by the surviving siblings will never fade away."[105] This scene can be seen as an allegory for the mass killings of Tibetans in the 1950s. By narrating their plight through metaphor Tsering Dhondup records the sudden shock of a historical situation and also preserves a national tale for posterity. As this chapter and the next demonstrate, through artistic representations of past traumatic events Tibetan writers and poets uphold the Tibetan expression:

ང་ཤི་རུང་རུས་པས་མི་བརྗེད༎
Even if I die my bones will not forget

NOTES

1. This Tibetan proverb records the arrival of the Chinese communists in Tibet and its repercussions. *Rgya nag po* is the abbreviation of *rgya ya nag po*. This word can literally be rendered as "dark adversary" or "dark enemy." It carries two connotations meaning bitter enemy or Chinese. Here it means both. It can also be rendered as "Chinese came up / Winds blew down."

2. Renan [1882] 1990: 19.

3. Alexander 2004: 1.

4. Ibid., 8, Smelser 2004: 37, and Sztompka 2004: 165.

5. Alexander 2004: 9–10.

6. Smelser 2004: 44.

7. Sztompka 2004: 165.

8. Eyerman 2004: 62.

9. For official Chinese accounts of the implementation of "democratic reforms" in Eastern Tibet see Panchen Lama [1962] 1997: 157–73 or *Tibet: 1950–1967*: 294–98, 321–46.

10. On "struggle sessions" see Smith 1996: 396 and Jamyang Norbu [1979] 1986: 133–34. In Tibet struggle sessions came to be widely used as a technique of public humiliation and terrorization during the Cultural Revolution. However, they had been employed as early as the late 1950s against certain elements of Tibetan

society. See Nags tshang nus blo 2007: 368–72 for a harrowing eyewitness account of a struggle session carried out against some Tibetan Lamas accused as "exploiters" and note also my mother's account in this chapter.

11. For the implementation of "democratic reforms" in Tibet and Tibetan resistance against it see Stag lha phun tshogs bkra shis 1995 Vol. 2: 217–50, Sperling 2008: 71–72, Zhwa sgab pa dbang phyug bde ldan 1976 Vols 1 & 2: 509–22, Tsering Shakya 1999: 136–44, Dawa Norbu 2001: 210–27, van Schaik 2011: 224–37, Smith 1994: 62–69, 1996: 387–450, Jamyang Norbu, March 7, 2009, [1979] 1986: 104–52, 'Jam dpal rgya mtsho 1997: 86–129, and Panchen Lama [1962] 1997. Violent insurrections against the Chinese communists started as early as 1949. For instance in Amdo Janza revolts took place in 1949 and 1952 (Bka' thub rgyal 2003: 17–92) and there were uprisings in Kham Gyalrong in 1952 and 1954 (Jamyang Norbu, March 7, 2009) and McGranahan 2010.

12. This is my translation of a passage cited by Bstan 'zin dpal 'bar (1994: 140) in Tibetan. The Chinese source text is entitled *A History of the Battles Fought by the 11th Infantry Division of the Chinese People's Liberation Army* (*Krung go'i mi dmangs bcing 'grol dmag rkang dmag hri bcu gcig pa'i dmag dpung gi dmag 'thab lo rgyus*).

13. For accounts of unprecedented death and destruction wrought by the suppression of Tibetan rebellion and the Great Leap Forward see Nags tshang nus blo 2007: 253–479, Bstan 'zin dpal 'bar 1994: 68–197, Panchen Lama [1962] 1997, Arjia Rinpoche 2010: 31–73, 'Gu log dam chos dpal bzang 200: 475–506, 526–34, Dikotter 2010: 114–15, 227, 311–12, and Rin bzang 2008 (this work will be briefly discussed below) and McGranahan 2010.

14. For instance, see Tashi Dhondup's *Dunglen* song cited at the end of the chapter, in which—like many Amdowas—he equates 2008 to 1958 in terms of historical momentousness and unleashing of political horror.

15. Ibid.: *Dgra nag po bod la thon gi lo.*

16. For a discussion of the historical significance of 1958 for the Amdo people see Makley 2005: 40–78.

17. 'Ju skal bzang 2009: 172–73.

18. Lopez 2006: 46–47.

19. Om 'bar 2008: 40–41.

20. One of the earliest poetic instances using *'brong* in this sense can be found in Jangbu's *The Cause of the Wild Yak's Death, 'Brong shi rkyen* (Ljang bu 1996: 126–7). An English translation of this poem by Heather Stoddard is available in Jangbu 2010: 112.

21. Rmog ru shes rab rdo rje 1998: 31–32.

22. *Phyi'i snod dang nang gi bcud kyis grub ba.* This phrase is derived from an Indic Buddhist cosmological idea called *bhājanaloka* in Sanskrit.

23. Gu ru don grub September 6, 2010–2011.

24. Information Office of the State Council of the People's Republic of China July 11, 2011.

25. Information Office of the State Council of the People's Republic of China 2001: 3.

26. Smelser 2004: 51.

27. Alexander 2004: 11, Smelser 2004: 38 and Eyerman 2004: 60–63.

28. Not only are the wild yak's sheer physical power and sharp horns regarded as awesome but also its tongue is feared as a deadly weapon. In some parts of Tibet it is fabled that a wild yak takes revenge by subjecting its enemy to a slow and painful death by licking it with its extremely coarse tongue. Tibetan nomads also used the dried tongue of the wild yak as a hairbrush.

29. Gnyan 2007: 49–52, 55.

30. For a commentary on a few praise poems see Hartley 2008: 14–22 and Chab 'gag rta mgrin 2007: 7–81.

31. Pema Bhum 2008: 114 (Translation by Ronald Schwartz).

32. Gu ru don grub posted this poem on his blog February 18, 2010, which was subsequently unavailable.

33 In which the Dalai Lama renounces the demand for Tibetan independence and champions the Tibetan exercise of meaningful devolutionary powers within the constitutional framework of the PRC. On Dalai Lama's "Middle Way Approach" and related statements visit: http://www.dalailama.com/messages/middle-way-approach

34. Bstan 'dzin dpal 'bar 1994: 140–41. Alak Tsayi used the name Bstan 'dzin dpal 'bar when he authored *The Tragedy of My Homeland*. On mass killings and arrests of the male population also see Rin bzang 2008: 9, 39 and 'Jam dpal rgya mtsho 1997: 122.

35. oM 'bar 2008: 41.

36. Rin bzang 2008: 7, Jamyang Norbu 1986 [1979]: 140, Bstan 'dzin dpal 'bar 1994: 144, 147, and also my mother's firsthand account (see below).

37. In a critical remark on Tibetan historians' tendency to adopt embellished language in their description of historical figures or events Mda' tshan pa (aka, Mgon po phyag gnyis pa: August 4, 2009) advises against the use of *rab btags kyi rgyan* in historical narrative. However, he lauds its literary merit inherent its ability to convey the ineffable.

38. For an illuminating reflection on metaphor see Arendt: 1978: 98–125.

39. An exposition of different categories of this "exaggerated poetic ornament" can be found in Bse tshang blo bzang dpal ldan 1984: 451–63. There are two ways of spelling this poetic device in Tibetan: *rab rtog gi rgyan*, and *rab btags kyi rgyan*.

40. Cohen 1978: 9.

41. Alvarez 2005: 85.

42. Indeed Borges's famous dictum goes: "Censorship is the mother of metaphor." Cited in Alvarez 2005: 85.

43. White [1974] 2001: 1721.

44. Bhabha April 14, 2004.

45. Skal bzang tshul khrims uses this popular Tibetan proverb in his daring audio-visual report on the absence of freedom in Tibet. In this report he traces the principal causes of the deplorable current situation to the forceful entry of the Chinese into Tibetan territories in the 1950s and the repressive rule that followed. The audio data and a Tibetan transcription of his appeal can be accessed at http://www.paldengyal.com/?p=908.

46. Lha byams rgyal 2010: 35–34.

47. In the 1950s and 1960s Tibetans were deported in theirs thousands to labor camps in the Tshadam (Salt Plains) in Northeastern Tibet. Tibetan elders often use the Chinese term Lo ge (Ch. *láogǎi*) to refer to these prison establishments for "reforming prisoners through labor," (*ngal rtsol bsgyur bkol*). A list of these facilities can be found in the Laogai Research Foundation 2008: 351–63. Tshadam as a labor camp location is also mentioned in the oral accounts recorded by Rin bzang 2008: 108–09 and Bstan 'zin dpal 'bar 1994: 439–40.

48. *Bya gtor* is a Tibetan term for the rite of sky burial. It can be rendered more literally as being "scattered to the birds" or "given to the birds."

49. Lha byams rgyal 2010: 48.

50. Woolf 2004 [1928]: 48.

51 This short story is published in book form (Lha byams rgyal 2010: 35–54) as well as online: http://www.sangdhor.com/pics_c.asp?id=3544.

52. Benjamin [1970] 1999: 84.

53. Tshe ring don grub 2006. For a short introduction of this novel and its author see Stoddard 2010b: 84–87. For Stoddard's English translation of an excerpt from it see Tsering Dhondup 2010: 88–91. Another brief mention of it can be found in Robin 2010: 39–41.

54. An excerpt from the first part of *The Red Wind Scream* was published as early as 2002 (*The Qinghai Tibetan News* February 20, 2002). The entire second half of the novel was serialised in the *Qinghai Tibetan News* from December 20, 2007 to June 30, 2008. Another excerpt is printed in a Tibetan literary anthology (Tshe ring don grub dang Bde skyid sgrol ma [eds.], 2004: 63–83).

55. Information attained through private communication with the author March 8–9, 2011 Siling.

56. Sztompka 2004: 158–59.

57. This is a reference to "minority" leaders's travels to Chinese political and economic centers such as metropolitan cities at the instigation of the Chinese state in the 1950s. In an insightful article on this practice, which still goes on in contemporary China, Bulag (2012) calls it "political tourism."

58. Preparatory Committee is a Chinese state agency for establishing Communist administrative rule in Tibetan areas for the first time. Almost every county and prefecture in Tibetan areas was first set up by such a body. The Preparatory Committee for the Tibet Autonomous Regions was the best-known of them all.

59. Tshe ring don grub 2006: 88–89.

60. Ibid., 185. "Historical prisoners" fear and loathe "common criminals" because the latter are given preferential treatment by prison staff and are also often used to persecute the former. Therein lies the genesis of Alak Drong's grudge: 107, 119–28.

61. Ibid., 69–70.

62. During the late 1950s many young Chinese from provinces such as Hunan, Anhui, Shandong, and Henan were sent to Tibetan areas for settling or to undertake agricultural production. Many died of disease and starvation. In Tibetan they are simply known as *na gzhon*, "youths," and their tragic fate is still remembered by local Tibetans today. For brief mentions of *na gzhon* see Rin bzang 2008: 24–25, 'Jam dpal rgya mtsho 1997: 126 and Bstan 'dzin dpal 'bar 1994: 136–37.

63. Tshe ring don grub 2006: 156.

64. *Zhwa gon* literally means the one who wears a hat. It denotes a serious criminal status symbolized by the forced donning of a dunce's cap. Once a person is labeled as a Hatted One then he or she is a target of constant persecution. See Arjia Rinpoche 2010: 76–77, and Rin bzang 2008: 18.

65. *Sgrol bstod* is a famous hymn written in praise of Tara in her twenty-one aspects. It is a popular and poetic Tibetan prayer that is either recited or sung out loud.

66. Tshe ring don grub 2006: 190–91.

67. Ibid.: 242–50.

68. Ibid.: 321–30.

69. Goodman 1981: 111.

70. Portelli 1998: 24.

71. For instance sketchy references to "the Harrowing Day" are found on pages 22, 92, 93–94, 109–18, 128–30, 176, 232–23, and 259.

72. Telephone conversation with Tsering Dhondup, May 30, 2012. Tsering Dhondup also expressed his admiration for world literary figures such as Charles Dickens, Victor Hugo, Gabriel García Márquez, George Orwell, Salman Rushdie, and Arundhati Roy. Although he read these authors in Chinese translation and encountered modern Western literature through Chinese intellectuals, when I asked him if he had been influenced by Chinese writers the answer was negative. This reluctance to acknowledge Chinese influence is a common tendency shared by contemporary Tibetan language writers. It seems to be driven by a patriotic desire to circumvent Chinese language mediation and an urge to establish a modern Tibetan literary identity within the context of world literature. As this book is primarily concerned with the endurance of the Tibetan literary and oral traditions and the presence of the Tibetan nation it fails to pay attention to this fascinating theme. However, future investigations into the Tibetophone writers' reception of Western and Chinese literatures would shed important light upon the development of modern Tibetan literature.

73. Ricoeur 1988: 133.

74. Telephone conversation with Tsering Dhondup, May 30, 2012. Salman Rushdie also makes a similar statement regarding the influence of oral narrative techniques on his disjointed and digressive narration of *Midnight's Children*, see Ashcroft, Griffiths, and Tiffin [1989] 2002: 181.

75. Levenson 2004: 201.

76. A private communication with Tsering Dhondup, March 8, 2011.

77. Nags tshang nus blo 2007: 253–479 and Rin bzang 2008.

78. For a brief report on the condition of Rinzang after his release from prison see Dge 'dun rab gsal 2009.

79. *Sangs rgyas bstan pa'i sku don dang/ yur kha skya mo'i 'gro don.*

80. I am grateful to Skab the lag lo, Kapthe the Armless One, for providing this information in a long recorded interview with him March 3, 2011.

81. This is a summary of a recorded account given by my mother August 7, 2003. My subsequent visits home (2005, 2007, 2009, and 2011) helped me to recheck some of the details with my mother and this written version is supplemented slightly. Like many Tibetans of my generation all my siblings grew up listening to this and other

similar stories about the "Chinese Raid in 1958" (*nga brgyad lo rgya rgyugs no'i skor*).

82. Armed tribesmen were called *mgon po'i lha dmag*, the Divine Army of the Protector, and PLA was called *phyi dmag*, the Army from the Outside or the Foreign Army.

83. *Ro shun phud* literally means stripping off the corpse or taking the clothes of the dead. This is done so as to expose the deceased to the natural elements and carrion birds. Tibetan nomads believe that if a proper sky-burial ceremony could not be carried out then the next best thing would be to leave the dead bodies naked in the wild. Thus many fighters fought stark naked on this day as a sign that they were absolutely resolved to die. It is believed that when they fell they would have already taken care of their bodies without having to trouble their families with the last rites.

84. Bstan 'dzin dpal 'bar 1994: 143–44.

85. Dikotter 2010: 227.

86. For similar mass killings in other Amdo areas in 1958 see Rin bzang 2008: 5–11, 29–41, Bstan 'dzin dpal 'bar 1994: 133–51 and 'Jam dpal rgya mtsho 1997: 121–22.

87. Bstan 'dzin dpal 'bar 1994.

88. Foucault 1977: 160.

89. Howe [1990] 2001: 1539.

90. Tshe ring don grub 2006: 153.

91. Tshe ring don grub 2006: 267–69.

92. Gray 1990: 311.

93. Ibid., 267–69.

94. Arjia Rinpoche 2010: 85–86 and Rin bzang 2008: 19.

95. Hartley's research into the translation and publication of Mao's works in Tibetan finds that in 1967 "[S]everal hundred thousand copies of Mao's *Selected Works* and more than one million copies of Mao's *Red Book* were printed." As a result, she states: "Given that the official Tibetan population at the time was four million, this meant that potentially every fourth Tibetan owned a copy of the *Red Book* (2003: 75)." As noted by McGranahan (2007: 190) these ubiquitous images and words of Mao were vital for legitimating socialism in Tibet.

96. Arjia Rinpoche 2010: 85.

97. Cited in Dikotter 2010: 19. Mao's March 1958 speech on the cult of personality is available at: http://www.marxists.org/reference/archive/mao/selected-works/volume-8/mswv8_06.htm.

98. Dikotter 2010: 19–21.

99. Tshe ring don grub 2006: 294–96.

100. Ibid.: 296.

101. Ibid.: 297–98.

102. Arendt [1961] 1993a: 8–9.

103. Nolan 2005: 159–60.

104. Kundera 2007: 156–57.

105. Tshe ring don grub 2006: 88–89.

Chapter 5

The Third Generation of Tibetan Poets and the Inescapable Nation

ཡབ་ཀྱི་མིག་རྒྱུ་ཡུམ་གྱི་རྡུལ་རྒྱུ

ཁྲག་གིས་བཏུམས་པའི་མ་ཎི་ཡིག་དྲུག

Father's tears, Mother's sweat
Six-Syllabled *Mani*, wrapped in blood[1]

The Third Generation (*mi rabs gsum pa*) was founded as a literary group in 2005. Their nonconformist literary attitude and writing have been greeted with criticism and praise. Their poetry seems to take contemporary Tibetan literature in a new direction in terms of both form and content. However, this chapter will show that their work does not escape the influence of traditional poetic genres nor older contemporary Tibetan poets like Jangbu. These young writers are working within socioeconomic, political, and technological conditions quite different from those of preceding generations. They have acquired a distinctive voice that is radical, iconoclastic, and critical of all types of authority, both "traditional" and colonial. Third Generation poets claim to have abandoned older forms of poetry and transcended even the influence of Dhondup Gyal, who is credited as the father of modern Tibetan poetry. Yet their works show that this is not the case. The poetic form of free verse pioneered by Dhondup Gyal is still their literary mode of choice, while older genres like *mgur* continue to inspire the themes and sensibilities of their poetry.

While their subject matter is often mundane and vernacular, and at times taboo and highly controversial, their iconoclasm and radicalism is not as unprecedented as it is asserted to be. And while a conspicuous rebellious spirit and individualism infuse their writing, it does not transcend the confines of the nation as asserted in their declaratory statements. A collective concern for Tibetan national identity courses thickly through their poetry. Although they may not employ the term "national pride" (*mi rigs kyi la rgya*) made popular by Dhondup Gyal, the thoughts and emotions in their poetry are informed by the fate of the Tibetan nation. This chapter will seek to affirm these assertions through the scrutiny of several representative poems after giving a brief account of the birth of the Third Generation along with their stated principles. Special attention will be accorded to the writings of Kyabchen Dedrol and Dhatsanpo to underline the innovative attributes of the Third Generation, Tibetan literary legacies, and the preoccupation with the nation.

BIRTH OF A NEW POETIC TRIBE

On July 6, 2003, the famed modern Tibetan poet Jangbu convened the first ever conference on Tibetan poetry called Waterfall of Youth in Siling (Ch-Xining). It was named after Dhondup Gyal's trail-blazing poem that introduced free verse to Tibetan literature.[2] As intended, the gathering became a biannual event attended by many leading writers and intellectuals of the Tibetan world. During the 2nd Seminar of Waterfall of Youth, on January 30, 2005, driven by a sense of their distinct identity and youthful zeal as a literary movement, a group of young Tibetan poets, led by Kyabchen Dedrol (Skyabs chen bde drol), founded "The Third Generation of Tibetan Poets" (*bod kyi snyan ngag pa'i mi rab gsum pa*).[3] It was initially composed of ten members, mostly young writers with varying literary credentials (which later grew into a quorum of up to twenty members). At its founding, Kyabchen Dedrol made a public announcement, in characteristically trenchant terms, declaring the reasons for the formation of the group and its principles. As a sign of the times, his statement was subsequently announced online, in journals, newsletters, and books, reaching a much wider and more critical audience. The very fact that there were now so many different modes of publicity and diffusion available underscored Kyabchen Dedrol's initial claim: that the new generation of Tibetan poets lived in a different world from their predecessors, that they had a different outlook, and that this necessitated the formation of a new kind of "tribe" (*shog kha*). It was asserted that this poetic community of kindred spirits was no longer in thrall to Dhondup Gyal's *Waterfall of Youth*. It was also maintained that a primary objective of its members was to make a "loud noise" (*ku co*) to cause a stir, create an impact. This "loud noise" was to be nothing like "the Great Path of Bright Light," "Happy Livelihood," and "Glorious Tasks" celebrated in Dhondup Gyal's most famous poem. On the contrary, it was to be a dystopian clamor of "gibberish, ennui, and aimlessness."[4] In this way the Third Generation challenged the ideals of Tibet's most celebrated modern poet. Ironically, it was a biannual conference newly established to honor Dhondup Gyal's poetic legacy, which served as the platform from which a tribe of new poets provocatively questioned his hallowed status.

In various publications, the Third Generation distinguished themselves from past poets and from older contemporaries by repeatedly declaring their dissatisfaction with the poetry of the past, including that of Dhondup Gyal and Ju Kalsang, and their total rejection of classical Tibetan poetics influenced by Indian *kāvya* tradition. These forceful assertions constituted what came to be considered the Manifesto of the Third Generation (*mi rabs gsum pa'i bsgrags gtam*) though there is no single document bearing that exact title. A spirit of individualism, assertiveness, and nonconformity characterize these statements. In the printed version of Kyabchen Dedrol's speech, he addresses the older generation of poets and critics of the Third Generation:

> You keep me next to you by force and would not let go. Is it because I need to offer you fragments of "praise" in return for your fragments of "advice" to me?
>
> If I cannot make it across this great concrete plain, I will not force myself to talk about distant snow-mountains and black yak-hair tents just to please you.
>
> If it transpires that I do not have even a palm-sized piece of land to live off, then it is possible that I may totally destroy the garden you have tended with loving care.
>
> I am not that bee attached to the lotus. I am not that person who examines if a beautiful woman has a waist or not. Neither am I that person who shouts orders to "charge" or "jump." Nor am I the dead butterfly used as a bookmark in the pages of "*Kāvyādarśa*."[5]

In this nuanced rhetoric, Kyabchen Dedrol announced a parting of company with certain established literary forms and practices. No longer are the Third Generation satisfied with the Tibetan literary tradition of "praise verses" (*bstod tshogs*), be they eulogies of Lamas, teachers, or the new communist rulers of Tibet. With it they also reject subservience to any literary authority as shown by the refusal to listen to any "advice." Like Western modernist poetry, which some of the Third Generation members imitate, their poetry is subjective and preoccupied with the present. Their immediate concern is to give expression to the experience of traversing the "great concrete plain": That is, the contemporary existence of Tibetans under the industrialized, urban conditions of China's developmental project. This current lived experience in the new towns and rapidly transforming countryside is perceived to be "distant" from the timeless "snow-mountains and black yak-hair tents" of Tibet's past.

This reluctance to speak in the metaphorical idioms of "snow-mountains and black yakhair tents"—that are so often patriotically evoked in the Tibetan poetry of their immediate predecessors—also reveals the Third Generation's desire not to be shackled by a nationalistically charged poetic conformism. Earlier in the same speech, Kyabchen Dedrol claimed: "The world under our pens is no longer the shared public world merely driven by 'national pride' and 'national characteristics' as before. Rather, it is one of inner consciousness and private life. As such it is rich with a diversity of literary techniques and a multiplicity of subject matters."[6] As is widely known, Dhondup Gyal had celebrated and advocated "national pride" in his poems like *Waterfall of Youth*, *Praise to Intellectual Heroes* (*Rig pa'i dpa' bo rnams la phul pa'i bstod tshig*), *Here is Another Live Heart Beating Wildly* (*'Di na yang drag tu mchong lding byed bzin pa'i snying gson po zhig*), and in his song *The Blue Lake* (*Mtsho sngon po*).[7] Subsequently, many writers did likewise, turning "national pride" into a dominant theme of contemporary Tibetan poetry and song. So much so, that in Amdo a highly prized type of *dunglen* has come to be known in popular parlance as "guitar songs of national pride."[8] The Third Generation regarded the forsaking of this literary trend as one of their defining characteristics. However, as we shall see in the subsequent sections of this chapter, a sense of the Tibetan nation continues to feature saliently in their poetry. Even poems tackling the most private matters are pregnant with national sentiment.

The Third Generation are keen to carve out an independent literary space and jealously guard their new literary territory, even if it means digging up the cherished garden nurtured by their predecessors. A further subversive connotative meaning may also lie within this garden metaphor, since the garden may also stand for the Chinese state, as it does for example in a Chinese primary school song *Our Country is a Flower Garden* (*wǒmen de zǔguó shì huāyuán*) taught to Tibetan and Chinese children alike. Like many Tibetans including myself when learning Chinese language for the first time Kyabchen Dedrol and his fellow Third Generation poets would have been exposed to this "social text" in which the sun shines warmly on brightly colored flowers and smiling children. Therefore, the destructive intent associated with the Third Generation's desire for an independent creative space is double-edged: subversive of received literary traditions and perhaps established political authority.

The Third Generation's repudiation of Tibetan *kāvya* tradition is far less ambiguous. Kyabchen Dedrol defines their movement in opposition to the stock imageries favored by classical *kāvya*-influenced poetry. He ridicules formulaic classical metaphors such as bee and the lotus for romantic infatuation, and "the waist-less female" (*sked med ma*) for the beautiful, slim woman. The rejection of Tibetan *kāvya* poetics is complete and resounding with the refusal to be associated with the "dead butterfly" of outdated poetry, a refusal to be a bookmark in an unread book.[9] In other words, they no longer defer to, nor even read the *Kāvyādarśa* (*Me long ma—Mirror of Poetics*) which dominated Tibetan classical poetry for centuries, until the 1990s or so. As far as they are concerned, the famous poetic figures of speech enlisted and expounded in this Indian-derived book of poetics are a dead butterfly—once beautiful but no longer with any vitality—and are rejected as an influence on their poetry.

In short, the Third Generation literary movement is characterized by the assertion of an independent, individualistic, subjective, and subversive spirit, spurning classical traditions and even Dhondup Gyal's authority as an exemplary modern poet. At the First Conference of the Third Generation of Tibetan Poets held in Siling, July 22–23, 2006, members reasserted these key principles and came to an agreement on the defining features of their literary movement, in a language far less obscure than the above statements by Kyabchen Dedrol. The members concurred that:

> In terms of both literary method and approach, the Third Generation has no particular object of reverence or attachment. It is a generation that does not surrender its rightful status on the literary platform to others. It is a generation that does not relish resting in the shadows of Dhondup Gyal, Ju Kalsang and others. It is a generation that is adept at distinguishing the poet from the orthodox "scholar."[10]

The validity of this polemical rhetoric of "the new" can only be verified by examining the literary output of these Third Generation writers. Such an examination reveals that there are indeed novel elements, with regards to literary techniques, use of images and choice of subject matter. However, at the same time, one can also detect continuities in terms of literary genre and imagery as well as the prominence of certain subject matters. Before looking at a few well-known poems, it is important to note that the Third Generation does also acknowledge the need to build upon the achievements of their immediate predecessors. Kyabchen Dedrol, for example, stated that in seeking new literary forms, that they should embrace the merits of the previous two generations and that as such "there is something to be continued."[11] Many Tibetan commentators have overlooked this important qualification as it has been drowned in a cacophony of polemical rhetoric about "the new."

CRUCIBLES OF INNOVATION AND CONTINUITY

What is "continued" by the Third Generation is primarily the poetic form of free verse introduced to Tibetan-language literature by Dhondup Gyal. I have read well over a thousand poems by the Third Generation and the majority of them are composed in free verse. No amount of bombastic talk about transcending the influence of Dhondup Gyal or the rejection of his poetic legacy can conceal the fact that their poetry has so far failed to come up with a new form. The emotive desire to escape from the "shadow of Dhondup Gyal" is undeniable, but in terms of form, their poetry is clearly written under the long shadow cast by this great poet. There is something like Harold Bloom's "anxiety of influence" at play here. Bloom maintains that any poets' endeavor to achieve originality is frustrated by the poetry of their great precursors. Original poetic work cannot be produced without an embattled interaction with poetic tradition. Outstanding poetic achievement can only be secured through serious engagement with the forerunners or through what Bloom calls "poetic misprision," a complex process of creative misreading of their poetry.[12] This echoes arguments advanced by Pound and Eliot, leading modernist poets, who believed in rigorous engagement with tradition as *sine qua non* for literary innovation.[13]

Just as in modern Anglo-American poetry, contemporary Tibetan poetry cannot eschew the influence of the works of their past masters and immediate predecessors. Although the Third Generation are reticent in acknowledgment of this, their poetry is still, at least partly, the outcome of an engagement with the past and older contemporary poets. This is not to deny that they have introduced innovative features to modern Tibetan poetry through foreign imports, nor to downplay their refinement of Tibetan free verse through the introduction of new techniques, themes, and idioms. Instead, aspects of continuity and innovation jostle, collide, and combust, as can be demonstrated by a well-known poem by Kyabchen Dedrol himself entitled *The Third Generation*. This poem is Kyabchen Dedrol's manifesto of the Third Generation in free verse. In it he again outlines, in oppositional and provocative language, the movement's key principles and attitudes and its challenge to established artistic authority and orthodoxy. It is a representative poem of the Third Generation literary movement not just in its confrontational and iconoclastic tone but in its innovative use of images, metaphors, arrangement of the lines, in its disregard of conventional punctuation, its preoccupation with the present, and in its worship of poetry itself.

Before presenting the poem in full translation, a few words are in order about its author. As noted already, Kyabchen Dedrol played the principal role in establishing the Third Generation of Tibetan Poets in 2005. He was born into a nomadic family in the Machu region in 1977 and by 2005 he had already received accolades for his poetry and had established a considerable literary reputation.[14] Alongside a prodigious literary output, he also founded the first Tibetan-language literary website in 2005 with his friend and colleague Kunchok Tsephel, who is now languishing in a Chinese prison for divulging "state secrets." Butter Lamp: Tibetan Literature Website (*Mchod me bod kyi rtsom rig dra ba*) initially faced state restrictions and was closed down several times. In English it is simply known as Tibetcm.com. It covers all genres of Tibetan literature from classical poetry and *mgur* to the Gesar epic and modern literary works. Even though Tibetan-language websites have proliferated since 2005 the popularity of this, Tibet's first literary website, remains undiminished. It was also the first website to promote Third Generation poetry and continues to do so alongside other online resources such as Gedun Choepel Literary Website.[15]

The poem below was first published to critical acclaim on this website. It not only introduces the principles and literary features of the Third Generation but also embodies its manifesto in its literary style. As can be seen in the following translation, the tone of the poem is defiant and combative and its language expressive and declarative:

The Third Generation

1
Father's tears, Mother's sweat
Six-Syllabled *Mani*, wrapped in blood
The real *bardo*—the term *bardo*
Startled by car horns
Mountain wolves amongst the ruins of pulverised snow-plains and crystal-mountains
The Third Generation—drinking—fornicating
Burning rage-like smoke and incense offering
Talking putrescent talk
Are stirring the brains of men and women, including themselves
Nursing the body, after consciousness has been flayed like the skin
All over the place—on the chest—along the spine
In the crotch—along the aged wrinkles of the Melodious Goddess
Within the depths of sunshine—in taverns—in hotels
In the hair of Prostitute Sangje Dolma
Deep inside grass and water
Into fat flesh and red lights
On wife's lips and before bosses
Are writing poetry—the Third Generation—
Are writing minute atom-like poetry

Every time that the Third Generation—
Like fine sunray piercing the weave of a dark brown yakhair tent
Like a tigress bolting out of the jungle
Like red lightning crushing red rocks
Sets forth from one's youth
In offices—bladders fully filled with boiled water
Those quarrelsome Tibetan cadres say
"They are dogs—they are ghosts

They are nothing
They can't even rival the pores of Dhondup Gyal's bodily hair"
Ah—Reasons reinforced by slaps
Sworn oaths presented as refutation
Hands prone to murdering
Theories composed of assumptions
Podiums tempered with heat
When all these clear away like ash and dust
The Third Generation will rise for the children like the sun
The Third Generation—will have made their preparations to die for poetry

2
Summer—the season of abundant rain and water
Yet the tears of the Third Generation stricken by drought
Winter—the season of bone piercing fierce winds
Yet the veins of the Third Generation strike sparks
Autumn—the season of sunshine sprinkling from grass tips
Yet the songs of the Third Generation burn the white clouds
Spring—the season of smile-blooming flowers
Yet the heart of the Third Generation is iced up

When the primordially pristine natural reality
Is blown in the wind like a tattered street rag,
And falls gently upon your window sill
Love-crazed Third Generation
Will burn moxa along the spine of the city
And fly poetry into the air of the meadow
Down and helloes scattered off poetry
Will be carried off higher and higher, to merge into emptiness
You can never catch it with the eyes of lust
Nor capture it by the camera of ignorance

When putrid milk and butter made of slogans and praises
Feed the flames of the plastic butter-lamps
Poetic diction, caught on the wing-tips of suicidal fire-divers[16]
Will slowly burn in the depth of the thick darkness
Those who mistake the smell of burning for the grace of the Melodious Goddess
Are not the Third Generation—but the wood-block print like old men
Directly opposite of the Third Generation

When the long tail formed of impetuosity and bigotry
Attempts to catch the yellow moon in the well
The watery droplets leaning on the branches of the slender tree
Will gently fall from the sockets of the long night
Those who mistake the squelch for the footfall of great men
Are not the Third Generation—but the traitor-like children
Directly opposite of the Third Generation

At that great theatre of the century
When people come to see a show with cheap passes
The Third Generation will perform a love play
Without chorus and clown
Will flaunt a nude body
Without representation and theme
Will make ritual offerings of poetry
Without offering and the object of offering
At that great theatre people's laughter
Will be imprisoned along with some insects and flies
And at times will resound like some wandering demon ghost

3
Like a shattered turquoise platter
Your meadow is strewn with bricks and ceramic fragments
My sky is overcast with dark smoke and clouds
Like a Chinese muskdeer hunter a man with his eyes, mouth,
Hair and chest caked with grey dust
Come running away as if frightened of something
Following him when each man holding a wine cup
And each woman leading a child approach
Out of the annals of history appears the 21st century
Not the Third Generation
They have already bound themselves up tightly
With the shackles taken out of poetry
And have entrusted the keys to you

Hey monk! The keys are already entrusted to you
Hey woman! The keys are already entrusted to you

After smashing the mirror they look at their bodies and say:
"Because poetry is not ornament but life
We've now turned into poetry.
Were the sound of the ancient bell the honk of the car horn
Now we could also, like a robot, charge at it."

Now the hostess has wandered off, the shack is dilapidated
Love stories gently seep
Into the sand hole amidst the tall grass
This fever-seized delirious land
Resembles the fever-seized delirious Third Generation
It is difficult to say that if misfortune struck
It would not take its own life for the sake of a single droplet of water[17]

   One obvious target of sustained attack in this poem is the Tibetan classical poetry dominated by Indian *kāvya* poetics. It is held in total disdain and rejected outright. As noted in chapter 1 the genesis of Tibetan *kāvya* poetry can be traced back to the Tibetan imperial period. It started flourishing in Tibet from the thirteenth century and since then it dominated Tibetan poetic compositions till the recent advent of free verse. It has undergone transformations and adapted to contemporary times, and is still being widely practiced. Dhondup Gyal's introduction of free verse undermined the dominance of Tibetan *kāvya* poetry, but he never dismissed it out of hand. Although he questioned some of its outdated features and constraining elements, he also acknowledged its merits and its contribution to Tibetan literature. As pointed out in chapter 1 and elsewhere, Dhondup Gyal in fact incorporated *kāvya* legacies into his own writings, including in his most influential poem, *Waterfall of Youth*.[18]

Kyabchen Dedrol's poem above has no time for the strict, regular metrical rules, the set imageries and similes, the rigorous technical schemes, and the formulaic themes celebrated and taught in *Kāvyādarśa*. All of these are seen as hindrances which only suffocate the new poet seeking to express a multiplicity of themes and the ambivalent emotions of the subjective consciousness. These require freer, more diverse, and less hackneyed poetic devices. The rejection of, and contempt for, Tibetan *kāvya* poetry is presented in allusive and metaphorical terms. It is difficult for those unfamiliar with the stock imageries of Tibetan classical poetry to fully appreciate the aggressive and condescending tone of this poem. A first volley of attack is detected in suggestion that the Third Generation write poetry "along the aged wrinkles of the Melodious Goddess" (*dbyang can ma*, Sarasvati). She is a goddess of wisdom (*shes rab kyi lha mo*) especially associated with inspiring music and poetry, a goddess who has been worshiped and praised almost throughout Tibetan literary history. Now, her inspiring luster is gone. She is aged and wrinkled. In a single phrase, the poet writes off Tibetan *kāvya* poetry by impugning the very goddess of the Indic *kāvya* tradition. Here, Sarasvati is no longer a muse for the new Tibetan poet. Her "wrinkles" serve only as lines to write the new poetry along.

Although Kyabchen Dedrol strikes a note of certitude when announcing the demise of the Melodious Goddess, it must be pointed out that she continues to inspire some of his fellow Third Generation poets. For instance, a long prose poem by Sakyil Tseta (Sa dkyil tshe bkra) is itself entitled *The Melodious Goddess*, and is both a paean and a supplication to her as a divine muse. In it, the poet "donning the seasons of homeland, stitches the wound of history with poetry" and calls upon the goddess to grant him solace and poetic inspiration in this dire time for his nation.[19] In Dhatsenpo's (Mda' btsan po)[20] *A Poem Dedicated to the Melodious Goddess*, Sarasvati is "a butter-lamp filled with wisdom and accompanied by compassion." Her song rings out through the poet—"The truth of your song resonates through the consciousness of my thighbone flute." In sum, Sarasvati dictates Dhatsenpo's poetry and the poet worships her with "jewels of words."[21]

In *The Third Generation*, the repudiation of Tibetan *kāvya* tradition is methodical and total. After consigning its divine muse to history, Kyabchen Dedrol undertakes an assault against the specific "poetic diction" (*tshig rgyan*) prized and promoted by *kāvya* poetics. On top of the observation of strict metrical rules and technical schemes, *kāvya* verse also dictates specific choices of words and poetic figures or ornaments.[22] This "poetic diction" principally consists of two types of poetic ornament, known as phonetic ornaments (*sgra rgyan*) and semantic ornaments (*don rgyan*). But the term *tshig rgyan*, literally meaning "ornaments of words," is not confined to just these two types. It also entails a range of prescribed metaphors using specific words and turns of phrase, and poetic formulations for the sentence structure which are deemed to beautify a poem or enhance its overall aesthetic appeal.[23] Mastery of this elaborate technical palette of poetic devices is considered indispensable for the perfection of *kāvya* verse and the effective communication of its content. The *Kāvyādarśa* and its Tibetan commentaries expound these ornaments at great length and with voluminous exemplification.[24] However, for the Third Generation, *kāvya* is "poetic diction caught on the wing-tips of suicidal fire-divers." The old generation of "wood-block"-like poets do not sense the death of these old poetic forms and deludedly cling to Sarasvati, whose diminished poetic powers have already been derided. The final, fatal blow struck to the poetic body of *Kāvyādarśa* in *The Third Generation* is the shattering of "the mirror" into pieces. This "mirror" is, of course, none other than the *Mirror of Poetics*, the *Kāvyādarśa* itself. Only after the destruction of "the mirror" can the Third Generation find the poetry within themselves:

After smashing the mirror they look at their bodies and say:
"Because poetry is not ornament but life
We've now turned into poetry . . ."

Individual subjective consciousness itself is poetry and individual creative freedom determines the poetic techniques, form, and themes used to express it. No external authority can define poetry and impose it on the individual like the promotion of "ornament" by *Kāvyādarśa*.

However, despite this broadside attack on the constraints of classical poetic form, in practice, Third Generation poetry does not totally jettison the legacy of *kāvya* poetic diction. In *To Prostitute Sangje Dolma*,[25] a defining poem for the Third Generation, Rekanglang (Re rkang gling) freely borrows conventional metaphors and the Indian mythological allusions employed by *kāvya* poetics. This is the same "Prostitute Sangje Dolma" in whose "hair" Kyabchen Dedrol's *Third Generation* writes poetry. That is to say that prostitution, a repressed and taboo theme, and prostitutes, marginalized members of society, are a prized subject matter for the new poets. Rekanglang's unconventionally themed poem is about a goddess-like prostitute. She is described in the throes of sexual ecstasy brought on by acts of autoeroticism accompanied by associated intimate memories. It is a poem abounding in symbolism and ambiguity, with a central focus on carnal pleasure. In it, the poet avails himself of typical classical metaphors and popular Indian legends for conveying the captivating beauty and sexual attraction of Prostitute Sangje Dolma. To cite just one example, the poem begins:

Because hazy red light
Blends with a blue light reflected off smooth silk
Behind the screen of the white bed
Sensual love flows with loving passion.
When she sings out passion like the howling of wild beasts
And like the eyes of the deer killed by a hunter
With passion her eyes incessantly quiver blinking
The Ascetic of Longevity in the flower garden
Renounces the Dharmic demeanor of a great longevity-attained hermit
And is revitalized by the roar of the solid world and its swaying riches
For the dream of passionate sexual union[26]

Ascetic of Longevity (Drang srong tshe ring) is one of the six Tibetan and Chinese symbols of long life. According to fables his paradisal abode is located somewhere in China and he is reputed to have attained the elixir of life.[27] Even this legendary sage gives up his spiritual quest and gives in to the sexual allure of Prostitute Sangje Dolma. The inability of sages or ascetics to resist temptations of beautiful women is a recurrent metaphor favoured by practitioners of Tibetan *kāvya* poetry. The poetic style and phraseology of Rekanglang's poem might diverge from the norms of *kāvya* versification, but they differ little in the application of time-worn metaphorical figures. For instance, Bod Khepa (Bod mkhas pa), a great exponent of Tibetan *kāvya* poetics, describes a stunning woman dancer as follows:

A figure brimming with youthful vigor
Entirely concealed in apt attire and jewelry
With a beautiful dance of virtuosity and style
Ruined the heart bliss of the Liberation Seeker[28]

Third Generation themes of seduction and lust are further conveyed in Rekanglang's poem by frequent allusions to Indian mythological characters or tales. The God of Desire with his five arrows is invoked, along with "the sorrow of the thousand-eyed Indra." The latter is a reference to the story of how Indra was punished for having an adulterous relationship with the wife of a certain sage named Gotama. When Indra's adultery is discovered Gotama curses his body to turn into a thousand female genitals. Accordingly, a thousand vaginas appeared on his body. After much repenting and imploring by Indra these are then transformed into a thousand eyes. Hence the epithet "thousand-eyed Indra."[29] This and similar legends are used in Rekanglang's poem to index the irresistibility of carnal pleasure. They form part of the repertoire of archetypal stories and stock characters and imagery employed in Tibetan *kāvya* poetry. So despite Kyabchen Dedrol's jettisoning of such classical poetic figures, in practice the influence of *kāvya* continues to echo in Third Generation poetry.

Returning to Kyabchen Dedrol's *The Third Generation*, we can see how he ridicules and reviles those who fail to recognize the literary achievements of the new tribe. In a derogatory passage, the poem accuses "quarrelsome Tibetan cadres" of hurling abuse at the Third Generation without rhyme or reason. The term "cadres" (*las byed pa*) has a negative connotation here as in "the cadres of the (Chinese) state" (*rgyal khab kyi las byed pa*), whose only concern is to earn a living and please the Chinese overlords. This tone of disparagement is reinforced by the reference to the indolent office environment of Tibet's new clerical classes. They while away their time drinking large quantities of hot water, idly pontificating and casting aspersions against the emergent poets. These "cadres" stubbornly claim that the Third Generation "can't even rival the pores of Dhondup Gyal's bodily hair" let alone his intellectual achievements. However, according to Kyabchen Dedrol these are idle and uninformed opinions, made without any knowledge or critical analysis of Third Generation poetry. Their criticisms are based not on insight, reasoning, or poetic sensitivity, but on violence, obduracy, laziness, and emotion:

Ah—Reasons reinforced by slaps
Sworn oaths presented as refutation
Hands prone to murdering
Theories composed of assumptions
Podiums tempered with heat

In these lines Kyabchen Dedrol is controversially suggesting that these figures conduct their argument in such a way that it is reminiscent of the *modus operandi* of their employer, the Chinese state.

DISTILLATION OF NEW IMAGES

In an article on the "jealous" detractors of the Third Generation, Kyabchen Dedrol identifies some of these "cadres" as Dhondup Tsering, Shogdung, and Dudlhagyal. These include university lecturers who are some of the leading social and literary critics inside Tibet. Kyabchen Dedrol accuses them of dominating the modern Tibetan cultural environment with their self-righteous, authoritarian, domineering attitudes and even attempting to monopolize the definition of what is "new." He bemoans their tendency to lecture and their unwillingness to listen to the opinion of others on equal terms.[30] He is especially disheartened by many readers' pedantic interest in the private identity of the Third Generation members rather than in their poetry. Kyabchen Dedrol asserts that "no analytical attention is paid to thematic representation, technical mastery and configuration of images in the Third Generation poetry."[31] Other commentators, both Third Generation poets and independent writers, have made similar remarks, stressing their distinctive use of imagery. For instance, Guru Dhondup (Gu ru don grub), a prominent Third Generation poet, praises his group's poetry in hyperbolic language and speaks of unique technical excellence, imaginative power and artistic sensibility.[32] Lhamkog (Lham kog—Old Shoe) a monk poet and critic, writes effusively on the distinctive use of images especially in the poetry of Kyabchen Dedrol and Rekanglang. Kyabchen Dedrol's peculiar use of images is said to have a mesmerizing effect on the reader, who needs a high degree of learning.[33] However, these observations of a unique use of images in the poetic writings of the Third Generation do not tell us how exactly it differs from other types of poetry. Apart from some emphatic statements, they do not demonstrate in any substantive way how the Third Generation poets use images, metaphors, and other literary devices.

The Third Generation is formed of many vivid images which, as in imagist poetry, are used to covey both thought and emotion. In 1913 Ezra Pound famously declared: "An 'Image' is that which presents an intellectual and emotional complex in an instant of time."[34] This instant "complex" of intellect and emotion is what makes the image the stuff of poetry or what Pound vaguely refers to as "the thing." The poetic image is then more than just a representation or a precise visual portrayal of an external object used to evoke a certain thought or feeling; images instead are the very substance of poetry. Peter Nicholls goes so far as to claim: "Far from being an object, this 'thing' is actually the 'complex' itself which constitutes the image, a verbal and affective assemblage whose syntax incorporates a literal spacing."[35] The poetic image precisely fuses a concise visual description with the internal intellectual and emotional state of the poet. The image is also the intellectual and emotional effect produced by a poem.[36] This modernist conception of the image is highlighted here, first because the use of imagery in Third Generation poetry seems to have been inspired by it. And second, because leading Third Generation poets publicly acknowledge their similarity with "modernism" (*deng rab ring lugs*) and one of its principal precursors, French symbolism, (*bsdus bjod ring lugs, mtshon rtags ring lugs*). They often speak of their own poetry in the same breath as Western modernism characterized by movements such as Imagism (*yid brnyan ring lugs*), Dadaism (*ta ta ring lugs*), Surrealism (*dngos brgal ring lugs*), and Futurism (*'byung 'gyur ring lugs*).[37] With characteristic vagueness, they do not give much detail about the concrete influence of these creative schools on their poetry, nevertheless, frequent mentions of these movements and key modernist poets in their writings and their translations of poems like Eliot's *The Waste Land*, reveal an engagement with modernist poetry and its poetic image.[38]

There are several images in Kyabchen Dedrol's *The Third Generation* that present a visual description with psychic and emotional loads. The way these images are employed is representative of the way imagery is used more broadly in Third Generation poetry as a whole. They attempt to convey the Poundian "thing" of a poem through precise visual distillation. In other words, *The Third Generation* expresses its content through the images that constitute it. For instance, right at the very outset of the poem the image of *Bardo* is employed to convey a liminal state of consciousness between the old and new, a space the Third Generation self-consciously seeks to occupy in Tibetan literary history. The sense of newness and disorientation associated with a transitional stage is also evoked through the novel and raw metaphor of "consciousness" being "flayed like the skin." The violent and destructive images of "Six-Syllabled *Mani* wrapped in blood" and the "pulverized snow-plains and crystal-mountains" describe the historically unique environment into which the Third Generation were born. These are also allusions to the fall of the Tibetan nation which will be explored later. Images of "car horns" and "the spine of the city" tell us that the Third Generation poets reside and practice their poetry in a modern urbanized world, treating the malady of urban existence with moxibustion "along the spine of the city," "writing minute atom-like poetry" in an atomized urban landscape. The subversive, oppositional, and dystopian spirit of the Third Generation and their almost suicidal obsession with poetry is illustrated through the evocation of the "bolting tigress," the dystopian antithetical experience of the four seasons, and the evocation of suicidal tendencies, and the states of fever and delirium.

In his *A Defence of Poetry*, Shelley underlines the power of poetry to heighten intellectual sensibility and expose it to new dimensions. "Poetry lifts the veil from the hidden beauty of the world, and makes familiar objects be as if they were not familiar" he writes.[39] T. E. Hulme, one of the first imagist poets, locates this illuminating quality more particularly in the creation of new images with metaphor and epithet.[40] These are seen as essential for conveying the "original visual effect" of something that has come to be concealed by stale time-worn metaphors. Unusual images or unusual juxtapositions of such images are employed in Third Generation poetry to enable the reader to perceive the subject in a new light. In *The Third Generation*,

Kyabchen Dedrol resorts to the image of *bsang*, the purifying ritual of smoke and fire offering, to convey the intense passions, camaraderie, and collective aspirations associated with the writing of their poetry. Burning of *bsang* is likened to the "rage" felt by the Third Generation as they write poetry "all over the place," meaning their poetry is without borders or inhibition, and that no topic is impermissible. Instead of scattering wind-horses (*rlung rta*) into the air as the traditional custom demands, the Third Generation "fly poetry into the air of the meadow." A traditional ritual is thus used as an image for the practice of a new kind of impassioned poetry.[41] The intensity and "collective effervescence" of the *bsang* ritual fuse into the writing of a new collective poetry and vice versa.

Another fresh simile is the likening of the "primordially pristine natural reality" to a windblown "tattered street rag." In conventional Tibetan Buddhist literature, primordial natural reality or the primordial mind is often likened to the expanse of an immaculate sky or infinite space. For instance, Ju Mipham follows this metaphorical tradition when he writes:

For no Buddha has seen concretely
The innate nature of space-like mind
One should ponder how help and harm
Brought to it by things of joy and woe[42]

In an exquisite *mgur* verse penned while in prison, Gedun Choepel departs from this beaten path and comes up with a fresh metaphor for the space-like mind trapped within flesh:

This mind is an infinite Goddess
This world is no home for the Goddess
Yet a little toe of the Goddess of Mind
Is tied fast by a thread to this body.
So until this thread snaps off,
The mind feels whatever the body feels,
Whatever good or harm comes to this little toe
Accordingly the Goddess feels joy and woe.[43]

In this *mgur* Gedun Choepel reflects upon the never-ending trials and tribulations of life with suicidal undertones. Nevertheless, in the concluding stanza of the poem he decides to comply with "the Commandment of the Queen of the Ultimate Reality" and live for a few more years "on this earth."[44] Similarly Kyabchen Dedrol's "tattered street rag" evokes a profane, samsarically embedded mind that is concerned with the here and now. It is a new and non-ethereal image that stresses the mundane and urban aspect of contemporary Tibetan condition. Yet, it still respects mind's potential to gain nirvana as demonstrated by the merging of the ever soaring "down and hellos scattered of poetry" with "emptiness." This line also seems to draw a parallel between poetry and Buddhist enlightenment. A tendency for abstraction and obscurity in Kyabchen Dedrol's poem makes it hard to appreciate this image fully, but it shows that a fresh visual representation provides a different perspective to view an extremely complex Buddhist concept.

Recurrent themes of Tibetan Buddhist literature, like mind, death, and emptiness, are also favored by Third Generation poetry. Dhatsenpo both utilizes the traditional sky/space metaphor for mind as well as introduces new visual depictions of it. His long poem in regular verse *A Song Revealing the Nature of Mind* is about death, impermanence, uncertainty, futility, gain, and loss that characterize the human condition.[45] It is an example of literary continuity from the past. Both in terms of content and form it bears the influence of religious *mgur* and a category of Tibetan gnomic literature known as "the elegant sayings" (*legs bshad*). It also deliberately imitates the message, cadence, and style of *Kache Phalu* (*Kha che pha lu*), a lyrical and catchy aphoristic work containing practical advice on living.[46] In this introspective and contemplative poem Dhatsenpo describes the mind and natural reality as flow:

The worldly riches that appear to be existential
Analysis reveals them as mere mental phenomena
When it's time to abandon the tax burden of pus and blood
Look how the empty hand of mind is reduced to shivering[47]

In another stanza Dhatsenpo gives a misty portrayal of the nature of reality and mind:

The so-called profound reality is empty
If unknown it hides at the edge of space
If known it is a light aspect of the mind
Amidst the mist-like phenomenon[48]

Thus Third Generation poetry presents abstract imagery even when dealing with old themes and employing traditional metrical composition. Kyabchen Dedrol's and Dhatsenpo's poetic works consist of free verse compositions as well as experimentations with traditional poetic forms and content. Such conscious borrowings from the past perpetuate Tibetan literary and oral traditions. However, contemporary subject matter, novel imagery, and simpler diction with a high degree of abstraction and obscurity make their poetry also distinct and representative of a new age.

Like Western modernist poetry, many of the poems of the Third Generation can be difficult. Often they are characterized by elaborate abstraction, obscure idiom, a kind of syntactic disintegration, and seemingly random juxtapositions of images. The Third Generation seem to embrace the famous advice of T. S. Eliot to his contemporary modernists that they "must be *difficult*."[49] Eliot qualifies his suggestion by stating: "Our civilization comprehends great variety and complexity, and this variety and complexity, playing upon a refined sensibility, must produce various and complex results. The poets must become more and more comprehensive, more allusive, more indirect, in order to force, to dislocate if necessary, language into his meaning." Alongside features like allusiveness, and an absence of syntax and narrative, what makes Third Generation poetry hard to comprehend is their frequent use of abstract imagery. With similes of "shattered turquoise platter" and a sky filled with "dark smoke and clouds" Kyabchen Dedrol perpetuates the theme of destruction and violence that manifests right at the outset of *The Third Generation*. However, what is puzzling is the juxtaposition of these visual representations with the enigmatic image of a frightened, dust-covered man who is running away from something. He is followed by men and women bearing, respectively, wine cups and children. What is being suggested by this chaotic scene? I can only cautiously surmise that it might be an allusion to September 11, based on the fact that this scene coincides with the advent of "the twenty-first century" ushered in by the terrorist attacks on the World Trade Center in New York.

Kyabchen Dedrol's *The Third Generation* displays obscure aspects throughout that are illustrative of Third Generation poetry. However overall, this poem is very accessible compared to the highly abstruse poems written by his fellow Third Generation poets. For instance, in poems such as *Shadow*, *Torture*, *Whip*, and *Last Grassland*, Dongbu (Ldong bu; aka, Chakdor Gyal, Lcags rdor ryal) appears to tackle themes of death, time, knowledge and ignorance, suicide, urbanity, repression, and resistance.[50] All of them convey a mood and tone associated with death, loss, and violence. Yet like Anglo-American modernist poems[51] their disparate images, dislocated syntax, lack of formal punctuation, and discontinuity or total absence of narrative prevents any simple paraphrasing or summarization. Consider, for example, the following randomly selected excerpt from Dongbu's poem *Shadow*:

The sword of magic
Hanging myriad colors on the wall
Weapons and armor suddenly appear empty

Black and white robe plaited out of hair for hanging oneself
A bizarre blood guitar being strummed by a fingerless hand
A page that is turning from red to black
And from black to red again
Half a head flung to the wind
Singing a pathetic dirge, whispering

Roar of the instant deceived by trust
Liberated from the volume of mud, kneaded by hooves
The pigeon that casts backward glances at the gate of seasons[52]

The poem continues in this vein, piling image upon abstract image. The poem is a montage of disparate images, a jumble of elliptical sentences lumped together under a single title.[53] There is no fluidity but a jagged stream of inscrutability. One detects themes of violence, suicide, and death through the imagery of blood, noose, and skull. The skull singing in the wind is a typical motif for death and defeat in Tibetan oral literature. In the epic narrative of Gesar one finds frequent references to the upper part of the skull singing in the wind and the lower part consuming sand.[54] Apart from sketchy information such as this, Dongbu's poems and many of its kind by his fellow Third Generation poets defy easy interpretation. The omission of formal Tibetan punctuation marks such as *shad* and *tsheg*, made popular by Jangbu's poetry, makes such poems even more baffling. For example, the nonobservance of usual Tibetan punctuation or grammatical rules engenders an indeterminacy as to which subject hangs "myriad colors on the wall." It could be the magical sword or the "weapons and armors," one cannot be certain. Lhamkog defends this opacity of Third Generation poetry by arguing that imaginative poetry is demanding because it plays tricks on the mind of the reader. He argues that as such it requires a "heightened artistic sensibility" for its comprehension.[55] As he does not elaborate his point it is hard to work out what this sensibility entails and how it would help us make sense of obscure poems formed of an assemblage of incomprehensible images. However, this extreme visual abstraction only affects a relatively small percentage of Third Generation poetry. Otherwise it would be extremely difficult to detect predominant themes such as the Tibetan nation.

NATION WITHIN THE POETIC SOUL

When Pound and his fellow imagist poets laid down the three fundamental technical principles of clarity, conciseness, and musical rhythm, they first of all prescribed the "direct treatment of the 'thing,' whether subjective or objective."[56] As noted earlier, "the thing" is the very substance of poetry that constitutes the poetic image. It is not only what is communicated but is itself, at the same time, the form of communication. Hence Pound believed that one should only write free verse "when the 'thing' builds up a rhythm more beautiful than that of set meters."[57] This Poundian "thing" is somewhat reminiscent of what Tibetans call "the poetic soul" (*snyan ngag gi srog*).[58] This too is a loaded concept that defies clear-cut interpretation, as it can either mean the central message imparted by a poem or the overall effect and mood it conveys. While being mindful of this conceptual ambiguity, it can be understood as referring to the essence of poetry conveyed through the combined force of literary devices and the subject matter. "The poetic soul" is an ineffable quality that pervades an entire poem with the subject matter at its heart, whether factual, fictional, intellectual, or emotional. What is also inherent within this concept is the expression and excitement of emotions along with the power to attract the mind of the reader or the listener. If we try to consider the "poetic soul" of the Third Generation poetry—its compelling life-force—the Tibetan nation is fundamental to it.

Despite the Third Generation's rhetoric of transcending the language of "national pride" and "national characteristics," Tibet as a nation is one of the themes that runs through their poetry as inescapably as it does through the poetic works of their immediate predecessors and other contemporary poets. Their talk of diversification of poetic themes cannot ultimately conceal their preoccupation with the Tibetan nation. This is not to deny that their poetry has not introduced new themes or at least novel treatment of existing themes. Their tackling of subjective experiences concerning death, loneliness, boredom, alcohol, and sex is noteworthy at times. Nevertheless, the better part of their poetry is concerned with communicating their reflections on or feelings about Tibet. For instance, a majority of the collected poems in the three published anthologies of Third Generation writings is clearly infused with patriotic sentiments. The Tibetan nation, with its history, culture, and current plight, breathes through these poems. They are about loss of homeland, and about the violence, destruction, pain, anguish, and despondency associated with that loss. Nostalgia for Tibet's imperial past, concern with its cultural and linguistic identity, and an embattled desire for national survival feature saliently. Even poems whose central themes are romantic love, loneliness, or something as mundane as a hangover are suffused with sentiments of the nation. In Third Generation poetry, these themes are presented in a more indirect, suggestive, and allusive manner, relying heavily on the use of concentrated images. Although the Tibetan nation pervades their poems it is not mentioned in straightforward or explicit terms like "national pride" or "snow-lion." Thoughts and feelings about the nation are expressed through constructing precise visual representations or by reemploying old motifs such as Lhasa city and Potala Palace, scripted with new implications.

For a group of poets who are professedly preoccupied with the present, it is understandable that the predicament of Tibet is evident in their writings. Their present is to a great degree defined by their national plight. To borrow a phrase of Hulme's, this "inevitableness" of Tibet in poetry can be demonstrated even in a manifesto poem like *The Third Generation*.[59] Kyabchen Dedrol's confrontational poem opens with a graphic description of Tibet in the mid-twentieth century. The Third Generation are depicted as inextricably linked to this blood-soaked, transitional, *Bardo*-like period of Tibetan history.[60] The famous mantra *Om ma ni padme hum*, recited throughout Tibet for hundreds of years, is "wrapped in blood." This national mantra is like an ancient national anthem condensed into just six syllables that effortlessly rolls off the tongues of both the young and old. It is an exclusive mantra for Tibetans to devote themselves to Avalokiteśvara (Spyan ras gzigs), Bodhisattva of Compassion, and the national deity of Tibet. Popular Tibetan parlance has it: "The six-syllabled *Mani* is the chosen Dharma of Tibet / The Lotus Holder is the chosen Deity of Tibet."[61] Its long history, sacredness, and popularity mean that it serves as a powerful national bond. Here, Kyabchen Dedrol exploits the historical and religious associations of the six-syllable mantra and gives it a violent injection of contemporary politico-historical morbidity. *Mani*—a conventional prayer for the dead or for the invocation of the Tibetan national deity—is here "wrapped in blood." This blood-soaked *Mani* acts as a distilled and potent image for the modern-day Sino-Tibetan encounter, and is still being sacrificed in Tibet along with "father's tears" and "mother's sweat." The poetry of Third Generation writers is written under the shadow of this blood-drenched *Mani* and among "the ruins of pulverised snow-plains and crystal-mountains" of Tibet.

Many of Kyabchen Dedrol's other poems also touch on Tibet with varying imagistic subtlety. This can be demonstrated by one particular poem, which functions as a kind of review of his entire poetic output. In it Tibetan history, past and present, takes center stage. The poem is narrated in the form of a play, in which the very act of narration is a dangerous undertaking, threatening life and limb:

To Take Me and My Poetry as an Example
I have built a great theatre
Have joined the stones with glass panes
Have lit the stars for lighting
The actors will come, tripping, but picking themselves up.
When some of them faint and do not come around
The MC will wet their faces with a few droplets of water.
First Act is called Birth of the Himalayas
Second Act is called Dynasties of Imperial Tibet
Third Act is called the Maw of the Machines
When a flower turns into a cannon
And a roar fills the sky,
It is the start of the Fourth Act.
The Himalayas, born of water
Will melt and turn back to water
The River Ganges will dry up, and Indians will flee in every direction.

And then
The theatre itself will also catch fire.
And me, I might be treated as a criminal and bound up with a chain.
I won't say "To be, or not to be" like Prince Hamlet
But, as I resolutely say that I want to live
The heat of my body
Will burn up the iron chain.

At that time the long shadow that stretches out
Into the distance on my right, will clap loudly,
The only remaining spectator.[62]

Historical reality shapes Kyabchen Dedrol's subjectivity. In this poem he intimates that his poetry is about the birth, rise, fall, and disappearance of Tibet. But it is also about survival and setting oneself free through the art of poetry. A historical identity of Tibet is constructed on a geological time scale by tracing the formation of Tibet to "the birth of the Himalayas" that resulted from the impact of the Indian Plate against the Eurasian continent about forty million years ago.[63] Another reference to this geological event is made by the phrase the "Himalayas, born of water." This phrase is also an allusion to legends found in Tibetan historical sources which say that primordial Tibet was either totally underwater or a fertile wetland dotted with lakes and crisscrossed with rivers.[64] The Second Act on the cherished Tibetan Empire is followed by the Third Act that records the violent fall of Tibet in the modern age of "machines." The current Tibetan situation, narrated through the roar of a cannon, signals Act Four, which depicts the dissolution of Tibet back into water in the age of global warming. The transformation of a flower into a cannon, that announces this last act, appears to be an inversion of the moment in the Buddha Śākyamuni's life story when he conquers Māra and attains enlightenment. In this often-told episode when Māra and his minions deploy their weapons including cannonballs (*sgyogs rdo*) at Siddhārtha (Tib. Don grub), he transforms them into flowers. In the poem Tibetan civilization steeped in the elightened teachings of the Lord Buddha falls prey to the modern cannon.

The use of the theater as a metaphor for life bears both Shakespearean and Tibetan Buddhist literary influences. In *Hamlet*, which the poem cites, life and play are imitations of one another, as evident in Shakespeare's use of the dramatic device of a "play within a play." This is not to mention other famous Shakespearean reflections on life as a play, some of which Kyabchen Dedrol spoke of admiringly when we had a long conversation on modern Tibetan literature in February 2011 in Labrang.[65] In Tibetan Buddhist literature life is often an illusory performance or likened to a magician's show. Indeed, the Buddha's illusory display of his body in a variety of forms (*sprul sku, nirmāṇakāya*) is also likened to a play or theatrical performance. In Ju

Mipham's excellent *Musical Play of Illusion* (*Glu bro rgyu ma'i rol mo*) which, by his own admission, had a lasting impact on Kyabchen Dedrol, life is often compared to a dance and a musical performance. This is illustrated by the following two stanzas from a song by the Great Sage who approaches some young performers lost in a show of dance, song, and music:

Oh! Busily engrossed in casting mutual glances
Here you enjoy like a peahen beholding clouds.[66]
Though residing near the jaws of fear and Death
Unsuspicious, you revel in song and dances.

The constantly changing nature of the dance play
Shows an example to the human heart,
Yet not knowing it, you still watch the dance play.
Don't you think that life is just like a dance play?[67]

Similarly, in Kyabchen Dedrol's poem, a play analogy is used to capture the insubstantiality, illusoriness, and impermanence of life. Yet within the poem one cannot detect any sense of resignation or despondency. It prophesies the eventual dissolution of Tibet just like any other phenomenon, like the River Ganges or the theater of poetry itself. However, Kyabchen Dedrol displays a steely resolution to live, and to live till the last moment and narrate Tibetan history through his poetry. The poet's personal zeal for life is intermeshed with his narrative of national survival and destruction. This harkens back to the old Tibetan notion of history as a fundamental constituent of both personal and collective identity. An oft-cited passage in Tibetan histories taken from the great Tibetan clan record of the *Rlangs* family (*Rlangs kyi po ti bse ru*) stresses this importance of historical consciousness. Before elaborating on the lineage of *Rlangs* it states: "A person who does not know his racial origins, is like a monkey in the forest; a person who does not know his familial lineage, is like a fake turquoise dragon; a person who does not know his ancestral nobility and archives, is like a lost boy from Mon."[68]

PILGRIMAGE THROUGH HISTORY TO LHASA

There is a prominent tendency in the poetry of the Third Generation to put the current predicament of Tibet within the context of its long history. Tibet is presented as a historical continuity with a glorious imperial past and a precarious repressive present. This point, along with the Third Generation's fixation with the Tibetan nation, can also be demonstrated by a brief analysis of a poem by Dhatsenpo, one of the most acclaimed poets of the movement. Dhatsenpo's *Tale of a Pilgrimage to U* (*Dbus la song ba'i sgrung*) is a long

free verse narrative poem about a pilgrimage to the sacred city of Lhasa.[69] It is
a journey that starts with hope, pride, devotion, and eagerness, and ends with
a disillusioned return from a tyrannized and disappearing Lhasa. The sheer
length, the rich figuration, the abstract phrases, and the tone of the poem defy
any easy paraphrasing. Nevertheless a summary of its narrative and imagery
is attempted here with a supplement of translated excerpts. A motley group of
pilgrims including the poet travel through the wilderness of Tibet. "This long
path to U"[70] is strewn with memories of Tibetan history from the imperial
past to Tibet's twilight in the bloody encounter with Communist China and
subsequent dark night-like times. They set off with great optimism, burning
purifying smoke and incense offering (*bsang*) that "blazes hotter than the life
itself," while cherishing their destination, Lhasa, within their bosoms like "lit
butterlamps." With great determination "these pilgrims to U" (*dbus ba*) make
their way to the holy city crossing "wound-like deep ravines" and fording rivers that gush out like blood from "extreme terrors of warfare and massacre."
The recent violent history of Tibet leaves no place unspoiled along the way
to Lhasa and it is what remains of the Tibetan imperial past:

During the time of warrior-kings
For the conquest of frontiers and lands beyond[71]
Strategies and weaponry transported along this path
Gar spread out the lifeblood of half his life[72]
At this site like sunshine, warm and brilliant

Now—apart from the pilgrims to U
Who are crawling along the black spine of dusk
No poem formed of perfect historical syllables can be seen
Even less—no pristine pastures can be found
That have not been splattered with the warm blood of men and wild beasts
Even if they were to be washed by ten thousand rivers[73]

The poet's reflections upon the distant Tibetan empire, the erosion of its
legacy, and Tibet's tragic recent history make him compare "the path to U"
to a wilderness. A wilderness where "everything is taken away by the bandit
of history" and where one cannot even find "the bones of the dead truth."
However, pilgrims continue their journey with pride and great ambition
along this path that is likened to "a ruined fortress of history." At this point
in the narration, night sets in, both during the pilgrimage, and allegorically
in Tibetan history. It is a night of death, pain, disappearances, crime, massacres, and lonely endurance. On this "night of shackles wrought of suffering
and solitude" the poet collects "the scattered blood of heroes" and calls upon
his beloved brothers to search for something that "burns like fire within the
heart/ and glistens like tears in the depth of blood and truth."[74] The image of

night and the quest sharpen into focus as the poem and pilgrims relentlessly proceed toward Lhasa:

From the wound of history
For long has wept nights and warm blood
Many shivering words
For long have also throttled me

Siblings—like words
That make my life force
And love-flames burn

Journeying along this path to U
That burns with more vitality than one's own veins

We must search for the lakes of vowels
Where swirls land's love
And the quivering snow-mountains of consonants
For storing words from the bosom

We must also search for the heavy load on the back of all lives
That's as sad as tears[75]

After this contemplation upon the night-like Tibetan present and welding of Tibet and Tibetan language, the pilgrims make it to Lhasa. Lhasa turns out to be a city of betrayals, fear, pretense, alcohol, distrust, love, and industrial construction:

For the truth of time
And tear-like flame of life

We've come to U
Like returning home from prison

After the heroic legend
"Lhasa of the victimized—Lhasa of betrayal
Lhasa of terror and suspicion"
Lhasa of drizzling alcohol and love

Oh—Lhasa that is
"Shivering
Ostentatious
Putrefying amid a few explanations"
Swaggering at the heart of a cemetery
Made of concrete[76]

In such a Lhasa, no trace of its imperial glory is found. It is hard to tell if the Potala Palace is an "empty bosom kneeling before some person" or "the

hardened suffering and exhaustion of a thousand year-old lone boulder."
Terror, murder, and machination crowd every nook and cranny of Lhasa,
as the poet roams its "wound-like streets" by night. Behind the night lurks
a killer that targets all the city's vital parts. The poet's beloved Lhasa is
unrecognizable. It is lost amid many languages and machines, a cacophony
of noise and bustle. Like a droplet of water, Lhasa is said to be losing itself
in "the hardness of concrete." Lhasa is transformed, a city under siege, and it
is dying and disappearing:

In reality—Lhasa is half a night
The initial essence of beauty
That has been burnt by electric light

In reality—Lhasa is a beloved corpse to me
Still out there
Because no-one can afford a coffin

When I think of Lhasa
More wrinkled with age than I myself

I want to lash with a whip
Those rocks of Lhasa devoid of groans and tears
And I want to burn this weak and powerless self
In the blood-drop like flames
That haven't ceased blazing in the depth of Lhasa's black earth

Oh—Lhasa that has seeped and is seeping
Through the crevices of loss[77]

Then the poem suddenly shifts register and adopts a Buddhist metaphysical
tone under the telling subtitle "*Mgur* of a Yogi." There is an urge to renounce
the self, which is driven by attraction and repulsion, and to embrace instead
an altruistic love that could provide imperishable warmth even to inanimate
objects like "earth, rock and mountains." With the refrain "my distant self,"
the poet calls upon a self that is beyond worldly egotism, to grant him love
and wisdom endowed with magnanimity and equilibrium. After ruminating
conflictual relations of "self and other," a realization sets in. It reveals that
deceptive "riches of existence" and "sufferings of samsara" "dissolve into a
seemingly non-existent realm of phenomena."[78] This abstract reflection upon
self continues in the concluding part of the poem titled "Return." When the
poet comes back home he seems to return from a distant self:

In reality
Like returning home from the darkness of cold winter
We have no place to go
Nor place to which we can return

In reality
When we've soaked disease-demon-like selves
With tears of woe
After wandering the great cemetery of the mind

Haven't we gone there
And come back?

Especially as for me
When some words, resembling broken fragments of history
Press heavily upon my chest

I've no choice but to go away
From this corpse-like wilderness

Come to think again
Where would I go without
Returning into this mother's tear-like suffering

Oh—My distant self[79]

Just as Kyabchen Dedrol appropriates the *Mani* mantra as a distilled image for modern Tibet, Dhatsenpo uses an age-old Tibetan religious custom to comment on Tibet's current situation within the context of its history, and to engage in introspective musing on nation and self. The traditional Tibetan practice of Buddhist pilgrimage links different places and people through both individual and collective spiritual quest. Pilgrimage is a spatial and psychic journey as it entails a person or persons' physical travel through specific territorial space accompanied by deep religious devotion and meditative absorption. It is also a form of territorial marking in that pilgrims reaffirm their relationship with their land and religion through rigorous mental and physical activities. For Tibetans it is a powerful means by which to lay claim to Tibet and other territories.[80] In their endeavor to accumulate karmic merits (*dge ba'i las*), attain enlightenment, and receive divine favors, Tibetans from all walks of life travel from one sacred place to another. These sacred sites range from monasteries, hermitages, and mountains to cemeteries, lakes, and rivers.[81] It is believed that these are places imbued with spiritual power because of their sacred geomancy as well as their intimate association with deities, Tibetan legendary figures, Buddhas, great Indian and Tibetan masters, yogis, scholars, and ascetics. Each and every one of them works as a sacred nodal point for bringing together Tibetans from all over Tibet in body and mind. In particular, great pilgrimage sites like Mount Kailash, Tsari, and historic monastic seats of learning function as national hubs for providing socio-spiritual cohesion to the Tibetan nation.[82] Observing this nationally cohesive function of Tibetan pilgrimage in the past, Kapstein speaks of the existence of a "national pilgrimage network, whose routes, extending throughout the length and breadth of geographic and cultural Tibet, helped to maintain communications among even the most far-flung districts."[83] Although Kapstein writes in the past tense this network is still very much alive today. Pilgrimage to Lhasa via "the long path to U" celebrated in Dhatsenpo's poem remains a central part of Tibet's "national pilgrimage network."

Dhatsenpo wrote this long poem after his own pilgrimage to Lhasa with his mother and some of his tribal people. By using it as a cohesive image and a narrative device, he furnishes the term pilgrimage with new senses while also keeping its conventional religious connotation. To put it in another way, Dhatsenpo's *Tale of a Pilgrimage to U* keeps a Tibetan tradition alive in two ways. The notion and practice of pilgrimage is preserved as a living spiritual practice entailing the body and mind of the poet himself, while also being used as a novel narrative image for the depiction of past and present Tibetan histories. There are at least two pilgrimages taking place simultaneously: a pilgrimage to Lhasa traveling through the vast and varied terrains of Tibet, and a journey through Tibetan history that ends with Tibet's precarious existence in the present symbolized by Lhasa disappearing in "concrete" and slipping through "crevices of loss." In the conventional sense, the poet and his fellow pilgrims begin their sacred journey in the traditional fashion with the burning of a purifying smoke and incense offering. In many Tibetan nomadic communities like the one alluded to in Dhatsenpo's poem, it is customary to commence a long journey or an important task with the offering of *bsang*. The pilgrims set forth on foot like in the old days, and traverse the "countless passes and plains" of Tibet. They make their way to Lhasa through the vast landscape of Tibet step by step, welcoming each evening with the ritual "flames of *bsang*." In parallel to this journey through the physical space of Tibet run memories of Tibetan history. This historical voyage begins with the imperial past when military "strategies and weaponry" and the great minister Gar traveled via "the path to U." Then centuries of Tibetan history are skipped over in an instant. The Tibetan imperial past, captured by images of "vajra-like ancestors" and "ancient heroes and scholars" immediately gives way to a bloody modern history and dark present. In the immense land of Tibet "no pristine pastures" left unstained by blood can be found. Night has set in, cloaking a killer in its darkness as the Tibetan capital almost buckles under fear, violence, and death.

There might also be a further kind of pilgrimage taking place within the poet, as suggested by the phrase "wandering the cemetery of the mind"—an inner pilgrimage. Here Buddhist notions are used to talk about a subjugated Tibetan nation in decline. Their conceptual complexity and obscurity make them ideal communicative vehicles for circumventing state censorship. The journey to Lhasa through Tibetan history abruptly ends with Buddhist philosophical ponderings on the nature of self. The pilgrimage to Lhasa proves to be a mental journey of self-discovery in which the individual self and the nation are codependent and coterminous. It makes the poet abandon an egocentric self and embrace a "distant self" that rises above the conflictual interests of "self and other." The poet aspires for an impartial and altruistic love that invokes Bodhisattava principles, thus enriching the poem with a nirvanic feel. However, at a more mundane level this might represent patriotic emotions that connect the individual to the religious and civilizational community of the Tibetan nation. It is the recent destructive history of Tibet, "broken fragments of history," which prompts the poet to transcend an egoistic self and reach the "distant self," a collective identity, immersed in historical consciousness and public-spiritedness. In all three dimensions, pilgrimage in Dhatsenpo's poem touches the Tibetan nation by fusing territory, history, religion, and subjective consciousness and is woven into the poetic narrative. Like Kyabchen Dedrol's *To Use Me and My Poetry as an Example* and other Third Generation poems, Dhatsenpo finds poetry crafted from the written Tibetan language indispensable for the narration of Tibetan history and reassertion of Tibetan identity.

MERGING LANGUAGE AND NATION

As we have seen in the speech that launched the Third Generation of Tibetan Poets as a group, Kyabchen Dedrol emphatically declares: "If I cannot make it across this great plain of concrete, I will not force myself to talk about distant snow-mountains and black yak-hair tents just to please you."[84] However, Dhatsenpo finds that one *can* write about contemporary Tibetan urban existence (concrete Lhasa) and snow-mountains at the same time, as they are equally emblematic of Tibet. In *Tale of a Pilgrimage to U*, Dhatsenpo uses the imagery of snow-mountains, retaining their traditional symbolic meanings, while also injecting fresh nuances. For him, snow-mountains signify Tibet just as they do in the prevalent phrase *Bod gangs ri ra bas skor ba'i zhing khams* (Tibet—The realm encircled by snow-mountains), but they also denote written Tibetan poetry. These two senses sometimes coalesce into one. Thus in Dhatsenpo's pilgrimage poem, Tibet's lakes represent Tibetan "vowels" and snow-mountains "consonants" that must be navigated and traversed in order to write poetry, which is itself Tibet. Snow-mountains then become both Tibet and poetry when Dhatsenpo writes:

With the flames within my bosom
I am lighting a shivering poem called snow-mountains
That tower at the cliff edge of the end of time[85]

This concern for Tibetan language, and even the identification of Tibet with the Tibetan alphabet, are common themes in Third Generation poetry.

In fact Third Generation poets declare with youthful energy that their move-ment upholds the "beauty of (Tibetan) consonants and vowels."[86] A similar sentiment is expressed on the first Tibetan literary website that promotes Third Generation poetry, *Butter-lamp*. On its homepage, a slogan at the top announces: "The undying butter-lamp: the beauty of thirty-four consonants and vowels."[87] Writing poetry in Tibetan is seen as both an expression of and a protection of Tibetan identity. Thus Mogru Sherab Dorje urges Tibetans to capture joys and woes of life in Tibetan language poetry in his *Looking for the Barmaid of Beauty*:

The barmaid is faraway
Is the winter still far off?
If one happens to be a person attached to homeland
Write a poem of thirty-four consonants and vowels
Life of shining light
Life of darkness
Whether eating a mouthful of tsampa
Or downing a gulp of liquor
Countless wounds are within the mind[88]

Like the Tibetan staple (as in the phrase "the black-headed tsampa-eaters"[89]), the written Tibetan language constitutes Tibetan identity. It also enables the poet to express his inner suffering concerning his wounded "homeland." A similar anxiety over Tibetan language and nation can be found in a poem by Kuchug Ngonmo (Khu byug sngon mo—Blue Cuckoo) entitled *Red Tear*. In it he asks:

Amid yesterday's betrayals
When those individuals carrying thirty-four consonants and vowels
Marched into the distance, gazing at light
Who felled them, one by one?[90]

In response, a portrait of Dhondup Gyal hanging on the poet's wall sheds "a red tear." This apprehension about the written Tibetan language is born of modern Tibetan experience under Chinese rule. Prior to the encounter with Communist China the survival of Tibetan language both written and spoken was taken for granted. When Tibetans took up armed resistance against the approaching Chinese army in the 1950s they fought for "Tibetan Dharma and political welfare" (*bod bstan ba chab srid*) or "native territory" (*rang sa rang yul*).[91] They did not speak in the idiom of linguistic freedom or rights as they do now. That was because Tibetans were yet to encounter the Cultural Revolution which nearly wiped out written Tibetan language and subsequent state language policies that have imposed restrictions.

Destruction of monasteries and scriptures which commenced in the 1950s reached a catastrophic culmination during the Cultural Revolution. During this tumultuous period, the teaching of Tibetan language was prohibited and even certain Tibetan phrases or letters were subjected to "struggle sessions" because they were deemed conservative or too religious.[92] During the 1980s there was a halfhearted adoption of Tibetan as a language of instruction in some schools by the Chinese state, especially in Amdo thanks to the endeavors of high-profile Tibetan figures and scholars.[93] However, the 1990s and the new millennium saw restrictions imposed on Tibetan language especially as a medium of instruction, and this unleashed unprecedented, large-scale language protests in Northeastern Tibet.[94] Alongside the cries for "Tibetan Freedom" and "the Return of the Dalai Lama" one of the most repeated demands of the Tibetan self-immolators is the call for language protection and language freedom.[95] The preoccupation with written Tibetan language in Third Generation poetry should be understood within this politico-historical context. It is concrete realities on the ground that inform contemporary Tibetan poetry and these realities are those faced daily by Tibetans living in the PRC.

The above poems by Dhatsenpo and Kyabchen Dedrol are only two samples from Third Generation poetry that revolve around the fate of the Tibetan nation. But poetic compositions of this kind are too numerous even to list here, let alone to comment upon them. It will suffice here to mention briefly a few noteworthy poems that typify this Third Generation obsession with the loss of Tibet and the current suffering of Tibetans. In *Four Different Poems Composed When Feeling Empty,* Jan Chelbar (Gcan ched 'bar) writes of a disappearing Tibet, forced silences, unspoken and unmourned deaths. The loss of homeland is likened to the owner of a hotel becoming its guest and renting a room. The Tibetan present is captured by images of the Amdo sky and earth that resemble coffins.[96] The poet Melong (Me long—Mirror), finds respite from loneliness and "countless pains" in his poem *Tonight I'm Alone Before the Potala.* On a still, deserted night amid historical memories, the speaker in the poem guards the Potala with his thought, his demands, his pen, his song, and his dreams.[97]

In *September and Incidental Poems* by Drongdrug ('Brong phrug—Wild-Yak Calf) the colors of Potala and the flag on its roof are drenched in the "red tears of the snow-mountain" that "surge out of the poet's heart." Such allusions to bloodshed in Tibet are accompanied by descriptions of fallen horsemen, lost grasslands, tattered mountains, a frail, aged wild yak, and half-recollected legends. The welfare of the individual and that of the collective fuse into one as the poet directly links the loss of his wife's smile to the plight of contemporary Tibet. The latter is distilled into the narrative of "a year of hardship spent in sorrow and exhaustion,"[98] an allusion to the

Tibet-wide 2008 protests and their aftermath. Unfathomable anguish deriving from the current situation in Tibet also saturates Drongdrug's other poems like *Homeland: Da Family* and *Speechless Snow-mountain.* In these poems a fallen Tibet is portrayed along with its silenced mountains, lakes, and poets, and images of Tibetan modernity cast in rapid urban and industrial developments assail the wild grasslands.[99]

Rekanglang's *This Current Life* and *Flower of Blood Presented by the Great Father* are haunted by the imminent death of the Tibetan nation. They allude to the arrival of Chinese Communists in terms like "barbarity and perversion" and "massacre and robbery." Ongoing dire conditions are evoked in the imagery of "starved snow-mountains turning to skeletons" that rattle in the wind. A despondent tone is commingled with a zeal for life and calls for national re-assertion and reawakening. The poet beseeches Tibetans to wear their father's gift, "flower of blood," on their chests and wrest back "the erased map of suffering on our foreheads"[100] and "the reproductive organ removed from our loins."[101] Similar aspirations are also apparent in a prose poem called *Golden Home* by Sakyil Tseta. It sings of a free, independent past, paints a present fraught with loss, deception, and agony, and eagerly awaits the return of a Great Goddess who would revitalize the "golden home."[102]

Tibet dominates many of Kuchug Ngonmo's poems including one with as unremarkable a subject as a hangover. In his *After Waking up (Cluster of Poems),* a personal feeling of emptiness following a night of heavy drinking is seen as an analogous to the emptying of the Potala Palace. Prolonged contemplation on the fall and disappearance of Tibet brings on a sense of losing oneself. The fall and subjugation of Tibet is equated to the psychological loss of the individual self. Thus the poet broods over the seizure of his gun, horse, and wife against the national backdrop of the stolen soul turquoise and the fallen flag.[103] In *My Tibet* Khuchug Nonmo celebrates Tibet's imperial past that still inspires contemporary Tibetans while bemoaning a modern Tibet plagued by internecine fighting, disunity, lack of progress, inactivity, and want of patriotism. The very structure of the poem breathes out Tibet as it is punctuated by and wrapped in the six syllables of *Om ma ni padme hum.* A central motif in the poem is Lhasa that still attracts devout pilgrims from afar, but amid "the flashes and clicks of cameras," has changed beyond recognition. It is not "yesterday's Lhasa smelling of butter and tsampa" but a Lhasa in dusk that engenders disillusionment in those Tibetans who flock to it with such devotion and anticipation.[104] Thus even a brief survey of some of the works by just six poets is adequate to demonstrate that Tibet is a salient subject matter in Third Generation poetry, with its capital Lhasa serving as a recurrent motif for the sense of self and the nation.

THE LHASA OF TIBETAN MODERNITY

Lhasa, as a beloved, sacred city and the celebrated capital of Tibet, has long served as a poetic theme in Tibetan artistic creations ranging from classical poetry to popular song. However, Lhasa as a precise visual representation of repression, bloodshed, and betrayal, standing for the modern fate of Tibet, is a new literary phenomenon.[105] Its genesis can be traced back to the poetry of Jangbu. Rekanglang maintains that the Third Generation poets have blazed a new literary path by making Lhasa a focal point of their poetry because "it brings out the aesthetic characteristics of the Tibetan people." Moreover, in Baudelairean terms he says it enables one to capture a "disoriented disposition" generated by the unique situation of Tibetan life and "depression and a sense of hollowness."[106] He continues that these poets express the happiness and suffering of Lhasa people, "the wound of loneliness" felt by Potala, the life-threatening terror of "the great concrete plains and the train's roar" and the influx of Chinese immigrants. However, he makes no mention of Jangbu. In Rekanglang's failure to acknowledge Jangbu we might detect a repressed "anxiety of influence." Although there are a number of noteworthy Third Generation poems featuring the Tibetan capital, Jangbu's poem *Lhasa* seems to be the trendsetter in this genre. Even though only a few Third Generation poets openly concede his influence it is clear that Jangbu's poetry serves as a model for many of them.[107]

Jangbu's economy of diction, deceptive linguistic simplicity, abstraction, suggestiveness, use of fresh images and metaphors, and an ever-present concern with the fate of contemporary Tibet are imitated or developed further in Third Generation poetry. Jangbu's novel portrayal of Lhasa as a modern place of intrigue and political manipulation shows his influence on Third Generation poetry. In the development of this motif we can also detect an undeclared yet conscious attempt by contemporary Tibetan poets to turn Lhasa into a motif of Tibetan modernity just as nineteenth-century Paris encapsulated a modernizing France for Charles Baudelaire. The theme of the city is nothing new in the Tibetan poetic tradition. *Kāvya* poetics recommends the city as a principal subject matter, but in *kāvya* tradition urban life represents glory, wonder, luxuriant riches, and ornate beauty.[108] Many modern Tibetan poets subvert this *kāvyic* city and express admiration for Baudelaire, who registers "the experience of shock" effected by the social alienation and sordid life of a Paris undergoing radical transformation.[109]

On several occasions Jangbu acknowledged, in conversation with me, his debt to Baudelaire and other French symbolists for their innovative use of imagery, philosophical self-reflection, and acute modern consciousness, especially regarding urban life.[110] My conversations with the likes of Dhatsenpo and Kyabchen Dedrol and my reading of the literature on the

Third Generation both reveal that Baudelaire is one of the most admired and frequently cited Western poets.[111] Needless to say Baudelaire and symbolists are not singular in influencing contemporary Tibetan poets, whose writings display intellectual debt to other great Western and Latin American poets such as T. S. Eliot, Ezra Pound, Dylan Thomas, Octavio Paz, Jorge Luis Borges, Pablo Neruda, D. H. Lawrence, and William Carlos Williams.[112] Following Baudelaire, Tibetan poets like Jangbu endeavor to depict Lhasa in a new light that would communicate contemporary Tibetan experience inside Tibet. They attempt to convey "the shock of the new" that constitute this experience through dark portrayals of the city. Baudelaire's city poems and these new Tibetan poems on Lhasa are alike in their treatment of the shock experience of modernity. However, while Baudelaire's concern is a modernizing colonial capital (a post-1848, Haussmann-era Paris of urban renewal and commodity fetishism) the shock of Lhasa is of a colonized city, undergoing unprecedented socioeconomic changes.

On the eve of the new millennium, Jangbu records the grim reality inside Tibet through the depiction of the stifling atmosphere of the Tibetan capital. In his poem *Lhasa* one senses a seemingly inexorable aggravation of an already brutal and decadent situation. As a ring of "entertaining taverns" (*nang ma*) forms a tightening noose around Lhasa, the poet feels the need to escape from a nightmarish world of violence, subjugation, and deception under a foreign power:

Lhasa
Behind the darkness
Assassinations and shivers
Among the crowd
Suspicion and the victimized
Putrefying amidst
Ostentatious explanations
Odors of sex, blood, wine
Tattered cloth of each night
Tacked with patches of Sichuan Restaurants
At the eve of a century
The circle of entertaining taverns completes
Where is the exit door?
The field of gargantuan poppies[113]

The Tibetan capital is characterized by violence, fear, secrecy, treachery, and debauchery. No trace of its famous spiritual aura, historical legacies, and natural and architectural beauty are found among the alcohol and drug-induced illusions. As the holy capital begins to fall apart, an alien power tightens its stranglehold through both coercive and deceptive means. The influx of

Chinese immigrants, epitomized by "Sichuan Restaurants," are patches on the tattered Tibetan body. The ever-increasing number of "entertaining taverns" distract and dull the Tibetan spirit and furnish it with a false sense of content-ment. Thus it seems a killer blow has been struck. The overall pessimistic tone of the poem changes when one deciphers a nuanced spirit of resistance. Jangbu's poet is neither cowed by intimidations and treacheries, nor deceived by overblown, ideological explanations and material inducements. The astute poet decides to look for the "exit door." This is the depiction of Lhasa that resurfaces in many of the poems penned by the Third Generation, be it at times in subtler guises.

As can be seen in the excerpts from *Tale of a Pilgrimage to U* it has several passages on Lhasa that more than echo Jangbu's portrayal of the holy city in terms of graphic imagery, simple language, and gloomy yet recalcitrant tone. In fact, Dhatsenpo acknowledges his debt by inserting borrowed phrases from Jangbu's poem in quotation marks. They are not verbatim citations but near verbatim reproductions of Jangbu's lines where the Tibetan capital is painted as "victimized," "shivering," "ostentatious," and "putrefying amid a few explanations." Dhatsenpo also imitates Jangbu's memorable use of olfactory sense to describe a decadent Lhasa, when he writes:

Odors of sex, blood, wine
Odors of Lhasa
Putrefying in the nostrils of the wind

Without killing myself
I find it hard to cross over the dried, rotten streets of Lhasa[114]

Yet for Dhatsenpo Lhasa is still a beloved city with the potential to inspire Tibetans because its "black earth" retains both recent historical memories and hope that resemble "blood-drop like flames." Acutely conscious of the importance of literary tradition on good poets, Eliot propounds a theory of indebtedness to other authors when he writes: "Immature poets imitate; mature poets steal; bad poets deface what they take, and good poets make it into something better, or at least something different."[115] Dhatsenpo's bor-rowings neither deface Jangbu's *Lhasa* nor efface his own unique, lyrical style that seamlessly weaves his lines with images, ideas and phrases from Jangbu or other poetic traditions.

We find Jangbu's *Lhasa* resurfacing in less obvious ways in other Third Generation poems. In Markhu Gyaltsen's free verse poem (Mar khu rgyal mtshan) *Grandma and Distant Lhasa,* the sacred Tibetan capital is distant from his grandmother on two levels.[116] First it is remote from her in terms of geographical space, and second, her imagined Lhasa as a city of gods (*lha sa*) is a far cry from contemporary Lhasa, which is also a residence for ghosts.

The speaker attempts to impart this knowledge of a transformed Lhasa through the Tibetan saying "wherever abound gods also abound ghosts"[117] but he could not sway his grandmother's conviction. Kyabchen Dedrol's *Let's Go to Lhasa* sketches an occupied Tibetan capital of pollution, decadence and Chinese counterfeit products.[118] On his journey, rather than being crippled by fear and despair in the face of military occupation—"Jowo's face under the gun"—the speaker finds strength and courage to go on in poetry—"Syllable *Ah* on the tip of the sword." Here Jowo refers to the holiest Buddha image in Tibet—Jowo Sakyamuni. The sacred syllable *Ah* (regarded as the essence of all mantras and the soul of all letters) adorns the sword tip of Manjushri, god of wisdom and poetry. Although he has been "robbed of everything" the speaker is adamant to make it to Lhasa with his "naked consciousness" so as, among other things, to speak "beer-guzzled Tibetan-like poetry." In his highly abstruse poem *Lhasa,* Rekanglang depicts the ancient Tibetan capital as devoid of beauty, courage, spiritual aura, or freedom. The Potala itself is an image of defeat and despondency in a desecrated Lhasa where the local Tibetan brew (*chang*) has been overtaken by mass-produced beer.[119] As already pointed out with the Eliotian notion of indebtedness, such imitations do not undermine the quality and distinctiveness of Third Generation poetry. Nor do they limit the subject matter.

TACKLING TABOO THEMES

Although the Tibetan nation in its many manifestations—history, language, and contemporary situation—permeates Third Generation poetry, its content is not confined within these themes. With their boisterous, oppositional attitude the Third Generation poets have brought dormant and subversive themes to prominence and have introduced new subject matter with their novel use of vulgarity. This is conspicuous in their embrace of sexual themes and their introduction of words and phrases hitherto deemed inappropriate for formal poetic composition. While admirers and detractors disagree regarding its literary merit, all concur that their poetry has exposed taboo themes and idioms. Kyabchen Dedrol pays tribute to this type of unorthodoxy when he announces on the behalf of Third Generation: "Everywhere we are puking out bloody words like 'prostitute,' 'widow,' 'coffin,' and 'ghost lice.'[120] And we are also beholding 'the realm of bliss,' 'the great mother,' and 'sky' through this forest of dirty, sludgy words."[121] In similar fashion Rekanglang salutes the use of such taboo terms, stating that through them, Third Generation writers bring to attention "the perversions of darkness and life of the lowly." It is seen as a bold endeavor to depict "the real experience of the lowly and the absurd."[122]

Tibetan critics like Lhamkog and Thoring (Tho rengs—Dawn) also praise the use of mold-breaking words like "genitals," "sex," "sperm and blood," "insects and flies" on the grounds that such themes are a close observation of real life and have the capacity to discomfit as well as attract readers.[123] For detractors of the Third Generation the potential to disturb ingrained mental habits and poetic treatment of new aspects of Tibetan life are negligible. Shogjang (Zhogs ljang—Green Morning) does not detect any literary innovation in Third Generation poetry apart from an excessive use of graphic, sexual terminology that helps undermine the "secular morality" of Tibetans.[124] Meje (Me lce—Tongue of Flame) also puts forward a moralistic argument and maintains that Third Generation boils down to a "poetry of dirty talk."[125] As such it is argued that they should be appropriately named "the Degenerate Generation" (*rgud pa'i mi rabs*).[126]

The treatment of erotic themes and the increasing use of graphic, sexual imagery have helped turn the Third Generation into a topic of heated debate, and sex into a permissible subject of portrayal and discussion in modern Tibetan literature, albeit with much resentment and reluctance from many established writers and scholars. Especially Dhatsenpo's sexually explicit poems known as "'dick' poetry" (*"mje" snyan ngag*) have compelled Tibetan writers, young and old, to discuss sex as a literary topic. It has both offended and inspired Tibetan poets.[127] As will be discussed in the following chapter, although Third Generation and other young poets have popularized sex, it is not as unprecedented and modern a subject matter as is assumed to be. Classical Tibetan literature and other written and oral art forms deal with it in various ways although not with the use of explicit vernacular vocabulary.

Third Generation poetry is also audacious and unique in its occasional treatment of homosexuality. Rekanglang's *To Prostitute Sangje Dolma* touches on lesbian sex alongside other taboo topics such as incest, masturbation, and sexual abuse.[128] While being enraptured by autoerotic ecstasy Prostitute Sangje Dolma recollects her sexual encounter with a nun including:

Her naked figure and fingers
Breasts that madden
And her lust-swollen tongue of speech
That entered furtively into her vulva[129]

In *When I Was Deluded* Tsering Kyi (Tshe ring skyid), the sole female member of the Third Generation, tackles the theme of a lesbian relationship along with unrequited love and sexual molestation.[130] A beautiful vase firmly clutches the stalks of some wilted flowers and to the poet's imagination this scene appears like:

A young woman
Coyly
Embracing
Another beautiful woman she loves[131]

This gentle imagery contrasts jarringly against the description of a pining young woman jilted by "a great man who fell out of love" and the subsequent lines on sexual assault. Like literary criticism offered by queer theory such poetry calls into question conventional notions of sexual identity and gender stereotypes.[132] In Tibetans it disturbs the established categories of desire by drawing attention to the hidden same-sex erotic relationship.

Tsobu Gade's *Getting Attached to Dhatsenpo* blurs the line between what Eve Sedgwick terms "homosociality"—social bonds between persons of the same sex—and homoeroticism.[133] Indeed it seems to highlight the unstudied continuum noted by Sedgwick between "homosociality" and homosexuality when Tsobu Gade writes to his fellow Third Generation poet Dhatsenpo:

If you were a woman
I would definitely be your lover
Who downs a glass of wine in loneliness
With a lowered head in the dark
My beloved friend[134]

These allusions are mostly sparing, but they tackle a theme that is rarely mentioned in traditional forms of Tibetan literature. Even in contemporary literary production it is hardly covered with the rare exception of Sangdhor's article on homosexual relations in monastic communities and the lively online discussions it generated.[135] One might be tempted to attribute this choice of such a rare subject matter to the Third Generation's tendency to court controversy and seek maximum publicity. The Third Generation can be described as the first publicity-conscious Tibetan poets who have exploited modern communications technology to promote themselves and their poetry. This can be seen in their successful use of websites, blogs, newsletters, and books. The coverage of their conferences online and in newsletters deliberately has a tabloid feel. Pictures of inebriated, chain-smoking poets are published alongside their provocative and experimental poems as a sign of nonconformity and self-criticism as well as self-promotion. However, it would be erroneous to reduce the audacity and willingness of the Third Generation to cover ultrasensitive topics to a penchant for self-publicity. Their pronouncements and poetic practice reveal their professed aspiration to write "atom-like poetry." That is to say, to write poems on a diversity of topics with an eye for fine detail and subtlety. Broadening the scope of subject matter also entails a desire to question established literary traditions and push the limit of permissibility within contemporary Tibetan society as a whole. Poetic depictions of neglected yet real aspects of Tibetan life supplemented by novel treatment of existing themes engender what Eliot highly prizes in good poetry as "the element of surprise."[136] This sense of surprise and strangeness detectable within some Third Generation poems also provides one with a different outlook on contemporary Tibetan existence.

CONCLUSION: SECRETING HISTORY

There was a different kind of surprise in store during the Fifth Conference of the Third Generation held at the lakeshore of Kokonor, June 13, 2011. Eight prominent members, led by Kyabchen Dedrol and Dhatsenpo, resigned from the group. This shock resignation was allegedly triggered by disagreement over the organization and its central principles.[137] It caused a great stir on the Tibetan literary scene. Some believe it sounded the death knell for the Third Generation while others think the group has split into two irreconcilable rival factions. It is too early to speak of what kind of Third Generation will emerge out of this incident. However, what is clear is that they have already made a considerable contribution to modern Tibetan poetry. While commenting on their breakup, Jangbu stresses the importance of poetry for Tibetan identity throughout the Tibetan written history and specifically for the preservation of Tibetan language today. He observes that although use of Tibetan language is restricted and limited in contemporary Tibet, unlike other fields of secular knowledge, poetry is promoted by journals, newspapers and websites. Jangbu puts this fact within historical context when he maintains: "Among the Tibetan language writers spanning the period between the historical genesis of the written Tibetan word till now, it would be hard to find anyone who has not translated or composed a stanza. What can be seen from this is the contribution made and efforts exerted by poets toward the strengthening of Tibetan language and its independence. In turn one can see how much attention this poetic people have paid to poetry. I believe that if poetry is given up it would be tantamount to chopping off a vital limb of this people."[138] Returning to the splitting up of the Third Generation, Jangbu concludes that "with regards to poetry *per se* what is important is not the group but the individual. And the individual is not important compared to what is written."

This survey of Third Generation poetry demonstrates that what is written is copious, creative, assertive, subversive, and at times imitative. It has advanced fresh themes, images, and diction but at the same time bears the marks of Tibet's poetic tradition. Contrary to self-assertive pronouncements, even *kāvya* imprints can be found in unlikely places and the Goddess of Melody (Saraswati) is still inspiring new poets. Although Third Generation poets shy away from the use of conspicuously patriotic terms like "national pride" the Tibetan nation manifests itself in a myriad of guises in their poetic writings. Tibetan history and culture prove to be a fundamental constituent of their "poetic soul," in which the nation and the individual seamlessly merge through history and the written Tibetan language. Just as for Sylvia Plath, whose poetry mingles public history and private tragedy, for many contemporary Tibetan poets "the self is a secretion of history."[139] Both past and present historical realities of Tibet inform and are narrated by the poetic works of the Third Generation. The written Tibetan language, out of which poetry is crafted, is also indivisible from the Tibetan nation as it is composed of "lakes of vowels" and "snow-mountains of consonants." The thirty consonants and four vowels that encapsulate the Tibetan language in the written form are seen as born of Tibetan soil, like its people. Thus when the Third Generation make "ritual offerings of poetry" this poetry is suffused with a Tibet constituted of history, culture, language, territory, people, and poets.

Some subject matters, like erotic themes and sexual imagery explored in the next chapter, feature noticeably in their poetry but these are dwarfed by an anxiety over and anguish for the Tibetan nation, whose land is being "pulverized" and whose "consciousness" is being "flayed like the skin."

NOTES

1. Skyabs chen bde grol 2008: 75.

2. A jo 2005: 14.

3. This chapter greatly relies upon the information on the Third Generation poets and many of their writings that are available at the special Web forums dedicated to the new group by Tibetan literary websites Mchod me bod kyi rtsom rig dra ba (http://www.tibetcm.com/) and Dge 'dun chos 'phel rtsom rig dra ba (http://www.gdqpzhx.com/bo/). The initial founding of the Third Generation is reported by Mi rgod 2008: 1–2 and A nag 2005: 11. Predating this official launch, the first appearance of the term "Third Generation" in print appears to be in a volume of poems by Tshe ring bkra shis (aka, Dhatsenpo) published in 2001. In its preface Kyabchen Dedrol announces the advent of "the Third Generation of Modern Tibetan Literature" (*bod kyi deng rabs rtsom rig gi mi rabs gsum pa*) and lists nine members including himself and Dhatsenpo (Skyabs chen bde grol 2001: 7–9).

4. Skyabs chen bde grol 2008: 5

5. Ibid., 8. For a collection of manifesto statements see *mi rabs gsum pa'i bsgrags gtam tshan bshus* at http://www.gdqpzhx.com/bo/html/third-generation/201106021186.html.

6. Ibid., 7.

7. Dhondup Gyal 1997: 90–94, 130–37, 147–56. For an English-language commentary on *Waterfall of Youth* and *The Blue Lake* see Tsering Shakya (2004: 188–96) and Stirr (2008: 305–31).

8. On *dunglen* music, see chapter 2.

9. This image is also an allusion to the Tibetan practice of using dead butterflies or dried flowers as bookmarks.

10. Skya bo and Khri sems dpa' 2008: 24.

11. Skyabs chen bde grol 2008: 7.

12. Bloom [1973] 1997: xxxiii, 30.

13. Eliot [1927] 1932: 13–22, Brooker and Perril 2001: 23. Exploring this line of argument Brooker and Perril (2001: 21–23) stress that Anglo-American modernism did not undergo a radical break with the past. Rather it had a complex relationship with a revised living tradition.

14. A brief biography of Kyabchen Dedrol and short introductions to his work can be found in Dge gnyen (eds.) 2006: 123; Skyabs chen bde grol 2006: 124–27; Bsam gtan 2006: 128–30; and Re rkang gling 2006: 131–36. A more detailed biography and a study of Kyabchen Dedrol's literary output in various genres are also provided by Bande Khar (Ban de mkhar 2012).

15. Gedun Choepel Literary Website has a special section dedicated to the Third Generation: http://www.gdqpzhx.com/bo/.

16. *Me lcebs*, literally suicidal fire-diver, is a kenning for moth.

17. Skyabs chen bde grol 2008: 75–80.

18. xx xxx 2011: 89–95.

19. Sa dkyil tshe bkra 2009: 137–46.

20. Dhatsenpo, mda' btsan po, is the penname of Tshe ring bkra shis.

21. Tshe ring bkra shis 2005: 44.

22. For an extremely useful compilation of *kāvyic* figures of speech collected from great Indian poetic works including *Kāvyādarśa* see Gerow 1971. See also Eppling 1989.

23. While advancing this broad conception of *tshig rgyan* Chapdak Lhamokyab (Chab brag lha mo skyabs) offers a very useful and accessible commentary on it in chapter 5 of his interpretative work on Tibetan *kāvya* tradition at http://www.chapda-klhamokyab.fr

24. Smith 2001: 201–08. Bse tshang blo bzang dpal ldan 1984.

25. The name Smad 'tshong ma sangs rgyas sgrol ma (*Prostitute Sangje Dolma*) literally translates as Prostitute Buddha-Tara.

26. Re rkang gling 2008: 9.

27. The remaining five entities of longevity are: Rock, Tree, River, Crane, and Deer. "The deer killed by a hunter" in Rekanglang's poem might be an allusion to this deer of long life (*sha tshe ring*). For a brief introduction of these prevalent symbols see Kun gzigs pan chen sku phreng dgu pa chos kyi nyi ma 2010 and Tshe skyid g.yang 'dzoms 2010.

28. Bod mkhas pa 2006: 454. "Heart bliss" is a literal rendition of *snying gi dga' ba*. Here it denotes spiritual bliss as opposed to worldly carnal pleasure. The former is pursued by "the Liberation Seeker," *thar 'dod*, which is a synonym for an ascetic.

29. For a Tibetan rendition of this Hindu myth see Bstan 'dzin (ed.) 1997: 51–52.

30. Skyabs chen bde grol 2008: 55–57.

31. Ibid., 57.

32. Gu ru don grub 2010.

33. Lham kog 2011.

34. Pound 1913: 200.

35. Nicholls 2007: 57.

36. Beasley 2007: 39.

37. Skya bo and Khri sems dpa' 2008: 22–23; Re rkang gling 2008: 44–47; 2009: 225–26 and Skyabs chen bde grol 2008: 54. In one of my interviews with Kyabchen Dedrol (now published online) he admits the influence of French symbolism and imagism on his poetry (Skyabs chen bde drol 2012). It must be pointed out that most Tibetophone writers originating from Tibet including Third Generation poets were introduced to these and other modern Western literary concepts and practices through Chinese writing and translations although many are reluctant to acknowledge this. A host of modern ideas—including Marxist literary theory, modernist and postmodernist thought, and radical Chinese literary movements such as the Obscure Poetry (*rab rib snyan ngag*. Chin. *Ménglóng Shī*)—have reached bilingual Tibetan intellectuals either through Chinese writers or re-translations via Chinese. Even during the early 1980s re-translations of works by the likes of Chekhov, de Maupassant, O. Henry, Faulkner, and Gabriel García Márquez served as sources of inspiration (Hartley and Patricia Schiaffini-Vedani 2008: xxi) for Tibetophone writers. A popularly received book is Kunga's translation of *Five Hundred Questions about Western Modernist Literature*, *Nub phyogs deng rabs smra ba'i rtsom rig gi dri gzhi lnga brgya*, which has introduced many monolingual Tibetan writers to modernist literary concepts (Kun dga' 2000). Due to matters of limited space and specific emphasis the current book does not explore the Chinese literary influence on Tibetan writers, but a consideration of the significance of such translations along with the Chinese political control of Tibet makes it an undeniable force in contemporary Tibetan writing.

38. Ldong bu (Trans. 2009), a Third Generation poet, translated Eliot's *The Waste Land* into Tibetan. It was based on a Chinese translation of the famous poem. A translated introductory essay on *The Waste Land* is also the centerpiece of the second issue of the Third Generation newsletter published in 2010. This is a reprint of a translation by Kun dga' 2010: 6–7. Incidentally Jangbu is one of the first Tibetan poets who claims to have been influenced by Eliot's poetry (Robin 2011).

39. Shelley [1821] 1968: 112.

40. Hulme 1938: 269; Beasley 36–37.

41. For an analysis of *bsang* ritual and *rlung rta* see Samten Karmay 1998: 380–422.

42. Ju mi pham 'jam dbyangs rnam rgyal rgya mtsho 2010: 411–12.

43. Dge 'dun chos 'phel 1994: 394. For a reading of this poem at two different levels see Hor gtsang 'jigs med 1999: 76–88.

44. An English translation of this poem in its entirety can be found in Lopez 2009: 22–25.

45. Mda' btsan po 2009: 37–44.

46. Mig dmar (ed.) 1992: *Kha che pha lu*. The authorship of this popular text is a contested issue. Some commentators attribute it to a great Islamic scholar. For instance, following accounts given by some Tibetan Muslims Dawa Norbu speculates

that the author's second name corresponds to a certain Farzur-alla in the preface to his English translation of *Kha che pha lu* (1987: xii). On the other hand, Hor khang bsod nams dpal 'bar attributes it to 'Brong rtse mkhas pa chen po, a famed teacher of the Seventh Panchen Lama (1999: 503–05).

47. Mda' btsan po 2009: 3.

48. Ibid., 43.

49. Eliot [1921] 1932: 289, italic original.

50. Ldong bu 2009: 128–35.

51. Nicholls 2007: 57–58.

52. Ldong bu 2009: 129.

53. This extreme abstraction, unexpected juxtapositions, and image obsession evident in a chaotic collage of surreal visual representations bear witness to the influence of modernist poetry on Dongbu, who has translated both Eliot's *The Waste Land* (Ldong bu 2009) and Octavio Paz's *Sunstone* (Ldong bu: Forthcoming) into Tibetan. Dongbu's debt to modernist poetry is also apparent in his MA thesis which explores modern Tibetan poetry through the theoretical lens of modernism. It is available in book format (Lcags rdor rgyal 2013).

54. For instance see *Hor gling g.yul 'gyel* 1980: 58, 288.

55. Lham kog 2010.

56. Flint 1913: 199.

57. Cited by Nicholls 2007: 57.

58. For the provenance of "poetic soul" and scholarly disagreements regarding this literary concept see Pad ma 'bum 1990: 35–50 and Bu bzhi bsam pa'i don grub 2008: 546–54.

59. Hulme 1938: 266.

60. According to Buddhist belief *Bardo* (*bar do*) is the liminal state between death and rebirth.

61. *Ma ni yig drug bod kyi chos skal yin/ phyag na pal mo bod kyi lha skal yin.* Phyag na pal mo, The Lotus Holder, is another epithet for Spyan ras gzigs. For a concise explanation of the spiritual significance of Spyan ras gzigs and the Mani mantra and their karmic relationship with Tibetans see Sngags 'chang rta mgrin rgyal 2002: 134–42. Although this is a religious text it shows how Tibetan national identity is also informed by a notion of Tibetan collective karma. See Dreyfus 2003: 492–522 for the importance of Spyan ras gzigs and other Buddhist deities in the formation of an early form of Tibetan collective identity.

62. Skyabs chen bde grol 2012: 156–57.

63. Kapstein 2006: 2.

64. Zhwa sgab pa dbang phyug bde ldan 1976: 18, *Bka' chems ka khol ma* 1989: 47, 'Gos lo tsa ba gzhon nu dpal 1984: 60 and Kapstein 2006: 2.

65. Kyabchen Dedrol saw similarities between Tibetan Buddhist writers' likening of life to an illusionary show and Shakespearean metaphor of life as play. While praising Ju Mipham's poetry (private communication, February 17, 2011) he made several references to famous passages from Shakespeare's plays such as the lines beginning with "All the world's a stage" (*As You Like It*, Act 2, Scene 7) and "Our revels now are ended" (*The Tempest*, Act 4, Scene 1).

66. This is a stereotypical *kāvya* simile. According to an Indian legend peahens conceive when they hear thunder. As such they are overjoyed to behold the approach of thunder and rain.

67. 'Ju mi pham 'jam dbyangs rnam rgyal rgya mtsho 2008: 406.

68. Ta si byang chub rgyal mtshan et al. 1986: 7. Mon (*mon*) usually denotes wild Himalayan borderlands of Tibet.

69. Mda' btsan po 2010: 59–80.

70. *Dbus lam ring mo* is the popular traditional name for the pilgrimage route from Amdo to Lhasa.

71. *Mtha' 'dul yang 'dul* is a well-known historical phrase that refers to the construction of eight great temples for pinning down the malevolent spirit of Tibetan territory that resembled a supine *srin mo*, demoness, during the reign of Songtsen Gampo. These consist of four temples for conquering the inner frontier and another four for the conquest of the outer frontier. A list of these temples can be found in Dung dkar blo bzang 'phrin las 2002: 1063, 1844.

72. Mgar is a reference to Mgar stong btsan, the powerful minister Gar who served under Songtsen Gampo.

73. Mda' btsan po 2010: 62.

74. Ibid., 67–68.

75. Ibid., 70–71.

76. Ibid., 71–72.

77. Ibid., 76–77.

78. Ibid., 77–79.

79. Ibid., 79–80.

80. As demonstrated by Toni Huber's claim of Tibetan "reinvention of Buddhist India" (2008) Tibetan pilgrimage also shapes the identity of territories that lie beyond the Tibetan plateau. Such identity-defining activities beyond the Tibetan plateau are not restricted to the sacred geography of India. Tibetan pilgrimage to the holy site of *Rgya nag ri bo rtse lnga*, Five Peaked Mount of China (Ch. *Wǔtái Shān*), is another example of Tibetans making their presence felt in a foreign land. For a collection of essays on Tibetan perception of and holy activities at *Wutai Shan* see Germano, David, et al. (eds.) 2011.

81. There is a prodigious Tibetan literature on sacred sites, *gnas yig*, and the practice of pilgrimage, *gnas skor*. Much of it displays fine poetic qualities. A sample of this can be seen in anthologies prepared by Karma rgyal mtshan et al. 2005 and Tshe ring dpal 'byor (ed.) 1995. In the latter collection one can find Jamyang Kyentse Wangpo's *Guide to the Sacred Sites of Central Tibet*, which was translated into English and elaborated on by Keith Dowman [1988] 1996.

82. On Mount Kailash see Ngag 'phrin 1995: 51–53, Dkon mchog bstan 'dzin 1992 (an English translation of Chapter 6 & 7 of this booklet can be found in Huber and Tsepak Rigzin 1999: 125–53), and Buffetrille who provides a French translation of Choeyang Dorje's (chos dbyings rdo rje) guidebook on Mt. Kailash (2000: 15–99). On Tsari see Bstan 'zin bzang po 1995: 61–134, and Huber 1999.

83. Kapstein 1998: 96.

84. Skyabs chen bde grol 2008: 8.

85. Mda' btsan po 2010: 69.

86. Skya bo and Khri sems dpa' 26.

87. *Mchod me bod kyi rtsom rig dra ba*, http://www.tibetcm.com/.

88. Rmog ru shes rab rdo rje 2009: 68.

89. *Mgo nag rtsam zan* is a popular epithet for Tibetans.

90. Khu phyug sngon mo 2009: 150.

91. These are terms widely used in both oral and written sources.

92. For instance, Rin bzang (2008: 17) notes that letters like *Ah* and *Ha* were written in large characters before being chained and denounced for their broad religious connotation. Also see two short memoirs by Pema Bhum (2001, 2006) that provide an insightful account of the precarious fate of the written Tibetan language during the Cultural Revolution.

93. For Tibetans' advocacy of Tibetan-medium education in the 1980s, its initial success, and its subsequent rejection by the state see Gser tshang phun tshogs bkra shis 2008: 374–85; Mda' tshan pa 2012 and Bass 1998: 229–49.

94. These massive language protests were reported by several international media outlets. For instance, see Wong in *New York Times* October 22, 2010; Branigan in *The Guardian* October 20, 2010; Rab 'byor on *Khabdha.org* and *Tibetan Review* March 17, 2012.

95. For instance, Trulku Solba from Golok, who self-immolated on January 8, 2012, prays for the restoration of the Dalai Lama's spiritual and temporal powers and stresses the preservation of Tibetan language and traditional customs in his written testament (Sprul sku bsod bha January 20, 2012). Sonam Darje from Rebgong is reported to have called for "the Return of the Dalai Lama and Freedom for Tibetan language" before succumbing to fire on March 17, 2012 (Shar phyogs khug rta March 20, 2012). Tsering Kyi, a middle school student from Machu, was passionate about the Tibetan language. She burnt herself to death on March 3, 2012, in protest against Chinese education policies that sought to eliminate the Tibetan language as a medium of instruction in schools (Skal bzang mchog sgrub March 6, 2012, Woeser June 12, 2012). In a written testament Dawu Jampal, a new arrival from Tibet who self-immolated in Delhi on March 25, 2012, demanded freedom for Tibetan religion, culture, and language (Tshe ring rgyal March 27, 2012). Kalsang Jinpa from Dowa, who self-immolated on November 8, 2012, left a written demand in which he calls for "Equality of Nationalities, Freedom for Tibet and the Promotion of Written Tibetan Language" ('Jam dbyangs dkar po November 8, 2012). Gonpo Tsering from Amchok shouted for "Freedom of Nationality, Freedom of Language and the Return of the Dalai Lama" before his death on November 10, 2012 (Tshe ring rgyal November 11, 2012). In a written will Nyingkar Tashi from Rebgong calls for Tibetan independence and lists "the freedom to study Tibetan language, and freedom to speak the mother tongue" among the reasons for his self-immolation on November 12, 2012 (Snying dkar bkra shis November 13, 2012).

96. Gcan ched 'bar 2009: 154–61.

97. Me long 2009: 163–66.

98. 'Brong phrug 2009: 173–80. It is highly likely that this "year of hardship" is an allusion to the Tibetan uprising in 2008 and suppression of it.

99. 'Brong phrug 2008: 95–97.

100. This is an allusion to the popular Tibetan phrase *thod pa'i ri mo*, "patterns (drawn) on one's forehead." It denotes one's karmic destiny as imprinted on one's forehead.

101. Re rkang gling 2009: 20–23.

102. Sa dkyil tshe bkra 2008: 135–41.

103. Khu byug sngon mo 2009: 147–52. On the significance of soul turquoise (*bla g.yu*) in Tibetan culture and rituals associated with it see Samten Karmay (1998: 310–38).

104. Khu byug sngon mo 2010.

105. In a study of Lhasa poems over the last hundred years Bande Khar also notes the fact that Lhasa has increasingly come to be associated with loss, pain, loneliness, despair, and colonial rule of Tibet (Ban de mkhar: Publication forthcoming). For a multifaceted reading of modern Lhasa enwrapped in the memories of the past and the present see Barnett 2006.

106. Re rkang gling 2009: 229–30. Although Rekanglang does not acknowledge it, this passage is an attempt to convey in Tibetan Charles Baudelaire's notion of ennui, the soul-deadening sense of boredom and depression that besets the modern man.

107. Ngal rdzi is one of the few Third Generation poets along with Dhatsenpo and Kyabchen Dedrol, who publicly admits Jangbu's influence. He specifically notes the impact of Jangbu's use of the vernacular on his poetry (Ldong bu dang Ngal rdzi 2009).

108. See Dandin's *Kāvyādarśa* 1964: 9. Bod mkhas pa 2006: 128–29.

109. For Baudelaire's treatment of the modern city with its resultant shock experience see Benjamin ([1970] 1999: 152–96, and for the use of the prosaic and alienating urbanity for his poetic modernity see Chambers (2005: 101–16).

110. Stoddard (2010a: xx–xxi) also notes Jangbu's fascination with Baudelaire and the French symbolist movement.

111. In one of my interviews with Kyabchen Dedrol (May 24, 2012) published on *Tibetcm.com* he openly expressed his admiration for Baudelaire and the symbolist movement. Similar sentiments are uttered by other Third Generation poets elsewhere: see Re rkang gling 2008: 49. Skya bo and Khri sems dpa' 2008: 23. Baudelaire's popularity is also demonstrated by the republication of a translated introductory essay on his *The Flowers of Evil*. It appeared both online and as the centerpiece for the first-ever issue of the Third Generation newsletter published in 2009. It was translated from the Chinese by Kun dga' 2009: 4–6.

112. For a catalogue of modern writers who inspired Jangbu see Stoddard (2010a: xx–xxii) and consult Chakdor Gyal (Lcags rdor rgyal 2013) for a study of modern Tibetan poetry within the theoretical context of Western modernism. For an introduction to Borges and translations of some of his poems (via Chinese) see Jan Metak (Gcan me stag 2010). See Dongbu for translations of Eliot's *The Waste Land* (Ldong bu 2009) and Paz's *Sunstone* (Ldong bu: Forthcoming), again via Chinese. Both Jan Metak and Dongbu are Third Generation poets.

113. Jangbu 2001: 43. For an English translation of some of Jangbu's poems and prose by Heather Stoddard see Jangbu 2010.

114. Mda' btsan po 2010: 74.

115. Eliot [1920] 1932: 206.

116. Mar khu rgyal mtshan 2009: 46–48.

117. *Lha mang sa na 'dre mang.*

118. Skyabs chen bde grol 2009: 1.

119. Re rkang gling 2008: 126–34.

120. In Tibet, widow, *yugs sa ma*, is associated with social stigma of untimely death, misfortune, woe and bad omen. *'Dre shig* is Tibetan for bed bug. Here a literal translation is adopted to convey its sinister connotation.

121. Skyabs chen bde grol 2008: 7.

122. Re rkang gling 2009: 225–26. Like other contemporary Tibetan poets Rekanglang uses the Tibetan phrase *ya ma brla'i sems tshul* for rendering the notion of the absurd in literature made popular by the works of Franz Kafka, Samuel Beckett, Eugene Ionesco and others. A literal translation of the Tibetan phrase would be "a psychological sense of meaninglessness."

123. Tho rengs 2009 and Lham kog 2011.

124. Zhogs ljang 2012: *mi chos kun spyod.*

125. *Kha gtsog gi snyan ngag* can also be more literally rendered as "dirty language poetry."

126. Me lce 2009.

127. Mi rgod and Skya bo 2008: 38, Mi rabs gsum ba 2008: 150–51, Seng ge rgyal bo 2011 and Seng rdor 2009 Ka.

128. Re rkang gling 2008: 9–19.

129. Ibid., 16.

130. Here Tshe ring skyid writes under the penname of Chu mig, Fountain, 2009: 83–85.

131. Ibid., 2009: 83–84.

132. For queer theory's challenging of conventional thinking on gender and sexuality see Bennett and Nicholas Royle 2009: 216–25.

133. Sedgwick 1985: 2.

134. Mtsho bu dga' bde 2009: 89.

135. Seng rdor 2009 Kha. For an instance of debates it generated see Lha sde gnam lo yag 2011. Also see the heated debate about homosexuality in monasteries triggered by the alleged abuse of a certain Kalu Trulku (Nam mkha' bstan 'dzin 2011).

136. Rainey 2007: 97.

137. Mchod me bod kyi rtsom rig dra ba 2011, Tshe ring skyid 2011.

138. Ljang bu 2011.

139. Smith 1982: 2. On the meshing of individual experience and public historical reality see chapter 9 on Sylvia Plath (ibid., 200–25).

Chapter 6

How Novel is Contemporary Tibetan Erotic Poetry?

རི་མཐོན་པོ་ཡོད་ན་དམའ་མོ་ཐོངས།།
ང་བྱ་རྒྱལ་ཁྱུང་ཆེན་འཕུར་གི་ཡིན།།

If there're high mountains around please lower your peaks
Because I, the Garuda, King of Birds, am going to fly[1]

In recent years there has been a proliferation of Tibetan erotic poetry that alarms traditionalists and delights a new generation of Tibetan writers and readers. Some of the finest and most nuanced pieces are penned by young, radical writers like Dhatsenpo and Sangdhor. Many of these poems are sexually explicit and deliberately provocative while others explore the fine line between carnal passion and love. Yet others question an individual's or society's attitude to sexuality. Most of them are controversial and work as "shock art" on the contemporary Tibetan literary scene. Many Tibetan critics regard erotic themes as a modern phenomenon and consider them too vulgar to be worthy of literary attention. Erotic poets counter such criticisms, saying that these themes constitute the flesh and blood of real life. The two opposing camps concur that such themes are indeed a novel characteristic of contemporary times and erotic poets attribute it to their own daring and innovativeness. However, this chapter will contend that, although today's erotic poems are relatively graphic and detailed, they are not without parallel in Tibetan literary history or oral traditions. A survey of erotically themed materials, ranging from Tibetan *kāvya* poetry and experiential spiritual songs to popular texts that fuse literary and oral sources, shows that it is unwise to regard poetic expressions of sensual desire as an exclusively modern phenomenon. Such a venture into previously uncharted literary waters will also demonstrate the literary and oral continuities between past and present, which are made more apparent when one considers the lasting legacy of oral art forms on contemporary erotic poets. It must be pointed out that although older forms of Tibetan literature provide an important literary-historical context for under-standing contemporary poetic production they do not totally dictate today's erotic poetry. The treatment of carnal passion and sexual acts by today's poets is distinct in its introspectiveness, its subversive and inflammatory intention, its employment of free verse along with more traditional poetic forms and its concern with the Tibetan nation.

SILENCING SEX

Tibetans are well aware of the fact that carnal passion is what makes the world go around. While Tibetan tantric Buddhism tells us that sexual desire is the root cause of samsaric existence, it instructs practitioners to harness this primordial energy to attain the ultimate bliss of spiritual liberation rather than rejecting it outright.[2] Themes of sex are not confined to esoteric tantric teach-ings. They are prominent in oral art forms, and ordinary speech is laced with them. Tibetan traditional *kāvya* poetry, which is often thought to carry only a Dharmic message, is not entirely free from sensual pleasures either. One can find bits and pieces of erotic poetry scattered throughout all the afore-mentioned genres. Here erotic poetry is understood as the creative expression of the passionate activities of the body and the mind driven by sexual desire. Despite this presence of sexual themes in Tibetan literary creations it is hard to come across any Tibetan scholarship on the phenomenon.[3] There might be several reasons for this Tibetan intellectual reluctance to explore the literary representations of sexual experience.[4] An overwhelming sense of shame asso-ciated with sexual speech in public and a strong conviction that sex is trivial as a literary or scholarly subject seem to be two key factors.

On the whole in Tibetan communities since I was a child talk of sex is kept within the limits of a confined, private space. Bawdy and sensuous speech is widely used within certain circles, but it cannot be uttered before one's family members or at a gathering where close relatives are present. It is an infringe-ment of a serious taboo to speak of ordinary romantic relationships before one's blood relations, let alone to divulge one's sexual fantasies. On rare occasions, communal festivals can turn into social gatherings where youth-ful love-singing and courtship take place. For instance, during the famous Lurol (*glu rol*) festivals of Amdo Rebgong[5] a variety of religious rituals are performed during the day, but by night it transforms into a more lighthearted event during which young people engage in witty and at times salacious love-song contests. However, in order for this transition to occur, permission must be asked in coded language. A singer covers his face with a flannel (literally hiding his shame) and sings a song akin to the lyrics quoted at the outset of this chapter. It warns parents (and siblings and other blood relations), "high mountains," to make themselves scarce before "the Garuda" of love songs and wooing takes to the air. The subsequent songfest episode is short-lived and brings the official festivities to a close. Young people continue their flirting and courtship elsewhere, free from the prying eyes of "high mountains." Thus the notion of shame places serious restrictions upon the expression of any sexual desire in public or familial space.

Creative literary production takes place within a public realm, be it at times only accessible to a highly literate audience with a rarefied taste. The above-mentioned constricting sense of shame is closely related to the second factor underlying Tibetan academic neglect of sexual themes in literary arts. Sex is regarded as a shameful subject matter unfit for public discourse. It is therefore also convenient to represent sex as a trivial matter in comparison with weightier issues such as religion, poetic diction, or the depiction of nature. In the rare instances of scholarly commentary on the depiction of graphic erotic scenes in Tibetan poetry, it is dismissed as an indecency or an embarrassment. For instance, many Tibetan commentators on *kāvya* poetics do not see sexual lust as an appropriate theme and instruct potential poets to eschew "speeches that cannot be uttered in public" at all times.[6] This phrase is an obvious euphemism for the graphic expression of the pleasures of the flesh. Meje, a young Tibetan scholar, condemns contemporary Tibetan erotic poetry as "poetry of dirty talk devoid of any decency." He is concerned that its dissemination, spearheaded by the Third Generation, will result in moral degeneration.[7] Meje's statement, although relatively muted, nevertheless captures the mood of many readers who take offense at the online publication of explicit erotic poetry, which they denounce with great vitriol in their posted comments.

This sense of moral shame and conscious intellectual marginalization of sexual desire might partly account for the surprising omission of *Treatise on Passion* (*'Dod pa'i bstan bcos*) from the two major editions of Gedun Choepel's collected works and from a volume of his selected writings.[8] In his book on desire, Gedun Choepel attacks sexual inhibition and celebrates carnal passion for its inducement of pleasure, procreative power, and nirvanic potentiality. His subversive audacity is apparent at the outset of the book when he casts away pretenses and speaks of sexual passion in the following stanza using the pronoun "this" for sex:

The beggar turns up his nose at gold
The hungry guest spits at food
With their mouths all condemn this
Yet within their hearts all love this[9]

Gedun Choepel anticipates criticism of his erotic work, yet is prepared to compose the text for the sheer significance of sexual ecstasy:

I am indeed insane these days
Those still sane may laugh at me
Yet it's no small matter to feel bliss
It's no small matter to produce young
Even more important it's no small matter
To nurture passion with Blissful Emptiness[10]

Treatise on Passion can be considered as one long poetic composition featuring instructions on sexual techniques, descriptions of carnal ecstasy verging on nirvanic bliss, and profound reflections on the human condition including, for the first time for Tibetans, the issue of gender equality.[11] It is written in a plain, lucid, and lyrical metrical composition, which is a hallmark of Gedun Choepel's poetry. Although novel in terms of accessibility, the diversity of sources, emphasis laid on worldly sexual pleasures rather than divine sexual bliss, and aesthetic qualities, this erotic treatise is not unprecedented. A translated prototype of such an erotic text can even be found in the Tibetan holy scriptures of the *Tengyur* (*bstan 'gyur*), the commentarial section of the Buddhist canon, which was penned by a certain Indian master called Lopon Zugsang (Slob dpon gzugs bzang).[12] Ju Mipham (1846–1912) composed a longer Tibetan version which Gedun Choepel claims to have surpassed with his own erotic volume.[13] Anyhow, Gedun Choepel's *Treatise on Passion* perpetuates these and the textual tradition of esoteric tantric sex manuals found buried in the works of many great tantric yogi scholars.[14] These manuals are couched in recondite language and are at times highly inaccessible, but to an ordinary reader uninitiated in tantric esotericism they are as sexually explicit as Gedun Choepel's book on passion. Yet, while these tantric sexual instructions are included in published works of great tantric adepts, Gedun Choepel's erotic text finds no space in the official editions of his collected writings. Sangdhor, a leading Tibetan writer and a great practitioner of erotic poetry, views this exclusion as indicative of contemporary Tibetan intellectuals' attitude toward sexual desire and finds it extremely depressing and irksome. In his "search for *Treatise on Passion*" Sangdhor is aghast to find that not only is it "banished from Gedun Choepel's (collected) works" but it is also concealed under a heap of various books "like something illegal" in Tibetan bookshops in Siling (Ch. Xining).[15] Another reason for the editorial omission and the surreptitious sale of this text might be the need to observe obscenity laws propagated and enforced by the CCP which, as shown by Gary Sigley, link the policing of sex-related issues to the maintenance of social stability and party authority.[16] Nevertheless, it is apparent that Tibetan academic eschewal of sexual themes continues in the twenty-first century.

While acknowledging the monumental achievement of cultural theory of having firmly established sexuality as a legitimate academic subject in the

West, Terry Eagleton ponders in amazement: "It is remarkable how intellectual life for centuries was conducted on the tacit assumption that human beings had no genitals."[17] He goes on to observe that academic obsession with all things to do with sex has now resulted in the trivialization of it.[18] In terms of Tibetan academic life, scholars still conduct themselves as if Tibetans have no genitals. Although Tibetan scholars have failed to turn human sexual desire and activities into legitimate objects of study, a young generation of contemporary Tibetan poets has succeeded in establishing them as valid subject matters for written poetry. The mushrooming of erotic poetry in the new millennium deserves scholarly attention. Scrutiny of this genre reveals that the current poetic representations of the erotic spirit have literary and oral antecedents. They are distinct in some aspects but are not as unprecedented as is commonly assumed.

SPINNING PASSION INTO POETRY

Some of the most critically acclaimed erotic poems have been penned by the Third Generation poet Dhatsenpo. In 2006, he released a cluster of poems on an Internet site called Butter Lamp: Tibetan Literature Website. It was the first and only Tibetan literary website in existence at the time and was and still is widely popular with an international Tibetan readership. Prior to their online publication, he presented some of his poems at the First Conference of the Third Generation of Tibetan Poets (Siling, July 22–33, 2006) where they received a mixed reception amid much excitement. Following their online release in 2007, the impact of these poems was immediate. Dhatsenpo burst onto the Tibetan literary scene and his name became inextricably associated with "poetry of sexual desire" (*chags sred snyan ngag*), even though the bulk of his poetry is of a nonerotic nature. This group of poems came to be known as Dhatsenpo's "'dick' poetry" (*"mje" snyan ngag*) and the poetic trend they set came to be called "poetry of the loins" (*lus smad snyan ngag*).[19] This is poetry that literally concerns with what Mikhail Bakhtin calls "the lower bodily stratum."[20] They became the topic of heated debates and social gossip to such an intense degree that the Third Generation of Tibetan Poets passed a resolution at their second conference in Rebgong (August 3–6, 2007) disassociating their movement from Dhatsenpo's erotic poems. It was concluded that this erotic genre was not the chosen model for Third Generation poetry. However, the group was quick to show admiration and support for Dhatsenpo's unique poetic style by showering him with the accolade of the 2007 "Representative Poet of the Third Generation."[21]

While appreciating the fine aesthetic qualities of Dhatsenpo's poetry, Jangmo Guzuk (Spyang mo dgu zug—The Howling She-wolf) singles out for specific praise his diversification of the subject matter of new Tibetan poetry. He believes that Dhatsenpo has enriched the contemporary "Tibetan poetic soul" by setting a trend with his erotic poem *Inside this Room*. This poem is believed to have introduced "terminology of lust" (*chags tshig*), such as "genitals" and "breasts" into new poetic compositions.[22] Draldo (Bsgral rdo), a Third Generation poet, concurs with this line of thought in a poem titled *Dhatsenpo*. He describes Dhatsenpo as a plain-speaking erotic poet who has "Spun vagina and penis / Formed of steel / Into the chain links of Tibetan literature."[23] It would be inaccurate to credit Dhatsenpo for being the first poet to introduce sexually explicit terms into Tibetan poetic writing. However, he has indeed played a pivotal role in the recent proliferation of erotic poetry and popularisation of "terminology of lust." This is epitomized by one of his signature erotic poems—*Inside This Room*:[24]

Inside this room
Pushing my trousers down to the nook of my knees
Saying there is no way to chop out this wretched dick
With a sackload of lust whom should I wait for?

Inside this room
Spinning my pubic hair into a cord
Would I give it, with a handful of love,
To a girl with shaking breasts that madden
Saying let it be a cord-belt for your trousers?

Inside this room
Putting my lips against a girl's
Thrusting my sex into hers
Saying here infernal torments are lost
And here heavenly bliss is found
Could I beget a sweetheart son?

As many Tibetan commentators have observed, Dhatsenpo writes in a playful, lucid and pleasant style. He often employs a simple yet expressive diction with fluid and flexible syntax.[25] In general, his poems display unique technical brilliance and verbal dexterity in tandem with a seemingly effortless fluency. These qualities are especially apparent in his long poems such as *A Song Revealing the Nature of Mind* and *Tale of a Pilgrimage to U*.[26] The former is a metrical composition in which Dhatsenpo displays his technical mastery of the *mgur* genre as he consciously and successfully borrows the melody and lyricism of *Kache Phalu*. The latter is a free verse narrative poem composed of memorable verbal combinations and balanced phrases marked by an overall fluidity and eloquence. As is evident in the above poem, Dhatsenpo also stands out because of his daring frankness and his willingness and ability to weave what are usually considered to be "vulgar words" (*tha shal kyi tha snyad*) into the fabric of his poetry. This manner of crafting poetry furnishes his poems with an element of surprise and brings variety to the content. In one of my interviews with Kyabchen Dedrol regarding Third Generation poetry, he also chose to highlight this quality of Dhatsenpo's poetic writings. He noted succinctly: "Dhatsenpo's poetry is predominately characterised by straightforward emotions and suffused with profanities."[27] The shocking appeal of Dhatsenpo's "dick poetry" is indeed assisted by a ruthless frankness and a subversive fondness for "vulgar" terminology. However, what goes unnoticed is that this appeal is enhanced by an aptitude for distinct imagery and use of specific vernacular words, which endow his poems with a novel tone and unique flavor.

Alongside the Tibetan phonic feel of *Inside This Room*, also lost in translation are the imagistic nuances and evocativeness of specific words that are vital for communicating the central feeling of the poem, erotic passion. These features reflect Dhatsenpo's nomadic roots and thus a certain degree of Tibetan pastoral sensibility enriches the reading of such a poem. John Stuart Mill's notion of "poetic laws of association" posits that ideas and images combine in the service of a dominant, preexisting emotion. He argues that in poetry thoughts and images are linked together in such a way so as to express the emotion which has called them into existence in the first place.[28] The pervasive emotion expressed in *Inside This Room* is the sexual desire consuming the "I" of the poem, with a subtext of loneliness. Dhatsenpo uses a cluster of images and colloquialisms to convey the rawness and intensity of this erotic passion. As soon as the violent idea of chopping off the penis at its root is relinquished, it is followed by the metaphor "a sackload of lust." My translation fails to convey that this metaphorical allusion to the scrotum is no ordinary bag. There is no equivalent term in the English language for the Tibetan word *sgye*. It is a large, hardwearing sack, woven of coarse yak-hair and much valued by nomads. It is usually larger and always more flexible than the *sgro ba*—another prized bag made of leather and a conventional euphemism for the scrotum.

The metaphor of a yak-hair bag is closely associated with other suggestive terms that make coarse hair a central image of the poem. A Tibetan word for "pubic hair" is *rlig rtsid*, which can literally be translated as "the coarse hair of the penis." *Rtsid* is the abbreviation of *rtsid pa*, meaning coarse yak-hair. Just as a nomad plucks out yak-hair by the "handful" and spins it into strong, useful threads or ropes, so the speaker of the poem spins his pubic hair into a "cord belt" as a token of love and lust. Here one must bear in mind that before the spread of modern leather belts, cords made of yak-hair and wool were commonly used for fastening nomads' trousers. Thus Dhatsenpo resorts to these rustic images and harsh-sounding words (that is, *chags sred sgye gang*, *rlig rtsid, brte dung spar mo gang, shed kyis rdzong* and *dmyal ba'i sdug bsngal* pronounced with a nomadic accent) to express sexual frustration and erotic intensity. He concludes the poem with a fusion of graphic sexual intercourse and procreative urges. However, even in the midst of strong sexual lust and the desire to have a baby the speaker of the poem utters deep-seated gender prejudice in Tibetan society. In the last line of the poem the traditional Tibetan preference of the birth of boys over that of girls is shown to be enduring even today.[29] This reading might be independent of authorial intention, but what also appears are the stereotyped gender roles of man as impregnator and woman as childbearer, entrenched in traditional Tibetan thinking.

When the online publication of *Inside This Room* and other poems in its genre caused shock and controversy and provoked virulent attacks, Dhatsenpo retorted in the only effective way at his disposal. In defiance he wrote a poem provocatively entitled *Even If You Don't Like It, So What? I Write Like This*:[30]

This is perhaps the noon
In terms of both age and sequence

I long ago erased
A rusted line of words

What remained was a paperless sky
Onto which I've written a poem
That is the light of semen dripping from the penis
And the supple softness of the unfolded vagina
In no way is it the twinned ancient sun and moon

The person who illumines the blade of intellect
Always dies without the time to wash the filth of certitude

In this rhetorical and somewhat cryptic poem he claims to have invented a new poetry through the employment of sexual themes and terminology. It passes judgment on the progress of modern Tibetan literature, which has only reached noontime. This does not mean it is at its zenith. On the contrary, "the noon" image implies that it is still at an early stage of development before it can evolve into a full day. "A rusted line of written words" alludes to traditional Tibetan literature, dominated by *kāvya* poetry which originated in India. The allusion becomes more apparent when we learn that the new poem inscribed on to "a paperless sky," the Internet, is not "the twinned ancient sun and moon." This is a subtle reference to *Kāvyādarśa* which shaped Tibetan classical poetry. Dandin's poetic treatise famously advises those attempting epic poetry to describe, among other themes, the risings of the sun and the moon.[31] However, as already noted, although Dhatsenpo's "dick poetry" has popularized sexually explicit poetic compositions, it is not as revolutionary as is intimated in this self-assertive poem.[32] As will be shown in the following section, even Tibetan *kāvya* poetry, which is mistakenly viewed as exclusively a vehicle of Buddhist teachings, features erotic poems replete with graphic descriptions of sexual desire and acts.

Before examining the treatment of carnal passion and the employment of sexual terminology in conventional forms of Tibetan literature, it is worth briefly mentioning Jangbu's erotic poetry. Jangbu appears to be the first modern Tibetan poet to deal with erotic themes in free verse. This undermines the claims of literary inventiveness by a younger generation of Tibetan poets like Dhatsenpo. Jangbu's first erotic poem is *Maple Leaves*, published in 1986. In this well-known poem two lovers meet under a maple tree in a still forest. Everything is silent except the occasional "Sound of unfolding petals / And the melody of two beating minds." A wind stirs "the liquid tree" and "a pair of maple leaves sprayed with dewdrops" get closer and closer and meet. At this point in the poem, the identities of the lovers are fused with the two maple leaves, "sparkling with the translucence of dewdrops." Then in the very instant lips meet "Two minds, redder than maple leaves, merge into one another / Like a droplet of blood merging into a droplet of blood / Like a tongue of flame merging into a tongue of flame." In the concluding part, the two maple leaves are locked into a single embrace and two minds are fused into one. All is still and quiet apart from the occasional "Sound of falling petals / And the melody of a single beating mind."[33] In a commentary on *Maple Leaves* Skyaba (Skya bha) expresses admiration for Jangbu's audacity and his employment of both lucid and abstract methods in the portrayal of erotic love. Skyaba observes that "given the particular circumstances of the time it is no easy task to traverse the great plain of love 'without inhibition' unless one resorts to such techniques."[34] Thus, through the use of novel imagery, Jangbu depicted sexual union in Tibetan free verse as early as 1986.

In some of Jangbu's later erotic poems he is less subtle and more graphic in his choice of words. Yet, semantically these poems are more abstract and introspective and peppered with philosophical reflections. They are found in his *Nine-Eyed Zi*, which has had a considerable impact upon a younger generation of Tibetan poets like Dhatsenpo and Kyabchen Dedrol. Because of their abstract nature and concentrated imagery, these contemplative poems resist summarization or easy interpretation, as can be seen in *The Fight*:

Once when I fell asleep, beside me
Like a copulating male and female couple
Two women were having a bloody fight
One woman stark naked
Was riding the belly of another, stark naked
One was squeezing the neck of the other

The other was biting back
Red blood stained nails and stained fangs

In reality on the wet liquid mattress
A woman was fighting with herself
In reality this woman with her paired fore and middle fingers
Was stirring, stirring inside her vagina
Like a skilled nomad woman churning butter
Odor of sweat, odor of rose
Menstrual blood-odor wailing—melody
As before, I fell asleep beside a woman
Yet, my perceptions could sense all these things[35]

The "I" of the poem either witnesses a bitter fight between two women or sees a menstruating, masturbating woman next to him. The indeterminacy concerning these two contrasting incidents is employed to portray an indefinite state of mind. The perception of a semiconscious mind sees a fight scene transform into a sexual act. Although an erotic theme is prominent in *The Fight*, it is also a poem about the subtle workings of mental and emotional consciousness. Eroticism and abstract thought commingle in another equally abstruse poem called *From a State of Bewilderment*:

Through the crack, red lightning streaked once
It was a white steed, or a white steed was born of it
Afterwards, like the final realization, it ossified
I, from a corner, inspected the velocity,
No amazing inspirations for me, I rode the steed
The blind steed that resembles the copulating woman on top,
Forgetting the aims and resonating groans in warm currents[36]

Once again Jangbu seems to be attempting to capture a mental process during sex. Although sexual intercourse and ecstasy come in the form of "red lightning" and a "white steed," the "I" of the poem is distant and cold. He is too caught up in thinking to surrender himself wholeheartedly to feeling. Like *The Fight* this poem captures both the intellect and the emotions. It is a quality reminiscent of Paul Valéry's poetry which gives equal weight to thinking and feeling, evident in *The Seaside Cemetery*.[37] Peter Broome and Graham Chesters are observant of this characteristic feature of Valéry's poems when they state: "In Valéry the intellect does not exclude the emotions. Indeed these two modes of human consciousness are seen in terms of each other, so much so that one often wonders whether the poet is intellectualizing the emotions or giving erotic and sensual expression to what is basically an intellectual observation."[38] The same can be said of Jangbu's erotic poems which weave carnal passion and intellectual contemplation into an integral poetic fabric. When eroticism features in traditional Tibetan *kāvya* poetry, on the other hand, it is in most cases directly concerned with the pleasures of the flesh, albeit couched in a rarefied figurative language.

EROTICISM OF TIBETAN *KĀVYA*

Both Tibetan and non-Tibetan scholars concur that Tibetan *kāvya* poetry has been an effective vehicle for the propagation of Buddhism in Tibet.[39] Sakya Paṇḍita, one of the first Tibetan scholars to import Indian poetics into Tibet, encapsulates this Buddhist didactic function of *kāvya* in an aspirational stanza in his highly influential *Entrance Door for the Learned*.[40] In it he declares his desire to make offerings of poetry to all enlightened beings and to be "a poet of the Buddhas" for eternity:

May I eternally make offerings [of poetry]
To the Buddhas and Sons of the Buddhas
And for all my future lives
Become a poet of the Buddhas[41]

However, the fact that Buddhism dominates conventional Tibetan *kāvya* compositions should not blind us to an appreciation of other thematic features like eroticism. In a reading of Tibetan *kāvya* commentaries Peter-Daniel Szántó rightly observes that "the naturalization of *kāvya*" was not a smooth process. He finds that Tibetan scholars embraced *kāvya* for advocating Buddhism and consequently sought to strip it of its original erotic and secular contents as part of a concerted effort to Buddhicize *kāvya*.[42] Szántó is correct to detect attempts to water down erotic elements in favor of the edifying function of *kāvya* poetry. Comparatively speaking, Tibetan commentaries contain far fewer erotic verses than Dandin's *Kāvyādarśa*, which mostly deals with romantic or erotic themes.

Erotic subjects and sexually explicit speech, although discouraged by some poet-scholars, are a detectable element in Tibetan *kāvya* poetry. Many of the poems that celebrate carnal passion are penned by celibate monks. When making sweeping generalizations about Tibetan *kāvya* many Tibetan critics also neglect this attribute and view it as a purely Buddhist pedagogic tool. For instance, Lhamkog, a contemporary Tibetan monk poet, claims that the introduction of *kāvya* to Tibet transformed Tibetan poetry into a "slave-like creature for the profound and prolific religion." In his opinion, it had a constricting impact as it tinged Tibetan poetry genres like *mgur* with a Buddhist ideology and restricted free expression of the "subjective passions and wonders of the individual."[43] Another Tibetan poet and critic, Jazhung Yangba (Bya gzhung dbyangs bha), asserts that the limitations of conventional Tibetan literature resulting from a predominantly Buddhist worldview led to the birth of "new Tibetan literature" in the late 1970s and early 1980s. He views all Tibetan literary production preceding this period as a mere "propaganda tool" for religion and contemptuously sums it up as "Buddha Dharma literature" (*thub bstan rtsom rig*).[44] It is surprising that such hyperbolic statements are still prevalent given the fact that *Kāvyādarśa* was written by a non-Buddhist as a guide for young aspirant poets of the Hindu court, and romance and eroticism are its most prominent themes. It specifically recommends lovemaking and the yearning of separated lovers as poetic themes.[45] As already noted, even though efforts were made within the Tibetan commentarial tradition to reduce the saliency of eroticism, it has undeniably infiltrated Tibetan *kāvya* compositions. A brief appreciation of Tibetan commentaries on *Kāvyādarśa* and *Kāvyādarśa*-influenced poetry sheds light upon this neglected aspect. Such an exercise also shows that there is a literary precedent to contemporary Tibetan erotic writings. Conventional Tibetan *kāvya* poetry is not only concerned with formal themes like Dharma or "the twinned ancient sun and moon," but it is also at times capable of producing sensual verses as explicit and shocking as those found in modern Tibetan poems.

Near the beginning of *Kāvyādarśa*, Dandin makes it clear that his poetics give equal weight to both spiritual and worldly affairs. For him, epic poetry (*snyan ngag chen po*)—by extension all genres of *kāvya*—is shaped by four goals or "fruits" of life (*sde bzhi'i 'bras bu*). These four categories of human experience are classified as material and intellectual wealth (*nor*), sensual pleasures (*'dod pa*), Dharmic quests (*chos*), and spiritual liberation (*thar ba*).[46] The first two types concern secular existence and the latter pair spiritual matters. According to Dandin the treatment of these principal themes must be accompanied by ornate descriptions of natural phenomena and various aspects of secular, human existence. Among these he lists representations of drinking parties, lovemaking, and the pangs of separation experienced by lovers.[47] Most of the exemplary verses in *Kāvyādarśa* deal with this category of "sensual pleasures." Tibetan *kāvya* commentators and poets, although driven by a religious mentality, do not shy away from mimicking Dandin's poetic figures of speech (*rgyan*) portraying erotic love and sexual ecstasy. A few notable examples, penned by acclaimed monk scholars, have been selected for consideration here, although it should be noted that these represent only a fraction of the materials available to support my argument.

Bod Khepa (Bod mkhas pa mi pham dge legs rnam rgyal, 1618–1685) was a celibate monk famous for his commentarial work on *Kāvyādarśa* and his refined verses that assimilated Dandin's technical and aesthetic prescriptions. He belonged to the Tibetan Buddhist school of Oral Transmission (*bka' brgyud pa*) and wrote his commentary at the age of sixty in 1678.[48]

Like most Tibetan commentators Bod Khepa expounds each poetic figure in *Kāvyādarśa* along with its technical terminology and Indian mythological allusions. This exegetical input is supplemented by his own exemplifying verses, which both imitate and illustrate Dandin's stanzas portraying specific figures. It is in his efforts to explain Dandin's poetic devices and teach them to aspiring Tibetan poets that we find such passionate lines as:

Oh Beauty, inside this garden of thy body
Blazes the youth of the immaculate lotus,
Veined arbor that devours innate particles
Reveling in all kinds of pleasure games[49]

To an untrained eye the erotic nature of this stanza is not obvious because of the use of a sophisticated language known as "poetic synonyms" (*mngon brjod*), which is a fundamental aspect of *kāvya* poetry. As the etymology of this term implies, it is a specific form of speech, a repertoire of kennings or compound expressions that reveal (*mngon*) or express (*brjod*) things and their qualities vividly and beautifully.[50] Once the artistic and technical terminology is explained, Bod Khepa's direct treatment of sexual desire and action is revealed in vivid detail. This illustrative stanza corresponds to Dandin's "ornament of metaphorical parallelism" (*sbyar ba'i gzugs rgyan*),[51] which is only one of twenty figures known as "metaphorical ornaments" (*gzugs rgyan*).[52] It is a decorative device that describes two separate objects or acts and fuses them together through their similar attributes. While comparing one thing (an object) to another (a metaphor) it depicts similar qualities belonging to both entities. As a result, verses adorned with such a figuration are open to two interpretations. Double entendre features at two levels: in the overall meaning of a verse, and in each metaphor used within that poem.

In Bod Khepa's verse, the portrayal of sexual climax becomes apparent when his "poetic synonyms" are deciphered. "The immaculate lotus" (*pad ma can*) is a common synonym for both woman and vagina.[53] "Veined arbor" or more literally "beautiful arbour of veins" (*rtsa yi mdzes spyil*), is another word for female genitals. This name is derived from the belief that the vagina is where thirty-two veins or nerves (*rtsa 'dab so gnyis*; Sanskrit: *nāḍi*) meet and merge, thus giving it heightened sensitivity. Here "veined arbor" can also be interpreted as the lotus which is seen as the distilled beauty of a plant (*rtsa*).[54] "Innate particles" or "innate dust" (*lhan skyes rdul*) has two connotations: it can denote both semen and the nectar of a flower. Thus, Bod Khepa simultaneously depicts the vagina *devouring* semen and an implied bee/male lover imbibing the lotus nectar/female sexual fluid. The above translation fails to capture this suggestiveness, but it intimates the second sense if we alternatively translate the third line as: "Innate particles of the veined arbor devoured." The double meaning of the metaphorical expressions lends his example some ambiguity, but its explicit sexual content is undeniable. Heeding the advice of Dandin's poetics not to portray erotic themes directly in simple vernacular language (*grong tshig*),[55] Tibetan *kāvya* poetry also avoids the use of plain or straightforward speech. Erotic themes, including graphic sexual intercourse, are reproduced through a literary idiom considered to be pregnant with aesthetic qualities.

Bod Khepa's commentary and verses abound in eroticism, but no lines are as novel, daring, and provocative as his famous stanza depicting the lassitude of a man who lacks sexual experience and drive:

Without having traversed the flower passage
Without having shafted the creeper thighs of youths
And without having exhausted the five petalled one
Woeful this collapse of the great pillar of consciousness[56]

This example is an imitation of a *kāvya* figure known as "cause of initial non-action" (*snga na med pa'i byed rgyu*), one of sixteen types of "ornaments of causation" (*rgyu'i rgyan*) that aim to poetically represent the intricate interplay between cause and effect.[57] As the name indicates, this particular figure depicts outcomes that result from an absence of conscious action. Lack of action is itself seen as the principal cause. Here Bod Khepa is referring to male impotency resulting from sexual inexperience and maybe also from old age. Once again one needs to decode the synonyms to reveal the graphic sexual content of the stanza. "The flower passage" (*me tog lam*) is an epithet for the female genitals because it is seen as a passage through which the flower of menstruation (*khams dmar*; literally red reproductive fluid) courses. The entwined "creeper" thighs belong to young men or boys. "The five petalled one" (*yal 'dab lnga ba*) is a synonym for the hand with its five fingers.[58] Now it should be clear that "the great pillar of consciousness" stands for the male sexual organ.

These lines could be interpreted as an autobiographical statement about Bod Khepa himself. He was a celibate monk of sixty when he wrote them down. What is striking is his unique audacity to mention homoerotic acts and male masturbation in the same breath as heterosexual desire. His stanza underlines the complexity and indeterminacy of sexual desire by questioning the conventional notion of it as a preserve of the opposite sexes. Such frank lines that expose homosexual tendencies in Tibetan society in general and monastic communities in particular are few and far between. On the rare occasions when homosexuality and autoeroticism surface in modern Tibetan poetry they almost exclusively concern lesbian sex or female masturbation, thereby denying through omission that such practices affect Tibetan men.

As touched on in the previous chapter this is evident in poems like Rekang-lang's *To Prostitute Sangje Dolma* and Tsering Kyi's *When I Was Deluded* and also in Jangbu's *The Fight* cited in the preceding section. Such sustained male gaze upon the female body (with the rare exception of Tsering Kyi's poem) and fascination with homosexual women reveal the persistence of a heterosexual, masculine conception of carnal passion in contemporary literary creations. Bod Khepa's stanza remains unique because it is one of the few poetic statements that disturb this macho eroticization of the female body and directs the male eyes elsewhere.

Thus Bod Khepa's temerity and willingness to treat sexual themes and taboos, albeit couched in highly literary terminology, is discomfiting to the Tibetan reader. For instance, the great scholar Tseten Shabdrung is appalled by the sheer quantity and explicitness of Bod Khepa's erotic *kāvya* exemplifications and advises aspiring Tibetan poets to eschew them. In a well-circulated article disapproving of sexually themed *kāvya* poetry, Tseten Shabdrung accuses Bod Khepa of breaking the boundary of Dandin's subtle erotic verses by employing "graphic sexual terms" (*'khrig thsig gsal rjen*).[59] He acknowledges that mildly erotic themes should be permissible, but it would be ethically appropriate to limit these to the praising of the youth of men and women. Otherwise, he continues: "extremely immoderate use of plain lustful speech without any terminological concealment (*tshig gi sgrib byed*) is difficult for a teacher to teach in a gathering and is difficult for listeners to listen to. In such a case it not only goes against the sacred Dharma but also completely goes against secular ethics."[60] Ethical and religious concerns and the notion of shame prompted Tseten Shabdrung to air critical views of erotic themes. He singles out for attack Bod Khepa's *kāvya* stanza cited above, seeing it as a source of unbearable embarrassment. He writes that even to cite this verse for the purpose of analysis and criticism reduces the fingers of a "thin-skinned" person like him to shivering.[61]

Tseten Shabdrung wrote this essay in 1983 after surviving the Cultural Revolution, and under politically ambiguous and precarious conditions. He was very aware of the CCP's "spiritual civilization" campaign that sought to tighten Party control over ethical and moral values in the early 1980s. In fact, by employing slogans like "Five Stresses and Four Beauties" Tseten Shabdrung attempts to cloak his attack in CCP idioms of moral guidance, even though it is clearly shaped by Tibetan moral and religious beliefs.[62] Given the uncertain and harsh circumstances of the time and his status as a senior Lama with great religious and moral scruples, his censuring of sexual themes in Tibetan *kāvya* verses mimicking Dandin's *Kāvyādarśa* is understandable. However, it is also undeniable that such a criticism deprives *Kāvyādarśa* of one of its fundamental attributes: the celebration of eroticism that Bod Khepa embraces. Bod Khepa is, of course, not alone in being affected by Dandin's erotic spirit. The Great

Fifth Dalai Lama's commentarial text also contains verses depicting carnal pleasure. Yet, for some reason they escape Tseten Shabdrung's critical attention. There is claimed to have been sectarian and intellectual rivalry between the Great Fifth and Bod Khepa, leading to the emergence of two schools of *kāvya* poetry. However, it is unlikely that prejudice stemming from this rivalry is the cause of Tseten Shabdrung's selective attention.[63] On the contrary, in his highly influential manual on *Kāvyādarśa*, Tseten Shabdrung commends Bod Khepa's commentary and even uses his *kāvya* exemplifications to illustrate specific similes and metaphorical figures.[64] He also demonstrates his admiration for Bod Khepa's technical mastery of *Kāvyādarśa* by composing his own illustrative verses in deliberate imitation of Bod Khepa's style.[65]

To use Tseten Shabdrung's notion of "terminological concealment," the Great Fifth may well be more adept at concealing erotic themes in specific phraseology than Bod Khepa. This might have been one of the factors, alongside the sheer religious and historical stature of the Great Fifth, that prevented Tseten Shabdrung from commenting on his erotic verses. Whatever the reasons may be, it is worth mentioning that even one of the most powerful celibate Lamas in Tibetan history composed erotic poetry, be it for the purpose of demonstrating certain figures in *Kāvyādarśa*. For the illustration of a figure known as "metaphorical ornament entailing the use of a simile" (*dpe'i gzugs rgyan*) the Great Fifth writes:

The all endowed tree of slim supple waist,
Leafy branches of thrilling passion swaying,
This bestowing of the buds of pleasure
Is like the nature of the wish-fulfilling tree.[66]

This stanza corresponds to the fifteenth of the twenty metaphorical ornaments listed by Dandin. It uses a metaphor to portray an object by initially fusing these two disparate entities through the pairing of their similar characteristics, and then concluding the verse by likening the object to the metaphor by using words that indicate similarity (*mtshungs pa gsal byed kyi sgra*) such as "like" and "as." Thus, in the concluding part of a four-line verse, the metaphor is turned into a simile. In the Great Fifth's example, a beautiful woman is seen as a great tree endowed with all good qualities (*yongs 'du'i shing*). Her limbs and body trembling with sexual arousal are compared to the swaying leaves and branches of this cornucopian tree. Her ability to give sexual gratification to the lustful is likened to "the wish-fulfilling tree" that gives abundant pleasures and riches to mankind.[67]

For the illustration of a figure called "ornament of effect before cause" (*'bras bu snga ba'i rgyan*) the Great Fifth composes another erotic verse that is more forthright and less ornate in its diction:

The young men of passion in their vibrant prime
After fully enjoying finely ripened, slim beauties
Behold their beautiful enchanting amorous looks
And yet again feel much unbearable maddening lust[68]

This particular figure is the fourteenth type of "ornaments of causation" and it reverses the natural sequence of cause and effect in such a way that it describes effect coming into existence before the cause. It is used to convey a sense of wonder caused by something unfamiliar or unexpected. In this example the Great Fifth expresses surprise at the insatiable sexual desire that follows, rather than precedes, passionate lovemaking. Here sexual arousal is seen as the cause and it should occur before what is regarded as its direct consequence, sexual intercourse. However, lovemaking does not result in gratification but fuels further desire thereby compounding the sequence of cause and effect. Thus the Great Fifth demonstrates the "ornament of effect before cause" through an intimate description of sex and intense carnal passion.

As in most verses of this type, the male gaze upon and eroticization of the female body are predominant. They are indicative of a patriarchal literary world where the woman poet is conspicuously absent and her desire is silent. As attested by most of the samples in this chapter Tibetan *kāvya* poetry favors a form of sexuality that borders on the sexual objectification of women. This is made possible by the male-dominated Tibetan literary culture in which women as author, reader, and imaginative characters are totally marginalized. Literature as a potent means of expression, representation, and creation has been usurped by Tibetan men for centuries. Tibet's masculine literary tradition hardly finds any space for the utterance of female experiences. One is hard pressed to find classical female *kāvya* poets and expositors when there are numerous old and authoritative *kāvya* commentaries composed by male authors and poets. Marginalization of the female voice is not just confined to *kāvya* poetry; it is glaringly obvious in the absence of women writers in the Tibetan literary canon as a whole. For example, popular and established anthologies of classical writing such as *Gold Ingot of Writings by Successive Great Scholars from the Land of Snows* (*Gangs ljongs mkhas dbang rim byon gyi rtsom yig gser gyi sbram bu*) used by Tibetan university students do not even feature a single female writer.[69] This is in spite of the fact that there are already established "literary foremothers" such as Yeshi Tsogyal (757–817), Machig Labdron (1055–1149), Migyur Paldron (1699–1769), and U-za Khadro (1892–1940) not to mention all the hidden female voices yet to be revealed by Tibet's future gynocritics. Although the literary merits of erotic Tibetan *kāvya* poetry are not questioned here it must be pointed out that the gaze fixed upon the female body within it belongs to the male viewer.

Erotic *kāvya* poetry is in no way limited to the imitations or pedagogic reproductions of similes and techniques in *Kāvyādarśa*. It is practiced in a multiplicity of literary genres like histories, plays, biographies, hymns, devotional songs, and so on. Commenting on this erotic literary phenomenon, Thupten Jinpa and Jaś Elsner write: "It is ironic, perhaps, since many of the poets were celibate monks, that the songs are often pregnant with sexual imagery."[70] They explain this presence of eroticism within the context of tantric mysticism. The sexual union of male and female is viewed as the most potent image to represent the tantric attainment of a mind within which bliss is fused with emptiness.[71] Mystic sexual union is undoubtedly a source for erotic poetic utterances but it is just a partial explanation. A large number of erotic passages found in the works of many distinguished classical poets are nothing to do with the mystic practice of tantric sex. They simply celebrate carnal pleasure or the potency of it as a poetic image. For instance, the poetry of Shangton, a great scholar-monk whose work has already been commented on in my analysis of Tibet's critical tradition, often employs vivid sexual imagery. The erotic references in his sublime biographical poem on Tara (*sgrol ma*) are too pronounced to be ignored by any reader.[72] Metrical variations, craftsmanship, sustained beauty, rich Indian mythological allusions, powerful and distilled images, and intensity of religious faith characterize this long poem. It consists of twenty-one sections corresponding to the twenty-one emanations or aspects of Tara. These sections deal with the enlightened activities and great deeds of deliverance undertaken by the revered female savior.

In section eight of the poem Tara delivers a beautiful courtesan from an attack by a poisonous snake.[73] The courtesan's stunning beauty (including her "heart-piercing" eyes and her petal-like lips) is described in ornate yet vivid and sensual language. As prearranged, at midnight she leaves for the place of a wealthy merchant who has pledged her immense riches for her services. On her way she rests against a tree lest too much physical exertion undermine her skills in the art of love. In no time at all she is caught in the coils of a deadly snake. Her feelings of sexual lust instantly give way to terror. Horrified she beseeches Tara with a trembling voice "like a lotus that has captured a bee." By the magical grace of Tara's mantra the venomous snake is instantly transformed into a garland of white flowers around her neck. Shangton is so taken aback by Tara's magical abilities that he utters them with a sense of disbelief in a verse that expresses admiration for Tara's providence and celebrates the courtesan's erotic power:

Or, has the snake been sweetly charmed by the touch of
Her soft, supple breasts with scratches left by lovers' nails
And has it turned its venomous self into forms of flowers
With such yearning for a long embrace? I'm in two minds![74]

In this stanza Shangton makes use of "exaggerated ornaments" (*rab rtog gi rgyan*), a *kāvya* figure favored by many Tibetan poets. As observed in chapter 3 this poetic adornment entails the attribution of animate qualities to inanimate objects or of the human faculty of thought to nonhuman beings. As such this figure carries an imaginative charge. It has three types and this stanza corresponds to "exaggerated ornament of the animate" (*sems ldan rab rtog*). Shangton attributes conscious human qualities to a snake so as to emphasize the irresistible erotic lure of the courtesan. The snake is enticed by the soft touch of her breasts exhibiting scratch marks left by lovers' nails, marks that heighten her attraction by bearing testament to her past sexual experiences. This image of amorous scratch marks is the use of an Indic *kāvyic* convention found in the *Kāma Sūtra* and other sexually charged texts. Bewitched, the snake consciously chooses to turn itself into a garland of flowers so as to give her a "long embrace." Her erotic beauty disarms a deadly snake and transforms it into an adornment. By praising Tara and the courtesan in the same breath and by expressing a slight doubt whether it was spiritual power or erotic charm that curtailed the snake attack Shangton's verse reveals a somewhat subversive undertone. It almost sacrilegiously suggests that the eroticism of the courtesan rivals the magical power of the bodhisattva-deity Tara. Such ambiguous statements found in the *kāvya* influenced traditional Tibetan literature also seem to presage the subversiveness of contemporary Tibetan erotic poetry which is not as unprecedented as it has been claimed.

In Shangton's work, as in that of many other Tibetan *kāvya* poets, erotic imagery is employed to depict phenomena totally unrelated to human sexuality. It is part and parcel of their poetic diction. The eleventh section of Shangton's biographical poem on Tara narrates the episode of her rescuing of merchants from a turbulent sea.[75] Three merchant ships brimming with precious cargos are homeward bound after a successful treasure hunt. However, a powerful storm suddenly gathers and turns "the great sea into a seething mass of violent waves" threatening to capsize the ships. Prayers to various gods all prove ineffectual with the exception of a recital of Tara's ten-syllable mantra by a sworn Buddhist (*dge bsnyen*).[76] At the very instant these sacred words are uttered the storm abates and the ships make it to terra firma overnight. As the ships return home with their cargos intact at dawn Shangton describes the break of day:

Then the temptress of the azure sky
Rolled up her skirt of darkness,
And the sun eager to embrace her
Stretched out its arms of dawn[77]

Here the object of poetic description is the moment immediately before sunrise, but Shangton selects erotic imagery and terminology for its depiction. This figure is another type of "exaggerated ornament" called "the exaggerated ornament of the inanimate" (*sems med rab rtog*). It entails ascribing attributes of human or other creatures to inanimate objects. This is akin to the rhetoric figure known as animism in English literary terminology, in which something lifeless is imbued with the qualities of life or spirit. In the above lines natural phenomena are eroticized through the femininity of the sky and the masculinity of the sun: the sky is personified as a seductive woman tempting the sun, a sexually aroused man with his outstretched "arms of dawn."[78] The *kāvyic* expressions of eroticism discussed in this section and their kind serve as a literary backdrop to contemporary Tibetan erotic writings, although this is not openly acknowledged.

THE *KĀVYIC* BEE STILL FLUTTERS

Tibetan *kāvya* poetry's use of similes, metaphors, regular meter, and erotic themes has been inherited by modern poets. The degree of this influence varies from one poet to another. It is obvious in some and subtle in others. Even the simple fact that one of the most frequently used names for the female breast in contemporary poetic writings is a *kāvya* epithet bears witness to this continuity. Today's young Tibetan poets have no qualms about employing the term *myos bum*, "breasts that madden" (literally vases that madden), for its descriptive and affective qualities—even though many of them are critical of *Kāvyādarśa*'s hold on Tibetan poetry. We find *kāvya*'s presence in contemporary poets who are acclaimed for their innovativeness and iconoclastic spirit. For instance, in Sangdhor's erotic poem *A Trio: Me, Tonight and the Lady*, the footfalls of *kāvya* can be heard right from the beginning:

Her eyes, bees ceaseless flutter
Her lips, flowers agape blossom
This lady who shoots white smiles
Is why the bedding is snug tonight

Over the soft body, dapples moist and wet
Round the firm chest whirls heat and fire
This lady with irregular heartbeats
Is why the night is fleeting tonight

Depths of flesh, bone, marrow all numbed
Hearts, livers and lungs all sent pulsating
This lady drunk with pleasure affirms
The enlightened narrative of my manhood tonight

Firm round breasts repeatedly caress
Loose supple belly frequently uplifts
This lady with eyebrows afloat on water
A testament to my muteness tonight

Each raindrop from mouth seeps into the mouth
Each blood-drop of tongue flows into the tongue
This lady assured with myriad magical skills
The sum of many stars that came out tonight

Ecstatic movements of flesh like soul nectar
The sound of groans delectable like jaggery
This lady, incarnate of utter wish-fulfilment
The legend of the quivering moon tonight

Like peacock plumage iridescent and shimmering
Like snowflakes virgin white and fleecy
This lady, a sight so beauteous, so enchanting
A witness to the cessation of snoring tonight

Amorous frolic shatters bedside thermos
Fluids red and white spoil cushions silken
This lady driven mad by passion wild
Preliminary act of my generosity tonight

This lady bestowed by Karma and encounter
This lady won by chance and fortunate accident
Is the sound of a patterned glass button dropping
Is the tear in the long white silk gown flowing

The flavor of life, bitter or sweet
Be the nature of Samsara, joy or woe
For a torch amidst the darkness of life
I will choose this lady lying next to me[79]

In this narrative poem of regular meter depicting an erotic encounter, Sangdhor uses commonplace images in tandem with new figurations. Age-old *kāvyic* metaphors paint the facial beauty of a woman the poet meets by chance. Portrayal of lips as flowers or petals and eyes as bees is a time-tested *kāvyic* practice. One of the most celebrated instances of this can be found in Tsongkhapa's (1357–1419) distilled and eloquent hymn to Sarasvati. In this devotional poem with sensual nuances Tsongkhapa praises and supplicates the Goddess of Melody:

Lotus-faced with fluttering bees of eyes
Luminous white moon tops blue tresses
Melodious Goddess poised in graceful dance
Grant woeful me the sublime power of speech[80]

Metaphorical recurrences such as Sangdhor's first stanza, busy with
motions demonstrate that such familiar images have retained their potency in
the modern age. Flying or quivering bees (*g.yo ldan*), a blossoming flower,
and darting smiles revealing a perfect row of shining "white teeth" (*tshems
dkar*) help capture the nonstop movements of a love-enraptured face.[81]
Other imagistic borrowings from Tibetan *kāvya* poetry like "soul nectar"
(*bdud rtsi*) and jaggery (*bu ram*) are used as synesthetic expressions to communicate the attraction power of the flesh and vocal utterances of pleasure.
Tactile and aural phenomena are presented as being ineluctable to one's
sense of taste.[82] "Utter wish-fulfilment"[83] and "peacock plumage" are other
images that display *kāvyic* genesis. Yet their descriptive power in portraying
"shimmering beauty" and a lover's capacity to bestow endless pleasure is
undiminished.

Although I am highlighting these *kāvyic* traces in Sangdhor's poem, it must
be stated that the poem itself is not dominated by figures and techniques of
kāvya poetry. It is quite unique in its embrace of narrative genre, use of novel
images, and lyricism (not to mention its frank depiction of an autobiographical incident).[84] What stands out is his creation of some exquisite images to
distill the erotic intensity of the occasion. To cite but a few, the image of float-
ing eyebrows imparts the beauty of the woman at an intimately close range
by poetically reconstructing the perspirations of passionate physical exertion.
This sweat along with saliva and blood-drops (signs of raw passion) and her
"myriad magical skills" are condensed into the picture of the numerous stars
that came out shining for the night. The night sky imagery continues in "the
quivering moon," mirroring powerful sensations of sexual ecstasy that reduce
human flesh to shivering. Images say things directly as well as leaving things
unsaid for the imagination. The sound of a falling glass button and a tear in
a flowing silk gown paint in words the process of undressing, but they also,
especially the latter image, hint at a tearing of the flesh. Above all, Sangdhor
uses concentrated images of precision to celebrate samsaric existence with
erotic love at its center. His adoption of religious terminology confirms this
point and also displays his characteristic cynical attitude to religion. By contrast, no such implicit criticism of religion can be found in the conventional
Tibetan *kāvya* verse, although at times ambiguous utterances carrying mild
subversion can be detected. Sangdhor's "enlightened narrative" (*rnam thar*)
and "preliminary act" (*sngon 'gro*) concern only sexual pleasure and virility
rather than dharmic deeds.[85] His preference for samsara is made emphatic in
the concluding stanza when the poet chooses the woman lying beside him
with which to face the human condition, be it "bitter or sweet." Thus sexual
passion transmutes into life-affirming romantic love.

Other modern poets commingle eroticism and spirituality in verses which
bear the imprint of *kāvya* poetry. In a playfully entitled poem *The So-called*

Heart-Essence of the Lustful Female Lover, Kyabchen Dedrol flaunts his technical virtuosity in *kāvya* poetics by writing a verse drawing on the "ornament of the twice duplicated syllable" (*zung ldan gyi rgyan*), a *kāvyic* rhyming scheme. As the poet describes a mind enraptured by a combination of earthly *eros* and divine *agape* again the *kāvyic* bees are in flight within the lines:

Sound of the fluttering bees of stunning eyes
Pierces sound-catching ears to the petalled heart
A mind beset by piercing pain beyond salvation
Will never be used by other things born of the mind[86]

This is a type of phonetic ornament (*sgra rgyan*) in which the end word or the end syllable of the first line of a poem is repeated at the beginning of the next line. It is often the case that, although the exact word is repeated, it has a different meaning every time it reappears. For instance, in the Tibetan original of this excerpt the first line ends with the one syllable word *sgra* (sound). *Sgra* is repeated at the beginning of the next line, but this time it combines with another syllable, *'dzin* (to catch) to form the word *sgra 'dzin*, which literally translates as "the sound catcher," a common kenning for the ear.

Such stylistic concerns involving a combination of rhyming and alliteration occupy a considerable space in *Kāvyādarśa*. In fact, Dandin is said to have given more attention to this phonetic element than most of his Indian contemporaries.[87] It is difficult to render the phonological aspects into English with any degree of exactitude, but my translation should show Kyabchen Dedrol's deliberate imitation of *kāvyic* rhyming and alliterative devices. However, in this poem his attempts to display technical mastery shroud its subject matter in obscurity. The form takes precedence over the content. As a result, it is difficult to ascertain if the poem celebrates a divine muse or an irresistible temptress or both.

This fusion of devotion and erotic desire is a recurrent theme in contemporary Tibetan verse. Lhamkog, a celibate monk, also writes a thematically similarly poem in his *Glorious Goddess*. This metrical composition describes the moving impressions made on him by a Tara painting by Amdo Jampa, who introduced photorealism to Tibet and is feted as the father of modern Tibetan painting. It is written in the melodious and rhythmic meter of *Tara Praises*, with borrowings of *kāvya* imagery and Gedun Choepel's musicality.[88] Spiritual love and sexual yearning induced by the painted goddess coalesce with poetic fluidity. This literary vogue for things both divine and erotic might also be echoing a certain genre of Tibetan experiential spiritual songs (*nyams mgur*) that mix sex and spirituality.

BLENDING SEX AND SPIRITUALITY

Unlike erotic *kāvya* poetry, Tibetan Buddhist spiritual songs on the whole do not conceal sexual themes in coded language or ornate expressions. Like contemporary Tibetan erotic poems they combine vernacular and formal idioms in their diction and use sexual imagery and language with subversive significance. As these erotic poem-songs are mostly composed by roaming tantric practitioners, who straddle the sacred and profane realms of Tibetan society, they communicate both spiritual and secular issues touching the lives of ordinary people. Although it is difficult to ascertain the degree of their impact upon contemporary literary creations, their extensive diffusion and popularity among the laity and the reverential esteem shown by today's writers to the singing yogis as great precursor poets underscore their literary legacy. For instance, Hortsang Jigme, an acclaimed poet and historian, acknowledges this literary continuity in a lighthearted poem dedicated to Drukpa Kunleg (1455–1529). He expresses his admiration for Drukpa Kunleg's sexually explicit songs and anecdotes centered around an omnipotent phallus and bemoans the death of this famed mad yogi by saying: "How woeful that you've departed for another realm/ Otherwise your dick would surely win us Independence!"[89] In fact, the life story of Drukpa Kunleg is a good starting point for an appreciation of erotic spiritual songs as another literary precedent. This also undermines the asserted novelty of the provocative use of graphic sexual language within contemporary Tibetan poetry.

There are several biographies of Drukpa Kunleg, the most famous mad yogi (*grub myon*) of Tibet.[90] Each is a treasure of Tibetan literature and spiritual insight. Here I have selected the most popular of them all called *Biography of Kunga Legpa, the Lord of Beings, Including the Accounts of his Conduct in Mon Padro ('Gro ba'i mgon po kun dga' legs pa'i rnam thar mon spa gro sogs kyi mdzad spyod rnams bzhugs so)*. It is a collection of orally transmitted anecdotes about his insane deeds and adventures.[91] It is written in a mixture of prose and verse. Prose narrates incidents and metrical songs transmit his teachings, which are often known as "Dharma of Copulation" (*rgyo chos*). His tales and songs are famous throughout Tibet because of their humor, sexual content, and sheer outrageousness mingled with religious messages. His style is simple and popular, his diction vernacular and expressive, his themes sexual, dharmic, and satirical. He frequently resorts to explicit sexual terminology and topics to teach both humans and demons a lesson. Tibetan Buddhists justify this bent for lewd language and conduct in religious terms. It is believed that such lascivious speech and action were to convey the essence of the dharma and help people to free themselves from the cycle of birth and death. The biography itself makes it apparent that the aim of his quirky, nonconformist behavior was either to effect spiritual realization or to instill Buddhist principles and values, such as justice, humility, and diligence. In some cases such acts are for the attainment of the enlightened rainbow body.[92] However, it seems that the ultimate target of Drukpa Kunleg's ribald wit and unorthodox behavior is the hypocrisy, corruption, and conformism of Tibet's clergy and their followers. He gets away with attacking established social norms and religious practices through songs and conduct that would be considered sacrilegious in a lesser person.

Drukpa Kunleg's subversive words and deeds are too many to be enumerated here. However, the use of the imagery of carnal passion to express his unconventional spirit can be highlighted through a few key examples. In a memorable scene near the beginning of his biography, Drukpa Kunleg ridicules the pomposity and misogynistic attitude of elite Tibetan monks. On one occasion, monks engaged in a dialectical debate are offended by Drukpa Kunleg's refusal to prostrate before them and their revered stupa. When the monks tell him that such a conduct is "heretical and goes against the words of the Victorious One (Buddha)" he responds by prostrating before a beautiful woman standing next to the stupa and sings sacred praises of her. The monks are repulsed and consider him insane. Unperturbed by their dismayed reaction, Drukpa Kunleg justifies his action stating:

> Generally speaking, because woman is the passage of all things good and bad she is the very nature of wisdom. In particular, when you virtuous masters (*dge ba'i bshes gnyen*) took disciplinary vows before monastic preceptors (*mkhan po*) making unstinting offerings of gold, silver and silk, you were ordained for guarding against what resides within the open and expansive mandala in the loins of this woman. And because she is no different from the stupa, I have prostrated before her.[93]

This rejoinder silences the monks and draws laughter from the lay onlookers. Along with the intellectual ostentation prevalent in monastic communities, Drukpa Kunleg mocks the vow of celibacy that enjoins monks to guard themselves against sexual desire, symbolized by the female abdomen. Denigrated carnal passion and despised women folk are revered over the monastic community and high learning. Moreover, for celibate monks, what lurks within the loins of a woman is more than just sexual temptation. Within it also "resides" the procreative power that would drag them back to the world of the laity. In a legalistic assessment of the Pali Vinaya's take on proscribed sex, Janet Gyatso observes that "what really made sex with a woman worse than any other kind was its practical upshot: marriage, children, the householder's life; in short, samsara, or what the Buddha calls 'village *dhamma*.'"[94] She concludes that monastic law's prohibition of sex with women is ultimately to ensure the existence of the monastic community rather than for any soteriological purposes.[95] Here Drukpa Kunleg might also, through his outrageous acts, be lampooning monks' fear of women resulting from such a desire for institutional preservation. His conduct and speech are not as unprecedented as they appear. He simply accentuates certain aspects of Tibetan tantric Buddhism that hold women as the source of wisdom and recommend embracing sexual passion for attaining the ultimate bliss of enlightenment.[96] Nevertheless, for most Tibetans who are not acquainted with complex tantric teachings and practices, such conduct and utterance help to question received attitudes toward women and sex.[97]

In another episode, Drukpa Kunleg upends the social mores that prohibit the mention of sex or sexually explicit terms in the presence of one's close relations. Akhu Tenzin, a rich and successful family head, asks him for a teaching beneficial to his impending death. Drukpa Kunleg instructs Akhu Tenzin to recite a specific Refuge Prayer without any inhibition whenever the old man thinks of him. He sings out this *Refuge Dharma for the Liberation from Samsara*:

I pay homage to the dick of the old man,
Fallen over at the root like an old tree, yet unable to let go of self-clinging.
I pay homage to the pussy of the old woman,
Fallen into great depths like a narrow ravine, yet unable to let go of lust.
I pay homage to the dick of the young tigerish man,
Fearlessly facing death when pride surges up from deep within.
I pay homage to the pussy of the young woman,
Fearless of decency and inhibition when ecstasy rolls like waves in her loins.[98]

Then Drukpa Kunleg tells the old man to recite this "Quadruple Refuge Prayer" once every time he comes to the latter's mind. Akhu Tenzin thanks his Lama for the invocation and asks for an aspiration prayer. He consents by uttering the following couplet:

For the great tree in the east is thick; its leafy branches seem to flourish and flourish
For the old dick of Kunleg is thick; this small pussy seems to tighten and tighten[99]

Drukpa Kunleg instructs the old man to learn these words by heart. His family is aghast when, during a mealtime, they hear the Quadruple Refuge Prayer for the first time. Totally embarrassed, they run out of the door with their eating bowls in their hands. Akhu Tenzin's wife thinks he has gone mad. She entreats him not to say the prayer in the presence of his family again, but the old man is adamant to recite it as instructed. As a result, he is made to move into a separate hut where he recites the prayers day and night for a month and eventually attains rainbow body.[100] Drukpa Kunleg's peculiar Refuge Prayer emphasizes the power of self-clinging, pride, and sexual lust that many Buddhist ascetics seek to renounce in their spiritual quests. It is not necessarily a message to abandon these emotions outright. At a mystical level it might also be construed as an indirect instruction to overcome such basic instincts by channeling them into emancipatory energies through yogic practices as taught by the tantric tradition. However, what is undoubted is the critical edge of the prayer. It mingles plain speech and religious idiom to unsettle both clergy and laity who hold fast to conventional social norms.

This critical spirit, imparted through an unconventional use of prurient language, becomes more apparent in other songs that interweave Dharmic principles and bawdiness. On one occasion devout patrons from Mon in the South request a specific teaching from Drukpa Kunleg that would start in the conventional way with the words: "'In the language of India' and 'in the language of Tibet.'" It needs to be easily transmissible while being persuasive enough on the laws of causality to move one to tears. It also needs to be interspersed with humor. Finally, this enlightening teaching must be simple, memorable, and able to effect liberation upon just hearing it. In response Drukpa Kunleg gives the following teaching:

In the language of India: "Darting dick darts, darts!"
In the language of Tibet: "Whistling pussy whistles, whistles!"
Homage to the Guru who thrusts, thrusts!

The Sermon on the Darting Dick and Whistling Pussy is composed of two parts: the ideal and the inadequate. Firstly, it's an ideal sermon because:

The bed is the wheel of copulation
It's ideal when comfy and wide
Knees are the messengers of copulation
They are ideal for dispatching in advance
Hands are the girths of copulation
They are ideal for gentle touch and gripping
Hips are the corvee labourers of copulation
They are ideal for driving around and around

Secondly, what it would not be ideal for is:

Even if one boasts a clitoris, triangular and exquisite
It wouldn't do as a pure, ritual offering object
Even if one boasts bum-hair, long and coarse
It wouldn't do as a thread for stitching sheepskin *chuba*s
Even if one boasts testicles, thick and large
They wouldn't do as a provisions-bag for the hermitage
Even if one boasts a dick, hard based and large headed
It wouldn't do as a hammer for striking in a peg

In between [the ideal and the not ideal] are the following laws of causality:

Don't let words be as sharp as a clitoris!
If words are as sharp as a clitoris
One falls out with and is hated by everyone.
Be gentle as a knob at the entrance of a pussy
And one gets along with everyone!

Don't be as unruly as pubic hair!
If one is as unruly as pubic hair
One offends and falls out with everyone.
People love those who are self-effacing
Like testicles that wade through warm fluids.

Don't roam around as much as the fart!
If one roams around as much as the fart
One falls out with everyone and causes ruin.
It's better to be shut like the black asshole.

Oh, for the clitoris is agile, it rides one astride,
For the knob is daring, it ventures inside,
For the testicles are meek, they remain outside.

The all-pervasive view of non-duality
Resembles the inner stretch of a pussy, long and wide.
The clear, empty meditation of non-grasping
Resembles the blood of a pussy, clear and red.[101]
The sixfold conduct of equilibrium
Resembles the blissful union of dick and pussy.
The tantras of the development stage and the mind of the completion stage,
Embrace them with great seriousness like donkeys copulating.

When putting them into practice
Be as fast as cockerels copulating.
When sealing retreat cells with cement
Make them as tight as dogs copulating.

Thus this sermon on worldly pleasure
Fuels the sexual lust of the young.
Let it refresh the past memories of old women,
And be the present practice of the tigerish youths.
It's the remorseless deeds of old men,
It's repulsive for the pure, disciplined monks,
It's the true statement of kings and chieftains,
It's the experiential practice of me, Kunga Legpa![102]

Tantric mysticism which pronounces that "[T]he wisdom of great sexual lust/ Grants enlightenment to the lustful"[103] would interpret this song at a deeper and more recondite level. For those of us who do not possess any specialized knowledge or spiritual experience in such esoteric matters, Drukpa

Kunleg communicates both religious messages and practical worldly advice framed within idioms of humor and ribaldry. Along with instructions on advanced meditative states and complex notions such as nonduality, we are told to uphold humility, patience, civility, and diligence. Nevertheless, as Aris argues, the popular appeal of this genre of literature lies in its expression of a critical, alternative voice against the established religious authorities. It is a voice that can easily be understood by the masses. In a study of a Bhutanese text on the "dharma of copulation" (that highly resembles Drukpa Kunleg's sermon), Aris observes that it "is precisely the inversion of the sacred which gives the story its whole effect: the formalism of monastic ritual and literature is continuously satirized. This presupposes an audience fully conversant with the orthodoxies that are being parodied, and so the audience is compelled."[104]

In Drukpa Kunleg's sermon the relentless parodying of the formal structure and language of monastic literature is evident at the outset. The sacred convention of starting a treatise with a phrase in Sanskrit followed by its Tibetan equivalent is imitated by inserting the names for male and female genitals as substitutes. The naming of sexual organs is made more graphic by adding reduplicated, onomatopoetic suffixes such as *mje sha ra ra* and *stu shu ru ru*. These reduplicated syllables are not purely for rhythmic or phonetic effect. They are descriptive of the shape, sound, and movement of the respective genitals.[105] Thus in accordance with the demands of the Mon patrons the sermon is memorable, eloquent, humorous, and religious. Most of all its language is deliberately crude and provocative throughout. As shown in Dhatsenpo's *Even If You Don't Like It, So What? I Write Like This*, contemporary erotic poets take pride in being the first artists to have introduced sexually explicit terms into Tibetan poetry. Many Tibetan writers accept such assertions without much critical reflection as they either praise or condemn young poets for bringing into poetic usage terms like "penis," "vagina," "testicles," and so on.[106] However, they seem to have suffered from a temporary amnesia when making such absolute statements. Unorthodox songs by the likes of Drukpa Kunleg abundantly demonstrate that graphic sexual terminology and imagery had already found their way into Tibetan poetry, even if such poets were in the minority. However, spiritual poem-songs, no matter how vulgar their language, almost always contain a religious message or an ethical principle. Modern Tibetan erotic poems are unambiguous about their emphasis on the carnal desires of the flesh. Even when they borrow religious terminology, as does Sangdhor in his poem cited above, it is injected with sensual connotations.

Needless to say that Drukpa Kunleg is not alone in conveying spiritual lessons through the vehicle of graphic sexual language. Other great Tibetan tantric practitioners show a penchant for sexual terminology in their spiritual songs. Unlike Drukpa Kunleg, whose maverick conduct and speech are approved by the Tibetan notion of the "crazy yogi" (*grub myon*), many of

these figures are accomplished practitioners and scholars held in high esteem
by the religious establishment. This shows that erotically charged poetry is
not confined to the songs of mad saints, but can also be found scattered in the
works of intellectual lamas and yogis. For instance, Nyingkyi Nangzad Dorje
(Nyang skyes snang mzad rdo rje; 1798–1874), a perspicacious tantric adept,
writes such a poem-song. He was a principal disciple of the great Shabkarpa
and was responsible for compiling the latter's works, which consist of thirty-
two volumes.[107] Nyingkyi usually writes in a *kāvya*-influenced style, employing formal terminology. Yet he occasionally switches to a less contrived and
more fluid style peppering the diction with colloquial speech. This can be
seen in the following excerpt, which is an internal dialogue with his sex:

I bow before the feet of my Great Lama,
Please bless me to dissolve the Three Poisons!
One night upon lying down in my bed
My vajra became so erect I was restless[108]
And many thoughts crowded my mind.
"Hey, you unfortunate vajra!" I said.
"You might have great virility
Yet, I, this Father, have an ugly face
No young beauty would ever desire me.
Because I don't live in a monastery
Where would I find the thighs of young monks?
Let alone any beautiful women
I wouldn't even find a pathetic nun.
Even if I were able to find one
I would break the self-liberating vows
And be disgraced as a breaker of the vows,
Ending up completely empty-handed.
I am fortunate among the unfortunates;
I don't need to climb rocky mountains
Nor do I need to feed sons and daughters.
Therefore, let us keep the vows,"
Thus I gave counsel to my vajra.
In response my vajra spoke as follows:
"Whatever woman, good or bad, comes into sight
As long as you don't set eyes upon her
How can I, the eyeless, attempt to behold her!"
Thus speaking its head collapsed.
My eyeless son has passed away
How wretched is this enemy—Desire![109]

In this song Nyingkyi writes about his grappling with the Three Poisons
(*dug gsum*) or the three root causes of suffering. After overcoming the poison

of desire, he successfully fights off the poisons of hatred and ignorance in the subsequent sections without employing sexual terminology. Although Nyingkyi's song ultimately negates erotic desire, it depicts the intensity of this emotion and various ways of gratification. The power of carnal passion can cause sleep deprivation and a restless mental state beset by licentious thoughts. Like Bod Khepa, Nyingkyi's voice is unique and daring in that he has the rare courage to mention homoerotic tendencies in monastic communities. His temerity also allows him to touch on the taboo of sexual intercourse with a nun (*jo mo*).[110] In short, the religious content of Nyingkyi's poem coexists with its portrayal of erotic intensity, the listing of potential sexual partners, and humorous yet precise description of the male sexual organ.

More often than not this erotic type of spiritual song, while conveying religious instructions, mirrors the humor and idiom of ordinary people. For that reason, such a genre functions as an artistic medium that blurs the already porous line between the sacred and the profane. It also blends literary language with common parlance, an attribute it shares with contemporary Tibetan literature. A collection of spiritual songs by the Second Shabkarpa contains many such instances, but to cite one example:

Yes, listen to me, my devout son!
The force of an unruly mind is like sex
No matter how much one indulges it
There's never a time one is satisfied.
The desire-afflicted mind is like a vagina
Nothing can fill it up, big or small,
So be contented, don't covet any riches
Pride of the conceited mind is like a dick
No matter how much one softens it
It only becomes stiffer and stiffer,
So it's better to stay humble and lowly.
All activities are like a loafer's testicles
No matter how frantic, they're all in vain,
So it's better to stay curled up in bed.
Ingratiating oneself with others is like a clitoris
No matter how hard one tries to catch it
One can never catch hold of it for long,
So it's better to be independent with purity.
A bad friend is like a heap of shit
The more time spent with him, the more he stinks
So it's better to throw him far way.[111]

It must be noted that this English translation belies the vernacular feel of the poem which mostly uses Amdo patois such as *g.yab* (sex or to have sex).

The Second Shabkarpa composed this poem for a certain Yeshi "in jest." It is a *mgur* that resembles the style and content of the elegant sayings genre (*legs bshad*) in its brevity, dispensation of practical advice and pithy expressions. An untamable mind, insatiable desire, egocentrism, banal activities, flattery, and bad company are discouraged. In the very same breath, common sense, contentment, humility, moderation, moral probity, and a wise choice of friendship are advocated. As in other verses of this kind, what is novel is that such traditional values are promoted through the unwonted medium of sexual language. Even the most sophisticated philosophical tenets and meditation practices are described using graphic sexual images. For instance, the practice of Dzogchen, the Great Perfection, consists of three aspects: "view, meditation, and conduct."[112] In another song, the Second Shabkarpa likens these tripartite elements to "vagina," "sexual union," and "dick at the entrance of a vagina" so as to encapsulate the expanse, blissful luminosity and all-penetrating liberating qualities of "view, meditation, and conduct" respectively.[113] A similar passage can be found in Drukpa Kunleg's sermon above. It is important to note that this erotically charged style is subversive but not revolutionary. It provocatively shows that both worldly and sacred wisdom can be conveyed through ordinary speech without resorting to recondite language. It implicitly criticizes the formalism of scholastic monastic literature, along with the ostentation and hypocrisy of the religious elite, but does not seek to overthrow the latent Buddhist worldview. The reliance upon spoken language and the use of crude humor demonstrate these works' heavy debt to secular Tibetan oral culture, locking it into an inseparable embrace with the literate sacred realm.

EROTIC UTTERANCES OF ORALITY

Many literary historians concur that the literature of any culture has its roots in artistic oral compositions. Reflecting this line of reasoning, in his short introduction to English literature Jonathan Bate observes that "all longstanding national literatures have their origins in oral tradition."[114] The roots of Tibetan literature are also deeply embedded in oral art forms. From archaic manuscripts buried in the Dunhuang caves to a plethora of literary creations in the form of life stories, spiritual experiential songs, religious teachings, ritual texts, genealogical accounts, and historical narratives, much Tibetan literature bears oral imprints of different kinds and to varying degrees. Tibetan erotic poetry shares this oral genesis. As can be inferred from the orally transmitted tales of Drukpa Kunleg, sexually explicit *mgur* and stories, in their use of vernacular language and ribaldry, draw on Tibetan oral culture, which is rich in erotic expressions. Unlike the *mgur* genre, which invariably displays a religious import, these verbal utterances are mainly direct treatments of sexual themes. They are for amusement and provocation rather than carrying ethical messages. For instance, the famous tales attributed to Akhu Tonpa include many episodes narrating his various sexual exploits, including his successful courting of celibate nuns and even an incestuous relationship with his sister. However, none of the officially sanctioned publications of Akhu Tonpa's adventures contains the sexually graphic anecdotes that one comes across in oral transmission.[115]

The omission of sexually explicit episodes in printed editions of oral literature is not limited to the tales of Akhu Tonpa. Neither is the erotic courtship of the King of Hor and Drukmo incorporated into the printed editions of *Battle of Hor and Ling*. In this episode of the Tibetan epic narrative, King Gesar of Ling wages a war with Gurkar, the king of the Hor tribe, over the abduction of his principal queen, Drukmo.[116] However, popular legend has it that although Gurkar is an evil and fainthearted king, his sexual allure and virility surpass those of Gesar. It is said that Drukmo preferred him in bed. In oral renditions, graphic tales detailing such features and Gurkar's relentless wooing of Drukmo and her eventual capitulation intermingle with the accounts of Gesar's and his warriors' deeds. For instance, as a young nomad boy I was mesmerized by a tale involving sexual organs with transmogrifying powers. According to this account, Drukmo, unswayed by Gurkar's sugared words of seduction, initially refuses to have sex with him. They vie with one another in magical displays and Drukmo turns her vagina into a great valley. Gurkar responds by transforming his penis into a great mountain. Then Drukmo turns her vagina into the eye of a needle, but Gurkar matches her magic trickery by transforming his organ into a strand of horsetail hair. This and similar sketches found in oral sources, such as Drukmo's comparative descriptions of her lovers' sexual organs, have not made it onto the printed page. Such omissions sanitize oral narratives by depriving them of sexual components. Common editorial excisions like these not only undermine the richness and artistic integrity of an oral composition, but also mislead the reader. To someone not immersed in Tibetan oral culture, the printed version of these narratives would give the impression of a very prudish society. Needless to say this is not an accurate representation.

As mentioned already, taboos prohibit sexual talk in specific familial or public spaces. However, outside these realms social discourse is often laced with "carnal speech" (*'dod gtam*) or "dirty talk" (*kha gtsog*). In addition to sexually themed tales, there are also many songs, ballads, proverbs, turns of phrase, and figures of speech that are erotically charged. Such erotic or sexual expressions are part and parcel of one's upbringing. For instance, as adolescent boys my friends and I used to memorize sexually suggestive songs and utterances from adults so as to engage in singsong contests or verbal sparring.

We used to sing songs such as the following whilst not being fully aware of their meaning:

Against your little bosoms
Let me put my little heart
Over your deep dark forest
Let me drag my scale weights

This genre of erotic songs is made memorable by metrical simplicity, an alternate rhyme scheme (a b a b), frequent alliterations and a riddle-like rhetoric device. It is composed in a popular seven-syllable meter with end rhymes, characteristic of many Amdo love songs. The first two lines are an explicit depiction of erotic intention. They are followed by two more cryptic lines describing sexual intercourse through the use of metaphors. Euphemistic expressions are used to inject the lines with an intriguing quality. For a proper comprehension of this oral verse one must work out that "scale weights" (*rgya rdo*) denotes testicles and "deep dark forest" (*rgya rdzong nags*) stands for the female genitals covered with hair. As part of an overall catchy phonetic pattern, the phoneme *rgya* is repeated to produce an alliterative effect, although conveying different meanings. The brevity, verbal artistry, and riddling quality of such oral versification make it an effective poetic vehicle for the oral diffusion of erotic themes. However, this type of oral art is not represented on the modern printed page. There are many laudable collections of Tibetan oral literature, including love songs, but so far I have not come across a single volume featuring erotic oral poetry. Once again the ever-present and potent notion of shame is at play. In what is otherwise an exceptional anthology of folk songs collected from Pari and its adjacent areas, the editors (although professedly preoccupied with cultural preservation) leave out the oral genre of erotic poetry.[117] In a versified preface for this volume, the famed scholar Pari Sangje (Dpa' ris sangs rgyas) justifies this omission as follows:

Only the genre of folksongs is printed out in this volume,
So that it can be picked up in assemblies of young and old.
Not a single love song depicting passions of men and women,
Can be found here, so don't tire yourselves out looking for it.[118]

The upshot is that it is a book that can be read in public without offending anyone. Such morally induced expurgations conceal a salient aspect of Tibetan oral culture in printed publications. This might also partly explain the shocked reaction to and seeming novelty of contemporary Tibetan erotic poetry. The world of the printed Tibetan word has suddenly been flooded by a flurry of erotic publications. It seems that, overwhelmed by this deluge, explicit treatment of sexual themes has appeared novel to Tibetan critics, who have forgotten both literary and oral precedents.

SEXUAL IMAGERY FOR THE NATION

It is clear that Tibetan poetry was no stranger to both subtle and explicit sexual themes prior to the proliferation of erotic poems in contemporary Tibetan literary production. What makes contemporary erotic poetry distinctive is the extended attention and space accorded to sexual themes and its dissemination through traditional modes of print media as well as Internet technology. The majority of contemporary erotic poems discussed here are widely available both in book format and online. As for traditional forms of Tibetan literature, with the exception of tantric sex manuals and Gedun Choepel's and Mipham's treatises on passion, no volumes or extensive sections of poetic works are dedicated just to sex, whereas in contemporary poetic writings sex is treated at great length. It is not used as mere metaphor nor mentioned briefly or in passing, but given undivided attention. For instance, Dhatsenpo's "dick poems" are the central feature of his second book of poems (2007) entitled *To Say Something Funny*. Through the use of erotic imagery and themes they deal with topics ranging from various aspects of lust, including sexual longing and frustration, to general dissatisfaction with life and the current sociopolitical situation. Likewise, erotic subject matter is the most striking feature of a volume of poems called *Death* by Gawu (Ge'u), a well-known member of the Fourth Generation of Tibetan Poets.[119] His poems capture the intensity of sexual desire and play through the employment of nomadic parlance, as well as depicting contemporary nomadic life in its myriad facets. Sangdhor gives a precise summary of this volume when he tentatively suggests that Gawu's book of poems might be saying that the definition of life is "to die after having sex many a time."

As demonstrated already, Sangdhor is himself a keen writer of erotic poems. Some of his most eloquent, musical and imagistically distilled poetic works concern aspects of sexuality. The first section of his long regular verse poem *Real Nomad Woman*, *'brog mo ngo ma*, provides a vivid portrayal of the female nomad aided by the poet's own pastoralist upbringing and attention to minute detail. Sangdhor uses his own carnal experiences to paint a sexually intimate picture of female Tibetan nomads. His observation is sharp, yet at times he reinforces stereotyped images of Tibetan nomads as unhygienic and rough by exaggerating unsavory qualities as can be seen in the following excerpt:

No custom of bathing before sex
No custom of wiping after sex
No cleaning tissues whatsoever
Wondrous is the real nomad woman

Inside her bed smells of grass
Her pretty hair smells of dung

Her mouth tastes of Tsampa
Wondrous is the real nomad woman

Dust cakes her pubic hair
Secretion seals her vagina
Earth sticks to her buttocks
Wondrous is the real nomad woman[120]

Sangdhor's portrayal of nomadic women with warts and all in this long and explicit poem would seem downright derogatory in parts were it not for its nuanced panegyric tone and applauding of pastoral beauty. He uses a technique very similar to that referred to by Tibetan *kāvya* poets as "the ornament of covert praise" (*zol bstod kyi rgyan*) in which the poet extols an object by pretending to denigrate its qualities (*smad pa'i zol gyis bstod pa*).[121] In *Real Nomad Woman*, Sangdhor praises the rustic simplicity and charm of nomadic women and their perceived harmonious relationship with nature. Underneath "dust" and "dung" lies a romanticized and idealized image of unchanging rustic beauty. This becomes more evident when the poem goes on to describe the nomadic woman as "unforgettable even after death," "with eyes that utter speeches" and "expressions that send love letters." As the poem progresses, sexual references give way to pastoral descriptions in which "butterflies flutter over her shoulders" and "bees bounce on her back." In another long poem called *Mask of Ordinary Life*, consisting of 124 four-line stanzas, Sangdhor celebrates sexual desire without supplementing it with other themes.[122] It is a highly subjective poem which contains frank confessions of the poet's various sexual encounters and advocacy of desire free of social and moral restrictions. In this poem bearing the influences of Gedun Choepel's *Treatise on Passion* and the compact syntax of classical poetry, Sangdhor uses subjective experience to unmask the wild face of lust unrestrained by morality or religion. Such unapologetic celebration of sexual passion from a purely secular perspective is indeed novel in written Tibetan poetry.

Another distinctive feature of modern Tibetan erotic poetry is the concern with today's Tibet. Poets are preoccupied with what occurs in the present and question the current sociopolitical status quo through the use of erotic imagery. In a poem called *When Attending a Meeting with Great Boredom, Sun snang chen pos tshogs 'dur zhungs na*, Dhatsenpo targets the CCP's political ritual of convening endless meetings throughout the year:[123]

With a feeling of one's own blood-drops dwindling
One feels that interminably sitting hunched up like this
Might end up crushing the two testicles

If the dignitaries run out of things to say here and now

One feels their flat tongues might turn into planks
Inside the cocooned bedding of their wives

Yet, the gazing of the thoughtful eyes of certain personnel
Who are too scared to strip naked
Or to sketch myriad drawings on their chests
Gives the impression that right now
They're relishing that small joy
Inside the cocooned bedding of their wives

Yet, in reality, here I am feeling
A heavy exhaustion
Like that which follows sexual intercourse

My private conversations with many Tibetans working for the Chinese government reveal that one of the most tiresome aspects of their job is the need to attend numerous conferences.[124] Government workers are made to participate in tedious political meetings, the frequency of which has increased since the 2008 Tibetan uprising. Here Dhatsenpo is attacking these kinds of compulsory meetings by depicting them as endlessly boring and soul-destroying. Sitting long hours in a hunched up position prevents smooth flow of one's blood, but here the metaphor of dwindling "blood drops" is used to paint more than an uncomfortable and unhealthy sitting position. It also conveys the purpose and content of these meetings that aim to indoctrinate and discipline the attendees into docility. They aim to shape the very consciousness of the attendees which is already weakened by the dwindling blood supply. The meeting incapacitates a person's independence both physically and intellectually. Unlike the "I" in the poem, some people fall for the ideological indoctrination symbolized by the long-drawn-out speeches given by the dignitaries. Due to their tireless work for the Party these speakers fall silent when it comes to the enjoyment of the only relatively autonomous private sphere in today's Tibet, the bedroom. Inside their nuptial beds their tongues turn into "planks" and cease to speak. Some listeners who are too scared to speak the truth ("to strip naked") and to have independent dreams and thoughts ("to sketch myriad drawings on their chests") are taken in by the political tirades and gaze with consenting "thoughtful eyes." They are brainwashed by the Party to such an extent that their facial expressions during the meeting give the impression of sexual ecstasy rather than sheer tedium. Here, the nuptial bed, the place of intimate sexual bliss, is a symbol of a space of freedom and independence from the prying eye of a totalitarian state. Yet, the poem suggests that such a space of freedom and comfort cannot be relished by contemporary Tibetans because of blood-draining political control. This hold on the Tibetan body and mind is distilled into the image of the exhausting meeting.

The current fate of the Tibetan nation finds a more direct and forceful expression in a recent poem by Dhatsenpo, infused with his trademark sexual imagery. In his dialogue poem *Sharpening Truth, Bden pa brdar ba*, Tibet suffers persecution and death, yet a spirit of survival and resilience prevails:

I said to a person:
"Lit undyingly in the heart of the earth
Donning armors of wind and rain,
Isn't it the ancestral soul snow-mountain?"

That awful person said:
"What you're talking about is an old corpse impaled by the knob of
military force and fallen into the vagina of dark punishment."

I replied:
"We have warm blood to represent warfare and tears to wash off suffering.
Therefore, recomposing legends for each lake vagina and reformulating
myths for each snow mountain penis, why can't we open wide the
cocooned pouch of the grassland representing the truth of time?"

That person stayed silent.

I continued:
"Isn't it said that 'Year by year the snow mountain rises ever higher'?"

Pointing to the steel-hard wall of black darkness, that person said:
"Yes. Don't we get home by just taking down this red door screen?"

At this point I uttered involuntarily:
"Colors of music played out on stones
With a skylight of sun, gushing light
Isn't this the palace at the heart of history?"[125]

Tibetan history, the cult of mountain worship, and undying hope for a better future are expressed through the violence and creativity of sexual intercourse. Two contrasting metaphors of sex are employed: one for Chinese aggression and the other for Tibetan survival. Destruction and repression unleashed by "military force" and punitive measures are countered by the creative energy of Tibetan lakes and grasslands that feed and enshrine "the snow-mountain." In other words, it is the race and culture of Tibet, embedded in its history and territory, that nourish its soul. Tibet's survival is ensured through physical procreation and the regeneration of culture for contemporary times. This is symbolized by the imagery of lakes and snow-mountains engaging in sexual union and the retelling of Tibet's rich and diverse legends and myths.[126] The sexual union of lakes and mountains also recalls a Tibetan Bon origin myth which recounts that such an act had produced cosmic eggs that in turn led to the birth of human beings. This cosmogonic tale continues to inform the lived realities of Tibetans as it is still being recited in the performance of the Tibetan marriage ritual.[127] As far as Tibetans are concerned mythologies are more than just a collection of fabulous tales from the past. They do not just serve as what Philip Larkin calls a "myth-kitty," out of which artists choose creative tools for uttering ineffable emotions.[128] They still inform a living culture and continue to be a source of social cohesion. They indeed provide what Ted Hughes, a great admirer of myths and shamanism, notes as "the deeper shared understandings which keep us intact as a group." Thus mythologies strengthen "the inner life of the group."[129]

In *Sharpening Truth*, a direct reference to one of the earliest and most popular *dunglen* songs by Palgon elaborates this mythic theme. Apart from the enduring influence of *dunglen* music, this allusion tells us that the snow-mountain in the poem is no ordinary mountain but the great Amnye Machen itself. It is a majestic sacred mountain considered by many to be "the soul mountain of snowy Tibet." According to legend a revered ancestral deity resides there. He has also been a national guardian of Tibet from ancient times.[130] Palgon's song confirms the religious and national significance associated with Amnye Machen when it starts:

The snow-mountain that resembles a crystal stupa
Is none other than the Machen Snow-mountain,
The soul mountain of the snowland of Tibet.
Year by year this snow-mountain rises ever higher,
An auspicious sign that Tibet will raise up its head.[131]

In a way, *Sharpening Truth* is a poem of quotations comprising a dialogue between two interlocutors in inverted commas. It is also bracketed within two stanzas excerpted from another patriotically charged poem by Dhatsenpo called *Love Embedded within Questions*, *Dri ba'i gting du zug pa'i brtse ba*.[132] Thus, the evocation of Palgon's song enriches the overall allusiveness while demonstrating the persistence of Tibetan collective consciousness in different art forms that are interpenetrative. A nationally unifying mountain deity (whose origins can be found in yet more unifying mythological accounts) that is still being worshiped and held dear in oral traditions and liturgical texts finds its presence in modern music and poetry. Although the use of harsh sexual imagery when depicting the current plight of Tibet might be jarring for the prudish, by alluding to Palgon's line Dhatsenpo reminds us that a familiar dream for Tibet is entertained by a young generation of Tibetan artists today. A dream to "raise up" Tibet's head.

Inside "the steel-hard wall of black darkness" enclosing Tibet the Tibetan poet once again finds encouragement and assistance in culture and history.

Mention of Communist Chinese rule, the "red door screen," and the possibility of regaining the homeland and reunion of Tibetans evokes an idealized image of traditional Tibetan houses made of stones with brilliant light flooding in through the skylight. Use of synesthetic phrasing makes the stone produce music and music display color. Thus in this poem Tibetan stones houses do not provide just shelter but they loudly (both in color and sound) express cultural vibrancy and the endurance of history. The greatest of these stone houses is, of course, the Potala Palace. Like many Tibetan poets Dhatsenpo sees it as a monument to Tibetan imperial history and Buddhist culture, "the palace at the heart of history." While reflecting upon the influence of history on modern Anglo-American poetry, Stan Smith observes that "if the poem is the creature of a moment . . . the life from which it arises is itself a historical creation."[133] He goes on to demonstrate that the past historical events and present historical circumstances under which a poet writes shape his or her poetry.[134] Likewise, the distant past and present histories inform Dhatsenpo's poetry. Tibetan imperial glory is contrasted against the contemporary history of bloodshed and repression.

As demonstrated in the chapters on cultural trauma and the Third Generation poetry, Dhatsenpo is not alone in being informed by past historical events and the present condition. However, some of his poems are unique in their employment of sexual imagery for the narration of Tibetan history and politics. National consciousness and aspirations are unconventionally expressed using sexual language as in the following poem called *Talking Dirty like Drukpa Kunleg, 'Brug pa kun legs ltar kha brla ba*:

Man says:
"I hang my two testicles, paired and spherical, for the sake of solidarity
And keep my old penis always erect for the sake of pride"

Woman says:
"I keep my vagina open for the sake of reunion,
And grow thick pubes for re-erecting the black yak-hair tent of history."[135]

In this dialogue poem Dhatsenpo acknowledges Drukpa Kunleg's literary legacy through conscious imitation of his sermon cited above. However, Dhatsenpo leaves his own mark by inverting one of the mad yogi's sexual imageries in order to represent his own time and place. On one occasion during the sermon, Drukpa Kunleg uses male and female sexual organs and bodily hair as metaphors for affectation and uselessness. On the contrary, Dhatsenpo sees national solidarity in the even number and spherical symmetry of "two testicles," pride in an erect penis, Tibetan reunion in an agape vagina and the reassertion of history in pubic hair. While Drukpa Kunleg mocks ostentation by ridiculing "long and coarse" "bum-hair" that cannot be used for "stitching sheepskin *chuba*s," Dhatsenpo finds "thick pubes" ideal for weaving anew the black tent of history, a tent made of woven yak-hair. Although they do so for different purposes, both Drukpa Kunleg and Dhatsenpo employ what Russian formalists call the device of "defamiliarization." This is an artistic technique through which a familiar theme or a subject of art is made unfamiliar or strange thereby renewing perceptions of it in the reader or perceiver.[136] Tibetan solidarity, pride, collective yearning for reunion, and desire to be the master of one's own destiny are recurrent themes in modern Tibetan literature. However, Dhatsenpo, by making these familiar themes appear unfamiliar and ambiguous through sexual imagery, elicits a fresh aesthetic response in the reader. In the process he also captures another collective concern, the need to ensure the survival of the Tibetan race through sexual reproduction. The parodying of Drukpa Kunleg in the use of imagery and biting humor while treating current Tibetan issues bears witness to the enduring legacy of the literary past and oral traditions.

CONCLUSION: PERENNIAL EROTIC LOVE

Smith avers that "A poem is produced at the intersection of two histories: the history of the formal possibilities available to the poet—conventions, themes, language—and the history of the individual as a particular expressive 'medium,' a product of his own time and place."[137] As can be seen in the poems cited in this chapter, modern Tibetan erotic poetry is a product of both Tibet's literary history and the particular sociopolitical circumstances within which contemporary poets live and work. Although today's erotic poets and their defenders and detractors concur that explicit sexual themes and use of vulgar terminology are a defining attribute of the modern, Tibetan literary and oral traditions paint a different picture. As evident in the cited works of the Great Fifth Dalai Lama, Bod Khepa, and Shangton, Tibetan *kāvya* poetry is not at all free from the erotic spirit embedded in *Kāvyādarśa,* which introduced classical Indian poetics to Tibet. Admittedly it employs a technical language that is often learned and recondite, but its treatment of carnal pleasure is direct and unapologetic. The genre of experiential spiritual songs that is rooted within orality relishes in erotic themes and crude vocabulary even though it always carries a moral or religious message. Oral art forms ranging from folktales to proverbs and popular phrases abound in erotic expressions.

These artistic traditions serve as literary precedents for modern Tibetan erotic poetry which bears imprints from all of them with varying nuances. Like *kāvya* erotic poetry, its treatment of sex is direct and frank; like *mgur,* its language is vernacular and vulgar; and like erotic oral utterances, it is popular and pervasive thanks to the print media and online publications. As with any

artistic creation, modern Tibetan erotic poetry is shaped by a preoccupation with the present which gives it its distinctive quality. It is informed by
contemporary sociopolitical issues including the idea of the Tibetan nation.
However, a contempt for and constrictive sense of shame associated with sex
in academic literature have so far deterred Tibetans from looking into their
erotic literary tradition. This chapter is a modest effort to address such scholarly negligence. It is also an attempt to underscore the essential eroticism of
the human condition expressed with humor and sarcasm by the following old
Tibetan ditty:

ཚོགས་ཆེན་འདུ་ཁང་ནང་ན།།
རྡུག་མེད་ར་བོ་འརྡོང་ཚོས་ཡ།།
འཇིག་རྟེན་འཁོར་བའི་ནང་ན།།
སྐྱིད་མེད་ར་སྲུང་བ་སྐྱིད་ལ།།

There's no suffering in the monastic assembly hall
Other than an aching bottom

There's no happiness in the perishable samsara
Other than joys of erotic love[138]

NOTES

1. From a traditional Tibetan love song.
2. Rdzogs chen chos dbyings stobs ldan rdo rje 2006: 218.
3. In one rare example Rakra T. C. Tethong (1995: 8) makes a brief mention of
physical love in his essay on *Love in Classical Tibetan Poetry* but chooses to leave it
at that rather than exploring it in depth.
4. Some discussions of the sexual practices of Tibetan tantric Buddhism can be
found in Western scholarship. For a psychological interpretation of the connection
between sexuality and Tibetan tantric practices see Campbell 2002: x–xv, 98–149. For
a reflection on the complex role of sexuality in the lives of celibate and noncelibate
Tibetan Buddhist practioners consult Jacoby 2009: 37–71.
5. For an account of this summer festival of ritual performances in one village
in Rebgong and its significance in local Tibetan history and identity see Epstein and
Peng Wenbin 1998: 120–38.
6. Tshe tan zhabs drung [1983] 2001: 6. Also see Muge Samten's (Bsam gtan
rgya mtsho 2009 Vol. 4: 13–340) deliberate avoidance of erotic verse examples in his
kāvya commentary text *Snyan 'grel yang gsal snang mdzod* which was specifically
written for the education of monks.
7. Me lce 2009.
8. To date there have been two major editions of Gedun Choepel's collected
works and one volume of his selected writings but none of them has incorporated
Treatise on Passion (Dge 'dun chos 'phel 2009; 1994; 1988). It is worth mentioning

here that Lopez's bilingual edition of Gedun Choepel's poetry in Tibetan and English includes a selection from *Treatise on Passion* (Lopez 2009: 155–67).

9. Dge 'dun chos 'phel 1969: 12. For a more literal translation of this verse by Hopkins and Dorje Yudon Yuthok see Gedun Choepel 1992: 180.

10. Dge 'dun chos 'phel 1969: 12–13. For an English rendition of these lines by Hopkins and Dorje Yudon Yuthok, see Gedun Choepel 1992: 181. Another English translation of this stanza can be found in Lopez 2009: 156.

11. Dge 'dun chos 'phel 1969: 13–17. For Hopkins and Dorje Yudon Yuthok's commentary on Gedun Choepel's treatment of the theme of sexual equality see Gedun Choepel 1992: 49–62.

12. Slob dpon gzugs bzang: a facsimile of this text found in *Sde dge bstan 'gyur* can be accessed via the website of Tibetan Buddhist Resources Centre at http://tbrc. org/?locale=bo#library_work_ViewByOutline-O00CR000800CR012959%7CW23703.

13. 'Ju mi pham 'jam dbyangs rnam rgyal rgya mtsho 2007 Vol 1: 97–126.

14. For instance, see Rdzogs chen chos dbyings stobs ldan rdo rje 2006: 218–45, 2000 Vol. 3: 459–503.

15. Seng rdor 2010.

16. For a discussion of the CCP's conservative attitude to sex throughout its history and its normative attempts to strictly regulate sexual issues see Sigley 2006: 43–61.

17. Eagleton 2003: 3–4.

18. However, Barfoot, who edited a collection of articles on the theme of sex and eroticism in English poetry (2006: ix), somewhat undermines Eagleton's assertion when she notes that several of the contributors to the volume found it difficult to convince their colleagues to take sex as a serious literary theme. It seems that even in Western intellectual life sex is still a frowned upon subject in some quarters.

19. Spyang mo dgu zug 2012 and Me lce 2009.

20. Cited in Ty 1994: 99.

21. Mi rabs gsum ba 2008: 150–51. Skya bo and Khri sems dpa' 2008.

22. Spyang mo dgu zug 2012.

23. Bsgral rdo 2010.

24. Mda' btsan po 2008 ka: 152–53. This poem can also be accessed at http://www.tibetcm.com/html/list_21/17668c7146d675fe2cb0f06858de5b28/.

25. Lham kog 2010, Gu ru don grub 2010, and Spyang mo dgu zug 2012.

26. Mda' btsan po 2009: 37–44; 2010: 59–80. See the preceding chapter for discussions of these two poems.

27. See a published version of this interview in Skyabs chen bde drol 2012.

28. Mill [1833] 1968: 355–67.

29. See a moving treatment of this theme and domestic violence in Dekyi Dolma (Bde skyid sgrol ma 2008: 42–49).

30. Mda' btsan po 2008 kha.

31. Slob dpon dbyug pa can (Dandin) and Bod mkhas pa: 2, Dandin 1964: 9.

32. Incidentally one of Dhatsenpo's favorite erotic phrases, *myos bum*, is popular *kāvya* kenning for breasts. It can be more literally rendered as "vases that madden."

33. Jangbu 1996: 26–27. For an English translation of this poem by Stoddard see Jangbu 2010: 72.

34. Skya bha 2008: 58.
35. Ljang bu 2001: 62–63.
36. Ibid., 66.
37. An English translation of this celebrated poem can be found in Valéry 2004: 97–105.
38. Broome and Chesters (eds.) 1976: 78.
39. Pema Bhum 2008: 120–21, Lham kog 2011, Bya gzhung dbyang Bha 2008: 15, Szántó 2007: 209–55, Kapstein 2003: 747–802, and Jackson 1996: 375–76.
40. On Sakya Paṇḍita's import of *kāvya* techniques, see Kapstein 2003: 776–82, Smith 2001: 202, and Jackson 1987.
41. Sa pan kun dga' rgyal msthan 1998: 25. See a brief interpretation of this aspirational verse by Ngag dbang chos grags in the same volume, who like many Tibetan scholars construes that the "offerings" (*mchod pa*) in these lines are made of poetic praises (Ibid., 328).
42. Szántó 2007: 209–55.
43. Lham kog 2011.
44. Bya gzhung dbyang bha 2008: 2–29.
45. Dandin 1964: 9–10. Bod mkhas pa 2006: 132–33.
46. Dandin1964: 8. For an explanation of this four-fold category see Bod mkhas pa 2006: 125.
47. Dandin 1964 : 9–10. Bod mkhas pa 2006: 125, 131–33.
48. Because of the term *mi pham* featuring in Bod Khepa's full designation he should not be confused with the well-known poet and scholar Ju Mipham (Ju mi pham 'jam dbyangs rnam rgyal rgya mtsho; 1846–1912) who also wrote a commentary on *Kāvyādarśa*.
49. Bod mkhas pa 2006: 438
50. *Mngon brjod* is valued for its descriptive power, aesthetic qualities and mnemonic function, and is also a source of rich Indian mythology. For an introduction and collection of Tibetan kennings see Dpa' ris sangs rgyas dang Nor bu kun grub (ed.), 2010.
51. An explanation of this figure, including an interpretation of the cited stanza, can be found in Bse tshang blo bzang dpal ldan 1984: 245–49.
52. For an extensive compilation of these and similar *kāvyic* figures of speech see Gerow 1971.
53. "Lotus endowed one" would be a more literal rendering of *pad ma can*. It also means one of the four types of women in Indian Tantric and erotic literature. A breakdown of this category can be found in Rdzogs chen chos dbyings stobs ldan rdo rje 2006: 220–21 and Ge 'dun chos 'phel 1969: 5–8.
54. Bse tshang blo bzang dpal ldan 1984: 248.
55. Ibid., 59–60.
56. Bod mkhas pa 2006: 455.
57. An illustration of all *rgyu'i rgyan* categories can be found in Bse tshang blo bzang dpal ldan 1984: 84, 463–505.
58. *Yal 'dab lnga ba* can alternately be rendered into English as "the five branched ones."
59. Tshe tan zhabs drung: [1983] 2001: 6.

60. Ibid., 6.

61. Ibid., 7.

62. Ibid., 2, 7 and 11. In the 1980s, the CCP repeatedly ordered people to adhere to the Five Stresses (*lnga spel*)—decorum, manners, hygiene, discipline, and morals; and to the Four Beauties (*bzhi mdzes*)—mind, language, behavior, and environment. For an explanation of these slogans see Murthy 1983: 3–11.

63. The poetry of the Fifth Dalai Lama is known for its grandeur and power while Bod Khepa is praised for his elegance, rich ornamentation and musicality. Their different writing styles led to the formation of two schools of Tibetan *kāvya* poetry. For an account of their intellectual rivalry and its legacy see Hartley 2008: 319–21.

64. Tshe tan zhabs drung: [1981] 2005: 7, 44, 76, 99.

65. Ibid., 81, 83.

66. Cited in Bse tshang blo bzang dpal ldan 1984: 249–50.

67. For an exposition of this figure, including an explanation of the cited verse by the Great Fifth, see Bse tshang blo bzang dpal ldan 1984: 249–51.

68. Cited in Bse tshang blo bzang dpal ldan 1984: 500.

69. Blo bzang chos grags dang Bsod nams rtse mo (eds.) [1988–1989] 2010. For instances of other widely used literary anthologies that leave out Tibetan women authors see Karma 'phrin las (ed) 2005 and Si khron zhing chen bod yig slob grwa (ed) [1991] 1998. At least within the last two decades this masculine dominance has been challenged by the welcome emergence of contemporary Tibetan women writers who bring into sharp relief the many silences of Tibet's male-dominated literary tradition. They tackle neglected themes such as motherhood, domestic violence, the betrayal of love and dereliction of paternal obligations, and lack of education and opportunities for girls. For samples of contemporary Tibetan women's writing see the voluminous anthologies covering poetry, fiction, prose, and critical essays edited by Palmo, Dpal mo (ed.) 2006, 2011ka, 2011kha and 2011ga.

70. Thupten Jinpa and Jaś Elsner (Trans) 2000: 20.

71. Ibid., 20–21.

72. Zhang ston bstan pa rgya mtsho 2004: 229–72.

73. Ibid., 242–44. According to conventional Buddhist accounts, Tara undertakes eight kinds of deliverances and as such she is popularly known as *sgrol ma 'jigs pa brgyad skyob ma*—Saviouress who delivers (humans) from eight fears. Although these attacks take the form of assaults on the human body by fearsome creatures or natural and manmade disasters, they represent afflictive emotions. A snake attack represents the torment of jealousy. A list of this and other fears and their symbolic significance can be found in a celebrated hymn to Tara by the First Dalai Lama, Rje dge 'dun grub (1993: 216–17). In his poem on Tara, Shangton adds eight more fears to this conventional categorisation.

74. Zhang ston bstan pa rgya mtsho 2004: 243.

75. Ibid., 248–50.

76. *Dge bsnyen* is lay Buddhist devotee who has taken vows to eschew killing, stealing, lying, sexual misconduct, and drinking.

77. Zhang ston bstan pa rgya mtsho 2004: 250.

78. For similar eroticisation of natural phenomena and treatment of erotic themes see Mdo mkhar tshe ring dbang rgyal 1979. An English translation of this

novel and an introduction to it by Beth Newman are available in Tshe ring dbang rgyal 1996.

79. Seng rdor 2006: 108–10.

80. Rje blo bzang grags pa 1993: 219.

81. *Tshems dkar*, white teeth, is another favorite *kāvya* term and image.

82. In Western literature synaesthetic expressions were idealized by Romanticism and popularized by French symbolism. They produce an effect by blending different kinds of sense-impressions. An effect experienced by one of the senses is expressed through naming the perception of another that is distinct from the former.

83. *Yid bzhin 'dod 'jo*, utter wish-fulfilment, fuses two different symbols of great abundance and satisfaction into one phrase. It abbreviates wish-fulfilling jewel, *yid bzhin nor bu*, and wish-fulfilling cow, *'dod 'jo'i ba*. Both are adopted Indian motifs akin to the Cornucopia that fulfils every desire.

84. This autobiographic content was confirmed by Sangdhor in a conversation on February 18, 2011, Siling.

85. Both of these terms are loaded with religious significance. *Rnam thar* is the sacred biography of a great Lama or other accomplished Buddhist practitioner that narrates their enlightened activities for the liberation of others. *Sngon 'gro* denotes preliminary religious practices or rituals that prepare one for more advanced spiritual quests.

86. Skyabs chen bde grol 2011. *Sems byung* literally means "what issues or arises from the mind." It denotes mental events and factors. A more literal translation of this stanza is adopted here so as to reflect the phonetic pattern of the poem.

87. Gerow 1977: 229, 232. For an exposition of phonic decorative devices see Bse tshang blo bzang dpal ldan 1984: 719–831.

88. This poem evokes the lyricism of *Tara Praises* (*sgrol bstod*; Sangs rgyas rnam par snang mdzad 1993: 200–205) and *'Du 'bral snying po med par rtogs pa'i glu* by Gedun Choepel (Dge 'dun chos 'phel 1994 Vol 2: 399–401).

89. Hor gtsang 'jigs med 2002 Vol. 5: 34.

90. For a collection of Drukpa Kunleg's biographies including his autobiography see 'Brug pa kun legs 2005.

91. 'Brug pa kun legs 1981. An English translation of Drukpa Kunleg's biography was provided by Keith Dowman and Sonam Paljor [1982] 2000. This was based on a compilation of anecdotes and songs undertaken by the Bhutanese scholar, Geshe Chaphu in 1966. The text consulted here is a similar compilation published in Tibetan in Dharamsala in 1981, covert copies of which can be found in Tibet. There are small variations between this and Geshe Chaphu's edition in the description of incidents and the song lyrics. On the whole, the latter seems to be more detailed and complete. A French translation of Drukpa Kunleg's life story and songs can be found in Stein (trans.), 1972. A German translation of his biography was undertaken by Andreas Kretschmar (trans.), 1981.

92. In the Tibetan *rdzogs chen* tradition (Great Perfection) it is believed that an accomplished practitioner attains enlightenment at the point of death as his or her physical body dissolves into rainbow light. For a brief discussion of the early development of this idea in *rdzogs chen* see Samten Karmay 1988: 190–96.

93. 'Brug pa kun legs 1981: 15–18.

94. Gyatso 2005: 280. Italics original.

95. Ibid., 281–88.

96. For a celebration of womanhood as wisdom see Rdzogs chen chos dbying stobs ldan rdo rje 2006: 218. Tantric Buddhism is, of course, not alone in identifying wisdom with femininity. Kabbalistic tradition also attributes the wisdom principle, the indwelling *Shekhinah* or Sophia, to the female (Bloom 2005: 6, Carr 2003: 142–43).

97. For an exceptionally witty and eloquent praise of the female over the male see 'Brug pa kun legs 2005: 70–72. However, it must be pointed out that Drukpa Kunleg is not free from the gendered language of a patriarchal Tibetan society. Like many male practitioners he also sometimes views women as obstacles in the path of spiritual progress and advises against keeping their company or living with "disobedient wives" (Ibid., 52, 62). On one occasion he even preaches: "Pay no respect to dogs, crows and women" (cited in Dowman and Sonam Paljor [1982] 2000: 139.

98. 'Brug pa kun legs 1981: 44–45.

99. Ibid., 46.

100. Ibid., 46–50.

101. *Stu khrag* is usually associated with menstrual blood.

102. 'Brug pa kun legs 1981: 57–61.

103. "'*Dod chags chen po'i ye shes 'dis / chags ldan rnam la byang chub ster*" cited in Rdzogs chen chos dbyings stobs ldan rdo rje 2006: 218.

104. Aris 1987: 152–53.

105. See chapter 3 for a brief comment on this unique poetic device.

106. For those who condone the use of sexual terminology, see Spyang mo dgu zug 2012 and Byang khu lo 2010; and for criticism of it see Reb gong ba 2011 & Me lce 2009.

107. For his short autobiography, written with great clarity and a unique attention to dates, see Nyang skyes snang mdzad rdo rje 2006: 1–52.

108. Here Vajra (*rdo rje*) is a tantric euphemism for penis.

109. Nyang skyes snang mdzad rdo rje 2006: 130–31.

110. *Jo mo* has several connotations: nun, queen, lady, or consort. In Amdo parlance it means a nun. Because Nyingkyi writes this poem mostly in Amdo vernacular language, here *jo mo* is understood as a nun.

111. Zhabs dkar pa sku phreng gnyis pa 2003: 125.

112. An accessible exposition of *lta sgom spyod gsum* (view, meditation and conduct or action) from the perspective of Dzogchen theory and practice can be found in the Dalai Lama 2000: 50, 58–91.

113. Zhabs dkar pa sku phreng gnyis pa 2003: 109.

114. Bate 2010: 27–28. Similar statements regarding the oral genesis of literatures can be found in many literary histories. For instance, see Carter and McRae 2001: 2.

115. Blo bzang 'jam dpal et al. (eds.) 2002 and Skal bzang mkhas grub (ed.) 2008.

116. For bowdlerized printed editions of *Battle of Hor and Ling* see *Hor gling g.yul 'gyed* 1980, 'Chi med rdo rje dang Tshe stobs (eds.) 1980.

117. Pari (*dpa' ris*) is situated in Northeastern Amdo, in today's Gansu province.

118. Dpa' ris sangs rgyas 2008: 1.

119. The Fourth Generation of Tibetan Poets was launched as a literary group in 2007 consisting of three members. Its membership rose to eight poets in 2013. Most of these poets appear to be younger than the Third Generation writers. Even though

they claim to be distinct from the Third Generation writers one cannot find any distinguishable features in terms of style or subject matter. For their literary outlook emphasizing individualism, defiance and free choice see Chos shul gsang bdag 2008.

120. Seng rdor, January 3, 2012.

121. An explanation of this poetic adornment and its three categories can be found in Bse tshang blo bzang dpal ldan 1984: 673–84. There is a famous illustration of it by Gedun Choepel (1990 Vol 2: 273) at the beginning of his *Klu grub dgongs rgyan* in which he praises Lord Buddha's patience and compassion by stressing his inability or reluctance to resist those who tried to kill him as he sat meditating at the foot of the Bodhi tree just before gaining enlightenment. In his commentary on this verse, Lopez fails to appreciate the use of a specific poetic figure and mistakenly interprets it as indicative of Gedun Choepel's unconventional or "different vision of the Buddha" (2006: 125–27).

122. Seng rdor, March 10, 2012.

123. Mda' btsan po 2008 ga.

124. According to some senior Tibetan officials they have to take part in at least one political meeting each week. Without exception they question the necessity and efficacy of such meetings.

125. Mda' btsan po 2013 ka.

126. By and large in terms of attributing gender to the natural physical environment Tibetans regard lakes and rivers as female and mountains as male. However, as noted by Charles Ramble in some cases this way of gender attribution might be reversed (1999: 5, 29).

127. For commentary on and a partial translation of this origin myth see Samten Karmay 1998: 147–53. This narrative recitation in original Tibetan can be found in Mkhar rme'u bsam gtan 2007 Vol 1: 337–44. Just to cite and translate three relevant lines from it: "Out of the sexual union of rock mountains and lakes / Emerged nine kinds of wonder foam / This foam rolled into eggs . . . " (*brag dang mtsho gnyis bshos pa las / ya mtshan wu ba dgu ru srid / wu ba la ni sgong du 'dril*).

128. Cited in Moulin 2005: 88.

129. Hughes 1994: 310.

130. I have briefly touched on the symbolic and religious significance of Amnye Machen in chapter 2.

131. Dpal mgon 2010: 18–19.

132. Mda' btsan po: 2011: 47.

133. Smith 1982: 2.

134. Ibid., 2–5.

135. Mda' bstan po 2013 kha.

136. Eichenbaum [1926] 2001: 1070. This notion of "defamiliarization" can be traced to European Romantic poets. For instance, Shelley regards it as a fundamental attribute of poetry ([1821] 1968: 112).

137. Smith 1982: 9.

138. In such folk love songs *snang ba* has both romantic and erotic connotations and in this translation the latter is emphasized.

Chapter 7

Conclusion

Whirlpools of Continuity and Creativity

ཕྱི་མ་གང་ཐུས་ད་ལྟའི་ལུས་ལ་ལྟོས།།
ཕྱི་མ་གར་སྐྱེ་ད་ལྟའི་ལས་ལ་ལྟོས།།

For past actions look to your present body
For future rebirths look to your present actions[1]

When I first embarked upon this research project I only had a vague grasp
of the intricate web of associations and continuities that shape modern Tibetan
literary creations. I had no idea how much and how often I would need to
engage with classical Tibetan literature, history, religion, and oral traditions
in my endeavor to understand these artistic productions. Such an engagement
demanded a wide range of reading and led me to fall back upon my Tibetan
nomadic upbringing, which had given me a deeply held love for oral art
forms. With its numerous challenges and revelations this research has been a
profound journey of intellectual discovery. As I grappled with a diversity of
oral and literary texts while immersing myself in modern Tibetan literature
and society I came to appreciate the persistence of Tibet's artistic past and living traditions in the creativity of the present. This has enabled me to address
some of the lacunae in existing scholarship by foregrounding the interwoven
nature of the past and the present, and the artistic continuities within the new.

Emphasis on the intertextual nature of modern Tibetan writing not only
brings into critical focus the complex interface between the Tibetan literary text and orality, but also calls into question the scholarly propensity for
clear-cut distinctions between the old and the new. This conclusion draws
together the arguments developed throughout my research to recapitulate its
two key contributions. First, I have drawn attention to the creative interplay
between the old and the new within both Tibetan poetry and fictional writing.

Second, I have shown that the Tibetan nation—constituted of history, culture, language, religion, territory, shared myths and rituals, collective memories, and a common sense of belonging to a troubled land—remains an enduring literary theme. For many contemporary Tibetan writers the Tibetan nation is their overriding preoccupation. It features prominently even when addressing other controversial subject matters like sexual desire.

THE INESCAPABLE PAST

A recurring theme of this book has been the importance of the past in present literary creations, and I have repeatedly taken issue with the prevailing notion of rupture within existing research on modern Tibetan writing. The intellectual tendency to view the 1980s as the point of "birth" of modern Tibetan literature and to present this period as marking an abrupt break with traditional forms of literature has inhibitive repercussions. As evident in many of the chapters, it deprives us of new insights by restricting the scope of research and predetermining its outcome. However, it is important to acknowledge that an initial necessity to define the uncharted field of modern Tibetan literary studies inevitably entailed latching onto and highlighting what seemed to be new and radical. It is therefore understandable that early efforts to establish this branch of knowledge in unambiguous terms involved a penchant for drawing sharp lines between the traditional and the modern and the past and the present. Such an approach, consisting of clearly defined dichotomies, might be somewhat limiting at times but it has made vital contributions to modern Tibetan literary studies. For instance, many of the essays in the noteworthy volume *Modern Tibetan Literature and Social Change* embrace a simple rupture position but are nevertheless illuminating with regard to the relationship between artistic creations and sociopolitical transformations.[2] My book benefits from and seeks to build on the insights of this existing scholarship. Another important factor that should not be forgotten when considering the adoption of the rupture perspective by Tibetan scholars still residing in Tibet is political exigency. Political circumstance and expedience make it a prerequisite for critics to toe the Party line and lay compulsory emphasis upon the Third Plenum of the Eleventh Chinese Communist Party Congress convened in 1978, which introduced relatively liberal policies and loosened the Party's restrictions on culture. Nevertheless, while being conscious of these factors, it is now time that we employed a more nuanced, multifaceted approach. Such a method reveals the immense debt that modern Tibetan poetry and fiction owe to Tibet's artistic past and its living oral and classical literary traditions.

In terms of form, modern Tibetan poetry generally presents itself in metrical composition, lyrics, prose, and free verse. In spite of this diversity many Tibetan and foreign scholars have come to regard free verse as the ultimate form of modern Tibetan poetry because of its apparent novelty. As a result, poems in free verse are usually the preferred examples for illustrating contemporary Tibetan poetic creativity. My research accepts free verse as a defining feature, but tries to contextualize its significance by citing and examining poetic writing in various forms, bearing diverse textual and oral imprints. Analyzing Tibetan free verse's fusion of vernacular and literary idioms, metric flexibility, and frequent use of classical terminology and metaphorical language has made it possible to discern links with Tibet's *mgur* genre and the Indian *kāvyic* tradition.

Even acclaimed free verse poems considered as representative of particular generations do not shake off the influence of the past. For instance, to cite just two examples, Dhondup Gyal's pathbreaking *Waterfall of Youth* is credited for introducing *vers libre* to Tibet,[3] and Rekanglang's sexually abstract *To Prostitute Sangje Dolma* is seen as a definitive poem of the Third Generation of Tibetan Poets.[4] Neither of these poems can be understood fully without a *kāvyic* literary consciousness. This is for the simple reason that they are embedded within the Tibetan *kāvyic* tradition, borrowing heavily from its poetic synonyms and Indic mythology. Literary precedents for the flexible meter, colloquialism, and subjectivity of free verse can be found in *mgur*, which has displayed these qualities for centuries. It appears that the literary legacies of *mgur* and *kāvya* function like Walter Benjamin's notion of the origin that compounds the past and the present. For Benjamin the origin "emerges from the process of becoming and disappearance"; it is "a whirlpool in the river of becoming [that] pulls the emerging matter into its own rhythm."[5] The origin is not the source of present artistic production, but a constitutive part of it. By calling attention to this "whirlpool" of Tibetan literary traditions, I am not denying the innovative attributes of Tibetan *vers libre*. In fact, most of the chapters in this volume recognize these attributes by highlighting features of high level abstraction, disjointed syntax, inversion, distillation of imagery, critical spirit, and emboldened treatment of controversial subject matter. However, I am suggesting that Tibet's literary tradition including elements of formal verse partly constitute the Tibetan free verse.

Another aspect of modern Tibetan poetry that is often overlooked is the persistence and pervasiveness of metric composition as a form. Formal verse does not merely manifest in fragments in Tibetan free verse, but it endures as a dominant poetic mode in its own right. Prevailing scholarly preoccupation with Tibetan free verse casts a shadow over the enduring popularity of Tibetan regular verse and its contribution to the development of modern Tibetan poetry. The referencing and analysis of formal metric poems in this work demonstrate how the techniques and principles of different systems of versification impinge upon modern poetic writing. Tibetan poets find rich pickings in verse forms ranging from *mgur*, folk songs and the Gesar epic to Buddhist scriptures, devotional verses, and *kāvya* poetics. The influence of these poetic categories is apparent in terms of style, theme, rhythm, cadence, diction, rhetorical devices, and poetic figures with, of course, the injection of contemporary subject matter. As can be seen in the reviewed poems of Dhatsenpo, Kyabchen Dedrol, Sangdhor, and others, individual poets differ from one another when it comes to appropriating specific verse forms and the display of subtle mimicry. Some poets make a deliberate effort to tap into all these poetic forms while attempting to come up with their own original metric verse. Sangdhor is one such poet whose distinctive verse poems exhibit a synthesis of diverse literary and oral resources.[6] He calls this type of poetry "new verse" (*bcad rtsom gsar ma*) and distinguishes it from metric compositions of *kāvya* and oral poetry.[7] However, he is quick to confess that "new verse" has developed out of all the conventional forms of verse and oral poetry. Admittedly, with its concentration on image construction, compact diction and the expression of subjective life experience in the vernacular,[8] this "new verse" has given a creative impetus to Tibetan regular verse poetry. Nevertheless, it is clear that "new verse" has emerged out of the "whirlpool" of Tibetan literary and oral traditions, as has modern Tibetan fiction.

Tibetan fictional writing in the form of the short story and the novel is yet another defining attribute of modern Tibetan literature. When this imaginative prose narrative, with its focus on individual experience, characterization, interiority, detailed description, and dialogism, was introduced to Tibet in the late twentieth century, it was indeed a new literary phenomenon. However, as fiction is steeped in real life, Tibetan short stories and novels have come to reflect the Tibetan world in both form and content. As demonstrated in chapters 3 and 4, they do so in part by appropriating language and rhetorical devices from traditional forms of narrative and by communicating the Tibetan condition. For instance, Dhondup Gyal's fictive narratives, some of the earliest examples of the Tibetan short story, carry imprints from Tibetan historical accounts, religious literature, the Tibetan biography, the Gesar epic, the *mgur* tradition, Tibetan *kāvya* poetry, Indic mythology, folklore and folk songs, proverbs, and other formulaic expressions. One can also detect the influence of Tibetan balladry in some of his short stories in their structure, lyricism and concern with social issues that plague Tibetan communities, such as tribal disputes and forced marriage. Likewise, the fictional works of Tsering Dhondup, one of the most celebrated Tibetan novelists, are also permeated with this multiplicity of literary and oral resources. This state of affairs makes it clear that the Tibetan literary text is the product of a multitude of interconnecting social and artistic relations.

In addition to the impact of literary and oral art forms, the Tibetan fictional text is shaped by social and cultural forces. This aspect is particularly observable in the critical content of the Tibetan short story and novel. In these fictional forms the art of storytelling is employed to reveal and attack injustices as well as to give voice to the oppressed and the silenced. Inheriting a rich Tibetan critical tradition found in *mgur*, the Gesar epic, and other types of oral poetry such as balladry, Tibetan fictional writing spares none from its censure. It exposes unequal social relations, tackles sensitive sociopolitical issues and mocks the abuse of power and privilege by established authorities, both Tibetan and Chinese. Tibetan society is criticized for its perceived conservatism, tribalism, religious corruption, and oppressive social practises. Often deploying a coded vocabulary, Chinese colonial rule is portrayed in an unflattering light that rejects the official Chinese narrative of modern Tibetan history and society. Tibetan fictional writing takes on many themes and issues, but in recent years Tibet's tragic encounter with Communist China has come into prominence. Through the literary form of the novel, writers like Tsering Dhondup capture this new Tibetan experience and thereby make intelligible within a public space sociopolitical events that are otherwise incomprehensible and unutterable.

THE INESCAPABLE NATION

As observed in chapter 2, the notion and the artistic expression of a culturally integrated Tibet are nothing new. What is new is the portrayal of a Tibet that has undergone a series of cultural traumas and radical social transformations since its bloody encounter with the CCP in the 1950s. Tsering Dhondup's *The Red Wind Scream* is one such novel that depicts this historical situation without losing its human content. Isak Dinesen is reported to have said: "All sorrows can be borne if you put them into a story or tell a story about them."[9] Hannah Arendt interprets this epigram as the redemptive power of narrative when she muses that it is the story that gives meaning to "an unbearable sequence of sheer happenings."[10] Tsering Dhondup's novel displays this redemptive quality as well as the critical function of the art of storytelling. It gives artistic expression to a traumatic and repressed Tibetan historical experience and critiques those who are deemed culpable. Contemporary Tibetan poetry deals with the tragic narrative of modern Tibet, but its treatment, although powerful and frequent, is short, compact, sketchy and momentary. Tibetan fictional writing, as we have seen in chapter 4, gives detailed introspective descriptions of recent national traumas by drawing on living oral narratives that record harrowing individual and collective experiences under Chinese rule.

This brings us to the omnipresence of the Tibetan nation in modern Tibetan writing. Alongside the embeddedness of modern literary practices within

Tibet's literary and oral traditions, another unavoidable feature of modern
Tibetan literature is the unfailing attention given to the Tibetan nation. The
Tibetan nation is manifested in a national consciousness that is expressed
through countless utterances, remembrances, celebrations, mournings, and
allusions within both poetry and fiction. What is more, it permeates the very
"body" of modern Tibetan literature. The following popular phrase is a useful conceptual tool with which to discern this: "For past actions look to your
present body/ For future rebirths look to your present actions." This is a statement conventionally employed in Tibetan Buddhist teachings to illustrate the
determining factor of karmic laws of causality on the physical form of life
that one's consciousness (*rnam shes*) takes in the present or future. Here it
can be used to explain the impact of the past on present creativity and that
of the present on the future. Past literary and extra-literary deeds including
oral compositions and what intertextualists call "social and historical texts"
have contributed to and are a crucial component of the literary corpus of the
present. As I have attempted to show throughout this book, the "body" of
contemporary Tibetan literature cannot be explored fruitfully without consideration of past artistic activities and socio-historical actions including the
arrival of the Chinese Communist Party and its army in Tibet. Likewise, the
direction that Tibetan literature will take in the future can only be surmised
through an examination of present literary, cultural and political activities,
combined with an awareness of past developments. The Chinese takeover has
been the most radically transformative process in the history of modern Tibet.
As such this sociopolitical reality that has shaped the modern Tibetan nation
is a constitutive component of the present Tibetan literary "body."

Finally, my findings also negate the modernist state-centric conception of
the nation. A nation may desire a state but it can still be a nation without a
sovereign political power of its own. Many Tibetans aspire for a state of their
own but their nation is not defined by it. On the contrary, as has been shown
in this research, Tibetan national identity flourishes in spite of the absence of
a centralized state. This study thus questions the overblown role attributed by
modernists to the state in the formation of national identities. Theorists of cultural nationalism have done a great deal to wrest away the nation from dominant state-orientated interpretations by stressing how vital cultural forces are
in the persistence of nations and nation-formations in the modern age.[11] My
analysis of modern Tibetan literature also highlights the role of culture in the
perpetuation and reinforcement of Tibetan national consciousness. This consciousness is not necessarily informed by "political nationalism"—a desire
for sovereign statehood. Admittedly, such a yearning features in the Tibetan
literary art, yet the Tibetan identity expressed by it transcends a narrow concern with an independent political community. As evident in all the chapters,
a preoccupation with Tibetan language, territory, history, shared myths and

rituals, collective memories, and cultural practices informs Tibetan national consciousness within modern Tibetan writing. The modern Tibetan literary text is itself national. It powerfully articulates Tibetan cultural identity, not only by cherishing the memories and practices of the past or remembering recent tragedies and current plights, but also through reviving, reusing and sustaining older forms of narrative and poetry in innovative ways. It contributes to the re-forging of the Tibetan nation by turning to these nationally cohesive forces, acting as a unifying mode of communication and a fertile locus where all things Tibetan are voiced, discussed, negotiated, debated, and proclaimed.

The frequency and the intensity with which the Tibetan nation features within modern Tibetan literature reflect the truth that it remains a source of both pain and pride for Tibetan writers today. They cannot help but write about their nation because, as a Tibetan saying puts it:

ཚ་ས་པོ་དེ་ཆེག་ཐུག་གི་འདུག་ག །
དགའ་ས་པོ་དེ་ཆེག་བཤད་གི་འདུག་ག །

One tends to touch where it hurts,
And talk about that which one loves.

NOTES

1. This is a popular phrase found in many Tibetan Buddhist teachings and is often recited by Tibetans as a proverb. Some versions of this phrase render the second line as *phyi ma gar skye da lta'i sems la ltos* (For your future rebirths look to your present mind.) However, this does not affect the overall meaning of the phrase because in Buddhism it is the mind that dictates actions.

2. Hartley and Schiaffini-Vedani (eds) 2008. For a review of this book see Lama Jabb 2011: 89–95.

3. See chapter 1.

4. See chapter 5.

5. Cited in Didi-Huberman 2005: 4.

6. See chapters 1 and 6.

7. Seng rdor 2010: 56–66. The term *bcad rtsom gsar ma* is often contracted to *bcad gsar*. Also see Sgo yon (2011) for an introductory commentary on *bcad gsar*.

8. Seng rdor 2010: 61.

9. Hannah Arendt ([1958] 1998: 175, [1961] 1993a: 262) attributes these words to Isak Dinesen although she does not provide any sources.

10. Arendt [1968] 1993b: 104.

11. For a cultural approach to nations and nationalism that counters modernists' obsession with the state see Hutchinson 1987, Leoussi and Grosby (eds.) 2007, and Smith 2008, 2009.

Bibliography

WESTERN LANGUAGE SOURCES

Aberbach, David. 2007. "Myth, History and Nationalism: Poetry of the British Isles." In Athena S. Leoussi and Steven Grosby (eds.), *Nationalism and Ethnosymbolism: History, Culture and Ethnicity in the Formation of Nations*. Edinburgh: Edinburgh University Press, 84–96.

Achebe, Chinua. [1958] 1986. *Things Fall Apart*. Oxford: Heinemann.

Adorno, T. W. 1984. "The Essay as Form." In *New German Critique*, No. 32 (Spring–Summer, 1984), 151–71.

Alexander, Jeffrey C. 2004. "Toward a Theory of Cultural Trauma." In Jeffrey C. Alexander, Ron Eyerman, Bernhard Giesen, Neil J. Smelser, and Piotr Sztompka. *Cultural Trauma and Collective Identity*. Berkeley: University of California Press, 1–30.

Alvarez, Al. 2005. *The Writer's Voice*. London: Bloomsbury.

Anderson, Benedict. [1983] 1991. *Imagined Communities: Reflections on the Origin and Spread of Nationalism*. London: Verso.

Andrugtsang Gompo Tashi. 1973. *Four Rivers, Six Ranges: A True Account of Khampa Resistance to Chinese in Tibet*. Dharamsala: Information and Publicity Office of His Holiness the Dalai Lama.

Arendt, Hannah. [1961] 1993a. *Between Past and Future: Eight Exercises in Political Thought*. New York: Penguin Books.

———. [1968] 1993b. *Men in Dark Times*. New York: Harcourt Brace & Company.

———. [1958] 1998. *The Human Condition*. Chicago: The University of Chicago Press.

———. 1978. *The Life of the Mind*. New York: A Harvest Book.

Aris, Michael 1987. "'The Boneless Tongue': Alternative Voices from Bhutan." In *Past and Present*, No. 115, 131–64.

Aristotle. 2001. "Poetics." In Vincent B. Leitch et al. (eds.), *The Norton Anthology of Theory and Criticism*. New York: W. W. Norton and Company, 90–117.

Arjia Rinpoche. 2010. *Surviving the Dragon: A Tibetan Lama's Account of 40 Years Under Chinese Rule*. New York: Rodale Inc.

Ashcroft, Bill, Gareth Griffiths, and Helen Tiffin. [1989] 2002. *The Empire Writes Back: Theory and Practice in Post-Colonial Literatures*. New York: Routledge.

Barfoot, C. C. 2006. *And Never Know the Joy: Sex and the Erotic in English Poetry*. Amsterdam: Rodopi.

Barnett, Robert. 2008. "Authenticity, Secrecy and Public Space: Chen Kuiyuan and Representations of the Panchen Lama Reincarnation Dispute of 1995." In Robert Barnett and Ronald Schwartz (eds.), *Tibetan Modernities: Notes from the Field on Cultural and Social Change*. Leiden & Boston: Brill, 353–421.

———. 2006. *Lhasa: Streets with Memories*. New York: Columbia University Press.

———. 2005. "Beyond the Collaborator-Martyr Model: Strategies of Compliance, Opportunism, and Opposition within Tibet." In Barry Sautman and June T. Dreyer (eds.), *Contemporary Tibet: Politics, Development, and Society in a Disputed Region*. London: M. E. Sharpe.

Bass, Catriona. 1998. *Education in Tibet: Policy and Practice since 1950*. London: Zed Books, TIN.

Bate, Jonathan. 2010. *English Literature: A Very Short Introduction*. Oxford: Oxford University Press.

Beasley, Rebecca. 2007. *Theorists of Modernist Poetry: T. S. Eliot, T. E. Hulme and Ezra Pound*. London: Routledge.

Benjamin, Walter. [1970] 1999. *Illuminations*. London: Pimlico.

Bennett, Andrew, and Nicholas Royle. 2009. *An Introduction to Literature, Criticism and Theory*. Harlow: Pearson Longman.

Benson, Sandra. 2007. *Tales of the Golden Corpse: Tibetan Folk Tales*. Northampton, Massachusetts: Interlink Books.

Berlin, Isaiah. 2000. *The Roots of Romanticism*. London: Pimlico.

Bhabha, Homi K. 1994. *The Location of Culture*. London and New York: Routledge.

———. April 4, 2004. "A Global Measure: Writing, Rights and Responsibilities." Lecture delivered at UC Santa Barbara. http://www.youtube.com/watch?v=yER4QwiSl14.

———. (ed.). 1990. *Narration and Nation*. London and New York: Routledge 1–7, 291–322.

Bloom, Harold. [1973] 1997. *The Anxiety of Influence: A Theory of Poetry*. Oxford: Oxford University Press.

———. 2005. *Essayists and Prophets*. Philadelphia: Chelsea House Publishers.

Branigan, Tania. October 22, 2010. "Tibetans Protest Against Language Curbs in Chinese Schools" at http://www.guardian.co.uk/world/2010/oct/20/tibetans-protest-language-chinese-schools.

Brooker, Peter, and Simon Perril. 2001. "Modernist Poetry and Its Precursors." In Neil Roberts (ed.), *A Companion to Twentieth-Century Poetry*. Oxford: Blackwell Publishers, 21–36.

Brooks, Cleanth. 1959. "What does Poetry Communicate?" In Harold Beaver (ed.), *American Critical Essays: Twentieth Century*. London: Oxford University Press, 1959, 249–61.

Broome, Peter, and Graham Chesters (eds.). 1976. *An Anthology of Modern French Poetry (1850–1950)*. Cambridge: Cambridge University Press.

Buffetrille, Katia. 1997. "The Great Pilgrimage of A myes rMa-chen: Written Traditions, Living Realities." In Alexander W. Macdonald (ed.), *Mandala and Landscape*. Delhi: D.K. Printworld, 75–132.

———. 2003. "The Evolution of a Tibetan Pilgrimage: the Pilgrimage to A myes rMa chen Mountain in the 21st Century." In *Symposium on Contemporary Tibetan Studies, 21st Century Tibet Issue, Collected Papers*. Taipeh, Mongolian and Tibetan Affairs Commission, 325–63.

———. 2000. *Pèlerins, lamas et visionnaires. Sources orales et écrites sur les pèlerinages tibétains coll*. Wien: Arbeitskreis für Tibetische und Buddhistische Studien Universität.

Buffetrille, Katia, and Françoise Robin (eds.) 2012. "Tibet is Burning—Self-immolation: Ritual or Political Protest?" In *Revue d'Etudes Tibétaines* 25, December 2012. http://himalaya.socanth.cam.ac.uk/collections/journals/ret/pdf/ret_25.pdf.

Bulag, Eradyn E. 2014. "Seeing Like a Minority: Political Tourism and the Struggle for Recognition in China." In *Journal of Current Chinese Affairs* 41(4).

———. 1998. *Nationalism and Hybridity in Mongolia*. Oxford: Clarendon Press.

Cabezón, José Ignacio, and Roger R. Jackson (eds.). 1996. *Tibetan Literature: Studies in Genre*. Ithaca: Snow Lion.

Campbell, June. 2002. *Traveller in Space: Gender, Identity and Tibetan Buddhism*. London: Continuum.

Carr, David M. 2003. *The Erotic Word: Sexuality, Spirituality, and the Bible*. Oxford: Oxford University Press.

Carter, Ronald, and John McRae. 2001. *The Routledge History of Literature in English: Britain and Ireland*. London and New York: Routledge.

The Central Tibetan Administration. "The Tibetan National Flag" at http://www.tibet.net/en/index.php?id=10&rmenuid=8.

Chambers, Ross. 2005. "Baudelaire's Paris." In Rosemary Lloyd (ed.), *The Cambridge Companion to Baudelaire*. Cambridge: Cambridge University Press, 101–16.

CNN. 2011. "Dadawa: China's pop idol turned U.N. ambassador." http://edition.cnn.com/2011/WORLD/asiapcf/01/19/talk.asia.dadawa/20 January 2011.

Cohen, Ted. 1978. "Metaphor and the Cultivation of Intimacy." In *Critical Inquiry* 5(1), Special Issue on Metaphor (Autumn 1978), 3–12.

Craig, Mary. 1999. *Tears of Blood: A Cry For Tibet*. Washington: Counterpoint.

Dadawa. 1996. *Sister Drum*. Zhe jiang dian zi min xiang chu ban she, ISRC-CN-D15-98-468-00/V. J6.

The Dalai Lama. 2002. *Dzogchen: The Heart Essence of the Great Perfection*. Translated by Geshi Thupten Jinpa and Richard Barron. Ithaca: Snow Lion Publications.

———. Middle Way Approach for Resolving the Issue of Tibet. http://www.dalailama.com/messages/middle-way-approach.

Dandin. 1964. *Kāvyādarśa*. Madras: V. Ramaswamy Sastrulu & Sons.

Davidson, Ronald M. 2004. "The Kingly Cosmogonic Narrative and Tibetan Histories: Indian Origins, Tibetan Space, and the bKa' 'chems ka khol ma Synthesis." *Lungta* 16, 2004: 64–83.

Dawa Norbu. 1988. "Chinese Communist Views on National Self-determination, 1922–1956: Origins of China's National Minorities Policy." In *International Studies* 25(4), 1988: 317–42.

———. 2001. *China's Tibet Policy*. Surrey: Curzon.

———. 1997. *Tibet: The Road Ahead*. London: Rider. .

———. (trans.) 1987. *Khache Phalu's Advice on the Art of Living*. Dharamsala: Library of Tibetan Works and Archives.

Deutsch, Karl W. 1994. "Nationalism and Social Communication." In John Hutchinson and Anthony D. Smith (eds.), *Nationalism*. Oxford: OUP, 26–29.

Dhondup, K. 1981. *Songs of the Sixth Dalai Lama*. Dharamsala: Library of Tibetan Works and Archives.

Didi-Huberman, Georges. 2005. "The Supposition of the Aura: The Now, the Then, and Modernity." In Andrew Benjamin (ed.), *Walter Benjamin and History*. London: Continuum, 3–18.

Dikotter, Frank. 2010. *Mao's Great Famine: The History of China's Most Devastating Catastrophe, 1958–62*. London: Bloomsbury.

Dowman, Keith. [1988] 1996. *The Power-Places of Central Tibet: The Pilgrim's Guide*. New Delhi: Timeless Books.

Dowman, Keith, and Sonam Paljor. [1982] 2000: Trans. *The Divine Madman: The Sublime Life and Songs of Drukpa Kunley*. Kathmandu: Pilgrims Publishing.

Dreyfus, George. 2002. "Tibetan Religious Nationalism: Western Fantasy or Empowering Vision?" In P. Christiaan Klieger (ed.), *Tibet, Self, and the Tibetan Diaspora: Voices of Difference*. Leiden: Brill Academic Publisher, 37–56.

———. 2003. "Cherished Memories and Cherished Communities: Proto-Nationalism in Tibet." In Alex McKay (ed.), *The History of Tibet: The Medieval Period: c. 850–1875 The Development of Buddhist Paramount*. London: Routledge Curzon, 492–522.

Dunham, Mikel. 2004. *Buddha's Warriors: The Story of the CIA-Backed Tibetan Freedom Fighters, the Chinese Invasion, and the Ultimate Fall of Tibet*. New York: Jeremy P. Tarcher/Penguin.

Eagleton, Terry. 1999. *Scholars and Rebels in Nineteenth-Century Ireland*. Oxford: Blackwell.

———. [1983] 1996. *Literary Theory: An Introduction*. Second Edition, Oxford: Blackwell.

———. 2003. *After Theory*. New York: Basic Books.

Eichenbaum, Boris. [1926] 2001. "The Theory of the 'Formal Method.'" In Vincent B. Leitch et al. (eds), *The Norton Anthology of Theory and Criticism*. New York: W. W. Norton and Company, 1062–87.

Eliot, T. S. [1921] 1932. *T. S. Eliot: Selected Essays*. London: Faber and Faber.

Emerson, Ralph Waldo. [1850] 1968. "Shakespeare; or, the Poet." In Edmund D. Jones (ed.), *English Critical Essays (Nineteenth Century)*. London: Oxford University Press, 458–77.

Eppling, John Frederick. 1989. "A Calculus of Creative Expression: The Central Chapter of Dandin's *Kāvyādarśa*." Madison: University of Wisconsin, Dissertation.

Epstein, Lawrence, and Peng Wenbin. 1998. "Ritual, Ethnicity, and Generational Identity." In Melvyn C. Goldstein and Matthew T. Kapstein (eds.), *Buddhism in Contemporary Tibet: Religious Revival and Cultural Identity*. Los Angeles & London: University of California Press, 120–38.

Erhard, Franz Xaver. 2007. "Magical Realism and Tibetan Literature." In Stephen Venturino (ed.), *Contemporary Tibetan Literary Studies*. Leiden, Boston: Brill, 133–46.

Erikson, Erik H. 1956. "The Problem of Ego Identity." In *Journal of the American Psychoanalytic Association* 4, 1956: 56–121.

Eyerman, Ron. 2004. "Cultural Trauma: Slavery and the Formation of African American Identity." In Jeffrey C. Alexander, Ron Eyerman, Bernhard Giesen, Neil J. Smelser, and Piotr Sztompka. *Cultural Trauma and Collective Identity*. Berkeley: University of California Press, 60–111.

FitzHerbert, George S. 2009. "The Tibetan Gesar Epic as Oral Literature." In Brandon Dotson et al. (eds.), *Contemporary Visions in Tibetan Studies: Proceedings of the First International Seminar of Young Tibetologists*. Chicago: Serindia Publications, 171–96.

Flint, Frank Stuart. 1913. "Imagisme." In *Poetry: A Magazine of Verse* 1(1), March 1913: 198–200.

Foley, John Miles. 1999. *Homer's Traditional Art*. University Park: Pennsylvania State University Press.

Foucault, Michel. 1977. "Nietzsche, Genealogy, History." In Donald F. Bouchard (ed.), *Language, Counter-Memory, Practice: Selected Essays and Interviews*. Translated by Donald F. Simon and Sherry Simon. Ithaca: Cornell University Press, 139–64.

Gedun Choepel. 1992. *Tibetan Arts of Love*, translated by Jeffrey Hopkins and Dorje Yudon Yuthok. Ithaca: Snow Lion Publications.

———. 2000. *The Guide to India*, translated by Toni Huber. Dharamsala: The Library of Tibetan Works and Archives.

Gellner, Ernest. [1983] 2006. *Nations and Nationalism*, Second Edition. Oxford: Blackwell.

———. 1998. *Nationalism*. London: Phoenix.

Germano, David. 1998. "Re-Membering the Dismembered Body of Tibet: Contemporary Tibetan Visionary Movements in the People's Republic of China." In Melvyn C. Goldstein and Matthew T. Kapstein (eds.), *Buddhism in Contemporary Tibet: Religious Revival and Cultural Identity*. Los Angeles & London: University of California Press, 53–94.

Germano, David, et al. (eds.). 2011. *Wutai Shan and Qing Culture*. In *Journal of the International Association of Tibetan Studies*, Issue 6 (December 2011), 1–428. http://www.thlib.org/collections/texts/jiats/#!jiats=/current/.

Gerow, Edwin. 1977. *A History of Indian Literature Vol. 5: Indian Poetics*. Wiesbaden: Otto Harrassowitz.

———. 1971. *A Glossary of Indian Figures of Speech*. The Hague: Moulton.

Giollain, Diarmuid O. 2005. "Folk Culture." In Joe Cleary and Claire Connolly (eds.), *The Cambridge Companion to Modern Irish Culture*. Cambridge: Cambridge University Press, 225–44.

Gladney, Dru C. 2004. *Dislocating China: Muslims, Minorities and Other Subaltern Subjects*. London: Hurst & Company.

Goldstein, Melvyn C. 1982. "Lhasa Street Songs: Political and Social Satire in Traditional Tibet." In *The Tibet Journal* 7(1 & 2), Spring/Summer 1982: 56–66.

Goodman, Nelson. 1981. "Twisted Tales; or, Story, Study, and Symphony." In W. J. T. Mitchell (ed.), *On Narrative*. Chicago: University of Chicago Press, 99–115.

Gramsci, Antonio. 1971. *Selections from the Prison Notebooks*. London: Lawrence and Wishart.

Gray, Jack. 1990. *Rebellions and Revolutions: China from the 1800s to the 1980s*. Oxford: Oxford University Press.

Gyatso, Janet. 2005. "Sex." In Donald S. Lopez Jr. (ed.), *Critical Terms for the Study of Buddhism*. Chicago and London: The University of Chicago Press, 271–91.

Habermas, Jürgen. 1992. *The Structural Transformation of the Public Space: An Enquiry into a Category of Bourgeois Society*. Cambridge: Polity.

Hartley, Lauran. 2008. "Heterodox Views and the New Orthodox Poems: Tibetan Writers in the Early and Mid-Twentieth Century." In Lauran R. Hartley and Patricia Schiaffini-Vedani (eds.), *Modern Tibetan Literature and Social Change*. Durham, London: Duke University Press, 3–31.

———. 2003. "Contextually Speaking: Tibetan literary discourse and social change in the People's Republic of China (1980–2000)." PhD dissertation, Indiana University.

Hartley, Lauran, and Patricia Schiaffini-Vedani. 2008. "Introduction." In Lauran R. Hartley and Patricia Schiaffini-Vedani (eds.), *Modern Tibetan Literature and Social Change*. Durham, London: Duke University Press, xiii–xxxviii.

Hartley, Lauran, and Pema Bhum. 2001. "A Show to Delight the Masses." In *Persimmon: Asian Literature, Arts and Culture* 1(3), Winter 2001: 58–77.

Hazlitt, William. 1998. Duncan Wu (ed.), *The Plain Speaker: The Key Essays*. Oxford: Blackwell.

———. 2000. *The Fight and Other Writings*. London: Penguin Books.

Hegel, G. W. F. 1975. *Aesthetics: Lectures on Fine Art*. Vol. II (T. M. Knox, Trans.). Oxford: Clarendon Press.

Henrion-Dourcy, Isabelle. 2005. "Women in the Performing Arts: Portraits of Six Contemporary Singers." In Janet Gyatso and Hanna Havnevic (eds.), *Women in Tibet*. London: Hurst & Co, 195–258.

Hilton, Isabel. 2006. "How an Exile defies China." In *The Guardian*, August 22, 2006.

Hobsbawm, Eric J., and Terence Ranger (eds.). 1983. *The Invention of Tradition*. Cambridge: Cambridge University Press.

Howe, Irving. [1990] 2001. "History and the Novel." In Vincent B. Leitch et al. (eds.), *The Norton Anthology of Theory and Criticism*. New York: W. W. Norton and Company, 1535–47.

Huber, Toni. 2008. *The Holy Land Reborn: Pilgrimage & the Tibetan Reinvention of Buddhist India*. Chicago: The University of Chicago Press.

———. 1999. *The Cult of Pure Crystal Mountain: Popular Pilgrimage and Visionary Landscape in Southeast Tibet*. Oxford: Oxford University Press.

———. 1997. "Colonial Archaeology, International Missionary Buddhism and the First Example of Modern Tibetan Literature." In Petra Kieffer-Pulz and Jens-Uwe Hartmann (eds.), *Bauddhavidyasudhakarah: Studies in Honour of Heinz Becher on the Occasion of His 65th Birthday*. Indica et Tibetica 30: Swisttal-Odendorf, 297–318.

Huber, Toni, and Tsepak Rigzin. 1999. "A Tibetan Guide for Pilgrimage to Ti-se (Mount Kailas) and mTsho Ma-pham (Lake Manasarovar)." In Toni Huber (ed.), *Sacred Spaces and Powerful Places in Tibetan Culture: A Collection of Essays*. Dharamsala: Library of Tibetan Works and Archives, 125–53.

Hughes, Ted. 1994. *Winter Pollen: Occasional Prose*. London: Faber and Faber.

Hulme, T. E. 1938. "Lecture on Modern Poetry." In Michael Roberts (ed.), *T. E. Hulme*. London: Faber and Faber Ltd, 1982, 258–70.

Hutchinson, John. 1987. *The Dynamics of Cultural Nationalism: Gaelic Revival and the Creation of the Irish Nation State*. London: Routledge.

Hutchinson, John, and David Aberbach. 1999. "The Artist as Nation-Builder: William Butler Yeats and Chaim Nachman Bialik." In *Nations and Nationalism* 5(4), ASEN: 501–21.

ICT. 2009. *A Great Mountain Burnt by Fire*. Washington, DC: International Campaign for Tibet.

Information Office of the State Council of the People's Republic of China. 2001. *Tibet's March toward Modernization*. Beijing.

———. July 11, 2011. *Sixty Years of Peaceful Liberation of Tibet*. http://news.xinhuanet.com/english2010/china/2011-07/11/c_13978644.htm.

Jackson, David Paul. 1987. *The Entrance Gate for the Wise (Section III): Sa-skya Paṇḍita on Indian and Tibetan Traditions of Pramāṇa and Philosophical Debate*. Wien: Arbeitskreis für Tibetische und Buddhistische Studien.

Jackson, Roger R. 1996. "'Poetry' in Tibet: Glu, mGur, sNyan ngag and 'Songs of Experience.'" In Jose Ignacio Cabezon and Roger R. Jackson (eds.), *Tibetan Literature: Studies in Genre*. Ithaca: Snow Lion, 368–92.

Jacoby, Sarah. 2009. "To be or not to be Celibate: Morality and Consort Practices According to Treasure Revealer Se ra mkha' 'gro's (1892–1940) Auto/Biographical Writings." In Sara Jacoby and Antonio Terrone (eds.), *Buddhism Beyond the Monastery: Tantric Practices and their Performers in Tibet and the Himalayas*. Leiden: Brill.

Jamyang Norbu. March 7, 2009. "March Winds: Remembering the Great Uprising of '56 And '59." http://www.phayul.com/news/article.aspx?id=24032&t=0.

———. December 27, 2007. "Freedom Wind, Freedom Song: Dispelling Modern Myths about the Tibetan National Flag and National Anthem." http://www.tibetwrites.org/?Freedom-Wind- Freedom-Song, December 27, 2007.

———. [1979] 1986. *Warriors of Tibet: The Story of Aten and Khampas' Fight for the Freedom of Their Country*. London: Wisdom Publications.

Jangbu. 2010. *The Nine-Eyed Agate: Poems and Stories*, translated by Heather Stoddard. Plymouth: Lexington Books.

Kapstein, Matthew T. 2002. "The Tulku's Miserable Lot: Critical Voices from Eastern Tibet." In Toni Huber (ed.), *Amdo Tibetans in Transition: Society and Culture in the Post-Mao Era*. Leiden, Boston Brill, 99–111.

———. 1999. "Dhondup Gyal: The Making of a Modern Hero." In Tashi Tsering (ed.), *Lungta: Contemporary Tibetan Literature* 12. Dharamsala: Amnye Machen Institute, 45–48.

————. 1998. "A Pilgrimage of Rebirth Reborn: The 1992 Celebration of the Drigung Powa Chenmo." In Melvyn C. Goldstein and Matthew T. Kapstein (eds.), *Buddhism in Contemporary Tibet: Religious Revival and Cultural Identity.* Los Angeles & London: University of California Press, 95–119.

————. 2006. *The Tibetans.* Oxford: Blackwell Publishing.

————. 2003. "The Indian Literary Identity in Tibet." In Sheldon Pollock (ed.), *Literary Cultures in History: Reconstructions from South Asia.* Berkeley: University of California Press, 747–802.

Knaus, John Kenneth. 1999. *Orphans of the Cold War: America and the Tibetan Struggle for Survival.* New York: PublicAffairs.

Kretschmar, Andreas. 1981. *'Brug pa kun legs: das wundersame Leben eines verrückten Heiligen.* Sankt Augustin: VGH Wissenschaftsverlag.

Kundera, Milan. 1982. *The Book of Laughter and Forgetting.* London & Boston: Faber and Faber.

————. 2007. *The Curtain: An Essay In Seven Parts.* London: Faber and Faber.

Laird, Thomas. 2006. *The Story of Tibet: Conversations with the Dalai Lama.* London: Atlantic Books.

Lama Jabb. 2009. Banditry in Traditional Amdo: The Story of Yidak Kela. In *Studies in the History of Eastern Tibet,* Wim van Spengen and Lama Jabb (eds.). Halle: IITBS, 209–22.

————. 2011. "The Consciousness of the Past in the Creativity of the Present: Modern Tibetan Literature and Social Change." In *International Journal of Asian Studies* 8(1), 89–95.

————. 2012. "Agir et s'exprimer au travers de la poesie tibetanine moderne." In *Tibet Creer Pour Resister, Monde Chinois,* Automne 2012: 78–86.

The Laogai Research Foundation. 2008. *Laogai Handbook: 2007–2008.* Washington. http://laogai.org/system/files/u1/handbook2008-all.pdf.

Leoussi, Athena S., and Steven Grosby (eds.). 2007. *Nationalism and Ethnosymbolism: History, Culture and Ethnicity in the Formation of Nations.* Edinburgh: Edinburgh University Press.

Levenson, Michael. 2004. "The Time-Mind of the Twenties." In *The Cambridge History of Twentieth-Century English Literature.* Cambridge: Cambridge University Press, 197–217.

Lin, Nancy G. 2008. "Dondrup Gyel and the Remaking of the Tibetan Ramayana." In Lauran R. Hartley and Patricia Schiaffini-Vedani (eds.), *Modern Tibetan Literature and Social Change.* Durham, London: Duke University Press, 86–111.

Lopez, Donald S. 2006. *The Madman's Middle Way: Reflections on Reality of The Tibetan Monk Gedun Choepel.* Chicago: The University Of Chicago Press.

————. (ed. and trans.) 2009. *In the Forest of Faded Wisdom: 104 Poems by Gedun Chopel.* Chicago and London: The University of Chicago Press.

Lord, Albert Bates. 1991. *Epic Singers and Oral Tradition.* Ithaca and London: Cornell University Press.

Lukács, György. 1974. *Soul and Form,* translated by Anna Bostock. Cambridge, Massachusetts: The MIT Press.

Macdonald, Ariane. 1997. "Une lecture des P.T. 1286, 1287, 1038, 1047 et 1290. Essai sur la formation et l'emploi des myths politiques dans la religion royale de

Sroṅ btsan sgam po." In Études tibétaines *dédiées à la mémoire de Marcelle Lalou*. Paris: Adrien Maisonneuve, 1971, 190–391.

Maconi, Lara. 2008. "One Nation, Two Discourses: Tibetan New Era Literature and the Language Debate." In Lauran R. Hartley and Patricia Schiaffini-Vedani (eds.), *Modern Tibetan Literature and Social Change*. Durham, London: Duke University Press, 173–201.

Makley, Charlene. 2005. "'Speaking Bitterness': Autobiography, History, and Mnemonic Politics on the Sino-Tibetan Frontier." In *Comparative Studies in Society and History* 47(1), 40–70.

Mao Zedong. March 10, 1958. *Talks at the Chingtu Conference*. http://www.marxists. org/reference/archive/mao/selected-works/volume-8/mswv8_06.htm.

Martin, Dan. 1997. *Tibetan Histories: A Bibliography of Tibetan-Language Historical Works*. London: Serindia Publications.

Marx, Karl. 1978. "The Eighteenth Louis Bonaparte." In Robert C. Tucker (ed.), *The Marx-Engels Reader*. New York: W. W. Norton & Company, 594–617.

McCartney, Jane. 2007. "Festival-Goers Ordered to Wear Fur or Face Fines as China Flouts Dalai Lama's Ruling." In *The Times*, July 27, 2007.

McGranahan, Carole. 2007. "Empire Out of Bounds: Tibet in the Era of Decolonization." In Ann Laura Stoler et al. (eds.), *Imperial Formations*. Santa Fe: New School for Advanced Research Press, 173–209.

———. 2010. *Arrested Histories: Tibet, the CIA, and Memories of a Forgotten War*. Durham and London: Duke University Press.

McGranahan, Carole, and Ralph Litzinger. 2012. "Self-Immolation as Protest in Tibet." In *Cultural Anthropology*'s Hot Spot Forum. April 11, 2012, //culanth. org/?q=node/526.

Mill, John Stuart. [1850] 1968. "Thoughts on Poetry and its Varieties." In Edmund D. Jones (ed.), *English Critical Essays (Nineteenth Century)*. London: Oxford University Press, 341–67.

Morcom, Anna. 2008. "Getting Heard in Tibet: Music, Media and Markets." In *Consumption, Markets and Culture*. Special Issue: *The Production and Consumption of Music* 11(4), 259–85.

———. 2010. "History, Traditions, Identities and Nationalism: Drawing and Redrawing the Musical Cultural Map of Tibet." In Saadet Arslan and Peter Schweiger (eds.), *Tibetan Studies: An Anthology*. [PIATS 2006: Proceedings of the Eleventh Seminar of the International Association for Tibetan Studies.] IITBS, 385–418.

Moulin, Joanny. 2005. "Ted Hughes: Anti-Mythic Method." In Joanny Moulin (ed.), *Ted Hughes: Alternative Horizons*. London and New York: Routledge, 86–92.

Murthy, Sheela. 1983. "Deng's 'Civilized' China of 'Five Disciplines, Four Graces and Three Loves." In *China Report* 19, 3–11.

Nicholls, Peter. 2007. "The Poetics of Modernism." In Alex Davis and Lee M. Jenkins (eds.), *The Cambridge Companion To Modernist Poetry*. Cambridge: Cambridge University Press, 51–67.

Nightingale, Andrea. 2006. "Mimesis: Ancient Greek Literary Theory." In Patricia Waugh (ed.), *An Oxford Guide: Literary Theory and Criticism*. Oxford: Oxford University, 37–47.

Nolan, Emer. 2005. "Modernism and the Irish Revival." In Joe Cleary and Claire Connolly (eds.), *The Cambridge Companion to Modern Irish Culture*. Cambridge: Cambridge University Press, 157–72.

Ong, Water J. 1982. *Orality & Literacy: The Technologizing of the Word*. London: Routledge.

Panchen Lama [1962] 1997. *A Poisoned Arrow: The Secret Report of The 10th Panchen Lama*. London: Tibet Information Network (TIN).

Paulin, Tom 1998. "Introduction." In William Hazlitt, *The Plain Speaker: The Key Essays*. Oxford: Blackwell Publishers, vii–xxiv.

Pema Bhum. [1991] 2008. "'Heartbeat of a New Generation': A Discussion of the New Poetry." In Lauran R. Hartley and Patricia Schiaffini-Vedani (eds.), *Modern Tibetan Literature and Social Change*. Translated by Ronald Schwartz. Durham, London: Duke University Press, 112–34.

———. 2008. "'Heartbeat of a New Generation' Revisited." In Lauran R. Hartley and Patricia Schiaffini-Vedani (eds.), *Modern Tibetan Literature and Social Change*. Translated by Lauran Hartley. Durham, London: Duke University Press, 135–47.

Phayul. 2006. "Burning the Animal Skin Revolution Sparked in Tibet." http://www.phayul.com/news/article.aspx?id=11881&t=1&c=1, February 18, 2006.

Portelli, Alessandro. 1998. "Oral History as Genre." In Mary Chamberlain and Paul Thompson (eds.), *Narratives and Genre*. London: Routledge.

Pound, Ezra. 1913. "A Few Don'ts by an Imagiste." In *Poetry: A Magazine of Verse* 1(1), March 1913: 200–8.

Radio Free Europe. June 4, 1957. *Colonization of Tibet*. Munich: Office of the Political Advisor.

Rainey, Lawrence. 2007. "Pound and Eliot: Whose Era?" In Alex Davis and Lee M. Jenkins (eds.), *The Cambridge Companion To Modernist Poetry*. Cambridge: Cambridge University Press, 87–113.

Rakra T. C. Tethong. 1995. "Love in Classical Tibetan Poetry." In *Lungta*, Winter 1995: 8–11. Dharamsala: The Amnye Machen Institute.

Ramble, Charles. 1990. "How Buddhist Are Buddhist Societies? The Construction of Tradition in Two Lamaist Villages." In *Journal of the Anthropological Society of Oxford* 21(2), 185–97.

———. 1999. "The Politics of Sacred Space in Bon and Tibetan Popular Tradition." In Toni Huber (ed.), *Sacred Spaces and Powerful Places in Tibetan Culture: A Collection of Essays*. Dharamsala: Library of Tibetan Works and Archives, 3–33.

———. 2009. "From 'Centre of this Earth' to 'Barbarous Borderlands' and Back Again: Spatial Self-Representation in Tibetan Politico-Religious Discourse." Lecture delivered at Wolfson College, University of Oxford on Friday, November 13, 2009.

Renan, Ernest. [1882] 1990. "What Is a Nation?" In Homi K. Bhabha (ed.), *Narration and Nation*. Oxon: Routledge, 8–22.

Ricoeur, Paul. 1988. *Time and Narrative*, translated by Kathleen Blamey and David Pellauer. Chicago: The University of Chicago.

Ridder, Knight, and Elizabeth Collins. 2006. "China Cannot Force People to Wear Fur." http://www.tibet.ca/en/newsroom/wtn/archive/old?y=2006&m=5&p=26_11, May 23, 2006.

Robin, Françoise (trans.). [2006] 2011. *Les Contes facétieux du cadavre*. Paris: Langues et Mondes—L'Asiathèque, collection "Bilingues L&M," 2nd edition.

———. 2007. "Stories and Histories: The Emergence of Historical Fiction in Contemporary Tibet." In Stephen Venturino (ed.), *Contemporary Tibetan Literary Studies*. Leiden, Boston: Brill, 23–41.

———. 2008. "'Oracles and Demons' in Tibetan Literature Today: Representations of Religion in Tibetan-Medium Fiction." In Lauran R. Hartley and Patricia Schiaffini-Vedani (eds.), *Modern Tibetan Literature and Social Change*. Durham, London: Duke University Press, 148–170.

———. 2010. "Tibetan Novels: Still a Novelty: A Brief Survey of Tibetan Novels since 1985." In *Latse Library Newsletter* 6, 2009–2010: 26–41.

———. 2011. "Ceci n'est pas un navire. Interprétations et lectures du poème de Jangbu (Ljang bu) Ce navire peut-il nous mener sur l'autre rive? (Gru gzings chen po 'dis nga tsho pha rol tu sgrol thub bam, 2000)." In *Impressions d'Extrême-Orient* [archive], 15 décembre 2011. http://ideo.revues.org/219#tocto1n3.

Samten G. Karmay. 1988. *The Great Perfection: A Philosophical and Meditative Teaching of Tibetan Buddhism*. Leiden: E. J. Brill.

———. 1998. *The Arrow and the Spindle: Studies in History, Myths, Rituals and Beliefs in Tibet*. Kathmandu: Mandala Book Point.

———. 2014. *The Illusive Play: The Autobiography of the Fifth Dalai Lama*. Chicago: Serindia Publications.

Sarin, Ritu, and Tenzing Sonam. (Directors) 1998. *The Shadow Circus: The CIA in Tibet*, a White Crane Films Production for BBC Television.

Sautman, Barry. 2006. "Colonialism, Genocide, and Tibet." In *Asian Ethnicity* 7(3), 243–65.

Schaedler, Luc. 2005. *Angry Monk: Reflections on Tibet*. Switzerland: Xenix Film-distribution GmbH.

Schiaffini-Vedani, Patricia. 2008. "The 'Condor' Flies over Tibet: Zhaxi Dawa and the Significance of Tibetan Magical Realism." In Lauran R. Hartley and Patricia Schiaffini-Vedani (eds.), *Modern Tibetan Literature and Social Change*. Durham, London: Duke University Press, 202–24.

Schwartz, Ronald D. 1994. *Circle of Protest: Political Ritual in the Tibetan Uprising*. London: Hurst & Company.

Scott, James C. 1990 *Domination and the Arts of Resistance: Hidden Transcripts*. New Haven & London: Yale University Press.

Sedgwick, Eve Kosofsky. 1985. *Between Men: English Literature and Male Homosocial Desire*. New York: Columbia University Press.

Shelley, Percy Bysshe. [1821] 1968. "A Defence Of Poetry." In Edmund D. Jones (ed.), *English Critical Essays (Nineteenth Century)*. London: Oxford University Press, 102–38.

Sigley, Gary. 2006. "Sex, Politics and the Policing of Virtue in the People's Republic of China." In Elaine Jeffreys (ed.), *Sex and Sexuality in China*. London and New York, 43–61.

Smelser, Neil J. 2004. "Psychological Trauma and Cultural Trauma." In Jeffrey C. Alexander, Ron Eyerman, Bernhard Giesen, Neil J. Smelser, and Piotr Sztompka.

Cultural Trauma and Collective Identity. Berkeley: University of California Press, 31–59.

Smith, Anthony D. 1991. *National Identity.* London: Penguin Books.

———. 1998. *Nationalism and Modernism—A Critical Survey of Recent Theories of Nations and Nationalism.* London and New York: Routledge.

———. 2008. *The Cultural Foundations of Nations: Hierarchy, Covenant, and Republic.* Oxford: Blackwell Publishing.

———. 2009. *Ethno-symbolism and Nationalism: A Cultural Approach.* London: Routledge.

———. 2010. *Nationalism.* Second Edition, Cambridge: Polity Press.

Smith, E. Gene. 2001. *Among Tibetan Texts: History and Literature of the Himalayan Plateau.* Boston: Wisdom Publications.

Smith, Stan. 1982. *Inviolable Voice: History and 20th Century Poetry.* Dublin: Gill and Macmillan.

Smith, Warren W. 1994. "The Nationalities Policy of the Chinese Communist Party and the Socialist Transformation of Tibet." In Robert Barnett and Shirin Akiner (eds.), *Resistance and Reform in Tibet.* London: Hurst & Company, 51–75.

———. 1996. *Tibetan Nation: A History of Tibetan Nationalism and Sino-Tibetan Relations.* Boulder: Westview Press.

———. 2010. *Tibet's Last Stand? The Uprising of 2008 and China's Response.* New York: Roman & Littlefield Publishers.

Snellgrove, David L., and Hugh Richardson. 1995. *A Cultural History of Tibet.* Boston & London: Shambhala.

Sorensen, Per K. 1990. *Divinity Secularised: An Inquiry into the Nature and Form of the Songs Ascribed to the Sixth Dalai Lama.* Wien: Arbeitskreis für Tibetische und Buddhistische Studien, Universität Wien.

Spencer, Richard. 2006. "Tibetans Clash with Chinese over Fur Bonfires." In *Daily Telegraph*, February 20, 2006.

Sperling, Eliot. 1994. "The Rhetoric of Dissent: Tibetan Pamphleteers." In Robert Barnett and Shirin Akiner (eds.), *Resistance and Reform in Tibet.* London: Hurst & Company, 267–84.

———. 2008. "Since Peaceful Liberation, What Policies has the Chinese Government Pursued in Tibet?" In Anne-Marie Blondeau and Katia Buffetrille (eds.), *Authenticating Tibet: Answers to China's 100 Questions.* Berkeley: University of California Press, 70–74.

Stein, Rolf Alfred (trans.). 1972. *Vie et chants de 'Brug-pa Kun-legs le yogin.* Paris: Maisonneuve et Larose.

Sternbach, Ludwik. 1976. *The Kāvya-portions in the Kathā-literature: An Analysis. Vol. III, Vetālapañcaviṁśatikā, mādhavānala-kāmakandalā-kathā, śukasaptati.* Delhi: Meharchand Lachhmandas.

Stirr, Anna. 2008. "*Blue Lake*: Tibetan Popular Music, Place and Fantasies of the Nation." In Robert Barnett and Ronald Schwartz (eds.), *Tibetan Modernities: Notes from the Field on Cultural and Social Change.* Leiden & Boston: Brill, 305–31.

Stoddard, Heather. 1985. *Le Mendiant De L'Amdo.* Paris: Societe D'ethnographie.

———. 1994. "Tibetan Publications and National Identity." In Robert Barnett and Shirin Akiner (eds.), *Resistance and Reform in Tibet*. London: Hurst & Company, 121–56.

———. 2010a. "Introduction." In Jangbu, *The Nine-Eyed Agate: Poems and Stories*, translated by Heather Stoddard. Plymouth: Lexington Books.

———. 2010b. "Tsering Dhondup and *The Red Wind Scream*." In *Latse Library Newsletter* 6, 2009–2010: 84–87.

Stoler, Ann Laura, and Carole McGgranahan 2007. "Introduction: Refiguring Imperial Terrians." In Ann Laura Stoler et al. (eds.), *Imperial Formations*. Santa Fe: New School for Advanced Research Press, 3–44.

Sujata, Victoria. 2005. *Tibetan Songs of Realization: Echoes from a Seventeenth-Century Scholar and Siddha in Amdo*. Leiden: Brill.

Szántó, Peter-Daniel. 2007. "Atra kim prayojanam? An Essay on the Reception and Naturalization of kāvya in Tibet: Tracing Texts, Reading Between the Lines and Other Vanities." In Csaba Dezso (ed.), *Indian Languages and Texts throughout the Ages: Essays of Hungarian Indologists in Honour of Prof. Csaba Tottssy*. New Delhi: Manohar, 209–55.

Sztompka, Piotr. 2004. "The Trauma of Social Change: A Case of Postcommunist Societies." In Jeffrey C. Alexander, Ron Eyerman, Bernhard Giesen, Neil J. Smelser, and Piotr Sztompka, *Cultural Trauma and Collective Identity*. Berkeley: University of California Press, 155–95.

TCHRD. 2008. *Uprising in Tibet 2008: Documentation of Protests in Tibet*. Dharamsala: Tibetan Centre for Human Rights and Democracy. This document can be obtained at http://www.tchrd.org/publications/topical_reports/uprising_in_tibet/uprising_in_tibet.pdf.

———. 2012. *Human Rights Situation in Tibet: Annual Report 2012*. http://www.scribd.com/doc/120758305/Annual-Report-TCHRD-2012.

Tibet: 1950–1967. 1968. Hong Kong: Union Research Institute.

Tibetan Review. March 17, 2012. "Massive Tibetan Student Protest Again over Switch to Chinese Language Education" at http://www.tibetanreview.net/news. php?id=10494.

Thom, Martin. 1990. "Tribes within Nations: The Ancient Germans and the History of Modern France." In Homi K. Bhabha (ed.), *Narration and Nation*. Oxon: Routledge, 23–43.

Thomas, Frederick W. 1935. "Tibetan Literary Texts and Documents Concerning Chinese Turkestan, Part 1." London: Luzac.

Thupten Jinpa, and Jaś Elsner (eds. and trans.). 2000. *Songs of Spiritual Experience: Tibetan Buddhist Poems of Insight and Awakening*. Boston and London: Shambhala.

TIN and HRW/Asia. 1996. *Cutting Off the Serpent's Head: Tightening Control in Tibet, 1994–1995*. London: Human Rights Watch.

Toelken, Barre. 1986. "Figurative Language and Cultural Contexts in the Traditional Ballads." In *Western Folklore* 45(2), April 1986: 128–42.

Tsering Dhondup. 2010. Excerpt from *The Red Wind Scream*, translated by Heather Stoddard. In *Latse Library Newsletter* 6, 2009–2010: 88–91.

Tsering Shakya. 1994. "Politicisation and the Tibetan Language." In Robert Barnett and Shirin Akiner (eds.), *Resistance and Reform in Tibet*. London: Hurst & Company, 157–65.

———. 1999. *The Dragon in the Land of Snows: A History of Modern Tibet since 1947*. New York: Columbia University Press.

———. 2004. *gSar rtsom: The Emergence of Modern Tibetan Literature Since 1950*. PhD dissertation, University of London.

———. 2008. "The Development of Modern Tibetan Literature in the People's Republic of China in the 1980s." In Lauran R. Hartley and Patricia Schiaffini-Vedani (eds.), *Modern Tibetan Literature and Social Change*. Durham, London: Duke University Press, 61–85.

Tsering Topgyal. 2012. *The Insecurity Dilemma and the Sino-Tibetan Conflict*. PhD dissertation, London School of Economics and Political Science.

Tshe ring dbang rgyal. 1996. *The Tale of the Incomparable Prince*, translated by Beth Newman. New York: HarperCollins Publishers.

Tuttle, Gray. 2007. "Interview with Pema Bum: Tibetan Literature and the Latse Tibetan Library." In Stephen Venturino (ed.), *Contemporary Tibetan Literary Studies*. Leiden, Boston: Brill, 147–57.

Ty, Eleanor. 1994. "Desire and Temptation: Dialogism and the Carnivaleque in Category Romances." In *A Dialogue of Voices: Feminist Literary Theory and Bakhtin*. Minneapolis: University of Minnesota Press, 97–113.

Upton, Janet L. 1999. "Cascades of Change: Modern and Contemporary Literature in the PRC's Junior-secondary Tibetan language and Literature Curriculum." In Tashi Tsering (ed.), *Lungta: Contemporary Tibetan Literature* 12. Dharamsala: Amnye Machen Institute, 17–28.

Valéry, Paul. 2004. "The Seaside Cemetery." In Mary Ann Caws (ed.), *The Yale Anthology of Twentieth-Century French Poetry*. New Haven & London: Yale University Press, 97–105.

van der Kuijp, Leonard W. J. 1996. "Tibetan Belles-Lettres: The Influence of Dandin and Ksemendra." In Jose Ignacio Cabezon and Roger R. Jackson. (eds.), *Tibetan Literature: Studies in Genre*. Ithaca: Snow Lion, 393–410.

van Schaik, Sam. 2011. *Tibet: A History*. New Haven and London: Yale University Press.

Virtanen, Riika J. (trans.). 2000. *A Blighted Flower and Other Stories*. Dharamsala: Library of Tibetan Works & Archives.

Warder, Antony Kennedy. 1992. *Indian Kāvya literature / Vol. VI, The Art of Storytelling*. Delhi: Motilal Banarsidass.

Watt, Ian. 1957. *The Rise of the Novel: Studies in Defoe, Richardson, and Fielding*. Harmondsworth: Penguin Books.

Weber, Max. 1994. "The Nation." In John Hutchinson and Anthony D. Smith (eds.), *Nationalism*. Oxford: OUP, 21–25.

White, Hayden. [1974] 2001. "The Historical Text As Literary Artifact." In Vincent B. Leitch et al. (eds.), *The Norton Anthology of Theory and Criticism*. New York: W. W. Norton and Company, 1712–29.

Wilde, Oscar. 1961. "The Critic as Artist." In Oscar Wilde, *Selected Writing*. Oxford World's Classics, London: Chancellor Press, 38–119.

Wildlifeextra.com 2009. "More Skins Being Burned in Tibet as Conservation Message Spreads." http://www.wildlifeextra.com/go/news/tibet-skins009.html#cr.

Woeser. 2009. "Us, Post-2008." In ICT (ed.), *Like Gold that Fears No Fire: New Writing from Tibet*. Washington, DC: International Campaign for Tibet, 9–20.

———. June 13, 2012. "Abolishing Tibetan Language Education for the Sake of 'Maintaining Stability.'" http://highpeakspureearth.com/2012/abolishing-tibetan-language-education-for-the-sake-of-maintaining-stability-by-woeser/.

Woolf, Virginia. [1928] 2004. *A Room of One's Own*. London: Penguin Books.

Wong, Edward. October 22, 2010. "Tibetans in China Protest Proposed Curbs on Their Language." In *New York Times*, October 22, 2010.

Wordsworth, William. [1802] 2001. "Preface to *Lyrical Ballads, with Pastoral and Other Poems*." In Vincent B. Leitch et al. (eds.), *The Norton Anthology of Theory and Criticism*. New York: W. W. Norton and Company, 648–68.

Yangdon Dhondup. 2008a. "Dancing to the Beat of Modernity: the Rise and Development of Tibetan Pop Music." In Robert Barnett and Ronald Schwartz (eds.), *Tibetan Modernities: Notes from the Field on Cultural and Social Change*. Leiden & Boston: Brill, 285–304.

———. 2008b. "Roar of the Snow Lion: Tibetan Poetry in Chinese." In Lauran R. Hartley and Patricia Schiaffini-Vedani (eds.), *Modern Tibetan Literature and Social Change*. Durham, London: Duke University Press, 32–60.

Yangtso Kyi. 2000. "Journal of the Grassland [Rtswa thang gi nyin tho]," translated by Lauran Hartley. *Manoa* 12(2).

Yeh, Emily T. 2012. "Transnational Environmentalism and Entanglements of Sovereignty: The Tiger Campaign across the Himalayas." In *Political Geography* 31(7), 408–18.

Yeshi Dhondup (trans.). 2009. *The Story of Golden Corpse*. Dharamsala: Library of Tibetan Works and Archives.

TIBETAN LANGUAGE SOURCES

Note: English translations of the following Tibetan titles might seem jarring to non-Tibetan ears as they deliberately remain faithful to the original. Here I adopt this approach whenever possible in order to reflect the distinctive Tibetan way of naming works, which is itself intellectually and culturally illuminating. With regard to titles that are already rendered into English, these are retained here as they appear in the published works.

གན་ཙྭ་བོད་རིགས་རང་སྐྱོང་ཁུལ་ཚོམ་སྒྱུར་ཁང་།)/<ༀ་ ⟨བསྐྱབ་རྒྱགཉིས་བསྒྲིགས། (*Selected Advice*) གན་ཙྭ་ བོད་རིགས་རང་སྐྱོང་ཁུལ་ཚོམ་སྒྱུར་ཁང་གིས་པར་དུ་བསྐྲུན།

ཀུན་གཟིགས་པ་ཚེ་ཆེན་སྐུ་ཕྲེང་དགུ་པ་ཚོམ་ཀྱི་ནི་མ། ༢༠༡༠། ⟨ཚེ་རིང་རྣམ་དྲུག་གི་ཁྱུང་བ་མདོར་བསྡུས་ཚིགས་སུ་ བཅད་པ།⟩ (A Brief Account of the Six Longevities in Verse) http://www.tsongchu.com/Article/Synthesize/201006608143.html.

གུན་དགས་བསྐྱར། ༢༠༠༠། ཉུབ་ཕྱོགས་དེང་རབས་རྩྭ་བའི་རྩོམ་རིག་གི་དྲི་གནའི་ལྔ་བརྒྱ། (*Five Hundred Questions on Western Modernist Literature*) བོད་གཞིས་ པེ་ཅིན། གུང་གོའི་བོད་ཀྱི་ཤེས་རིག་དཔེ་སྐྲུན་ཁང་།

———. ༢༠༠༢ ༼མི་དགེ་མེ་ཏོག་༽ ཅེས་བྱ་བའི་སྙན་ངག་དེབ་ཀྱི་ངོ་སྤྲོད་རྒྱས་པ། (A Detailed Introduction to a book of poems called *The Flowers of Evil*) ༼མི་རབས་གསུམ་པ་༽ གསར་འཕྲིན་ ༡ (*The Third Generation of Tibetan Poets*) Newsletter 1. ཤོག་ངོས་ ༩ནས་༡༤།

———. ༢༠༡༠། ཨེ་ལེ་ཡུའི་ཐབ་སྙན་ངག་རིང་མོ་ ༼ཐང་ཆད་ཐང་༽ སྐོར་ཀྱི་ངོ་སྤྲོད་རྒྱས་པ། (A Detailed Introduction to Eliot's Long Poem *The Waste Land*) ༼མི་རབས་གསུམ་པ་༽ གསར་འཕྲིན་ ༢ (*The Third Generation of Tibetan Poets*) Newsletter 2. ཤོག་ངོས་ ༩ནས་༡༥།

དགོན་མཆོག་བསྟན་འཛིན། ༡༩༩༢། ༼གངས་རིའི་གནས་བཤད་ཤེས་དཀར་མེ་ལོང་༽ (*Sacred Guidebook for the Snow-mountain: The White Crystal Mirror*) བོད་ལྗོངས་མི་དམངས་དཔེ་སྐྲུན་ཁང་།

བགའ་ཕྲུག་རྒྱལ། ༢༠༠༣། ༼གསུང་དུ་མེད་པའི་རྨ་ཁ། ཨ་འཇུང་རྡོ་རྗེ་ཚེ་རིང་ངམ་རིག་འཛིན་གྱི་བགྲོད་ལམ་རིང་མོ་༽ (*Indelible Wound: The Long Path Traversed by Ajung Dorje Tsering, Aka, Rigzin*) བོད་ཀྱི་རྩོམ་པ་པོས་མཉམ་ཚོགས་ནས་དཔར་བསྐྲུན་འགྲེམས་སྤེལ་བྱས།

བགྲ་ཤེས་རྒྱལ་མཚན་གྱིས་བདམས་ཏེ་བསྒྲིགས། ༡༩༩༢། ༼རོགས་འཐེན་རྡོ་རྗེའི་ཚེ་མདུད་༽ (*The Eternal Vajra Knot of Romantic Ballads*) ཟི་ལིང་། མཚོ་སྔོན་མི་རིགས་དཔེ་སྐྲུན་ཁང་།

གཉྭ་མཁན་འཐུས་དང་བགྲ་ཤེས་རྒྱལ་མཚན་གྱིས་ཚོམ་བསྒྲིགས་བྱས། ༡༩༩༥ཀ། ༼གཉེན་བཟང་ཐོས་པ་ཀུན་དགའ།༽ (*All Pleasing Wedding Recitals*) ཟི་ལིང་། མཚོ་སྔོན་མི་རིགས་དཔེ་སྐྲུན་ཁང་།

———. ༡༩༩༥ཁ། ༼གཉེན་རྒྱའི་ཚེ་ལོ།༽ (*Nagyi Tselo*) ཟི་ལིང་། མཚོ་སྔོན་མི་རིགས་དཔེ་སྐྲུན་ཁང་།

གཉྭ་རྒྱལ་མཚན་ཚོགས་སོགས། ༢༠༠༥། ༼མདོ་ཁམས་གནས་ཡིག་ཕྱོགས་བསྒྲིགས་དང་བསྐུལ་ལྔ་དབང་ཌ་རྒྱ་ཞེས་བ་བཞུགས་སོ།༽ (*Inspirational Drum Call of Indra: Collected Guides to Holy Sites in Dokham*) པེ་ཅིན་ མི་རིགས་དཔེ་སྐྲུན་ཁང་།

གཉྭ་འཕྲིན་ལས་ཀྱིས་ཚོ་བསྒྲིགས་བྱས། ༢༠༠༥། ༼སྔ་ཚོ་གཅེས་བསྒྲིགས།༽ (*Selected Pre-modern Writings*) པེ་ཅིན་ མི་རིགས་དཔེ་སྐྲུན་ཁང་།

སྐལ་བཟང་མགོས་གྲུབ་ཀྱིས་ཚོ་སྒྲིག་བྱས། ༢༠༠༢ ༼ཨ་ཁུ་སྟོན་པའི་སྒྲུང་།༽ (*Tales of Akhu Tonpa*) ཧྲ་རས་ས་ལ། བོད་གཞུང་ཤེས་རིག་དཔར་ཁང་།

སྐལ་བཟང་མཆོག་སྤྲུལ། ༢༠༡༢ ཟླ་ ༡ ཚེའི་ ༥། ༼ཚེ་རིང་སྐྱིད་ལགས་ཀྱི་ཕུང་པོ་རྫོང་མི་དམངས་སྨན་ཁང་དུ་བཙན་ཏུར་བྱས་འདུག༽ (Tsering Kyi's Body Kept in the County People's Hospital by Force) ཁ་བྱཌ། http://www.khabdha.org/?p=26292.

སྐལ་བཟང་རྒྱལ་ཁྲིམས། ༢༠༠༧། ༼བོད་ལ་རང་དབང་མེད་པའི་སྐོར་ཀྱི་སྙན་ཞུ།༽ (*A Report On The Lack of Freedom In Tibet*) མཆོད་ དཔལ་ལྡན་རྒྱལ་གྱི་ཟིན་བྲིས། //www.paldengyal.com/?p=908.

བྱ་བོ་དང་བྱི་མེམས་དཔལ། ༢༠༠༤། ༼སྲས་རང་དང་བོའི་བོད་ཀྱི་སྙན་ངག་པའི་མི་རབས་གསུམ་པའི་བགྲོ་གླེང་འདུ་ཚོགས་བོང་ཁྱེར་ཟི་ལིང་ནས་བསྐུས་པ།༽ (*The First Seminar of the Third Generation of Tibetan Poets Held in the City of Siling*) ༼མི་རབས་གསུམ་པ།༽ (*The Third Generation of Tibetan Poets*) ཤོག་ངོས་ ༢༡ནས་༢༣།

རྨ་བྱ། ༢༠༠༤། ༼བོད་ཀྱི་དེང་རབས་ཚོ་རིག་ལས་ན་གཞོན་ཚོ་པ་པོ་འགའི་སྙན་ངག་བརྩམས་ཚོས་བཤད༽ (*Comments on the Poetic Works of Some Young Writers of Modern Tibetan Literature*) ༼ཀྲུང་གོའི་བོད་རིག་པ།༽ (*China Tibetology*) ༢༠༠༤འི་དེབ་གསུམ་པ། ཤོག་ངོས་ ༤༩ནས་༥༠།

སྣུབས་ཆེན་བདེ་གྲོལ། ༢༠༡༢། ༼མི་རྟག་པ།༽ (*Impermanence*) གན་སུའུ་མི་རིགས་དང་སྐྲུན་ཁང་།

———. ༢༠༡༢ ཉི་རབས་གསུམ་པའི་སྐོར་ནས་ཞིབ་འཇུག་པ་ཞིག་གི་དྲི་བར་ལན་བཏབ་པ། (Answering a Researcher's Questions about the Third Generation) http://www.tibetcm.com/html/degrol/201205244510.html.

———. ༢༠༡༡ ཚགས་ཕྲན་དགའ་མའི་སྙིང་ཐིག་ཅེས་བྱ་བ། (*The So-called Heart-Essence of the Lustful Female Lover*) http://www.tibetcm.com/html/degrol/201110123679.html.

———. ༢༠༠ཁ ལྷ་སར་འགྲོ། (Let's Go to Lhasa) ཉི་རབས་གསུམ་པ། གསར་འཕྲིན་ ༡། (*The Third Generation of Tibetan Poets*) Newsletter 1. ཤོག་ཙོག༡།

———. ༢༠༠༤། ཉི་རབས་གསུམ་པ་ཞེས་པའི་སྐོར་གྱི་ལབ་སྟེང་ཕྲན་བུ། (A Few Words About the so-called Third Generation) ཉི་རབས་གསུམ་པ། (*The Third Generation of Tibetan Poets*) ཤོག་ཙོ་ར་ནས་ར།

———. ༢༠༠༢ ཉི་རབས་གསུམ་པ། (The Third Generation) ཉི་རབས་གསུམ་པ། (*The Third Generation of Tibetan Poets*) ཤོག་ཙོ་ལྤ་ནས་རㅇ།

———. ༢༠༠ཆ། རང་གི་གསར་ཚོམ་དང་འབྲེལ་བའི་གཏམ་ཕྲང་ཕྲང་། (A Brief Remark Regarding my Literary Creations) མཚོ་སྔོན་བོད་ཡིག་གསར་འགྱུར་ཁང་གིས་བསྒྲིགས་པའི་ ཞགས་སྐོང་ལུ་ཕྲུག་འདྲ་ གནས། (*The Deep Forest Abode of Cuckoos*) པེ་ཅིན་ མི་རིགས་དཔེ་སྐྲུན་ཁང་། ཤོག་ཙོ་༡༢ནས་ ༡༢༡།

———. ༢༠༠༢ རྐྱ༡༢ཆོས༡༢ ། རྨ་ཆུའི་ཉིན་ཐོ་ཕ། (Machu Diary: Six Entries) མཚོད་མའི་བོད་ཁྱུག http://www.cmbod.cn/u/skyabchen/archives/2009/16776.html

———. ༢༠༠༡ ས་ཆེན་གྱི་གླུ་བ། (Singer of the Great Land) ཚེ་རིང་བཀྲ་ཤིས་ཀྱིས་བརྩམས་པའི་ སྒྱུ་ འཕྲུལ་གྱི་མཆོད་མེ། (*The Illusory Butter Lamp*)ཞེས་པར། ཞིང་ཀང་གི་ཤིང་དཔེ་སྐྲུན་ཁང་། ཤོག་ཙོ་ ༡ནས་༡༢།

ཁ་བ་སྐྱ་མོ། ༢༠༡༢ ང་ལ་མིག་ཆུ་མི་འདུག། (I've No Tears) http://www.sangdhor.com/blog_c.asp?id=5964&a=kawa

ཕུ་ཐུག་སྤྲིན་མོ། ༢༠༡༠ ང་ཡི་བོད། (My Tibet) http://www.gdqpzhx.com/bo/html/third-generation/20100515686.html.

———. ༢༠༠ཁ ཀྲ་ཉིད་ལས་སད་རྗེས་སྙན་ཚོམ། (After Waking up: A Cluster of Poems) ཉི་རབས་གསུམ་པ། (*The Third Generation of Tibetan Poets*) ཤོག་ཙོ་༡༢ར་ནས་༡༤༢།

མཁར་སྲེབ་བསམ་གཏན། ༢༠༠ཆ། མདའ་དང་འཕང་། (*The Arrow and The Spindle*) སྡོང་ཆ་རྒྱུང་བོའི་ བོད་རིག་པ་དཔེ་སྐྲུན་ཁང་།

འཁྲུངས་སྲིང་མེ་ཏོག་ར་བ། (*The Flower Garden of Ling Gesar's Birth Story*) ༡༠༠༡ མི་རིགས་ མི་རིགས་དཔེ་སྐྲུན་ཁང་།

གུ་རུ་དོན་གྲུབ། ༢༠༡༠ རྨ་༡༡ ཚེས་ ༤ ། འཆི་བ། (Death) དགེ་འདུན་ཚོས་འཕེལ་ཚོ་རིག་དྲ་བ། http://www.gdqpzhx.com/bo/html/third-generation/201107021233.html.

———. ༢༠༡༠ རྨ་༢ ཚེས་༡༤། ཕ་ཡར་ལགས། ང་ལ་བསྒུ་བྲིད་མི་གཏོང་རོགས། (Please Stepfather, Do Not Deceive Me) http://blog.amdotibet.cn/geriduanzhi/index.aspx.

———. ༢༠༡ཁ ཐོད་བརྒལ་དང་ཕྱིར་ཏོག་བར་གྱི་གནད་མིག - མི་རབས་གསུམ་པ་བ་ཞིག་གི་མིག་གིས་མི་རབས་ གསུམ་པར་མིག་བཞེར་བྱས་པ། (Pressure Points Between Transcendence and Introspection: Casting a Glance over the Third Generation with the Eyes of a Third Generation Poet) http://www.tibetcm.com/html/list_21/201103122973.html.

བུ་ར་ལྩ་ཀྲན་སྐྱོང་བ། ཉ(ཤར2ཉ) ༡(ཤ2) བཀའ་ཐང་སྡེ་ལྔ། (*Five Categories of Royal Chronicles*) པེ་ཅིན། མི་རིགས་དཔེ་སྐྲུན་ཁང་།

གུང་ཐང་བསྟན་པའི་སྒྲོན་མེ། ༡༠༠༢། (ཡང་སྤྲུལ་དེ་ཉིད་གསལ་བྱེད།) (*Revealing the Truth about Rein-carnations*) སྤྲོས་ཞེན་ཟླ་བའི་སྐད་ཡིག་ཚོག་སྒྲིག་ཁྱུ་ཡོན་སྐྱེན་ཁང་གིས་བསྒྲིགས། (སྐད་ཡིག) (*Language*) ལོ་རིག་དགུ་པའི་སྐད་ཆ། དེ་ཡིག། མཚོ་སྔོན་མི་རིགས་དཔེ་སྐྲུན་ཁང་། ཤོག་ཙོང་རེབས༡༠ཤབ།

————. ༡(ཤར2) (ཡང་སྤྲུལ་དེ་ཉིད་གསལ་བྱེད།) (*Revealing the Truth about Reincarnations*) གཏན་ཚོ་ཕོད་རིགས་རང་སྐྱོང་ལྗུལ་ཚོ་སྐྱར་ཁང་གིས་པར་དུ་བསྐྲུན། (བསླབ་བྱ་གཅེས་བསྡུས།) (*Selected Advice*) ཤོག་ཙོ་ར2ཉན2 (2ཤབར།

དགེ་གཉེན་ཕོགས་ཀྱི་ཚོ་སྐྱིགས་བྱམ། ༡༠༠༦། (ཉགས་སྒོང་ཉུ་ཕྲུག་འདུ་གནས།) (*The Deep Forest Abode of Cuckoos*) པེ་ཅིན། མི་རིགས་དཔེ་སྐྲུན་ཁང་། ཤོག་ཙོང་༡༢རཉ2ན༡༢2།

དགེ་འདུན་ཚོས་འཕེལ། ༡༠༠༡། (ཉབས་དབང་དགེ་འདུན་ཚོས་འཕེལ་གྱི་གསུང་འབུམ་བཞུགས་སོ།) (*The Collected Works of the Great Scholar Gedun Choepel*) སྤོ་ཁ། སྐྲ་ཁ། སི་ཁྲོན་མི་རིགས་དཔེ་སྐྲུན་ཁང་།

————. ༡(ཤར2) (དགེ་འདུན་ཚོས་འཕེལ་གྱི་གསུང་ཚོག) (*Writings of Gedun Choepel*) དེབ་གསུམ། ཕོད་སྤོལས་ཕོད་ཡིག་དཔེ་སྐྲུན་དཔེ་ཇེ་ཁང་ནས།

————. ༡(ཤརར2) (ཉབས་དབང་དགེ་འདུན་ཚོས་འཕེལ་གྱི་གསུང་ཚོ་ཤྲོགས་སྤེག) (*Collected Writings of the Great Scholar Gedun Choepel*) སི་ཁྲོན་མི་རིགས་དཔེ་སྐྲུན་ཁང་།

————. ༡(ཤ2) (ཉདོད་པའི་བསྟན་བཅོས།) (*Treatise on Passion*) ཟླ་མེ།

དགེ་འདུན་རབ་གསལ། ༡༠༠2། (ཤབལ་ཏིའི་ཡུལ་དང་སྐད་ཏོ་སྤོད།) (*Introduction to Baltistan and its Language*) ཁ་བརྡ། http://www.khabdha.org/?p=1913.

————. ༡༠༠2། (རིན་བཟང་སྤོན་པར་བཏང་འདུག) (*Rinzang Driven Mad*) ཁ་བརྡ། http://www.khabdha.org/?p=4334.

————. ༡༠༠༡། (ཕོད་ཀྱི་ཚོ་རིག་བྱུང་བ་བཙོད་པ་རབ་གསལ་མེ་ཕོང་ཞེས་བུ་བ། ལྲ་རྲ་ཆ་སི། ལྲ་ཆ་དབུས་ཕོད་ཀྱི་ཚོ་མཚོའི་གཙོག་ལག་སྤོང་གཉེར་ཁང་། (*History of Tibetan Literature*).

འབྲུ་ལོག་དར་ཚོས་དཔལ་བཟང་། ༡༠༠༡། (འབྲུ་ལོག་གི་ལོ་རྒྱུས་གཉན་པོ་གཡུ་ཚའི་བསང་དུད།) (*A History of Golok: The Purifying Smoke-offering of Nyanpo Yutse*) སྐད་ཁ། རྲ་ཪ་ས་ལ། ཕོད་ཀྱི་དཔེ་མཚོད་ཁང་།

འགོས་ལོ་ཚ་བ་གཞོན་ནུ་དཔལ། ༡(ཤར2) (དེབ་ཐེར་སྔོན་པོ།) (*The Blue Annals*) སྤོད་ཁ། སི་ཁྲོན་མི་རིགས་དཔེ་སྐྲུན་ཁང་།

བསྐལ་དོ། ༡༠༡༠། (མི་རབས་གསུམ་པའི་ཕུར་ཇེང་།) (*The Clamor of the Third Generation*) http://www.tibetcm.com/html/list_21/201007062306.html.

རྒྱ་ཡེ་བག་སྐོང་གཙོ་སྲིག་བྱས་པ། ༡༠༠༢། (ཕོད་ཀྱི་ཚོ་རིག་ལོ་རྒྱུས་སྐལ་བཟང་མིག་སྤོན།) (*A History of Tibetan Literature: A Lamp for the Eye of the Fortunate Student*) ཟི་ལིང་། མཚོ་སྤོན་རིགས་དཔེ་སྐྲུན་ཁང་།

རྒྱ་ཡེ་བག་སྟོ། (༡༠༠༡། ༡༠༠2 (དུན་ཧོང་ནས་ཐོན་པའི་ཕོད་ཀྱི་ལོ་རྒྱས་ཡིག་ཚེ་ཕོད་ཀྱི་"བླ་བརྡུང་"ཞེས་པར་དཔྱད་པ།) (*An analysis of the term "bla brdung" found in Tibetan Historical Man-uscripts from Dunhuang*) (ཀྲུང་གོའི་ཕོད་རིག་པ་"ལོ་འཁོར་༡༠ཡི་དཔྱད་ཚོ་བདམས་བསྒྲིགས།) (*Selected Critical Essays from 20 Years of "China Tibetology"*) པེ་ཅིན། ཀྲུང་གོའི་ཕོད་རིག་པ་དཔེ་སྐྲུན་ཁང་། ཤོག་ཙོས་༡༠ར2ན༡༡།

རྒྱལ་ཁབ་མི་རིགས་ལས་དོན་ཀྱུ་ཡོན་ལྷན་ཁང་གི་སྲིད་ཇུས་ཞིབ་འཇུག་ཁང་གིས་ཚོམ་སྒྲིག་བྱས་པ། ༡༩༩༠ ཞི་རིགས་སྲིད་ཇུས་སྐོར་གི་གཏམ་བཤད། (Speeches on Nationality Policies) མི་རིགས་དཔེ་སྐྲུན་ཁང་།

བློ་ཡོན། ༢༠༡༡ ཞིབཅད་ཚིག་གསར་མ་ཞེས་པའི་ཚིག་ལྷུག་ཀྱི་གོ་དོན་བརྗོད་པ། (An Interpretative Commentary on New Verse) མཚོ་མེ་བོད་ཀྱི་ཚིག་རིག་དྲ་བ། http://www.tibetcm.com/html/list_15/201102182897.html.

དགའ་འཕྲིན། ༡༡༥༽ གནས་ཆེན་གངས་རི་མཚོ་གསུམ་རྒྱ་པོ་བཞི་དང་བཅས་པ་གཏན་ལ་དབབ་པ་ལུང་དོན་སྟོན་བར་བྱེད་པའི་མེ་ལོང་། (Mirror of Prophetic Expositions: Great Holy Sites of the triad - Snow mountain, the Mountain and the Lake, and the Four Rivers) ཚེ་རིང་དཔལ་འཛོར་གྱིས་བསྒྲིགས་པའི། བོད་ཀྱི་གནས་ཡིག་བདམས་བསྒྲིགས། (Selected Guides to Holy Sites in Tibet) བོད་ལྗོངས་བོད་ཡིག་དཔེ་རྙིང་དཔེ་སྐྲུན་ཁང་། ཤོག་ངོས་༡༣ནས་༥༽

དགེ་འདུན་རྒྱ་མཚོ། ༡༦༥༽ རྃ་ཧོར་གྱི་བརྗེ་དགག་དངང་སློ་བཟང་རྒྱ་མཚོའི་འདི་སྣང་འཁྲུལ་པའི་རོལ་ཆེད་དྲ་གོས་བརྗོད་ཀྱི་ཚུལ་དུ་བཀོད་པ་དུ་ཀུ་ལའི་གོས་བཟང་ཞེས་པ། (The Exquisite Divine Robe: Illusive Play of Sahor Paṇḍita Lobsang Gyatso's Worldly Existence in the Form of a Biography) འཕགས་པ་འཇིག་རྟེན་དབང་ཕྱུག་གི་རྣམ་སྤྲུལ་རིམ་བྱོན་གྱི་འཁྲུངས་རབས་དེབ་ཐེར་ནོར་བུའི་ཕྲེང་བ། (Life Stories of Successive Reincarnations of the Dalai Lama: A Rosary of Chronicle Jewels) དེབ་གཞིས་པ། ར་རམ་ས་ལ། ཤོག་ངོས་༢༢༼ནས༣༠༽

———. ༡༥༽ བོད་ཀྱི་དེབ་ཐེར་དཔྱིད་ཀྱི་རྒྱལ་མོའི་གླུ་དབྱངས། (The Tibetan Annals: Song of the Spring Queen) པེ་ཅིན། མི་རིགས་དཔེ་སྐྲུན་ཁང་།

སྒྲགས་འཆང་དྷ་མཥིན་རྒྱལ། ༢༠༠༢ བོད་ཕྱུལ་འདི་རྗེ་བཙུན་སྤྱན་རས་གཟིགས་ཀྱི་གདུལ་ཞིང་ཡིན་པའི་རྒྱ་མཚན་གནད་བསྡུས། (A Concise Explanation of Why Tibet is the Divine Dominion of the Supreme Avalokiteśvara) སྒྲགས་མང་ཞིབ་འཇུག (Ngakmang Research) ༢༠༠༢ ལོའི་དེབ་དང་པོ། ཟི་ལིང་། སྒྲགས་མང་ཞིབ་འཇུག་ཚོམ་སྒྲིག་ཁང་། ཤོག་ངོས་༡༢༼ནས༩༢༽

གཅན་ཆེད་འབར། ༢༠༠༼ སེམས་པ་སྟོང་པའི་དུས་སུ་བྲིས་པའི་སྣན་ངག་ཁག་བཞི། (Four Different Poems Composed When Feeling Empty) མི་རབས་གསུམ་པོ། (The Third Generation of Tibetan Poets) ཤོག་ངོས་༡༥༼ནས༽

གཅན་མེ་སྟག ༢༠༡༠ མི་ལོང་དང་གཏན་པའི་ཕོ་བྲང་། རྗེ་ལྷ་དང་མིག་ལོང་བོད་ཀྱི་སྟོར་དེ་ཟེ། (Mirror and Labyrinth: Borges amidst Dreams and Blindness) ཧྲོར་ཧེ་ཟིའི་སྣན་ཚིག་འགའ་ཡི་འགྱུར། (Translations of some Poems by Borges) དགའ་འདུན་ཚོམ་འཕེལ་ཚིག་རིག་དྲ་བ། http://www.gdqpzhx.com/bo/html/photo/20100615711.html.

སྒྲགས་ཏོར་རྒྱལ། ༢༠༡༢ བོད་ཀྱི་དེང་རབས་སྣན་ངག་རིག་པ། (Modern Tibetan Poetry Studies) ཟི་ལིང་། མཚོ་སྔོན་མི་རིགས་དཔེ་སྐྲུན་ཁང་།

ཆབ་འགག་ལྷ་མཁྱིན། ༢༠༠༽ བོད་ཀྱི་དེང་རབས་ཚོམ་རིག་ལོ་རྒྱུས། (A History of Modern Tibetan Literature) པེ་ཅིན། མི་རིགས་དཔེ་སྐྲུན་ཁང་།

ཆབ་བྲག་ལྷ་མོ་སྐྱབས། ༢༠༡༡ བཀའ་ཐང་སྡེ་ལྔ། (Five Categories of Royal Chronicles) http://www.chapdaklhamokyab.fr/མཆོགས-ས-ར/བཀའ-ཐང-ས-ལ/.

———. ༢༠༡༡ ལེའུ་ལྔ་བ། སྣན་དག་གི་རྒྱན་ནམ་སྒྱུ་རྩལ་མཚོན་ཐབས་བཤད་བཏད་པ། (Chapter 5: On Poetic Ornaments or Artistic Techniques) http://www.chapdaklhamokyab.fr

ཚེས་སྐྱོང་། ༢༠༠༥། ཤེང་གྲོལ་ཞིབ་འཇུག དོན་གྲུབ་རྒྱལ་གྱི་མི་ཚེ་དང་གསར་གཏོད་ཀྱི་སྙིང་སྟོབས། (*Rangdrol Studies: Dhondup Gyal's Life and His Courage for Innovation*) གན་སུའུ་མི་རིགས་དཔེ་ སྐྲུན་ཁང་།

ཚེས་ཕྱུག་གསང་བདག ༢༠༠༤། ཨ་རབས་བཞི་བ་ཚོ་ལ་བསྐྱར་དུ་བསྐྱར་པོ། (A Review of the Fourth Generation) http://www.tibetcm.com/html/list_03/798cc30237d22fa97f51b2a2f1 2aa83a/.

མཆོད་མེ་བོད་ཀྱི་ཚེས་རིག་དྲ་བ། ༢༠༡༡། ཨིམ་འར་བཙན་པོ་སོགས་མི་རབས་གསུམ་པ་ནས་བུད་པོ། (Dhat-senpo and Others Leave the Third Generation) http://www.tibetcm.com/html/ news/201106203344.html.

འཆེ་མེ་དྲེ་རྗེ་དང་། ཚེ་སྐྲོབས་ཀྱིས་ཚོམ་སྒྲིག་བྱས་པ། ༡༦༥༠། ཧོར་གླིང་གཡུལ་འགྱེད། (*The Battle of Hor and Ling*) ཕྱ་ས། བོད་ལྗོངས་མི་རིགས་དཔེ་སྐྲུན་ཁང་།

འཇམ་དཔལ་རྒྱ་མཚོ། ༡༦༦༢། སྐྲོབ་དཔོན་ཆེན་པོ་པཎ་ཆེན་རིན་པོ་ཆེ། (*Great Master Panchen Rinpoche*) ཧ་རམ་ས་ལ། བདེ་སྤྱང་བོད་གཞན་ཞམས་ཞིབ་ཁང་།

འཇིམ་དབྱངས་དཀར་པོ། ༢༠༡༢ ཟླ་༡༡ཚེས་༢། སྐྱལ་བཟང་སྦྱིན་པ་ལགས་ཀྱིས་རང་ཕྱག་བཏང་སྐོར་གནས་ཚུལ་ཁུངས་ ཕྱན་བ་སྟོན་ཅིག (Reliable Supplementary Information About the Self-immolation of Kalsang Jinpa) http://www.khabdha.org/?p=35969

ཀུན་མཁྱེན་འཇིགས་མེད་དབང་པོ། ༡༦༧༩། ཀུན་མཁྱེན་འཇམ་དབྱངས་བཞད་པའི་རྣམ་ཐར། (*Biography of Kunkyen Jamyang Shepa*) གན་སུའུ་མི་རིགས་དཔེ་སྐྲུན་ཁང་།

འབྲུ་སྐྱལ་བཟང་། ༢༠༠༠། གངས་གྲོང་གི་རླུང་བུ། (*Wind of the Snow-Mountain Village*) ཟི་ལིང་། མཚོ་ སྔོན་མི་རིགས་དཔེ་སྐྲུན་ཁང་།

————. ༡༦༦༠། བོད་ཀྱི་སྙན་ངག་གི་རྒྱུན་འཛིན་དང་འཕེལ་རྒྱས་སྐོར་རགས་ཚམ་སྙིང་བ་གཟུར་གནས་རིག་པའི་ འཇུག་ངོགས། (*A Brief Reflection on the Preservation and Development of Tibetan Poetry: An Entrance for the Impartial Intellect*) སྙན་ངག་གི་རྣམ་བཤད། (*A Categorical Exposition of Poetry*) ཟི་ལིང་། མཚོ་སྔོན་མི་རིགས་དཔེ་སྐྲུན་ཁང་། ཤོག་ངོས་༡༩༤༡༦༡།

————. ༡༦༥༠། ཏུང་ཧོང་ཡིག་རྙིང་ལས་བྱུང་བའི་བོད་ཀྱི་གནའ་རབས་སྙན་ངག་སྐོར་རགས་ཚམ་སྙེ་བ། (A Brief Discussion of Archaic Tibetan Poetry found in the Old Dunhuang Manuscripts) http://www.tibetcm.com/html/list_15/bafe544addafc8d909a13884dc462ca0/

————.   ༡༦༦༡།   ཤིང་རབས་སྙན་ངག་ཏོ་སྐྲོད་རགས་བསྒྲས་ལོག་རྟོག་མུན་པ་སེལ་བའི་སྐྱ་ རེངས། (A Brief Introduction to Modern Tibetan Poetry: A Dawn Dispelling the Darkness of Misunderstanding) http://www.tibetcm.com/html/list_15/ edb60d1ce35bb31e071c774d874c6f1c/.

འཇུ་མི་ཕམ་འཇམ་དབྱངས་རྣམ་རྒྱལ་རྒྱ་མཚོ། ༢༠༡༠། སྒྱུ་རྩ་སྣའི་རོལ་མོ། (Musical Play of Delusion) བློ་བཟང་ཚོམ་གྲགས་དང་བསོད་ནམས་རྩེ་མོ་བསྒྲིགས་པའི། གངས་ལྗོངས་མཁས་དབང་རིམ་བྱོན་གྱི་ཚོམ་ཡིག གསེར་གྱི་སྦྲམ་བུ། (Gold Ingot of Writings by Successive Great Scholars from the Land of Snows) སྐུད་ཁ། མཚོ་སྔོན་མི་རིགས་དཔེ་སྐྲུན་ཁང་། ཤོག་ངོས་༨༠༤༨ས༢༩།

————. ༢༠༠༧། འདོད་པའི་བསྟན་བཅོས་འཇིག་རྟེན་ཀུན་དུ་དགའ་བའི་གཏེར། (*Treatise on Passion: A World Pleasing Treasure*) ཨི་ཕམ་རྒྱ་མཚོའི་གསུང་འབུམ། (*The Collected Works of Mipham Gyatso*) པོད་དང་པོ། ཁྲི་ཧུ༠། གནས་ཚན་རིག་གཞུང་དཔེ་སྐྲིག་རྒྱུན་སྤྱོབས་སྐྲུན་ཚོགས།

ཇེ་དགེ་འདུན་གྲུབ། ༡༡༽ ཁྱིགས་ཏྲེ་མ་བཞུགས་སོ། (The Exquisitely Written) བསྟོད་སྨོན་ཕྱོགས་བསྒྲིགས། (Collected Praises and Devotional Prayers) ཤོག་དོ་༢༢༢ནས་༢༢༤ མཚོ་སྔོན་མི་རིགས་དཔེ་སྐྲུན་ཁང་། ཤོག་དོ་༢༢༢ནས་༢༢༤།

ཇེ་བློ་བཟང་གྲགས་པ། ༡༡༽ དབྱངས་ཅན་མའི་བསྟོད་པ་བཞུགས་སོ། (Praise to Sarasvati) བསྟོད་སྨོན་ཕྱོགས་བསྒྲིགས། (Collected Praises and Devotional Prayers) ཤོག་དོ་༢༡༠ མཚོ་སྔོན་མི་རིགས་དཔེ་སྐྲུན་ཁང་།

ལྗང་བུ། ༢༠༠༡། སྤྱན་ཚིགས་གཟི་མིག་དགུ་བོ། (Nine-eyed Zi Poems) Tim Ma Book Company Limited.

———. ༡༡༩། ལྗང་བུའི་ཚོམ་བཏུས། སྙན་ངག་དེབོ། (Jangbu's Collected Writings: Poetry Volume) གན་སུའི་མི་རིགས་དཔེ་སྐྲུན་ཁང་།

———. ༢༠༡༡། མི་རབས་གསུམ་པའི་དོན་རྐྱེན་གྱིས་དྲན་སྐུལ་བསླངས་བོ། (A Recollection Prompted by the Third Generation Incident) མཚོ་མི་བོད་ཀྱི་ཚོམ་རིག་དྲ་བ། http://www.tibetcm.com/html/list_21/201106233347.html.

སྟོངས་ཞིང་སྡེའི་སྐད་ཡིག་ཚོམ་སྒྲིག་ལུ་ཡོན་སྐྲུན་ཁང་གིས་བསྒྲིགས། ༢༠༠༥ སྐད་ཡིག (Language) བོ་རིག་བདུན་པའི་སྐྲུན་ཁ། ཟི་ལིང་། མཚོ་སྔོན་མི་རིགས་དཔེ་སྐྲུན་ཁང་།

ཉུང་སྐྱེས་སྣང་མཛད་རྡོ་རྗེ། ༢༠༠༨། ཉུང་སྐྱེས་སྣང་མཛད་རྡོ་རྗེའི་གསུང་ཚོམ་ཕྱོགས་བསྒྲིགས། (The Collected Writings of Nyingkyi Nangzad Dorje) ཟྭགས་མང་དཔེ་ཚོགས། པེ་ཅིན། མི་རིགས་དཔར་སྐྲུན་ཁང་།

གཉན་༢༠༠༧། འབྲོང་དྲན་པའི་ཟིན་ཐོ། (Notes on Remembering the Wild Yak) གངས་རྒྱན་མེ་ཏོག (Snow Flower) ༢༠༠༧། ༤ སྦྲིའི་དེབ་གྲངས་༢༡༠། ཤོག་དོ་༤འནས་༥༥།

སྙིང་དཀར་བཀྲ་ཤིས། ༢༠༡༢ ཟླ་༡༡ ཚེས་༡༢། དི་རིང་ཚེས་༢༢ཉིན་མཚོ་སྦྱང་རེ་གོང་ནས་རང་ཤིག་བཏང་བའི་སྙིང་དཀར་བཀྲ་ཤིས་ལགས་ཀྱི་ཞལ་ཆེམས་ཕྱག་བསྐུར་མ། (The Handwritten Testament of Nyingkar Tashi who Self-immolated Today, November 12) http://www.khabdha.org/?p=36279.

དྲུ་མི་བྱང་རྒྱལ་རྒྱལ་མཚན་སོགས། ༡༡༤། རྐྱངས་ཀྱི་པོ་ཏེ་བཻ་ཌུ་རྒྱས་བོ། (The Expanded Edition of the Rhino-horn Book of Rlang) སྐ་མ། བོད་ལྗོངས་མི་དམངས་དཔེ་སྐྲུན་ཁང་།

ཏ་མགྲིན་ཚེ་རིང་གིས་ལེགས་སྒྲིག་བགྱིས། ༡༡༽ འིངན་ཆགས་མི་ཚོམ་སུ་བཤད་པ་རིག་པའི་གཏེར་མཛོད། (The Treasury of Intellect: Narrating the Worldly Tale of the Winged Ones) གན་སུའི་མི་རིགས་དཔེ་སྐྲུན་ཁང་།

ཕྱག་ལྭ་ཕུན་ཚོགས་བཀྲ་ཤིས། ༡༡༧། མི་ཚེའི་བྱུང་བ་བརྗོད་བོ། (Narrating A Life Story) དེབ་གཉིས་པ། ཏ་རྭ་ས་ལ། བོད་ཀྱི་དཔེ་མཛོད་ཁང་།

བསྟན་འཛིན་གྱིས་བསྒྲིགས། ༡༡༩། རིག་བྱེད་གཏམ་རྒྱུད་བདམས་བསྒྲིགས། (Selected Vedic Tales) མཚོ་སྔོན་མི་རིགས་དཔེ་སྐྲུན་ཁང་།

བསྟན་འཛིན་དཔལ་འབར། ༡༡༣། ཕའི་ཕ་ཡུལ་གྱི་ཡ་ང་བའི་བོ་རྒྱུས། (The Tragedy Of My Homeland) ཏ་རྭ་ས་ལ། སྣར་ཐང་པར་ཁང་།

བསྟན་འཛིན་བཟང་པོ། ༡༡༧། ཚ་རི་ཊ་ཡེ་ཤེས་ཀྱི་འཁོར་ལོའི་ལྟེ་བ་མཚོ་དཀར་སྤྲུལ་པའི་པོ་བྲང་གི་གནས་ཡིག་གསལ་བའི་སྒྲོན་མེ་ཞེས་བྱ་བ་བཞུགས་སོ། (Illuminating Lamp of Sacred Guides to the Miraculous Palatial White Lake at the Hub of the Wisdom Wheel of Tsari) ཚེ་རིང་དཔལ་

འབྲོང་གིས་བསྒྲིགས་པའི། ཁོད་ཀྱི་གནས་ཡིག་བདམས་བསྒྲིགས། (Selected Guides to Holy Sites in Tibet) བོད་ལྗོངས་བོད་ཡིག་དཔེའི་རྙིང་དཔེ་སྐྲུན་ཁང་། ཧོག་ཙོ་ལྗ་ནས་ཉ༢༢ལ།

ཐར་ཆེན། ཉ༢༤ནས་ཉ༥༢། ཕྱལ་ཕྱོགས་སོ་སོའི་གནས་འཁྱུར་མེ་ལོང་། (The Tibet Mirror) http:// www.columbia.edu/cu/lweb/digital/collections/cul/texts/ldpd_6981643_000/.

ཚོ་རིངས། ༢༠༠༥། རྙིང་ཞེན་གྱི་ཀླད་ཞ་གསར་གཏོང་གིས་བཀྲུས་པའི་མི་རབས་གསུམ་པ། (The Third Generation That Has Washed Off the Brains of Conservatism with Innovation) http:// www.tibetcm.com/html/list_21/ad9eb4dc9e22baaa056fbf4ccb5dc4fc/.

དུང་དཀར་བློ་བཟང་འཕྲིན་ལས། ༢༠༠༢། ཁུང་དཀར་ཚིག་མཛོད་ཆེན་མོ། (The Dungkar Encyclopaedia) པེ་ཅིང་། ཀྲུང་གོའི་བོད་རིག་པ་དཔེ་སྐྲུན་ཁང་།

——. ཁྱིམ་རྫ། ༢༠༠༩། རྙིན་བཀལ་འཇུག་སྒོའི་ཚོན་ཚོན་རྒྱན་རིག་པའི་སྒོ་འབྱེད། ཀ (Unlocking the Door of Poetic Diction: An Introduction to Kāvya Poetics) པེ་ཅིན། མི་རིགས་དཔེ་སྐྲུན་ཁང་།

དོན་གྲུབ་རྒྱལ། ཉ༥༢། ཁ་དཔལ་དོན་གྲུབ་རྒྱལ་གྱི་གསུང་འབུམ། (The Collected Works of Dhondup Gyal) པོད་དྲུག པེ་ཅིན། མི་རིགས་དཔེ་སྐྲུན་ཁང་།

དོར་ཞི་གདོང་དྲུག་སྙེམས་བློ། ཁྱིམ་རྫ། ཉ༥༢། རྗེས་དྲན་གྱི་གདུང་པད་དཀར་རྒྱུ་པོ། (An Obituary: A Bouquet of White Lotuses) དཔལ་དོན་གྲུབ་རྒྱལ་གྱི་གསུང་འབུམ། པོད་གསུམ་པ། དཔྱད་ཚོམ་ཕྱོགས་བསྒྲིགས། (The Collected Works of Dhondup Gyal: Volume 3, Critical Essays) པེ་ཅིན། མི་རིགས་དཔེ་སྐྲུན་ཁང་། ཧོག་ཙོ་ཉ༣ནས་ལབར།

——. ༢༠༠༩། ཁདྲྱང་ཚོམ་སྐྲུན་འཛོམས་ཚོར་ཕུའི་ཕྲེང་བ། (Critical Essays: A Rosary of Jewels for Dispelling Darkness) གང་སུའུ་མི་རིགས་དཔེ་སྐྲུན་ཁང་།

——. ཉ༥༢༢། རྙིན་གྱི་ཕོ་ཉའི་ཚིག་འགྲེལ། (A Word by Word Interpretive Commentary on The Cloud Messenger) མི་རིགས་དཔེ་སྐྲུན་ཁང་།

བདུད་ལྷ་རྒྱལ། ༢༠༠༩། འབྲུམ་རམས་པའི་ཆེད་ཚོམ། ཁོད་ཀྱི་བརྩམས་སྒྲུང་གསར་བའི་གནས་སྟངས་དང་དེའི་དགག་སྒྲུབ། (The Status of New Tibetan Fiction and a Critique of It) ལན་གྲུ་ནུབ་བྱང་མི་རིགས་སློབ་གྲྭ་ཆེན་མོ།

བདེ་སྐྱིད་སྒྲོལ་མ། ༢༠༡༡། རྟ་ཕོ་རྒྱ་མོ་དགུ་མདུད། (Nine-eyed Knot: A Monthly Record) ཁོ་ཕོ་བརྩེ་བའི་ཞགས་པ། (Lasso of Love: A Record of a Year) དཔལ་ཚོས་ཚོམ་སྒྲིག་བྱས་པའི་དེང་རབས་བོད་རིགས་བུད་མེད་ཀྱི་དེའི་ཚོགས་ལས། (Contemporary Tibetan Women's Series) རྙིན་ཚོམ་ཕྱོགས་བསྒྲིགས། (Collected Poems) པེ་ཅིན། ཀྲུང་གོའི་བོད་རིག་པ་དཔེ་སྐྲུན་ཁང་། ཧོག་ཙོས་པ་འནས་ ཕ༥དང་ ཕ༢ནས་ཙ༢།

——. ༢༠༠༢། ཁར་ཐས་ཟིམ་སྦུག་ལང་ལོང་། (Gentle Rain and Swirling Mist) ལན་གྲུ་གན་སུའུ་མི་རིགས་དཔེ་སྐྲུན་ཁང་།

མདའ་བཙན་པོ། ༢༠༡༢ ཀ ཁ་བོན་པ་བཟར་བ། (Sharpening Truth) http://www.sangdhor.com/list_c.asp?id=10429.

——. ༢༠༡༢ ཁ ཁ་འབྲུག་པ་ཀུན་ལེགས་ལྟར་ཁ་བཀར་བ། (Talking Dirty like Drukpa Kunleg) http://www.sangdhor.com/list_c.asp?id=10429.

——. ༢༠༡༡། ཁ་མཛེས་པར་བརྒྱུས་པའི་མེ་ཏོག་གི་ཕྲེང་བ། ཞེས་པ་ལས། (A Garland of Flowers Threaded Through Beauty) ཁྱི་བའི་གཏིང་དུ་བྲལ་བའི་བརྩེ་བ། (Love Embedded within Questions) རྙ་ཟེར། (Moonlight) ༢༠༡༡ལོའི་དེ་ཟེར་གསུམ་པ། སྟེའི་དེ་གྲངས་ཉ༠ཁ ཧོག་ཙོ་ ༢༢ནས་ ༢༡།

———. ༢༠༡༠། ཁ་བྲལ་ལ་སོང་བའི་སྐྱིད། (Tale of a Pilgrimage to U)

———. ༢༠༠། སེམས་ཀྱི་རྡོ་པོ་གསལ་བྱེད་ཀྱི་གླུ། (A Song Revealing the Nature of Mind) ཞི་རབས་གསུམ་པ། (The Third Generation of Tibetan Poets) ཐོག་ཏོས་དགུ་ནས་༢༢།

———. ༢༠༠༨། ཀ ཁང་པ་འདིའི་ནང་ནས། (Inside This Room) http://www.tibetcm.com/html/list_21/17668c7146d675fe2cb0f06858de5b28/.

———. ༢༠༠༨། ཁ ཁྱེད་རང་མི་འཐད་ནའང་ངས་འདི་ལྟར་བྲིས་ན་ཅི་རེད། (Even If You Don't Like It, So What? I Write Like This) www.tibetcm.com.

———. ༢༠༠༦། ག ཕྱུན་སྐྱང་ཆེན་པོས་ཚོགས་འདུར་ཞུགས་ན། (When Attending a Meeting with Great Boredom) www.tibetcm.com.

———. ༢༠༠༧། སྐད་ཆ་བསྐོར་མོ་རེ་བཤད་ན། (To Say Something Funny)

མདའ་ཚན་པ། ༢༠༡༠། གཉེན་དཀར་ཕྱོགས་ལས་རྣམ་རྒྱལ་ཏེ་གང་ན་ཡོད་པ་རེད། (Where is the Snow-Mountain of Ultimate Victories?) http://www.khabdha.org/?p=7601.

———. ༢༠༠༨། གོར་མོ་ང་འདུའི་གྲོས་ཤིག་བྱེད། (Let's Have a Round Drum-like Discussion) http://www.khabdha.org/?m=200809&paged=2.

———. ༢༠༠༩ ཟླ་༢ ཚེས་༢། མགོན་པོ་ཕྱུག་གཉིས་པས་བེ་རི་འཇིགས་མེད་ཀྱིས་བརྩམས་པའི་ཆུ་སྐྱང་བོ་རྒྱལ་དང་ཐེང་གཉིས་པ། ༡ ཞེས་པར་བཏབས་པའི་མཆན་ཞིག (An online comment on Beri Jigme's A History of the Four Rivers and Six Ranges, Volume II) http://www.khabdha.org/?p=3436#comments.

———. ༢༠༠། མགོན་པོ་ཕྱུག་གཉིས་པས་དགེ་འདུན་རབ་གསལ་གྱི་ཁུལ་ཏིའི་ཡུལ་དང་སྐད་ཏོ་སྐོད། ཅེས་པར་བཏབས་པའི་ད་མཆན་ཞིག (An online comment on Gedun Rabsal's Introduction to Balistan and its Language) ཁ་བརྡ http://www.khabdha.org/?p=1913.

———. ༢༠༡༢། དགེ་རྒན་སངས་རྒྱས་རྒྱལ་རྗེས་སུ་དྲན་པོ། (Remembering Teacher Sangje Rgyal) ཁ་བརྡ http://www.khabdha.org/?p=28268.

མདོ་ལམབར་ཚེ་རིང་དབང་རྒྱལ། ༡༨༢༨། གཞོན་ནུ་ཟླ་མེད་ཀྱི་གཏམ་རྒྱུད། (The Tale of the Peerless Youth) པོད་སྟོངས་མི་དམངས་དཔེ་སྐྲུན་ཁང་།

རྡོ་རྗེ་རྒྱལ། ༡༨༢༠། དགེ་འདུན་ཆོས་འཕེལ། (Gedun Choepel) གན་སུའུ་མི་རིགས་དཔེ་སྐྲུན་ཁང་།

ལྷུན་འགྲུབ། ༢༠༠། གྲིབ་གཟུགས། (Shadow) མནར་གཅོད། (Torture) ལྕགས་ཚན། (Whip) མཐར་ཐུག་གི་རྩྭ་ཐང་། (Last Grassland) ཞི་རབས་གསུམ་པ། (The Third Generation of Tibetan Poets) ཐོག་ཏོས་༡༢་ནས་༡༤།

ལྡོང་བུ་བསྒྱུར། ༢༠༠། T.S ཨེ་ལིའི་" རྒུ་དབ་ཐང་"། (The Waste Land by T. S. Eliot) http://www.gdqpzhx.com/bo/html/photo/2009/11/01/398/.

ལྡོང་བུ་བསྒྱུར། པར་སྐྲུན་བྱ་རྒྱུ་ཡིན་པ། ཨོ་ཁུ་ཐེའུ་པོ་པ་ཟའི་། རྡོ་ཉི་མ། (Sunstone by Octavio Paz).

ལྡོང་བུ་དང་ངལ་རྗེ། ༢༠༠། ལྡོང་བུ་དང་ངལ་རྗེའི་སྙན་ངག་སྐོར་གྱི་ད་ཐོག་ཁ་བརྡ།(Dongbu and Ngalzi's Online Conversation on Poetry) http://www.gdqpzhx.com/bo/html/third-generation/2009/10/19/381/.

ནགས་ཚང་ནུས་བློ། ༢༠༠༧། ནགས་ཚང་ཞི་ལུའི་སྐྱིད་སྡུག (The Joys and Woes of the Naktsang Boy) ཟི་ཁྲི། མཚོ་སྔོན་ཟི་ཁྲིང་པར་ཁང་གིས་དཔར།

ནུབ་མཚོ་མི་རིགས་སྒྲ་བརྙན་པར་སྐྲུན་ཁང་། ༢༠༠༩། ཀུན་གྱི་སྐར་མ་དང་སྨན་ཚོང་ཚེ་སྐྱིད། (Karma of Ganja and Tsekyi of Mantsong) ISBC CN-H12-06-0006-0/V.B5.

ནས་མཁའ་བསྐུན་འཛིན། ༢༠༡༡། ཁོ་དགོན་པ་ནས་བཙན་གཡེམ་བྱས་ནས་སྡོད་དུ་མ་བཅུག་ཐབས་ཟེར། ༎ (It is alleged that due to being raped he could not remain in the monastery) ཁ་བརྡ། http://www.khabdha.org/?p=23597.

ནས་མཁའ་དང་དར་མཚོ་གཉིས་ཀྱི་རྡུང་ལེན་ཚེད་བསྒྲིགས། ༢༠༠༠། ས་ཆེན་པོའི་མིག་ཆུ། (Tears of the Great Land) ཕྱུ་ནུ་སྒྲ་བརྙན་པར་སྐྲུན་ཁང་། ISRC CN-H09-08-305-00/V.J6.

ནས་མཁའི་རྡུང་ལེན་ཚེད་སྒྲིག ༢༠༠༥། ཁ་བ་ཅན་གྱི་གླུ་བོ། (Singer of the Land of Snows) རྔུབ་མཚོ་མི་རིགས་སྒྲ་བརྙན་པར་སྐྲུན་ཁང་། ISRCCN-H12-04-315-00/V.J6.

པད་མ་འབུམ། ༢༠༠༡། རྫ་བོ་སྙིང་དྲུག་མེ་འཁྲིག (Six Stars with a Crooked Neck: Tibetan Memoirs of the Cultural Revolution) ཟ་རངས་ལ། བོད་ཀྱི་དུས་བབས་གསར་ཁང་།

——. ༡༩༩། མི་རབས་གསར་པའི་སྙིང་ཁམས་ཀྱི་འཕར་ལྡིང་། སྣན་དག་གསར་པའི་སྐོར་སྐྲིང་བ། (The Heartbeat of a New Generation: A Discussion of the New Poetry) Dharamsala: Amnye Machen Institute, 5–43.

——. ༡༩༩༽ ཀ ཁུན་ཧོང་ཡིག་རྙིང་གི་མགུར་ལ་དཔྱོད་པའི་སྟོན་འགོ། (A Preliminary Study of Song-poems in the Old Dunhuang Manuscripts) In Per Kvaerne (ed.), Tibetan Studies: Proceedings of the 6th Seminar of the International Association for Tibetan Studies, Fagernes 1992. Vol. 2. Oslo: The Institute for Comparative Research in Human Culture, 640–648.

——. ༡༩༩༽ ཁ། དོན་འགྲུབ་རྒྱལ་གྱི་མི་ཚེ་ སྐར་མདའ་ མཚན་མོའི་ནས་མཁའ་འོད་ཀྱིས་གཤེགས་ནས་ཡལ། (The Life of Dhondup Gyal: A Shooting Star that Cleaved the Night Sky and Vanished) པད་མ་འབུམ་གྱིས་རྩོམ་སྒྲིག་བྱས་པའི་ དོན་གྲུབ་རྒྱལ་གྱི་ལང་ཚོའི་རབ་རྒྱ་དང་སྐྱངས་རྩོམ་བདམས་སྒྲིག (Torrents of Youth and Selected Writing by Dhondup Gyal) ཟ་རངས་ལ། ཨ་སྐྱེས་རྨ་ཆེན་ བོད་ཀྱི་རིག་གཞུང་ཞིབ་འཇུག་ཁང་། ཤོག་ངོས་ ༼ཞསཔཡན།

——. ༢༠༠༽ རྫ་བོ་རྡོ་རིང་མ། (Stone Pillar of a Memoir) ཟ་རངས་ལ། བོད་ཀྱི་དུས་བབས།

——. ༡༩༩༠། སྙན་དག་གི་སྲོག་གི་སྐོར་ལ་དཔྱོད་པ། (Investigating the Poetic Soul) ལྗང་གཞོན། (Green Seedling) སྤྱི་ལོ་༡༩༩༠ ཟླ་༡༢ སྟེའི་འདོན་ཐེངས་༡། ཟ་རངས་ལ། ཤོག་ངོས་༤༢ནས་༥༠།

དཔའ་བོ་གཙུག་ལག་ཕྲེང་བ། ༡༩༨། ཆོས་འབྱུང་མཁས་པའི་དགའ་སྟོན། སྡོད་ཆ། (A Religious History: A Feast for the Learned) བོད་དང་པོ། པེ་ཅིན། མི་རིགས་དཔེ་སྐྲུན་ཁང་།

དབང་རིས་སངས་རྒྱས། ༢༠༠༤། སྤྲིང་གཞི། (Preface) འཇའ་མོ་གནམས་བཏགས་ཚེ་རིང་གིས་ཚོམ་སྒྲིག་བྱས་པའི་ ཁོད་གླུ་ནོར་བུའི་རྒྱ་མཚོ། (Tibetan Songs: An Ocean of Jewels) གན་སུའུ་མི་རིགས་དཔེ་སྐྲུན་ཁང་།

དབང་རིས་སངས་རྒྱས་དང་ནོར་བུ་ཀུན་གྲུབ་ཀྱིས་བསྒྲིགས། ༢༠༡༠། མཚོན་བརྗོད་ཁྱད་བཅུན་རྒྱ་མཚོ། (An Ocean of Definitive Poetic Synonyms) གུང་བོའི་བོད་རིག་པ་དཔེ་སྐྲུན་ཁང་།

དཔལ་མགོན། ༢༠༡༠། སྤྲིང་སྟོངས་མེ་ཏོག་འཁྲིགས་པའི་སྤྲིང་ཁང་། དཔལ་མགོན་གྱི་གླུ་སྣན་ཤིང་ལེན་གཉེས་བསྡུས། (The Rainbow Tent of Swirling Meadow Flowers: Selected Dunglen Songs of Palgon) མི་རིགས་དཔེ་སྐྲུན་ཁང་།

དཔལ་མགོན་འདབགས་པ་གྲུ་སྒྲུབ། ༢༠༠༽ རོ་སྒྲུང་། (The Tales of the Corpse) ལྷ་ས། བོད་ལྗོངས་མི་དམངས་དཔེ་སྐྲུན་ཁང་།

དཔལ་མོས་ཚོ་སྒྲིག་བྱས། ༢༠༠༥། དེང་རབས་བོད་ཀྱི་བུད་མེད་ཚོ་པ་པོའི་སྣན་ཚོ་གཉེས་བཏུས། (Selected Poems of Contemporary Tibetan Women Writers) བཞོ་ལྱང་། (Milking Toggle) པེ་ཅིན། མི་རིགས་དཔེ་སྐྲུན་ཁང་།

———. ২০০৬། དེང་རབས་བོད་ཀྱི་སྐྱེས་མའི་བརྩམས་ཆོས་བདམས་སྒྲིག (Selected Writings of Contemporary Tibetan Females)/དཔྱད་རྩོམ་ཕྱོགས་བསྒྲིགས།\ (*Collected Critical Essays*) པེ་ཅིན། ཀྲུང་གོའི་བོད་རིག་པ་དཔེ་སྐྲུན་ཁང་།

———. ཀ ২০১১། དེང་རབས་བོད་རིགས་བུད་མེད་ཀྱི་དཔེའི་ཚོགས་ལས། (Contemporary Tibetan Women's Series) /སྙན་ངག་ཕྱོགས་བསྒྲིགས།\ (*Collected Poems*) པེ་ཅིན། ཀྲུང་གོའི་བོད་རིག་པ་དཔེ་སྐྲུན་ ཁང་།

———. ཁ། དེང་རབས་བོད་རིགས་བུད་མེད་ཀྱི་དཔེའི་ཚོགས་ལས། (Contemporary Tibetan Women's Series)/སྒྲུང་ཚོམ་ཕྱོགས་བསྒྲིགས།\ (*Collected Fiction*) པེ་ཅིན། ཀྲུང་གོའི་བོད་རིག་པ་དཔེ་སྐྲུན་ཁང་།

———. ག དེང་རབས་བོད་རིགས་བུད་མེད་ཀྱི་དཔེའི་ཚོགས་ལས། (Contemporary Tibetan Women's Series)/སྤྱོད་ཚོམ་ཕྱོགས་བསྒྲིགས།\ (*Collected Prose*) པེ་ཅིན། ཀྲུང་གོའི་བོད་རིག་པ་དཔེ་སྐྲུན་ཁང་།

སྤྲུལ་སྐུ་བསོད་སྦ། ২০১২ ཟླ་༡ ཚེ་༢༠། /སྤྲུལ་སྐུ་བསོད་སྦའི་འདའ་ཁའི་ཞལ་ཆེམས།\ (The Last Testament of Trulku Solba) གཡུ་ཤུན་དྲ་བ། http://youshun12.com/?p=5627.

སྐྱུང་མོ་དགུ་ཐུག ২০১২། /བོད་ཀྱི་སྙན་ངག་པའི་དབྱུང་མི་རབས་གསུམ་པ་སྐོར་བ། (On the Third Generation of Tibetan Poets) http://www.gdqpzhx.com/bo/html/third-generation/201202251688.html.

བན་དེ་མཁས། ২০১২། /སྐྱབས་ཆེན་བདེ་གྲོལ་ཞིབ་འཇུག\ (A Study of Kyabchen Dedrol) ཟི་ལིང་། མཚོ་ སྔོན་མི་རིགས་དཔེ་སྐྲུན་ཁང་།

———. པར་སྐྲུན་བྱ་རྒྱུ་ཡིན་པ། /ལྷ་བཅུའི་ལྔ་སའི་སྙན་ངག་གི་ཞིབ་འཇུག\ (A Study of One Hundred Years of Lhasa Poems) ཟི་ལིང་། མཚོ་སྔོན་མི་རིགས་དཔེ་སྐྲུན་ཁང་།

བུ་བཞི་བསམ་པའི་དོན་གྲུབ། ২০০༢། /སློབ་དཔོན་དཎྜིའི་སྙན་ངག་ཏུ་སྒྲོག་གི་རྣམ་གཞག་བསྟན་ཡོད་མེད་ཀྱི་དོགས་ དཔྱོད།\ (An Enquiry into Whether Master Dandin's Poetics Feature the Category of Poetic Soul) /"ཀྲུང་གོའི་བོད་རིག་པ"ལོ་འཁོར་২༠ཡི་དཔྱད་རྩོམ་བདམས་བསྒྲིགས།\ (*Selected Critical Essays from 20 Years of "China Tibetology"*) ཀྲུང་གོའི་བོད་རིག་པ་དཔེ་སྐྲུན་ཁང་། ཤོག ངོས་༤༨༩ནས་༤༤༩།

བོ་ཐར་བཀྲ་ཤིས་ཚོས་འཕེལ་དང་། བག་དབང་ཚོས་གྲགས། ༡༨༢། /ས་པཎ་མཁས་འཇུག་རྩ་འགྲེལ་བཤུགས།\ (*Sakya Paṇḍita's Entrance Door for the Learned and its Exposition*) པེ་ཏུན་མི་རིགས་ དཔེ་སྐྲུན་ཁང་།

བོད་མཁས་པ། ২০০༤། /སྙན་ངག་མེ་ལོང་དང་བོད་མཁས་པའི་འགྲེལ་པ་བཞུགས་སོ།་\ (*Mirror of Poetics and its Exposition by Bod Khepa*) མཚོ་སྔོན་མི་རིགས་དཔེ་སྐྲུན་ཁང་།

འབའ་པ་ཕུན་ཚོགས་དང་རྒྱལ། ২০০༥། /ཨར་ལེ་སི་རིང་ལུགས་ཀྱི་མི་རིགས་ལྟ་བའི་སྐོར།\ (*On the Marxist Conception of Nationality*) http://www.sangdhor.com/pics_c.asp?id=618, 2009.

བྱ་གཞུང་དཔལ་སྐྱབས། ২০০༤། /ཚོམ་རིག་དང་མི་ བོད་ཀྱི་ཚོམ་རིག་གསར་བའི་དགག་པ།\ (*Literature and Man: A Critique of New Tibetan Literature*) ཀན་སུའི་མི་རིགས་དང་སྐྲུན་ཁང་།

བྱང་ལོ། ২০১༠། /མི་རབས་གསུམ་པའི་དགེ་མཚན་སྐོར་བ།\ (On the Merits of the Third Generation) http://www.tibetcm.com/html/list_21/201012302806.html.

/ཁྱུང་བདུད་ཀླུ་བཙན།\ (*Lutsan the Northern Demon*) ২০০২། སྐྱང་མགར་བསམ་གྲུབ་ཀྱིས་ཕབ་པའི་སྐྱེ་ ཀེ་གེ་སར་རྒྱལ་པོའི་སྐྱང་། བོད་བརྒྱ་ཆིན་པ། བོད་ལྗོངས་བོད་ཡིག་དཔེ་རྙིང་དཔེ་སྐྲུན་ཁང་།

བྲག་དགོན་པ་དཀོན་མཆོག་བསྟན་པ་རབ་རྒྱས། ༡༨༣། /མདོ་སྨད་ཆོས་འབྱུང་།\ (A Religious History of Amdo) ཀན་སུའི་མི་རིགས་དང་སྐྲུན་ཁང་།

འབྲུག་པ་ཀུན་ལེགས། ༡༩༨༠། ཁྲོ་བའི་མགོན་པོ་ཀུན་དགའ་ལེགས་པའི་རྣམ་ཐར་མོན་སྤྲོ་སོགས་ཀྱི་མཛད་སྤྱོད་ རྣམས་འཁྲབས་སོ།། (*Biography of Kunga Legpa, the Lord of Beings, Including the Accounts of his Conduct in Mon Padro*) རྡ་རམ་ས་ལ། བོད་གཞུང་ཤེས་རིག་པར་ཁང་།

———. ༢༠༠༤། ཁབྲུག་པ་ཀུན་ལེགས་ཀྱི་རྣམ་ཐར། (*Biographies of Drukpa Kunleg*) ལྷ་ས། བོད་ ལྗོངས་མི་དམངས་དཔེ་སྐྲུན་ཁང་།

འཕོང་ཕྱུག་ ༢༠༠༡། རྐ་དགུ་དང་ཕོར་གྱི་སྙན་ངག (*September and Incidental Poems*) ཁྱི་རབས་ གསུམ་པ། (*The Third Generation of Tibetan Poets*) ཤོག་ངོས་ ༡༢༢ནས༡༢༠།

———. ༢༠༠༡། ཕ་ཡུལ། བདའ་ཚང་། (*Homeland: Da Family*) མི་རབས་གསུམ་པ། (*The Third Generation of Tibetan Poets*) ཤོག་ངོས་ ༡༠ནས༡༢།

འཕོས་སྟོན་པ་རྒྱལ་བའི་འབྱུང་གནས། ༢༠༡༠། མི་ཚོས་གནད་ཀྱི་ཕྲེང་བ། (*A Rosary of Essential Secular Ethics*) བློ་བཟང་ཚོས་བྱགས་དང་བསོད་ནམས་རྗེ་མོས་བསྒྲིགས་པ། ཁངས་ལྗོངས་མཁས་དབང་རིམ་བྱོན་གྱི་ ཚོས་ཡིག་གསེར་གྱི་སྤུ་གྲི། བེ་ལིང་། མཚོ་སྔོན་མི་རིགས་དཔེ་སྐྲུན་ཁང་།

བློ་བཟང་ཚོས་བྱགས་དང་བསོད་ནམས་རྗེ་མོས་བསྒྲིགས། ༢༠༡༠། ཁངས་ལྗོངས་མཁས་དབང་རིམ་བྱོན་གྱི་ཚོས་ཡིག་ གསེར་གྱི་སྤུ་གྲི། (*Gold Ingot of Writings by Successive Great Scholars from the Land of Snows*) སྟོད་ཁ། སྨད་ཁ། བེ་ལིང་། མཚོ་སྔོན་མི་རིགས་དཔེ་སྐྲུན་ཁང་།

བློ་བཟང་འཇམ་དཔལ། ཚེ་རིང་སྐྱོལ་མ། མིག་དམར་བཀྲ་ཤིས་ཚོས་སྒྲིག་བྱས་པ། ༢༠༠༢། ཁུ་ཏུ་སྟོན་པ། (*Akhu Tonpa*) བོད་ལྗོངས་མི་རིགས་དཔེ་སྐྲུན་ཁང་།

མར་ཁུ་རྒྱལ་མཚན། ༢༠༠༡། རྫོ་མོ་དང་རྒྱང་ཐག་རིང་བའི་ལྷ་ས། (*Grandma and Distant Lhasa*) མི་རབས་ གསུམ་པ། (*The Third Generation of Tibetan Poets*) ཤོག་ངོས་ ༩༢ནས༩༣།

མི་ཉོད། ༢༠༠༤། བོད་ཀྱི་སྙན་ངག་པའི་མི་རབས་གསུམ་པའི་ག་སྒྲིག་བགྲོ་སྟེང་ཚོགས་འདུ་མཚོ་སྔོན་པོའི་ཉེ་འགྲམ་ ནས་ཚོགས་པ། (*The Preparatory Seminar of the Third Generation of Tibetan Poets Convened at the Lakeside of Kokonor*) ཁྱི་རབས་གསུམ་པ། (*The Third Generation of Tibetan Poets*) ཤོག་ངོས་ ༡ནས་ ༣བ།

མི་ཉོད་དང་རྒྱ་པོ། ༢༠༠༤། སྐབས་གཉིས་པའི་བོད་ཀྱི་སྙན་ངག་པའི་མི་རབས་གསུམ་པའི་བགྲོ་སྟེང་ཚོགས་འདུ་རེབ་ གོང་ནས་ཚོགས་པ། (*The Second Seminar of the Third Generation of Tibetan Poets Convened in Rebgong*) ཁྱི་རབས་གསུམ་པ། (*The Third Generation of Tibetan Poets*) ཤོག་ངོས་ ༣བནས་ ༤༡།

མི་རབས་གསུམ་པ། ༢༠༠༤། མཐའ་བཅན་པོའི་ "མཇེ" སྙན་དག་གི་སྐོར། (*On Dhatsenpo's "dick" poetry*) ཁྱི་རབས་གསུམ་པ། (*The Third Generation of Tibetan Poets*) ཤོག་ངོས་ ༡༤༠ནས༡༤༡།

ཁི་རོ་རྩེ་སྒྲུང་། (*The Tales of the Golden Corpse*) ༡༩༨༠། མཚོ་སྔོན་མི་རིགས་དཔེ་སྐྲུན་ཁང་།

མིག་དམར་གྱིས་ཚོས་བསྒྲིགས་བྱས། ༡༩༩༢། ཁ་ཆེ་ཕ་ལུ། བོད་ལྗོངས་མི་དམངས་དཔེ་སྐྲུན་ཁང་།

མི་རྗེ། ༢༠༠༩། ཁི་སྙེས་མི་རབས་གསུམ་པར་བྲིས་པ། (Meje's Written Message to the Third Generation) དགེ་འདུན་ཚོས་འཕེས་དྲ་བ། http://www.gdqpzhx.com/bo/html/ third-generation/2009/05/06/92/.

———. ༢༠༡༠། དགེ་ཚོས་རྒྱང་མཐའ་ལ། (*Beholding Gechoe from a Distance*) ལན་བྲུ་གན་སྤུའི་མི་ རིགས་དཔེ་སྐྲུན་ཁང་།

མི་ལོང་། ༢༠༠༩། དོ་ནུབ་ང་པོ་ཏ་ལའི་མདུན་དུ། (*Tonight I'm Alone Before the Potala*) ཁྱི་ རབས་གསུམ་པ། (*The Third Generation of Tibetan Poets*) ཤོག་ངོས་ ༡༤༤ནས༡༤༥།

ཌངུལ་སྦྲིང་སྐུན་པ་རང་གསལ་བ༎ (*The Spontaneous Illumination of the Infernal Realms*) ༡༡༤༢། ཟི་ལིང་། མཚོ་སྔོན་མི་རིགས་དཔེ་སྐྲུན་ཁང་།

ཆོག་རུ་ཞེས་རབ་རྡོ་རྗེ། ༢༠༠༤། ཌཀླུ་གཞུང་ནས་འཕུར་བའི་ངང་ཕྲུག༎ (*Gosling Flown from the Plains of the Machu River*) གན་སུའུ་མི་རིགས་དཔེ་སྐྲུན་ཁང་།

———. ༢༠༠༠། ཌམཛེས་པའི་ཆང་མ་འཚོལ་བ༎ (*Looking for the Barmaid of Beauty*) ཌམི་རབས་གསུམ་པ༎ (*The Third Generation of Tibetan Poets*) ཤོག་ངོས་ ༦ ཞེས་ ༢༠།

སྦོན་ལས་རྒྱ་མཚོན་ཞུ་དག་བྱས། ༡༡༤༡། ཌབཀའ་ཆེམས་ཀ་ཁོལ་མ༎ (*Royal Testament of the Pillar*) གན་སུའུ་མི་རིགས་དཔེ་སྐྲུན་ཁང་།

ཙོང་ཁ་ལྷ་མོ་ཚེ་རིང་། ༡༡༤༢ཎ༤༠༠༤། ཌབཙན་རྒོལ་རྒྱལ་སྐྱོབ༎ (*Resistance and National Defense*) ཕོད་དྲུག

ཆབ་མདའ་སྒྲུག ༢༠༡༡། ཌཕྱིར་རྟོག༎ (*Introspection*) གན་སུའུ་མི་རིགས་དཔེ་སྐྲུན་ཁང་།

ཆེ་སྐྱེང་གཡང་འཛོམས། ༢༠༡༠། ཌཚེ་རིང་རྣམ་དྲུག་གི་མཚོན་དོན༎ (*Symbolism of the Six Longevities*) http://blog.amdotibet.cn/caiji/archives/744.aspx.

ཆེ་ཏེན་ཞབས་དྲུང་། ཌ༡༡༤༠། ༢༠༠༥། ཌསྙན་ངག་སྤྱི་དོན༎ (*An Overview of Kāvya Poetics*) གན་སུའུ་མི་རིགས་དཔེ་སྐྲུན་ཁང་།

———. ཌ༡༡༤༠། ༢༠༠༡ ཌསྙན་ངག་མེ་ལོང་གི་འདོད་པའི་གཏན་ཚིགས་ཕྱོགས་སུ་གཞོལ་བའི་དཔེར་བརྗོད་ཀྱི་དཔྱད་པ་བབ་ཡོད་གོས་ཀྱི་ཞས་བུ༎ (*A Garment of Decency: An Analysis of Sexually Charged Exemplifications in Kāvyādarśa*) ཤོག་ངོས་ ༡ ནས་ ༡༢། སྦྲང་ཚར་ལོ་འཚོར་ ༢༠༡༤འི་ཆོགས། ཌདྲུང་ཆོས་ཆངས་པའི་ཐིག་རིས༎ (*Brahmā Line of Critical Essays*) ཟི་ལིང་། མཚོ་སྔོན་མི་རིགས་དཔེ་སྐྲུན་ཁང་།

ཆེ་རིང་བཀྲ་ཤིས། ༢༠༠༥། ཌམི་རྐྱང་གི་ཕྱི་ནང་༎ (*The Inside and Outside of a Bachelor*) ཟི་ཆིང་། མི་རིགས་དཔེ་སྐྲུན་ཁང་།

———. ༢༠༠༡། ཌསྒྱུ་འཕྲུལ་གྱི་མཆོད་མེ༎ (*The Illusory Butter Lamp*) ཞང་གང་གི་ཟིང་དཔེ་སྐྲུན་ཁང་།

ཆེ་རིང་སྐྱིད། ༢༠༡༡། ཌམི་རབས་གསུམ་པས་འཁན་འཛི་མེད་པའི་བྱ་སྤྱོད་མ་སྟེལ་རོགས༎ (*The Third Generation, Please Do Not Advocate Irresponsible Behavior!*) མཆོད་མེ་ཕོད་ཀྱི་ཚེམ་རིག་དྲ་བ། http://www.tibetcm.com/html/list_21/201106223345.html.

———. (aka རྒྱ་མེ།) ༢༠༠༠། ཌང་འཁྲུལ་ཤོང་བའི་སྐབས་དེར༎ (*When I Was Deluded*) ཌམི་རབས་གསུམ་པ༎ (*The Third Generation of Tibetan Poets*) ཤོག་ངོས་ ༤༢ནས་ ༤༡།

ཆེ་རིང་རྒྱལ། ༢༠༡༢ ཟླ་༤ ཆོས་༢༧། ཌརྒྱལ་གཅེས་དཔའ་བོ་འཇམ་དཔལ་ཡེ་ཞེས་ལགས་ཀྱི་ཞལ་ཆེམས༎ (*The Testament of National Martyr Jampal Yeshi*) ཕོད་ཀྱི་དུས་བབས། http://www.tibettimes.net/news.php?showfooter=1&id=5803.

———. ༢༠༡༢ ཟླ་༡༡ ཆོས་༡༡། ཌམདོ་སྨད་ལ་མཆོག་ཏུ་རང་ལུས་མེར་བསྲེགས༎ (*Self-immolation in Amchok, Amdo*) ཕོད་ཀྱི་དུས་བབས། http://www.tibettimes.net/news.php?showfooter=1&id=6888.

ཆེ་རིང་དོན་གྲུབ། ༡༡༤༦། ཌཚེ་རིང་དོན་གྲུབ་ཀྱི་སྲུང་ཐུང་བདམས་བསྒྲིགས༎ (*Selected Short Stories of Tsering Dhondup*) ཟི་ཆིང་། མཚོ་སྔོན་མི་རིགས་དཔེ་སྐྲུན་ཁང་།

———. ༡༡༤༠། ཌཚེ་རིང་དོན་གྲུབ་ཀྱི་སྲུང་འབྲིང་ཕྱོགས་བསྒྲིགས༎ (*Collected Medium Length Short Stories of Tsering Dhondup*) གན་སུའུ་མི་རིགས་དཔེ་སྐྲུན་ཁང་།

———. ༢༠༠༡། ཌམེས་པོ༎ (*Ancestors*) ཟི་ཆིང་། ཞང་གང་གི་ཟིང་དཔེ་སྐྲུན་ཆོང་ཡོད་གུང་ཟི།

———. ༢༠༠༢། ཌསྨུག་པ༎ (*Fog*) ཟི་ཆིང་། ཞང་གང་གི་ཟིང་དཔེ་སྐྲུན་ཆོང་ཡོད་གུང་ཟི།

————. ༢༠༠༦། རླུང་དམར་འུར་འུར། (*The Red Wind Scream*)

————. ༢༠༠༢ ཟླ་༢ ཚེས་༢༠། ༢༠༠༠ ཟླ་༡༢ ཚེས་༢༠ནས་༢༠༠༢ ཟླ་༤ ཚེས་༢༠། ["རླུང་དམར་འུར་འུར་"ཚན་ བཞིས།] (Serialization of *The Red Wind Scream*) (མཚོ་སྔོན་བོད་ཡིག་གསར་འགྱུར།) (*The Qinghai Tibetan News*) ཟི་ལིང་།

————. ༢༠༠༩། ["རླུང་དམར་འུར་འུར"] སྤུང་རིང་ཚན་བཞས།] (An excerpt from the novel *The Red Wind Scream*) (ཚེ་རིང་དོན་གྲུབ་དང་བདེ་སྐྱིད་སྒྲོལ་མས་བསྒྲིགས་པའི, རྨ་ལྷོ་སོག་རྫོང་གི་རྩོམ་རིག་ བཅམས་ཚོམ་བདམས་བསྒྲིགས།] (*Selected Literary Writings from Malho Mongol County*) ཟི་ལིང་། མཚོ་སྔོན་མི་རིགས་དཔེ་སྐྲུན་ཁང་། ཤོག་ངོས་༤ནས་༔༡།

ཚེ་རིང་དཔལ་འབྱོར་གྱིས་བསྒྲིགས། ༡༌༡༼། ཁྲིད་ཀྱི་གནས་ཡིག་བདམས་བསྒྲིགས།] (*Selected Guides to Holy Sites in Tibet*) བོད་ལྗོངས་བོད་ཡིག་དཔེའི་རྙིང་དངེ་སྐྲུན་ཁང་།

མཚོ་བྱུ་དགའ་བདེ། ༢༠༠༠། [མཁའ་བཅན་པོར་ཆགས་པ།] (Getting Attached To Dhatsenpo) [མི་རབས་ གསུམ་པ།] (*The Third Generation of Tibetan Poets*) ཤོག་ངོས་༤ནས་༔༠།

ཆོགས་ཆེན་ཆོས་དབྱིངས་སྤོབས་ལྡན་རྡོ་རྗེ། ༢༠༠༦། [ཡང་གསང་རྟ་ཕག་ཡིད་བཞིན་ནོར་བུའི་ཆོགས་ཆེན་ཁྲིད་ཡིག] (*A Manual for the Wish-fulfilling Gem of Most Esoteric Hayagriva and Varahi Dzogchen*) པེ་ཅིན། མི་རིགས་དཔེ་སྐྲུན་ཁང་།

————. ༢༠༠༠། [མདོ་རྒྱུད་རིན་པོ་ཆེའི་མཛོད།] (*Precious Treasury of Sutra and Tantra*) དེབ་ གསུམ་པ། ཁྲེང་ཏུའུ། སི་ཁྲོན་མི་རིགས་དཔེའི་སྐྲུན་ཁང་།

ཞང་སྟོན་བསྟན་པ་རྒྱ་མཚོ། ༢༠༠༩། [ཞང་སྟོན་བསྟན་པ་རྒྱ་མཚོའི་གསུང་འབུམ་བཞུགས་སོ།] (*Collected Works of Shangton Tenpa Gyatso*) བོད་དང་པོ། གསུམ་ང་དང་བཞི་བ། ཀཱ་སྦུ་མི་རིགས་དཔེའི་སྐྲུན་ཁང་།

ཉྭ་སྐྲབ་པ་དབང་ཕྱུག་བདེ་ལྡན། ༡༌༡༼། བོད་ཀྱི་སྲིད་དོན་རྒྱལ་རབས།] (*An Advanced Political History of Tibet*) རྡེགས་བས་གཉིས། ཨྀ་ལི།

ཞབས་དཀར་བ་སྐུ་ཕྲེང་གཉིས་པ། ༢༠༠༣། [ཞབས་དཀར་བ་སྐུ་ཕྲེང་གཉིས་པ་རོང་སྟོན་རིག་འཛིན་རྒྱ་མཚོའི་མགུར་ འབུམ།] (*Spiritual Songs of Shabkarpa Rongnyon Rigdzin II*) (སྔགས་མང་ཞིབ་འཇུག) (*Ngakmang Research*) འཛིན་སྐོངས་དྲུག་པ། ཤོག་ངོས་༡༠༠ནས་༡༥༔།

ཚོགས་ཤྲྭང་། ༢༠༡༢། [མི་རབས་གསུམ་པ་དང་འབྲེལ་ཡོད་བསམ་ཚུལ།] (Opinions Concerning the Third Generation) སེང་ཏོར་ད་ཊ http://www.sangdhor.com/blog_c.asp?id=6104&a=3.

གཡང་མཚོ་སྐྱིད། [ཀ༌ར༌༡། ༢༠༡༡། [རྩྭ་ཐང་གི་ཉིན་ཐོ།] (Diary of the Grassland) དཔལ་ཚོས་ཚོམ་སྒྲིག བྱས་པའི་དེང་རབས་བོད་རིགས་བུད་མེད་ཀྱི་ཚོགས་ལས། (Contemporary Tibetan Women's Series) སྤྱུང་ཚོམ་སྤྱོགས་བསྒྲིགས།] (*Collected Fiction*) པེ་ཅིན། ཀྲུང་གོའི་བོད་རིག་པ་དཔེ་སྐྲུན་ཁང་། ཤོག་ངོས་༤༌ངས་༔༡།

རྒས་ར་བགྲེས་མཛོར་ཕྱུག་བསྐུན་ཚོམ་དང་། [ཁུ་འདུན་ཆོས་འཕེལ་གྱི་ལོ་རྒྱུས།] (*The Story of Gedun Choepel*) ཉ་རས་མ་ལ། བོད་ཀྱི་དཔེ་མཛོད་ཁང་གིས་དཔར་སྐྲུན་བྱས།

རབ་འབྱོར། ༢༠༡༠། [སྐད་ཡིག་སྲུང་སྐྱོབ་ཀྱི་དོ་ཁོལ་ཁྲོན་སྐོར་ལ་ཐོག་མར་ཐོན་པའི་འབྲས་བུ།] (The Initial Outcome of the Language Protection Protests) ༦་བ༔ http://www.khabdha.org/?p=12914#more-12914.

རིན་བཟང་། ༢༠༠༢། [ངའི་ཕ་ཡུལ་དང་ཞི་བའི་བཅིངས་གྲོལ།] (*My Home and Peaceful Liberation*)

རེ་ཀང་སྐྱིད། ༢༠༠༠། [ཨིག་མཐུན་གྱི་འཚོ་བ་འདི།] (This Current Life) (ཡབ་ཆེན་གྱིས་བསྟལ་བའི་ཁྲག་གི་མེ་ ཏོག] (Flower of Blood Presented by the Great Father) (མི་རབས་གསུམ་པ་བ་ཞིག་གིས་བོད་ཀྱི་

སྐྱེན་དབག་གསར་བའི་སྐོར་ལ་མིག་བཞེར་ཞིག་བྱས་ན། (A Third Generation Poet Casting a Glance over New Tibetan Poetry) ཨི་རབས་གསུམ་པ། (The Third Generation of Tibetan Poets) ཤོག་ངོས་ ༢༠༩ནས་༢༢ དང་། ༢༡༢ནས་༢༢༡།

———. ༢༠༠༢། ཆུང་འཚོང་མ་སངས་རྒྱས་སྒྲོལ་མར་ཕུལ་བ། (To Prostitute Sangje Dolma) ཧྲ་ས། (Lhasa) ཨི་རབས་གསུམ་པ། (The Third Generation of Tibetan Poets) ཤོག་ངོས་ ༡༥དང་ ༡༢༤ནས་༡༢༥།

———. ༢༠༠༧། སྐྱབས་ཆེན་བདེ་གྲོལ་དང་ཁོང་གི་བརྩམས་ཆོས། (Kyabchen Dedrol and his Work) མཚོ་སྔོན་བོད་ཡིག་གསར་འགྱུར་ཁང་གིས་བསྐྲུན་པའི་ ཆགས་སྡོང་ཁུ་བྱུག་འདུ་གནས། (The Deep Forest Abode of Cuckoos) ཕེ་ཅིན་ མི་རིགས་དཔེ་སྐྲུན་ཁང་། ཤོག་ངོས་ ༡༢༢ནས་༡༢༢།

རེབ་གོང་བ། ༢༠༡༡། ཨི་རབས་གསུམ་པ་དང་ཚེ་རིང་སྐྱིད། (The Third Generation and Tsering Kyi) http://www.tibetcm.com/html/list_21/201106283363.html.

ཞིང་བཟང་སྨན་བཟང་ཆོས་ཀྱི་རྒྱལ་མཚན། ༡༥༢༠། བོད་སོག་ཆོས་འབྱུང་། (A Religious History of Tibet and Mongolia) ཕེ་ཅིན་ མི་རིགས་དཔེ་སྐྲུན་ཁང་།

འཕར་ཕྱོགས་ཁྲག་ཁུ། ༢༠༡༠ ཟླ་༢ ཚེ་༢༠། རྭ་རྒྱ་ཀི་ཏི་སོགས་ནས་རེབ་གོང་དུ་འཚམས་འདི། (People Come from Different Areas including Ragya and Kirti to Offer Condolences) ཁ་བརྡ http://www.khabdha.org/?p=27074.

ཞེས་དཀར་སྐྱིད་པ། ༢༠༡༠། ཧྲ་ས་དྲན་སྒྲོ། (A Song of Longing for Lhasa) དཔལ་མགོན་གྱིས་ཚོམ་སྒྲིག་བྱས། སྤང་སྐྱོངས་མེ་ཏོག་འཁྲིགས་པའི་སྐྲེ་ཁང་། དཔལ་མགོན་གྱི་སྣ་སྣན་སྲུང་ལེན་གཅེས་བསྡུས། མི་རིགས་དཔའི་སྐྲུན་ཁང་། ཤོག་ངོས་ ༡༥༤ནས་༡༧༡།

ས་དཀྱིལ་ཚེ་བག། ༢༠༠༦། དབྱངས་ཅན་མོ། (The Melodious Goddess) ཨི་རབས་གསུམ་པ། (The Third Generation of Tibetan Poets) ཤོག་ངོས་ ༡༢༢ནས་༡༢༧།

———. ༢༠༠༤། གཡིར་མགོ་གི་རང་ཁྱིམ། (Golden Home) ཨི་རབས་གསུམ་པ། (The Third Generation of Tibetan Poets) ཤོག་ངོས་ ༡༢༤ནས་༡༢༡།

ས་པཎ་ཀུན་དགའ་རྒྱལ་མཚན། ༡༥༢༤། པོ་ཟར་བག་ཤེས་ཆོས་འཕེལ་དང་ངག་དབང་ཆོས་གྲགས། ཤེས་པ་མཁས་འཇུག་རྩ་འགྲེལ་བཞུགས། (Sakya Paṇḍita's Entrance Door for the Learned and its Exposition) སི་ཁྲོན་མི་རིགས་དཔེ་སྐྲུན་ཁང་།

ཤེ་ཐོན་ཞིང་ཆེན་བོད་ཡིག་སློབ་གྲྭ་བསྒྲིགས། ༡༥༢༤། ཡིག་གཆོས་སྙིང་བསྡུས། (A Collection of the Finest Writing) ཕེ་ཅིན། མི་རིགས་དཔེ་སྐྲུན་ཁང་།

སངས་རྒྱས་སྐྱབས། ༡༥༡༡། སྔོན་འགྲོའི་གཏམ་བ། (Preface) འགྱུར་མེད་ཀྱིས་བསྒྲིགས་པའི་ བོད་ཀྱི་དེང་རབས་ཙོ་རིག་དཔེ་ཚོགས་ རྟ་ནག་ལྒོག་འགྲོས། (Modern Tibetan Literature Series: Gait of the Black Hobbled Horse) ཟི་ལིང་ མཚོ་སྔོན་མི་རིགས་དཔེ་སྐྲུན་ཁང་། ཤོག་ངོས་ ༡ནས་༡༤།

སངས་རྒྱས་རྣམ་པར་སྲུང་མཛད། ༡༥༢། རྗེ་བཙུན་འཕགས་མ་སྒྲོལ་མ་ལ་བསྟོད་པ་བཞུགས་སོ། (Praise to the Supreme Lady Tara) བསྟོད་སྤྲིན་ཕྱོགས་བསྒྲིགས། (Collected Praises and Devotional Prayers) མཚོ་སྔོན་མི་རིགས་དཔའི་སྐྲུན་ཁང་། ཤོག་ངོས་ ༢༠༠ནས་༢༠༥།

སེའི་རྒྱལ་པོ། ༢༠༡༡། ཨི་ཚེ་ལྭགས་ཀྱིས་མི་རབས་གསུམ་པར་བྲིས་པའི་ལན་དུ་བྲིས་བ། (A Written Reply to Meje's Written Message to the Third Generation) མཆོད་མི་བོད་ཀྱི་ཙོས་རིག་དུ་བ། http://www.tibetcm.com/html/list_21/201102192901.html.

སེང་རྡོར། ༢༠༡༢འོའི་ཀླུ་དངོས་༡༠། ཆེར་མའི་འདུ་འབགས་ཅེས་བྱ་བ་བཞུགས་སོ། (Mask of Ordinary Life) http://www.sangdhor.com/blog_c.asp?id=5905&a=sangdhor.

———. ༢༠༡༢འོའི་ཀླུ་༡ཚེས་༢། ཁ་བྲོག་མོ་ངོ་མ། (Real Nomad Women) http://www.tibetcm. com/html/special/201201034033.html.

———. ༢༠༡༠ འོའི་ཀླུ་རྐེས་༡༢། སྐྱིང་ཡང་ཡིན་ལ་མགུར་ཀྱང་ཡིན། (It's a Story as well as a Song) http://www.sangdhor.com/blog_c.asp?id=1743&a=sangdhor.

———. ༢༠༡༠། སོ་སྐྱེས་སྐད་སྒྲ། (Voice of an Ordinary Person) ལན་གྲུ་ཀན་སུའུ་མི་རིགས་དཔེ་སྐྲུན་ཁང་།

———. ༢༠༠ཀ། ཀ། ཨི་རབས་གསུམ་པ་ཕེབས་ཤོག (The Third Generation, Please Come Along!) མཚོ་མེ་བོད་ཀྱི་ཚེམ་རིག་དུ་བ། http://www.tibetcm.com/html/list_21/385428f764 10a40c87c12c3d799bfbcd/.

———. ༢༠༠ཀ། ཁ། ཁུ་བ་གང་དགར་གཏང་བའི་དགེ་བཤེས་ཚོ། (Geshis Who Discharge Semen at Will) སེང་རྡོར་དུ་བ། http://sangdhor.com/list_c.asp?id=121.

———. ༢༠༡༠། ་འདོད་པའི་བསྟན་བཅོས་་འཚལ་བ། (In Search of *Treatise on Passion*) http://www.sangdhor.com/blog_c.asp?id=1771&a=sangdhor.

———. ༢༠༠༤། ཆུལ་པོད། (Audacity) ལན་གྲུ་ཀན་སུའུ་མི་རིགས་དཔེ་སྐྲུན་ཁང་།

———. ༢༠༠༢ འོའི་ཀླུ་༡༢ཚེས་༢༤། ཀླུ་སྒྲུབ་དགོངས་རྒྱན་གྱི་རྒྱུ་མ་འདི་རེད། (These are the Innards of *The Ornament of Nagarjuna's Thought*) http://www.sangdhor.com/blog_c.asp?id=36 &a=sangdhor.

———. ༢༠༠༦། སྒྲུ་ཟུར་གྱི་གསལ་སྐྲིབ། (Clarity and Obscurity in the Corner) ལན་གྲུ་ཀན་སུའུ་མི་རིགས་དཔེ་སྐྲུན་ཁང་།

གསེར་ཚང་ཕུན་ཚོགས་བཀྲ་ཤིས། ༢༠༠༤། བོད་རིགས་ས་ཁུལ་དུ་བོད་ཀྱི་སྐད་ཡིག་སྤྱོད་རྒྱུའི་སྐོར་གྱི་དོན་གནད་འགའ་ཞིག་ལ་དཔྱད་པ། (An Analysis of Some Issues Concerning the Use of Tibetan Language in Tibetan Areas) ཀྲུང་གོའི་བོད་རིག་པ་་ལོ་འཁོར་༢༠ཡི་དཔྱད་ཚོམ་བདམས་བསྒྲིགས། (*Selected Critical Essays from 20 Years of "China Tibetology"*) པེ་ཅིན། ཀྲུང་གོའི་བོད་རིག་པ་དཔེ་སྐྲུན་ཁང་།

ཁགསེར་མཚོ་དང་བློ་གྲོས་ཀླུ་བ། ༢༠༠ཀ། ཀླུ་༡༠། ཚེས་༢༦། (Sertso and Lodroe Dawa) སེང་རྡོར་དུ་བ། http://www.sangdhor.com/list_c.asp?id=114.

བསམ་གཏན། ༢༠༠༦། ཆུ་བོ་སྐྱབས་ཆེན་བདེ་གྲོལ་སྐྲེ་བ། (Talking About Little Brother Kyabchen Dedrol) མཚོ་སྔོན་བོད་ཡིག་གསར་འགྱུར་ཁང་གིས་བསྒྲིགས་པའི་ནགས་ཁྲོད་ཁུ་བྱུག་འདུ་གནས། (*The Deep Forest Abode of Cuckoos*) པེ་ཅིན། མི་རིགས་དཔེ་སྐྲུན་ཁང་། ཤོག་ངོས་༡༢༢ནས་༡༣༠།

བསམ་གཏན་རྒྱ་མཚོ། ༢༠༠ཀ། བསམ་གཏན་རྒྱ་མཚོའི་གསུང་འབུམ་ལས། སྙན་འགྱེལ་ཡང་གསལ་སྣང་མཛོད། (*An Exposition of Kāvya Poetics: An Illuminating Treasury of Light:*) པོད་བཞི་པའི་ཤོག་ཙོས་༡༢ནས་༢༩༠ བྲེ་ཏུབྱ་སུ་ཐོན་མི་རིགས་དཔེ་སྐྲུན་ཁང་།

བལེ་ཚང་བློ་བཟང་དཔལ་ལྡན། ༡༢༤༢། ཚངས་སྲས་བཞད་པའི་སྒྲ་དབྱངས། (Melodious Laughter of *Sarasvati*) ལན་གྲུལ་ཀན་སུའུ་མི་རིགས་དཔེ་སྐྲུན་ཁང་།

སློབ་དཔོན་དབྱུག་པ་ཅན། བོད་མཁས་པ། ༢༠༠༦། སྙན་ངག་མེ་ལོང་དང་བོད་མཁས་པའི་འགྲེལ་བ་བཞུགས་སོ། (Mirror of Poetics and its Exposition by Bod Khepa) མཚོ་སྔོན་མི་རིགས་དཔེ་སྐྲུན་ཁང་།

སློབ་དཔོན་གཉགས་བཟང་། ཁུ་དགེ་བཀའ་འགྱུར་ལས་ "འདོད་པའི་བསྟན་བཅོས་ཞེས་བྱ་བ་" ("Treatise on Passion" from The Derge Kagyur) http://tbrc.org/?locale=bo#library_work_View-ByOutline-O00CR000800CR012959%7CW23703.

ཧོར་ཁང་བསོད་ནམས་དཔལ་འབར། ༡༤༤། ཧོར་ཁང་བསོད་ནམས་དཔལ་འབར་གྱི་གསུང་རྩོམ་ཕྱོགས་བསྒྲིགས། (Collected Writings of Horkhang Sonam Palbar) པེ་ཅིན། ཀྲུང་གོའི་བོད་ཀྱི་ཤེས་རིག་དཔེ་སྐྲུན་ཁང་།

ཧོར་གླིང་གཡུལ་འགྱེད། (The Battle of Hor and Ling) སྟོད་ཆ། སྨད་ཆ། ༡༤༩༠ ཟི་ལིང་། མཚོ་སྔོན་མི་རིགས་དཔེ་སྐྲུན་ཁང་།

ཧོར་གཙང་འཇིགས་མེད། ༢༠༠༤། མདོ་སྨད་ལོ་རྒྱུས་ཆེན་མོ། (The Greater History of Amdo) པོད་དང་པོ་དང་གཉིས་པ། ཟི་རཝ་ས་ལ་བོད་ཀྱི་དཔེ་མཛོད་ཁང་།

——. ༢༠༠༧། ཁྲག་ཐིགས་ལས་སྐྱེས་པའི་ལྗང་རྒྱུག དེང་རབས་བོད་ཀྱི་རྩོམ་རིག་དང་དེའི་རྒྱབ་ལྗོངས། ༡༩༨༠- ༢༠༠༠། (Green Shoots Born of Blood-Drops: Modern Tibetan Literature and its Background, 1980–2000) གཡུ་རྩེ་དའི་འབྲུམས་ཁང་ནས་བསྐྲུན།

——. ༡༤༤། ཧྲུང་བདེན་གྱིས་བསླུས་པའི་སྤྲང་པོ་བ། མདོ་སྨད་པ་དགེ་འདུན་ཆོས་འཕེལ་གྱི་མི་ཚེ་དཔྱད་བཟོད། ཟི་རཝ་ས་ལ་གཡུ་རྩེ་དའི་འགྲེམས་ཁང་ནས་བསྐྲུན།

——. གདོན་འཕྲུལ་སྟ་ཕུའི་བཟི་བ། (As Intoxicating as Demonic Sorcery) ཧོར་གཙང་འཇིགས་མེད་ཀྱི་སྙན་རྩོམ་ཕྱོགས་བསྒྲིགས། དེབ་ཕྲེང་ལྔ་བ། (Collected Poems of Hortsang Jigme, Volume 5) ཟི་རི་ཆང་གཡུ་རྩེ་དཔར་སྐྲུན་ཁང་།

སྦྲ་སྟེ་གནས་ལོ་ཡག ༢༠༡༡། ཟིང་ཧོར་དང་མཆན་མཐུན་འཁྲིག་སྤྱོད་རིག་པ་གཉིས། (Sangdhor and Homosexual Studies) སེང་ཧོར་དྲ་བ། http://sangdhor.com/blog_c.asp?id=4189&a=admin.

སྐྱ་བྱམས་རྒྱལ། ༢༠༡༠། ལམ་གྱི་ཉི་འོད། (Sunshine on the Path) ཟི་ལིང་། མཚོ་སྔོན་མི་རིགས་དཔེ་སྐྲུན་ཁང་།

སྐྱ་གོག ༢༠༡༡། བོད་ཀྱི་རྩོམ་རིག་དང་མི་རབས་གསུམ་པ། (Tibetan Literature and the Third Generation) http://www.tibetcm.com/html/list_21/201105113204.html.

——. ༢༠༡༠། མི་རབས་གསུམ་པའི་སྙན་ངག་པ་ཀཾ་སྒྲིང་ལ་སྒྲིང་གཤོལ་བྱས་པ། (A Conversation with the Third Generation Poet Rekanglang) http://www.tibetcm.com/html/list_21/201007202368.html.

སྤྲུན་འགྲུལ། ཤ་དཀར། ༡༩༩། རྟ་ནག་སྒོག་འགྲོས། (Gait of the Black Hobbled Horse) འགྱུར་མེད་ཀྱིས་བསྒྱིགས་པའི། བོད་ཀྱི་དེང་རབས་རྩོམ་རིག་དཔེ་ཚོགས། རྟ་ནག་སྒོག་འགྲོས། (Modern Tibetan Literature Series: Gait of the Black Hobbled Horse) ཟི་ལིང་། མཚོ་སྔོན་མི་རིགས་དཔེ་སྐྲུན་ཁང་། ཤོག་ངོས་༢༡ནས༢༢།

ཨ་ཚོ། ༢༠༠༥། སྤྲུན་དག་འདུ་ཚོགས་ལང་ཚོའི་ནབ་ཅུའི་གནས་ཚུལ། (Information about Waterfall of Youth, a Conference of Poets) ད་ལྟ་བ། (Present) ༢༠༠༥། འཛིན་ཐེངས་༢པ། ཟི་ལིང་། ཤོག་ངོས་༡༨།

ཨ་ཏི་ཤ། ༢༠༠༦། ཇོ་བོ་རྗེ་དཔལ་ལྡན་ཨ་ཏི་ཤའི་གསུང་འབུམ། (Collected Works of the Glorious Lord Atisha) པེ་ཅིན། དཔལ་བརྩེགས་བོད་ཡིག་དཔེ་རྙིང་ཞིབ་འཇུག་ཁང་།

ཨ་ནན། ༢༠༠༥། སྤྲུབས་གཉིས་པའི་སྐྲ་དག་འདུ་ཚོགས་སྐོར་གྱི་ཉིན་ཐོ། (Diary Entries on the Second Seminar of the Conference of Poets) ད་ལྟ་བ། ༢༠༠༥། འཛིན་ཐེངས་༢པ། ཟི་ལིང་། ཤོག་ངོས་༡༠ནས༡༡།

ཨ་བུ་དཀར་ལོ་སོགས། ༢༠༠༢། ༼ཨ་ཀྱེས་རྨ་ཆེན་གྱི་གནས་ཡིག༽ (*Sacred Guides to Amnye Machen*) མགོ་ ལོག་ཁུལ་ཡུལ་སྐོར་ཐུན་དང་རྨ་ཡུལ་བོ་སར་རིག་གནས་སྟེ་གནས་དཔེ་ཚོགས།

ཨོ་འབར། ༢༠༠༤། ༼ད་ཐེ་མགོ་ཅན་གྱི་གཏམ་སྟེང་སུ་འབྱང་མོ༽ (Streaming Words Beginning with the Letter "*da*") ༼ཤར་དུང་རི༽ (*The Eastern Snow Mountain*) སློབེ་དེབ་བཟངས་ཞར་གཅིག་པ། ༢༠༠༤། ལན་རྡུག

Index

About the Author

Lama Jabb was born and brought up in the Dhatsen tribe, a nomadic community in Amdo, Northeastern Tibet. He left Tibet at the age of fourteen to attend school in India. Since 1995 he has lived in London, UK. He received a BA Honors degree in political science and MSc in international relations from the University of London, and completed his DPhil in modern Tibetan literature at the University of Oxford. Lama Jabb currently holds the Junior Research Fellowship in Tibetan and Himalayan Studies at Wolfson College, Oxford University, where he also teaches.

www.ingramcontent.com/pod-product-compliance
Lightning Source LLC
Chambersburg PA
CBHW030632110726
47901CB00002B/418